FIRST SEA LORD

FIRST SEA LORD

An Authorized Biography
of Admiral Lord Fisher

RICHARD HOUGH

SEVERN HOUSE

First published in Great Britain in 1969 by Unwin
Brothers Ltd. This 1977 Edition from Severn House
Publishers Ltd, 144–146 New Bond Street,
London W1Y 9FD.

ISBN 0 7278 0293 3

Printed in Great Britain by litho at
The Anchor Press Ltd and bound by
Wm Brendon & Son Ltd, both of
Tiptree, Essex

TO CECIL SCOTT, WITH AFFECTION

PREFACE

John Arbuthnot Fisher, First Baron Fisher of Kilverstone in Norfolk (1841–1920), was a man of deep passions, strong beliefs and limitless ambition and patriotism. He was brave, impetuous, impatient; brusque and even vindictive with his opponents and with those who failed to match up to the standards he set for himself—and that meant total loyalty to the Fisher creed, itself an uneasy blend of selflessness and self-aggrandizement. He adored all beautiful women; better still if they were intelligent, best of all if they were witty, well-informed and willing to dance the night through. Women loved him in return, for his vigour and decisiveness and charm. He could also electrify a committee of hard-bitten politicians, and renew the batteries of a minister as young and vibrant as Winston Churchill, or as old as Lord Salisbury.

In an age when the grip of patronage and privilege was still exclusive and tenacious, Fisher brashly fought his way through to become at the age of sixty-three the controller of the most powerful single force of destruction in the world, and on familiar terms with the influential at home and the crowned heads of Europe.

When Fisher came to power in the Royal Navy, the service which had held back Napoleon's Grand Army a century earlier and changed the face of Europe at Trafalgar was stiff in the joints, asthmatic and reactionary in the few warlike beliefs it held. The Royal Navy was weary with inaction. By its statistical strength, Britannia still ruled the waves. But the monolithic power of the British Empire and its navy was in jeopardy even as its size and wealth reached its zenith.

Fisher was among the first to recognize that the real danger to the peace of Europe lay across the North Sea rather than the English Channel; and he was the leader in spirit and in rank to alert the Royal Navy—the service to which he had offered his life at the age of thirteen —to the imminence of war.

His enemies jostled about him and sniped with deadly effect as he did so. Some held sincere doubts about his methods and his plans. The motives of others were less worthy. The hellish ordeals of the reformer at last wore out 'Jacky' Fisher's Dreadnought-like constitution, and he was driven from power, bequeathing to the nation a Navy which sustained the security of Britain as effectively, if less dramatically, as the navy of his hero Nelson had done a century earlier.

Professor Arthur J. Marder first suggested to me in 1961 that I should write a biography of Admiral Lord Fisher. With the completion of the third volume of Fisher's letters and the publication of the first volume of his monumental work *From the Dreadnought to Scapa Flow: The Royal Navy in the Fisher Era, 1904–1919,* the time appeared to be ripe for a reassessment of the man who (to quote Marder's Preface to the above work) 'dominated the Navy as it has never been dominated by a single individual'. It required the added enthusiasm of my friend, wise counsellor, and editor, Cecil Scott, finally to persuade me to take on the task.

Thanks very largely to Marder's own researches in this field since 1938, much new material unused by Admiral Bacon for his official biography[1] has become available. In writing this present volume I have drawn heavily on Marder's three major published works, the Letters, *The Anatomy of Sea Power: British Naval Policy, 1880–1905* (London, 1941), and volumes 1 and 2 of *From the Dreadnought to Scapa Flow.* I have also retraced many of his old tracks, guided from time to time across this territory by the directions of the pioneer explorer. My debt to Professor Marder is therefore an immense one. But I would not like to give the impression that this work carries, so to speak, the Marder imprimatur. Steady and faithful guide though he has been, he has never attempted in any way to influence my judgments or weights of emphasis. Any errors and unbalanced conclusions are mine alone.

I have concentrated my own researches on The Fisher Papers at Kilverstone Hall, Lennoxlove, and the Navy Department Library in London. My special thanks are due to the third Baron Fisher for allowing me free access to his grandfather's papers and correspondence, and for much helpful advice and hospitality; and to the fourteenth Duke of Hamilton for opening up the Fisher Papers, in the care of his family at Lennoxlove, at a particularly inconvenient time. My old friend Lieutenant-Commander P. K. Kemp, o b e, until recently the Navy Department Librarian and head of the Historical Department, helped me directly and indirectly in countless ways. Not only did the two volumes of *The Fisher Papers* which he edited for the Navy Records Society simplify my searches; he also guided me through many published and unpublished sources in his care, among them *The Robinson Papers, The Tweedmouth Papers* and *The Crease Papers.* My tasks at the Navy

[1] Admiral Sir R. H. Bacon, *The Life of Lord Fisher of Kilverstone* (2 vols., London, 1929).

Department Library were also greatly lightened by the diligent detailed researches and correcting hand of the late Commander W. B. Rowbotham.

Among the many people who gave me advice, guidance and their time, I would like to single out the tenth Earl of Selkirk, Captain Stephen Roskill, DSC, Captain John Creswell, Rear-Admiral H. E. Dannreuther, DSO, Bertram E. Sargeaunt Esq., Fisher's nephew; Mrs Philip Dumas, widow of Admiral Philip Dumas (*The Dumas Papers*); Mrs George Anson, David Nielson, Esq., and Ernest Bletcher, Esq. (*The Wilmot-Horton Papers*); Rear-Admiral E. M. Eller, USN, of the Naval History Division, USN, Washington, DC; that matchless proof-reader and indexer, G. Norman Knight, Esq.; and the staff of the London Library, the Public Record Office, the British Museum Reading Room, the Beaverbrook Library and other libraries.

For permission to quote copyright material I am indebted, firstly, to Jonathan Cape Ltd., the publishers of the three volumes of Fisher letters, *Fear God and Dread Nought*, edited by Arthur J. Marder, for the use of numerous letters and extracts from letters and certain intro-ductory matter from these volumes. My thanks are also due to the following publishers, agents and individuals: Hodder and Stoughton Ltd (*Records* and *Memories* by Admiral of the Fleet Lord Fisher, *The Life and Letters of David, Earl Beatty* by Rear-Admiral W. S. Chalmers); Macdonald and Co. Ltd and the Macmillan Company of America (*Yesterday's Deterrent* by Jonathan Steinberg); Harcourt, Brace and World Inc. and Faber and Faber Ltd (*The Reign of King George V* by D. C. Somervell); Eyre and Spottiswoode (Publishers), Ltd, (*The Life and Letters of Lord Wester Wemyss* by Lady Wester Wemyss) and, with The Macmillan Company of America (*Recollections of Three Reigns* by Sir Frederick Ponsonby); John Murray Ltd (*My Working Life* by Colonel Lord Sydenham, *Parliamentary Reminiscences and Reflections* by the Rt Hon Lord George Hamilton, *King George V: a Personal Memoir* by John Gore, *Life of Admiral of the Fleet Sir A. K. Wilson* by Admiral Sir E. E. Bradford) and, with E. P. Dutton and Co. Inc. (*King Edward VII* and *Gladstone* by Philip Magnus); The Hamlyn Publishing Group, Ltd and Charles Scribner's Sons (*The World Crisis* by Winston S. Churchill); George G. Harrap and Co. Ltd (*Pull Together* by Admiral Sir Lewis Bayly), Seeley, Service and Co. Ltd (*British Battleships* by Oscar Parkes); Frederick Muller Ltd (*Naval Strategy* by Admiral Sir R. H. Bacon and Francis McMurtrie); H. F. and G. Witherby Ltd (*A Great Seaman: the Life of Admiral of the Fleet Sir Henry F. Oliver* by Admiral Sir William James); Nigel Nicolson, Esq and Constable and Co. Ltd (*King George V* by Harold

11

Nicolson); The Hutchinson Publishing Group, Ltd (*Who Goes There?* by Sir Archibald Hurd, *A Naval Scrapbook* by Admiral Sir R. H. Bacon, *Sailors, Statesmen and Others* by J. M. Kenworthy, and *Gone for a Sailor* by Lionel Dawson); The Beaverbrook Foundation (*Politicians and the War* by the Rt Hon Lord Beaverbrook); Viscount Esher (*Journal and Letters of Reginald, Viscount Esher*, by Mauric V. Brett and Oliver, Viscount Esher); Miss Bacon, A. P. Watt and Son and Hodder and Stoughton Ltd (*The Life of Admiral Lord Fisher* by Admiral Sir R. H. Bacon); Margery, Lady Pentland, A. P. Watt and Son and the Hutchinson Publishing Group Ltd (*The Life of the Rt Hon Sir Henry Campbell-Bannerman* by J. A. Spender); Peter Dawnay Ltd (*Charlie B.* by Captain Geoffrey Bennett).

Letters and related textual extracts without source references are from *Fear God and Dread Nought: the Correspondence of Admiral of the Fleet Lord Fisher of Kilverstone*, Edited by Arthur J. Marder (3 vols., London, 1952–9), which is so well arranged and indexed that precise identification is unnecessary.

PREFACE TO THE SECOND EDITION

Like his hero, Horatio Nelson, 'Jackie' Fisher will always be a subject for controversy. There was so much that was good in the man and his accomplishments. But there was also his destruction of the Royal Navy's priceless 'band of brothers' spirit which had been so carefully fostered by Nelson himself.

I received more letters on the publication of the first edition of this book than for any other biography I have written. Besides pointing out several minor errors, more or less politely, in the engaging way people have, some of my more august correspondents gave their opinion of Fisher or quoted others'. Admiral Sir Angus Cunninghame Graham wrote that, after putting down my book, he was still 'left wondering whether he was worthwhile, concluding that perhaps on balance he was'. He continued: 'His drive and intellect would have been so much more valuable had he not retained so much of the mentality of your colliding Admiral Tryon,[1] a mentality of the later 19th century and early 20th century which caused elders and seniors to put on a cloak of infallibility. They were unwilling and incapable of using a Staff and allowing its members to argue their proposals.'

Commander W. M. Phipps Hornby, R.N. (Retd.), wrote of his famous grandfather, Admiral of the Fleet Sir Geoffrey Phipps Hornby, that 'he was very much alive to Fisher's exceptional capabilities, and availed himself of them'. But he also quotes his grandfather as saying of Fisher, when he was still a young officer, 'Jack Fisher would make a good servant but a bad master'. This was not the view of his most illustrious admirer, Winston Churchill, who chose him as 'master' again in 1914, when unfortunately 'Jackie's' powers were past their zenith.

As evidence of the continuing interest in this unique and colourful naval officer since the publication of *First Sea Lord* we have had Ruddock Mackay's very detailed and scholarly biography, *Fisher of Kilverstone* (1973), and the splendid entry in *The Oxford Companion to Ships and the Sea* (1976) by Arthur Marder, the foremost authority on the subject, who earlier edited the three volumes of Fisher's letters, *Fear God and Dread Nought*.

Richard Hough
December 1976

[1] *Admirals in Collision* (1959)

CONTENTS

ILLUSTRATIONS

FIGURES

PART ONE

Chapter 1

THE FAVOURED MIDSHIPMAN

John Arbuthnot Fisher was separated from his parents at the age of six and never again saw his father. As an old Admiral he cherished the most romantic and tender memories of them. His mother, he wrote at the age of seventy-six, was 'a most magnificent and handsome, extremely young woman, who married for love exactly nine months before I was born!' Sophie Lambe was the daughter of a London trades-man, a wine merchant in New Bond Street. Fisher, who from early childhood deeply admired Horatio Nelson, enjoyed recalling that one of his mother's grandfathers had served under Nelson at Trafalgar, and that Emma Hamilton, when still a young housemaid, used once to scrub the front steps next door in New Bond Street. For Fisher this compensated in large measure for her rather humble background 'in trade'.

While she was still a young girl, Sophie was sent out to Ceylon to keep house for her brother Frederick in Colombo. Her charm and looks brought her many admirers. In April 1840 she married a tall, splendid-looking Army officer, Captain William Fisher, of the 78th Highland Regiment, 'also very young, also especially handsome and also equally unmindful of worldly advantages in satisfying the desires of his heart, for my mother had only beauty and he had only his splendid body!' Fisher added to this highly coloured autobiographical fragment, 'Why I am ugly is one of those puzzles of physiology which are beyond finding out!'

The Fishers were of grander stock than the Lambes, being an old Warwickshire family 'going back to the dark ages'. There was a Sir Clement Fisher in Charles II's time who married Jane Lane; and then the baronetcy lapsed 'as my ancestor after Sir Clement Fisher's death wouldn't pay £500 in the nature of fees, I believe'.[1] Fisher's own paternal grandfather was Rector of Wavendon in Buckinghamshire,

[1] Admiral of the Fleet Lord Fisher, *Records* (London, 1919) 2. (Hereafter cited as *Records.*)

and his brother fought at Waterloo, where he was mortally wounded alongside the Duke of Wellington. His dying wish was that his young nephew, Fisher's father, should be granted a commission. Fisher himself inherited from his great uncle the watch he had carried at Waterloo, and it bore the dent of the bullet which had killed him. William Fisher sailed out to Ceylon in 1831 with his promised commission as an ensign in command of the Governor's Guard.

The Governor of Ceylon, Sir Robert Wilmot-Horton, was evidently attached to the young officer and appointed him his A D C. But from the time of his marriage to Sophie Lambe, William Fisher's life was dogged by misfortune. Soon after 'Jack' was born he was tempted by the money being made from coffee planting to buy himself out of the Army. His estates prospered only briefly. He was soon in debt and spent the rest of his life in a state of unceasing anxiety about money and the ever-growing size of his family. There were eleven children in all, four of whom died in infancy or early childhood.

We are left with the impression that William Fisher was kindly and ineffectual and improvident, and that the main responsibility for the management of the family, through pregnancy after pregnancy, was left to the redoubtable Sophie. Certainly it was from his mother that Fisher inherited his vigour, vitality, tenacity and sharp intellect. Long after her death, when Fisher was appointed First Sea Lord in 1904, a naval correspondent wrote of Sophie Fisher that 'she was no ordinary woman. She was strong with a moral courage she has given to her son, and her powerful mind, organizing capacity and taste for power, are characteristics faithfully reproduced in her family'.[1] This was no doubt true of her when she was bringing up her numerous children. But as a widow, when she returned to England, she became fat and less attractive and worried incessantly, and with good reason, about money. Fisher in his middle age took against her, though with feelings of awful guilt, and at this time had 'none of the feelings of a son for his mother'.[2] She was always worrying him for money for herself and her daughters at a time when Fisher was struggling to bring up his own family on his pay alone. Until the end Fisher found it difficult to forgive his improvident family for calling on him for money. They did not believe that anyone so famous could also be penurious.

John Arbuthnot Fisher was born at Rambodde, Ceylon, on 25 January 1841. 'I attribute my present vitality', he once wrote, 'to the imbibing

[1] Unsigned article in the *Pall Mall Gazette,* October 1904.
[2] Admiral of the Fleet Lord Fisher, *Memories* (London, 1919) 77. (Hereafter cited as *Memories.*)

of my mother's milk beyond the legal period of nine months.' The vast good fortune that accompanied him through so much of his life, in such strong contrast with his poor father, began when the Governor's wife, Lady Wilmot-Horton, agreed to stand as his godmother. She was, by all accounts, a most remarkable woman, blessed by a huge inheritance and an influential circle of friends. Fisher, who would lovingly recount how his earliest thoughts were associated with her, wrote that 'She was *very, very* beautiful even as an old lady, and as good as she was beautiful. A saint on earth!' It was of Lady Wilmot-Horton that Byron wrote:

> She walks in beauty, like the night
> Of cloudless climes and starry skies . . .

Soon after Fisher's birth, Sir Robert died, and Lady Wilmot-Horton returned to the family seat at Catton Hall near Burton-on-Trent. Her young godson providentially followed her to England soon after, in order to live with his Uncle Frederick, who had left Ceylon soon after Sophie's marriage. But it was Fisher's godmother who really took charge of him for the next six years of his life, and school holidays from Knight's School in Coventry were spent at Catton Hall, and in marked contrast with the worrying austerities of life in Ceylon. 'I had happy days there. The Trent flowed past the house and I loved being on the river and catching perch.' The art of finding the target and shooting straight, with which he was to become preoccupied for so much of his life was first exercised at Catton at the age of about ten years. But 'having shot the butler instead of a rabbit, I was disallowed a gun. It was his fault', claimed Fisher. 'He told me never to hesitate, but always to shoot at anything I saw moving! I saw the tall grass moving and I shot!'

Of young Fisher's many natural advantages, the exceptional fascination he held for women was one of the most potent influences towards the early success of his career. He was quick to recognize its value and it served to sustain him all through his life. As a boy the innocence of his charm was irresistible, and this same boyish innocence—the eager vivacity, the curious blend of wide-eyed egotism and heart-warming evidence of his interest in the beauty and charm of his companion— brought him the affection and support of many women of influence right up to his death.

Lady Wilmot-Horton, the first of many women who played such a large part in his life, adored her precocious and lively godson. His presence at Catton Hall gave joy to her widowhood, and she would have done anything for his happiness and future. When Fisher expressed an enthusiasm for going to sea, Lady Wilmot-Horton's connections at once proved effective. The last survivor among Nelson's captains lived nearby, at Shenstone Lodge on the other side of Lichfield. He was Admiral Sir William Parker, a distinguished and influential old sailor. When he became Port Admiral at Portsmouth, Admiral Parker received automatically two nominations for entering the Royal Navy. He was easily persuaded by Lady Wilmot-Horton to part with one of these for Fisher when he reached the age of thirteen. Fate was characteristically profligate in doubling his nominations. Admiral Parker's second nomination was by chance given to another elderly lady who had also fallen under the boy's charm. She was a niece of Lord Nelson, no less. There could hardly be a neater foundation for the career of a boy who was to become the most famous sailor since Nelson himself. The last foundation stone fell into place on 12 June 1854, almost forty-nine years after Trafalgar, when John Arbuthnot Fisher joined Nelson's old flagship *Victory* at Portsmouth.

*

When he became a famous Admiral, Fisher enjoyed telling his friends how simple were the rules for entering the Navy when he was a boy. 'I wrote out the Lord's Prayer and the doctor made me jump over a chair naked, and I was given a glass of sherry . . .' It was nearly but not quite as sketchy as that. Fisher had forgotten in his enthusiasm for embellishment that he had first been summoned to the Royal Naval College at Portsmouth where he was given some dictation and briefly tested in basic arithmetic, and had been examined to ensure that he was 'free from defect of speech, defect of vision, rupture, or any other physical disability'. He had then returned briefly to Catton Hall before being appointed a cadet in the *Victory*. Early in June 1854 he left Catton Hall again, bearing a letter of introduction from Lady Wilmot-Horton to Admiral Parker. 'I arrived as a little boy alone at Portsmouth and went to the outfitters, who gave me a bed.' The brief cadet's examination followed, and he was then allowed ashore to take his letter to the Port Admiral. 'He asked me to dinner, but I told him I thought I had better get on board my ship! He was amused,' Fisher later recalled, 'and told me to dine and sleep at his house, and he told me all about Lord Nelson, who he had served under a great many years.'

Fisher's active service life began the following morning, without any preliminary training, and at the age of thirteen and a half years. Admiral Parker 'sent me off to my ship with the Admiral's coxwain, and as I stepped on board I had a bucket of salt water over my feet'. It was a mild beginning to a harsh conditioning process endured by all naval cadets at that time. They were holystoning the decks of the *Victory* and the First Lieutenant roared at him 'like a Bull of Bashan'. On the same day he saw eight men flogged, and fainted at the sight. Captain C. D. Hay had been recently tried by court martial for cruelty after flogging an entire crew. His zeal was evidently undiminished. Commander Alexander Boyle, the first officer, was no better. He would padlock the men to a ringbolt and have buckets of salt water hurled at them. The *Victory's* Captain and Commander were both brutes by any standards. 'All the same, I loved him [the Commander], and the Captain also, and both loved me till they died. They were each of them great for war; but, alas! peace was their portion.'[1]

Fisher's arrival at Portsmouth with a letter of introduction to the Port Admiral made an impressive start for the young cadet. But judging from the few facts known about this period in his life, the few early privileges that came his way were earned by his appealing charm and liveliness and not because he curried favours or had a special relationship with the Port Admiral. On that very first day, the Lieutenant who had shouted so harshly at him when he stepped aboard later offered him an orange. Although Commander Boyle made him walk the break of the poop with a coil of rope round his neck because he said the boy was born to be hanged, this same officer made him his aide-de-camp. His duties included daily taking a boat ashore to bring Boyle on board. 'He had a very lovely young wife,' Fisher lovingly recalled, 'and she used to give me Devonshire cream and jam every morning. . . . She really was a very lovely woman—only seventeen.'

The Navy had changed little since the days of Nelson. Life on shipboard was still brutalizing, the basic diet at sea, after the perishable stores had been consumed, was still salt beef, and biscuit that was likely to be weevil-ridden. Admiral Parker coming on board the *Victory* or any of the other wooden men-of-war in Portsmouth harbour would see little evidence of any change since he had fought at Trafalgar half a century earlier. A line-of-battle ship still sailed under the same rig as in Nelson's time, and carried tiers of smooth-bore guns which boasted little more accuracy, range or power. The *Victory* herself, nearly 100 years old, was still kept ready for sea, and she could have given a good account of herself in battle. The great technical revolutions in warship design, signalled by the advent of the shell, steam power and armour plate were still in their infancy or a decade or more away. The 18-inch gun, the aircraft carrier, the submarine and fast minelayer were all introduced in Fisher's lifetime and there was no more active and enthusiastic advocate of these new and fearful twentieth-century weapons. But

[1] Admiral Sir R. H. Bacon, *The Life of Lord Fisher of Kilverstone* (London, 1929, 2 vols), i. 7. (Hereafter cited as *Bacon.*)

as a senior officer he derived lasting satisfaction from having served afloat under the same conditions as Nelson had known, when 'we midshipmen were allowed only a basin of water to wash in, and the basin was inside one's sea-chest; and if anyone spilt a drop of water on the deck he was made to holy-stone it himself'[1]; when 'there was a fiddler to every ship, and when the anchor was being weighed, he used to sit on the capstan and play, so as to keep the men in step and in good heart'.

Fisher often cited 'the inestimable benefit of sending little boys to sea when they are young! What splendid Nelsonic qualities were developed!' It was a matter of 'survival of the fittest among those little Midshipmen. . . . In the first ship I was in we not only carried our fresh water in casks, but we had some rare old Ship's Biscuit supplied in what were known as "bread-bags". These bread bags were not preservative; they were creative. A favourite amusement was to put a bit of this biscuit on the table and see how soon all of it would walk away. In fact one midshipman could gamble away his "tot" of rum with another midshipman by pitting one biscuit against another. Anyhow, whenever you took a bit of biscuit to eat it you always tapped it edgeways on the table to let the "grown-ups" get away . . . I didn't grow tall because in the days I went to sea the poor little Midshipmen were kept in three watches with insufficient food . . . Yes, at that infantage, and measuring about 4 feet nothing, the poor little boys had to walk the quarter-deck in their "watch-keeping" from 8 p.m. till midnight one night and from midnight till 4 a.m. the next night! and always very hungry all the time! They never had a whole night's rest ever! and their little bellies were never full! I still remember falling over the 32-pounder brass carronades on the quarter-deck (they had been used at Trafalgar) as I walked up and down the quarter-deck, almost in my sleep! So how on earth could I expect to be as tall as my father and mother, for she was very tall also!'[2]

While Fisher was undergoing these first rigours of his early service a few words of stern but affectionate encouragement arrived from his father in Ceylon.

FROM CAPTAIN WILLIAM FISHER

Kandy, Ceylon
May 15th, 1854

My dear Jack,

. . . You must recollect I am very poor and that you have a great many brothers and sisters, and that I cannot give you much pocket money. But I will give you

---

[1] *Records*, 10.   [2] *ibid.*, 5–8.

what I can afford, and, mind you, never get into debt. If you do, you will never get on in the Navy or anywhere, and recollect never to tell an *untruth as long as you live*. Never mind what happens, *always* tell the truth, whether you have done right or wrong. Always make friends with the best fellows and *gentlemen*, and always dress well and be *very clean* in your person and dress.

From all I have heard of you from Mr Knight[1] and Lady Horton, you are a very good boy and very clever, and I expect you will get on well. Perhaps you may see some fighting.

Never forget your religion and your prayers, and don't let any bad fellows laugh at you for being better than they are.

God help you, my dear Jack. Ever your affectionate father,

W. Fisher

*

In 1854 there was a good chance that Fisher might see some fighting. The Crimean War had just broken out, and the Royal Navy which had not known a major war for so many years was grinding ponderously into action. A vast and lamentably inefficient naval force under the command of the aged Vice-Admiral Sir Charles Napier had headed for the Baltic Sea, while the Mediterranean Fleet, under the equally senile and indolent Vice-Admiral James Dundas, made its hesitant way into the Black Sea. The conduct of the naval campaigns which followed provided Fisher with early evidence of the decay in fighting efficiency to which a great service could succumb in a long period of peace. He was already storing away the shot and shell he would need for his own personal bombardments, which so effectually prepared the ground for his later reforms. For Fisher there was to be no fighting in the Crimean War. It was an exhilarating time all the same. His first seagoing experience was in the 84-gun 2-decker *Calcutta*. In February 1855 she sailed from Plymouth, and the weather was so bad that seven days later they were off the Scilly Isles instead of being half way up the Channel.

The record of his experiences at this time is tantalizingly incomplete, but what has been left (including memories of frequent seasickness) offers clues to the development of his character at fourteen years. There is, for example, the violin anecdote. In the *Calcutta*, it seems, there was a proficient violin player, a contemporary of Fisher, who gained attention in the wardroom by playing popular airs. At first Fisher had to be content with voice accompaniment. He decided that this was not good enough, saved enough to buy an instrument for himself, persuaded a bandsman to give him lessons and by close application and determination was soon able to rival the performance of his fellow cadet. A

[1] His headmaster.

furious exasperation at his inadequacy must have driven him to take up this difficult instrument, and only exceptional zeal, determination and competitive spirit could have got him through those early lessons. Poor bandsman!

Even during these early years the shadow of Nelson was always at his side: Nelson the fighting sailor, bold and vigorous, passionate in his patriotism and all his loyalties. Copenhagen was one of Fisher's favourite Nelson actions. Every Nelsonic characteristic he most admired was magnificently demonstrated during this battle—the boldness to the brink of rashness; independence of spirit; the stubborn refusal against all the evidence of his single eye to accept the superiority of the enemy. 'His audacity! His imagination! His considered rashness!'[1] No wonder that Fisher's first sea-going voyage into the Baltic, off to fight Britain's enemies, was a youthful pilgrimage, and the memory of his hero's voyage there in the *St George* before Copenhagen comforted him through all the adverse weather.

'When we went up the Baltic in this old sailing 2-decker to take part in the Russian War,' he once wrote, 'it reminded one so of the time, I remember, of how Nelson used to get his ships replenished with water at odd places. We went into a little place, the island of Nargen . . . And there we digged for water and sent the casks ashore as in Nelson's time to be filled by the "watering party".'[2] There is the romantic Fisher. But here is Fisher the practical realist, with a touch of youthful humour, writing of the same uncomfortable passage. 'I remember I made poetry while I was seasick!

> Now sailors all take my advice
> Let steamships be your motta
> And never go to sea again
> In the sailing ship *Calcutta*'

Fisher was back from the Baltic before the autumn of 1855, and when the *Calcutta* was paid off a few months later, he was appointed to the modern screw ship *Agamemnon* in the Mediterranean. She carried a full spread of sail, of course, and her steam engines were still regarded strictly as an auxiliary means of propulsion, but the fact that he sailed out to her in the second-rate ship-of-the-line *Impregnable* which was nearly fifty years old and indistinguishable from the men-of-war at Trafalgar, gives some hint of the wide variety of *matériel* in the Royal Navy at that time. It was an uneventful passage out to the Mediterranean, and again there was to be no combat. The war with Russia was

---

[1] *Records*, 161.   [2] Lennoxlove MSS.

over, the *Agamemnon* was loaded with soldiers on their way back from the Crimea. She was, for the present, just a trooper. But at least Fisher had his first taste of the Mediterranean, of seeing some of the places where Nelson had prepared his plans to hunt down Villeneuve, and of sailing close past the scene of his hero's last magnificent victory half a century earlier. For another half-century the Mediterranean was to remain the real seat of British sea power, and in later years Fisher was to become familiar with its every mood, with every port and roadstead, every bay and cape. In this sea he was to experience action as a Captain, was to institute dramatic reforms as a Commander-in-Chief, and to prepare his plans for his most notable *matériel* revolutions. In 1856, as a junior cadet under Captain James Stopford, he was still accustoming himself to the strenuous living conditions, still adjusting himself to shipboard life and learning basic seamanship and gunnery.

On his return to England Fisher was promoted to Midshipman. Until he received his Peerage and was made an Admiral of the Fleet, this was Fisher's only unremarkable step up the ladder. One reason why he was later so frequently singled out for his qualities by those in authority over him was the unfailing accuracy of his judgement of his seniors. He could probe character with a sharp scalpel and with the speed of a deft surgeon. He knew how to handle a troublesome grey-haired First Lieutenant, left behind in his advancement, or a cruelly vindictive Commander who flogged his men because of a bad hangover. Equally, he admired warmly and readily those above him, and let them see it; although it was as impossible for him deliberately to ingratiate himself with one kind of officer as it was to conceal his contempt for those deserving of it. His evident intelligence and cheerfulness, his ebullient eagerness to take on responsibility and face danger, his clear-headed articulateness, all recommended him to his superiors. These were the qualities that made themselves evident, and brought him distinction, during the next period in his life, when he met many dangers, made warm friends, and established lasting loyalties. From the summer of 1856 when he sailed for the Far East, until the late summer of 1861, more than half the man and more than half the Admiral were made.

*

War with Russia and war with China in successive years did not carry the same implications of ultimate armageddon in the 1850s as they would have done 100 years later. The war with Russia in 1854–5 scarcely touched the lives of the common people of France, Britain or

Russia; it was an affair of rather squalid local violence during which, on the British side, a mere twelve per cent of the casualties resulted from enemy action. The Russian war was a traditional western war of power politics and nationalism. The Second China War of 1856–60 was a trade war, with origins going back to the conflict between traditional Chinese xenophobia and sense of superiority and the further stimulus to the western urge to trade provided by the industrial revolution. The disorders and corruption in China which had increased during the second quarter of the nineteenth century had led to the First China War—or 'Opium War'—of 1839–42 which sought to break down the barriers to trade and European penetration imposed by the Chinese. The Treaty of Nanking in 1842 permitted trade to be carried on by British merchants, under much more liberal conditions, at five large Chinese ports, the Treaty Ports. But the intransigence of the more violent and nationalistic elements in China, and the increasing demands of British traders, backed by diplomatic pressure and men-of-war, made more bloodshed an increasing certainty.

The French were equally exasperated by the hazards and uncertainties of the trading situation, and they were especially incensed by the persecution of their Catholic missionaries. The defeat of Russia in the Crimea at once released naval and military reinforcements for the Far East and increased the danger of Russia attacking China from the north to console herself for her losses in the west. The arrest by Chinese officers at Canton of twelve of their own countrymen, on piracy charges, from a ship flying the British flag, led to the outbreak of fighting which was to continue, on and off, for nearly four years, broken by the most tortuous diplomatic machinations and face-saving exercises.

Fisher became personally and most dangerously involved in the China War towards its closing stages in 1859. Almost to the end he served under Captain Charles Shadwell in the corvette *Highflyer*, which sailed for the Far East from England in July 1856. Under Shadwell's paternal care and tuition, Fisher acquired new wisdom, nautical knowledge and invaluable experience in naval practice, from handling a small boat in a gale to facing with courage the fire of a more numerous enemy. Fisher repaid this officer with loyalty and affection, and gratitude that lasted throughout his life.

Charles Shadwell was the fourth son of the late Vice-Chancellor of England, Sir Lancelot Shadwell, 'who used to bathe in the Thames with his seven sons every morning', according to Fisher's own characteristically graphic account of the officer in his *Records*. 'My Shadwell was about the greatest Saint on earth. The sailors called him, somewhat profanely, "Our Heavenly Father". He was once heard to say, "Damn," and the whole ship was upset. When, as Midshipmen, we punished one of our mess-mates for abstracting his cheese, he was extremely angry with us, and asked us all by what right we had to interfere with his cheese. He always had Midshipmen to breakfast with him, and when we were seasick he gave us champagne and gingerbread nuts. As he went in mortal fear of his own steward, who bossed him utterly, he would say: "I think the aroma has rather gone out of this champagne. Give it to the young gentlemen." The steward would reply: "Now you know very well, Sir, the aroma *ain't* gone out of this 'ere champagne"; but all the same we got it. He always slept in a hammock, and I remember he kept his socks in the head clews ready to put on in case of a squall calling him suddenly on deck. I learned from him nearly all that I know. He taught me how to predict eclipses and occultations, and I suppose I took more lunar observations than any Midshipman ever did before.'[1]

Fisher loved to tell stories of his favourite Captain's fearlessness in the minor actions on the coast and up the rivers which frequently occurred on the China station at this time. Once they went up a river 'to capture a pirate stronghold. Presently the pirates opened fire from a banana plantation on the river bank. We nipped ashore from the boats to the banana plantation. I remember I was armed to the teeth, like a Greek brigand, all swords and pistols, and was weighed down with weapons. We took shelter in the banana plantation, but our Captain stood on the river bank. I shall never forget it. He was dressed in a pair of white trousers, yellow waistcoat and a blue tail coat with brass buttons and a tall white hat with a gold stripe up the side of it, and he was waving a white umbrella to encourage us to come out of the bananas and go for the enemy. He had no weapon of any sort. So (I think rather against our inclinations, as the gingall bullets were flying about pretty thick) we all had to come out and go for the Chinese.'[2]

When Fisher's beloved Shadwell was sent home, he asked what he could do for the young Midshipman. 'I loved him so, I asked him to give me a set of studs with his motto on them: "Loyal au mort.".' Fisher wore them daily for over sixty years. 'His sole desire for fame was to do good.' Fisher summarized him, 'and he requested for himself when he died that he should be buried under an apple tree, so that people might say: "God bless old Shadwell!" He never flogged a man in his life.'[3]

No doubt Shadwell was as near to being a saint as was possible at

[1] *Records*, 12–13.   [2] *ibid.*, 13.   [3] *ibid.*, 14.

that time for a ship's commander; but Fisher's memory of him in after years paints the officer a shade too white, for elsewhere there is a record of Fisher writing of him at the time: 'He was rather put out the other day. He had to flog a couple of men and disrate ½ a dozen, and that always upsets him for 24 hours afterwards. I got one of them 3 dozen, thank goodness. The blackguard ran away from my boat on duty, and when Harcourt-Smith went to fetch him in the morning with a lot of marines, he began abusing him, so Harcourt-Smith went up to him and knocked him down, made a hole in his skull 1½ inches long. It stunned him beautifully. The old Skipper said, "Mr Smith, you ought to have cut him down with your sword.". . .'

Fisher's loss of maternal affection had found its compensation in Lady Wilmot-Horton. Far from Catton Hall and the delights it offered during school holidays, with no expectation of a return to England for a long time, he was in need of the comfort and warmth and flattery only an understanding married woman could offer. He discovered these in a Mrs Edmund Warden. It was not unusual at this time for young Cadets and Midshipmen on distant foreign stations for long periods to acquire for themselves some form of unofficial foster-mother and domestic headquarters to which they could return after strenuous and dangerous service. Mrs Warden, the wife of the Far East manager of the P. & O. shipping company provided a home-from-home for many of the boys during the Second China War. Her relationship with Fisher was especially warm and intimate, and they exchanged many long and affectionate letters. None of Mrs Warden's have survived, but a number of Fisher's have been found, and these serve to show how quickly he was developing, how successfully he was managing his career, and how endearingly pleased with himself he was becoming. They also demonstrate the incisiveness of his mind as well as the strength of his emotions and his will. In later years, when his responsibilities were so great and the need for discretion in his writing was often so important, his friends used sometimes to despair at the way he wrote (so swiftly, in his magnificent rounded hand) the transparently honest thoughts as they came to his mind, destroying reputations, concealing nothing. He knew that the consequences of this practice could sometimes be serious, and would appeal to many of his correspondents: 'BURN THIS!' thrice underlined. But this same forthrightness, clarity and lack of discretion in 1859 when he was a Midshipman offers the reader today a hauntingly clear picture of the boy, and at that time could compromise no one, except possibly Mrs Warden herself. For when proper allowance is made for the contemporary extravagance of expression, the richness of his endearments was open to misinterpretation.

TO MRS EDMUND WARDEN

H.M.S. Highflyer, at sea
Off Shantung Promontory
June 15th, 1859

My dear Mams,
. . . We had to anchor on the night of the 10th on account of the wind falling light. I felt particularly miserable that night. I kept thinking WHERE I was the night before and wishing myself back again. I saw it was no good keeping on like that, because it was impossible for me to get back, so I went down below and ate 26 gingerbread nuts to keep my PECKER up, had a glass of grog, and turned in. Just fancy! I have only smoked 2 cigars all the time we have been out. I can hardly believe it myself. We had it blowing like old boots the second day after we were out, going 12 knots with the *Banterer* in tow. We hauled her right through it. It is such beautiful weather now, just like May in England, a little cooler perhaps, and the sea breezes so jolly, but the old Skipper has got an idea in his head to make us all smart, so he does nothing but exercise, shortening and making sail, shifting spars, etc. etc. Now I come to think of it, I am afraid you understand but little of the foregoing, but you must take it for granted that it is something very horrid. We saw the Admiral [James Hope] in the *Chesapeake* on the 13th. It was great fun, we beat him sailing with a gunboat in tow. At last he got up steam and beat us and left his own two gunboats to make the best of their passages.

Hills is all right and bully, *which I am certain you will be glad to hear. I am quite well*, but I am afraid that *that* is uninteresting news. The examination is finished and I am 200 ahead of all of them. (I am not bragging, Mams!) . . .

June 16th
Here we are, dear Mams, off 'Toki' in the Gulf of Pecheli . . . The old Skipper is getting up all about the movements of armies and the regulation of advanced guards and rear guards, etc. He is making me do the same, because I am his A.D.C. . . .

I have got to go and relieve Harcourt-Smith now; it is my next watch. The old Skipper behaves like a brick and lets me keep Lieutenant's watch at sea. I nearly carried some of the yards away the other day. Got caught in a squall.

June 18th
Here we are, riding to an anchor a few miles from the mouth of the Peiho, blowing half a gale of wind. We shipped a sea just now; it came right into our berth and wet us all through. We are knocking about tremendously, so that must account for my bad writing. The Admiral has gone up the river with all the gunboats to reconnoitre. I dare say I shall be able to tell you all the news before the vessel with the mail goes . . . This is horribly disgusting work. We are all but *battened* down and it is blowing and raining, and the old 'hooker' is turning herself inside out. The galley fire is put out, so I have been making my tea off red herrings and beer . . .

We had a tremendous squall yesterday morning, split our foretopsail, blew part of our main topgallant sail away, etc., etc., and a lot more you don't understand, so you see, there is no yacht-sailing up here. It is just like the Black Sea as regards weather . . .

At the age of eighteen, then, Fisher had already been selected for special favours both on shore and at sea: at Shanghai the apple of Mrs Warden's eye, in his ship the A D C to Chaptain Shadwell, who also let him keep a Lieutenant's watch. Moreover, a testing time of extreme endurance and hazard was imminent, and this again would serve to draw attention to him. The operations that lay ahead were to test his courage and bring him closer to death than any other experience in his life, and to sever him from his beloved Captain.

The action of the British naval squadron off the Peiho Forts in June 1859 was one of those rare events in Victorian colonial history when a well-equipped and well-led British force was out-gunned and out-fought, and whose defeat resulted in severe casualties. On 20 June the British, French and American envoys in China arrived off the mouth of the River Peiho, intending to make their way to Pekin, there to ratify the terms of the treaties of Tientsin which had been agreed to with the Chinese authorities the previous year. The Chinese had meanwhile had a change of heart and decided to have nothing to do with them. They were also militarily in better shape. The envoys intended to proceed up-river as far as Tientsin, and thence overland to Pekin. There had been plenty of trouble here in the past, and it was not expected that the envoys' journey would be entirely peaceful this time. A large Anglo-French naval force had therefore assembled in the gulf of Pechili so that, if necessary, a passage could be forced up the river. It was soon discovered that the river was indeed defended against foreign invasion, first by a series of obstructions across the water, and then by some very professional-looking forts. 'There were three booms or obstructions', one account described the situation. 'The first, or lowest, was of iron piles; the second was of heavy spars of wood, apparently moored ahead and stern, and cross-lashed with cables; the third consisted of large timber baulks, well cross-lashed together, tied with irons, and forming a mass about 120 feet wide and 3 feet deep. It was made in two over-lapping pieces . . . and the opening between these might have just admitted the passage of a gunboat, though the strength of the current would have rendered it difficult and even dangerous for such a craft to attempt to get through.'[1] Demands made to the Chinese to clear these

---

[1] Sir W. Laird Clowes *et al.*, *The Royal Navy: a History* (7 vols, London, 1897–1903), vii, 124–5. (Hereafter cited as *Clowes*.)

obstructions and to allow the envoys to proceed were ignored, and on 24 June the commander of the naval force, Rear-Admiral Sir James Hope, determined to force a way through and capture the forts. For this operation he selected nine little gunboats each of around 250 tons, and two rather larger vessels. The force was divided into two, under the overall command of Admiral Hope, Captain Shadwell being given command of the vessels on the right. Midshipman Fisher was in the gunboat *Banterer* under Lieutenant John Jenkins.

Before the assault force sailed, the officers and men had some inkling that serious combat lay ahead, but were in no doubt at all of the outcome. On 18 June Fisher wrote, 'We reached the rendezvous yesterday. Directly we got in, the Admiral made signal for the squadron to weigh and form line of battle, and then brought us up to the Peiho here after performing all kinds of wonderful evolutions. He had just sent orders down to make a lot more scaling ladders, so I suppose something is up.'

The attack began at 2·00 p.m. on 25 June, with one of the gunboats pulling up the first boom, and when this had been cleared others moved up-river to the second obstruction. All were at once met by a fierce and sustained fire from some forty guns of the forts, firing at close range. Admiral Hope, flying his flag in the gun vessel *Cormorant*, gave orders to engage. For five hours a heavy fire was exchanged between the well-protected forts and the helplessly vulnerable naval vessels. The casualties on the British side mounted alarmingly, and the Admiral himself was badly wounded. Several of the gunboats were driven into the mud, where they made an even better target for the excellent Chinese gunnery. One after another they were disabled. 'In the last part of the action,' wrote Fisher, 'I was the only one left to carry the orders about . . . We had a hard fight of it, but what could we do against such a fearful number of guns? and us poor little gunboats inclosed in such a small place, not much broader across than the length of our ship. . . .'

The strength and skill of the defenders were far higher than anyone had expected, and afterwards there was much dark talk about professional Russian assistance, and even active participation. As to the British, they fought quite alone. The French had no suitable vessels, and the Americans were, strictly speaking, neutrals in the quarrel. But they could not ignore entirely the sounds of battle, and accounts soon reached them of the severe drubbing the British were taking.

Commodore Josiah Tattnall, USN, could not bear to stand by while his friends were shot to pieces, even though he had fought against the British in the war of 1812. Tattnall had himself rowed in a cutter up river, and through shot and shell made his way to the *Cormorant*, where he found his friend Admiral Hope lying wounded in his cabin, While the battle raged, the party of American sailors 'watched the . . . weary bluejackets working intermittently at the bow gun'. Idleness under the circumstances was unbearable. 'At length, one of the Americans, and then others, climbed shyly on deck, and began to help, saying little or nothing, but gradually relieving the proper gun's crew, until the gun was wholly manned by Tattnall's men.' At this point the Commodore reappeared and pointed out to his men that they were supposed to be neutrals. '"Beg pardon, sir," said one of the Americans, drawing off shamefacedly with his mates to the boat, "they were very short-handed at the bow-gun; and so we thought we'd lend them a hand for fellowship's sake.".'[1]

Perhaps it was either at this stage of the action, or later when Tattnall helped to remove the injured, that (so the story goes) the much quoted expression 'Blood is thicker than water' was first used. Accounts vary, and it does not matter very much which one is true. The important thing about this American intervention was that Briton fought alongside American, however briefly, and the bloody disaster off the Peiho forts did much to seal Anglo-American friendship for years ahead.

In spite of the casualties his force had already suffered after some five hours of combat, Admiral Hope ordered out the assault party by 7.00 p.m. They were towed in their boats up the river by small steamboats (one of them was reported to be Tattnall's), and comprised about 350 Royal Marines and sailors.

Fisher was alongside Captain Shadwell during the advance up to the forts, a frightful business carried out through a jungle of sharp stakes and ditches, ankle- or knee-deep in stinking river mud, and against a heavy fire from guns, gingals, rifles, and even bows. Men fell on all sides, and many who were only lightly wounded suffocated in the mud. A few of them reached the bastion of the south fort, worn out and with their ammunition sodden from wading through the mud and five-foot deep ditches.

A few extracts from Fisher's breathless letter to 'Mams' offer a fragmentary picture of the whole murderous business in which nearly half the total force of 1100 engaged were killed or wounded.

'. . . I don't know whether I can give you a description of it, I feel in such a state of excitement. My poor old Skipper keeps his pecker up. I was with him all day till he was wounded in the mud and then I brought him out to the ship . . . I had to fling all my arms away coming

[1] *Clowes*, vii, 128.

back from the forts and was nearly smothered once, only one of our bluejackets was kind enough to haul me out. You sank up to your knees *at least* every step, and just fancy the slaughter going 500 yards in the face of that fire of about 30 pieces of artillery right in front of you and on each flank. It was dreadful, horrible work but, thank God, I came out all right . . . They had horrid fire-balls firing at us when we landed. I saw one poor fellow with his eye and part of his face burnt right out. If a piece struck you, it stuck to you and regularly burnt you away till it was all gone. . . . '

The picture of the whole ghastly business remained vivid in Fisher's memory all his life, and he would often talk about that race through the Peiho mud, the cries of the wounded, the sudden collapse of his Captain at his side—though he rarely mentioned that he had dragged Shadwell back to the boat in the retreat.

The tragic event provided Fisher with his first experience of personal danger and bloodshed on a large scale. For a boy of eighteen the pitching overboard 'as they are killed or dead' of his shipmates ('one soon gets used to it'), the sight of men dying in agony, of the decapitated heads of the dead stuck on the walls of the forts the next day, of the sunk gunboats lying in the mud, the assault on the Peiho forts, all provided him with a great impetus into manhood. 'I am certain I am not born to be shot,' Fisher wrote five days after the action; a wonderfully powerful assertion for a boy of eighteen to make. But it is clear from what he wrote at the time, and later, that the proof of his courage and conduct throughout the action added greatly to his self-confidence.

His experience of Chinese strength and numbers at the Peiho forts, and on many other occasions during his period in the Far East, provided the genesis of the conviction developed in later life that 'the yellow peril' must one day become a reality. 'When by-and-by the Chinese know their power,' he wrote at the age of seventy-eight, 'they have only to walk slowly westwards and, like the locusts in Egypt, no Pharaohs in Europe with all their mighty boats will stop them. They won't want to fire guns or bombs. They'll just all walk along and smother Europe.'

For the next six months the state of Captain Shadwell's wounded foot was a source of anxiety to Fisher. He was not only genuinely fond of 'my old Skipper', but was quick to recognize the handicap to his advancement the death or departure of Shadwell would be. He had now served under him for nearly three years and was the Captain's favourite as well as his ADC.

For the first few days after the retreat down the Peiho, Shadwell remained, suffering considerable pain, in his cabin. Here Commodore

Tattnall visited him every day, and Fisher also spent much time with him. 'The Captain asked me why on earth I did not shave!!! I told him as I should most likely have some more shore work, the more like a *military man* I looked the better,' Fisher told Mrs Warden. This sort of cheerful puckishness, taken to the nicely calculated limit of respect for his senior officer, eased the burden of convalescence for Shadwell, just as it had endeared the boy to him over the past years. The foot still failed to heal properly, and in October Fisher witnessed a further and more drastic operation on it.

A retired surgeon 'had a look at the foot and recommended that it should be cut in two places and deeper than before. So one fine morning they gave him chloroform and did it. Two awful gashes they were too, right across the bottom of his foot and right down the middle, to the bone each way. They performed the operation all right and the Captain had recovered from the chloroform and was feeling as well as he could under the circumstances, and the bandages had all been put on, and the doctors were congratulating one another at the GLORIOUS CUTS they had made, when the principal artery of his foot broke adrift and the whole place was filled with blood. Courtney had to cut another piece out so as to be able to reach it with his tweezers, and they hauled it out and tied it up. They had not time to give him chloroform, so you can fancy the agony the poor old gentleman endured, and the old fellow said quite innocently afterwards, "Well, Fisher! I am afraid I made a great deal of noise this morning," as if anybody could help making a noise when they feel a man's hand hauling the inside of your foot out . . .'

Miraculously, Shadwell's foot seems to have improved after this rough treatment. By early November 'the swelling has gone down and not more than a teaspoonful of matter comes out of a day'. A month later it was worse again, and at Hong Kong Admiral Hope came on board and told Shadwell that he should give up his command and sail home in January. The news was an awful blow for Fisher. 'I can hardly realize the fact of the old buffer going,' he wrote. 'I'd give anything for him to stop.'

In spite of his wound, the manner of Captain Shadwell's going was appropriately colourful. He gave the Midshipmen a dinner in his cabin, and the Midshipmen invited him back (this was Fisher's own idea, and 'the fellows in the wardroom don't like it, because it is what *they* ought to have done'). On Christmas Eve 1859 'there was great fun in the Captain's cabin . . . The Skipper served out all his stock among the Midshipmen, and you saw fellows walking out of the Captain's cabin loaded with brown Windsor soap, tooth brushes (*new ones of course!!!*), nail brushes, combs, looking glasses, etc. etc. etc.' For Fisher, besides the engraved set of studs, there was a present of all Shadwell's books, beautifully bound. 'Isn't it jolly of the old gentleman?' Fisher wrote to Mrs Warden. 'Directly he gets well he has been promised a line-of-battle ship, and he told me he should take care I was with him there.' Fisher was also present on the day Admiral Hope came to say good-bye to his Captain, and the Admiral asked Shadwell if there was anything he could do for him. Of this occasion Fisher wrote in the last months of his life, 'He turned his suffering body towards me and said to the Admiral: "Take care of that boy." And so he did.'[1]

Shadwell's departure had a surprisingly favourable effect on Fisher's fortunes. Admiral Hope's motto was 'Favouritism is the secret of efficiency', which Fisher later included among the most useful in his renowned collection of aphorisms, and he experienced its benefits even before the Admiral left the *Highflyer*. Fisher was ordered to the flagship 'and everyone in the Fleet saw this Midshipman going into the Admiral's boat. He took me with him to the Flagship: and I got on very well with him . . .' This was the beginning of a long and profitable association.

A further lesson in the value and meaning of power of another kind was established in Fisher's mind that winter at Hong Kong. There was much press criticism of the failure of the British forces to overwhelm the Peiho forts. Admiral Hope was the target of critical comment, but the most harshly treated was Captain Shadwell. Perhaps this, as much as his foot injury, was why he had been relieved of his command. 'I see some of the papers are trying to lay the blame on old Shadwell,' wrote Fisher from Hong Kong. 'It's just like them. There wasn't a single thing old Shadwell did that day without a positive order from the Admiral, especially the landing, and now these confounded quill-drivers want to get the old gentleman into a row. If the best of them had as much sense in their whole bodies as old Shadwell has in his little finger . . .' When Fisher later acquired power and authority, his view of the press remained ambivalent: he could at one moment condemn it and in the most extravagant terms, at the next praise it warmly for its considered wisdom. His attitude depended on whose side it was on; and the key to this was in the proprietor and the journalist. What he was never to forget from this time was the importance and the *power* wielded by the press. When it became necessary he cultivated its attention with all his charm and experience, and numbered among its ranks his closest friends and (when he failed) his most implacable enemies.

For the present, as a Midshipman soon to face his examinations for

[1] *Records*, 14.

promotion to Mate (the equivalent rank to Sub-lieutenant today), Fisher was chiefly preoccupied with his personal ambitions and his delight in his new privileged status in Admiral Hope's flagship. Soon his position was to be further substantially improved. On 25 January 1860, his nineteenth birthday, Midshipman Fisher took his examinations for Mate. 'I went up . . . before the three Captains, and they gave me a regular bounce out. It took altogether three days and . . . I had the satisfaction of getting a *first-class* certificate . . . Oh, Mams!' he continued to Mrs Warden, who had now returned to England, 'you should see me in my scales and full-dress coat, such a beauty! (I don't mean the coat.) One can't help hearing as one walks along people saying, "Who's that? By George, a handsome fellow!" I don't wish to brag, but I don't think they are far out, do you?' Soon after he was told of his success, the senior Post-captain told Fisher he would be 'mentioned to the admiral'. Admiral Hope then sent for him 'and told me he was very pleased to see I had passed such a good examination, and that as a reward for it and on account of old Shadwell's report of me, he should take me as his Flag Mate, and that he would take care to look out for me always'.

This appointment finally confirmed the recognition of his qualities as an officer. For the remainder of his period in the Far East Fisher— ever more lively, industrious, shrewd and resourceful—continued to earn the good opinion of those about him. It was impossible to overlook the youth. Whenever an opportunity offered for him to demonstrate his qualities, he rushed in to seize it with the spirited eagerness of Ariel's 'What shall I do? say what; what shall I do?' No one else had a chance of getting in first. What was most important, he earned the affection and approval of Admiral Hope as he had of Captain Shadwell before him.

When Admiral Hope appointed Fisher as his Flag mate he was 51, 'a great man, very stern and stately, the sort of man everybody was afraid of',[1] wrote Fisher sixty years later. 'His nickname was composed of the three ships he had commanded: "Terrible . . . Firebrand . . . Majestic." ' And there is a brief but telling contemporary glimpse of him through Fisher's eyes in another of his letters to Mrs Warden: '. . . I went all round Hong Kong the day before yesterday with the Admiral in his yacht, a kind of picnic affair. The worst of it was I had to take one end of the table, and I felt so precious uncomfortable accordingly. He is an awful proud old fellow, but he is very kind at the same time. Post-Captains have to run after him like little dogs. It is such fun to see the cool way in which he treats them.' What admirable training and

[1] *Records*, 14.

experience for a future Admiral of the Fleet! Fisher revelled in every moment of it, and gleefully recorded the rigours of his tasks with a touch of hyperbole—a weakness he was later scarcely able to control.

'I have nothing to do with anyone in the ship except the Admiral himself, and, no mistake, he keeps me going. He hardly takes off his boots without sending for me and informing me officially of it. I have to call him at 5 a.m., be in his cabin dressed by 7 a.m., ready to receive orders as to what the different ships are to do. At 8 o'clock I take him a load of papers, which takes me 2 hours of the previous evening to make out, and follow him about like a dog whenever he leaves his cabin. It is very jolly in one way. I can give some of these Lieutenants a good snubbing sometimes. They dare not say anything to me, because the Admiral has given strict orders that no one is to interfere with his Staff on any pretence what-sum-dever . . .'

The relationship between the youthful mate and the middle-aged Admiral developed rapidly. On 7 February 1860, for example, he went for a sail with Hope. They landed 'about six miles away from the ship and [he] asked me if I would go [for] a walk with him. Of course I said I should be extremely happy, and away we went about 7 miles an hour. He kept me at almost a run the whole way, he has got such awful long legs. You would never think, to see him walking, that he had a hole in his thigh you could shove both fists into. [A result of his wounds at Peiho]. I had an awful long confab with him and he finished up very jolly. He asked me to dinner. They are very jealous of me on board because I have got into such a good berth. . . .'

By the standards of today, the favouritism of Admiral Hope appears excessive, but it was not unusual at that time for a youth in the services with exceptional promise to be selected for special treatment and privileges on the scale Fisher enjoyed. Fisher's letters to Mrs Warden continue through 1860 to recount these in detail, and his own puckish response. It is evident, from several references at this time, that Admiral Hope sensibly made use of the boy's special appeal to women. On a Sunday evening in February 1860, Fisher wrote to Mrs Warden, after assuring her that 'like a good boy', he had been to church: 'The Admiral made me go and call on Lady Robinson, the Governor's wife. How I did bless her! though she is a very nice person. While I was there Mrs Coutts came to call, so I was off like a shot. Lady Robinson sung out after me, but it was no good. Just fancy facing two strange females all by myself . . .' There can be no doubt that he would have handled the pair of them with as much skill and diplomacy as he was already learning to manage his own affairs.

Admiral Hope had determined to promote his young protegé at the earliest opportunity. On 11 February he sent for Fisher and told him he had a blank commission to give away. He told him that he intended giving it to Fisher, 'but there was a Mate just arrived on the station who on the way out had jumped overboard when the ship was going 10 knots and saved a man, and he wished very much to reward him for it, and he had been a very long time a Mate. So he gave it to him. But he told me something would be sure to turn up soon and he would take care not to forget me.' Fisher added generously, in his letter to Mrs Warden, 'I don't begrudge it, because I think he deserves it more than I do'. This Lieutenant's name was Edward Seymour, later Admiral of the Fleet Sir Edward Seymour, who became one of Fisher's strongest opponents and lived to be described by him as 'a senile ass' and 'a d—d fool'.

Fisher knew that he had not long to wait for his commission. 'Just fancy,' he wrote exultantly to Mrs Warden in England, 'I might be a Lieutenant at home this time next year. Won't I come and tease you. I'll have a dance with you then with my epaulettes on.' But he wisely turned down the next opportunity, which came little more than a month later. On 24 March 1860 Admiral Hope offered him a Lieutenant's commission on the *Esk*, a gunboat similar to his old ship, the *Highflyer*. But Fisher knew that more fighting was imminent, and that when it occurred the little *Esk* was likely to be left behind. So he declined, and Admiral Hope told him he was quite right to do so. 'Besides which,' wrote Fisher ingenuously, 'it is a first-rate thing to be with an Admiral as I am—not for the good I gain now by it, but what I shall gain hereafter in having a powerful friend to back me . . .'

Four days later Fisher's promotion came through. He at once told Mrs Warden, adding 'I am too excited to write'. A fuller account had to wait until later, and meanwhile much had happened to 'Lieutenant Fisher!!!!', as he announced himself, and which he now described with effervescent enthusiasm to Mrs Warden:

TO MRS EDMUND WARDEN

H.M.S. Pearl, at sea
April 4th, 1860

My dear old Mams,

Lieutenant Fisher has at last a little spare time to devote to Mrs Edmund Warden. I thought directly I became a Lieutenant I should have nothing whatever to do, but ever since I came on board here they have been keeping me hard at it. We left Hong Kong the same day as I sent my last letter, with a horrid old troopship in tow called the *Cressy* to take up with us to Chusan. You can imagine what kind of job we have before us to sail up with a ship in tow against the N.E. Monsoon. The day after we left we fell in with a regular gale of wind. It was my first watch, i.e. from 8 p.m. till midnight, the first night watch I ever kept as 'Officer of the Watch.' Some of the sails blew away, the wind being so strong. I was howling away the whole four hours. I quite astonished the old Skipper with MY GRUFF voice. You may laugh if you like, but you have no idea what a noise I made. The Skipper is such a rough old fellow, so different to old Shadwell. He is one of the regular old school. . . . The old Admiral was so kind to me when he gave me my commission. He said he was very sorry indeed to part with me, but that it was for my own benefit, and that I might depend upon his keeping his eye upon me. He told me he would send me as Naval A.D.C. to Mr Bruce in case he wanted one, which will be a splendid berth. But I am very much afraid that he won't want one. At any rate, he has sent me into Mr Bruce's ship, the *Furious*, and I must try there and work round old Bruce.

I forgot to tell you that the Admiral gave me *command* of the *Coromandel* for four days, and I took her up to Canton and back. I was regular Captain of her. We passed close by the old *Highflyer* on our way up and down. Old Purvis and all the fellows up there could hardly believe their eyes. I was very sorry to leave the *Chesapeake*. I came to consider myself as the next man to the Admiral, but, *really*, no one dared to say anything to me, not even the Captain, because everything nearly I did the Admiral himself told me to do. It seems so strange now to call the First Lieutenant just by his name instead of saying 'Mr So and So,' or 'Sir'. Well, I really can't think, Mams, how it is that I am so lucky. I am in a dreadful fright that something will happen soon to take me down a peg or two. I have done nothing much to serve such good fortune. Well! We shall see all in good time.

I can't write any more to-day. The ship isn't very easy and I have a little headache. Just fancy the '*boy*' having a headache, isn't it preposterous! You don't believe it, do you? I forgot to tell you that I was very nearly SEASICK. Just fancy a fine Lieutenant being seasick, but I wasn't regularly. I took a stiff glass of grog and I was all right. I expect I am rather a donkey for being so candid. You will only chaff me by and by. Well, I don't mind a little *private* chaff. If you say anything to anyone, I will never speak to you again, *there!* . . .

The intimate nature of Fisher's letters to Mrs Warden at this time suggest his need for a proxy mother to replace Lady Wilmot-Horton, herself an inadequate correspondent. He wrote rarely to Ceylon, and received few letters from his family. The remoteness of son from his parents is revealed in a passage from a letter to Mrs Warden sent soon after he had received his commission:

'. . . My mother sent me her picture last mail [he wrote] but when I came to open the box I found it broken in three places. I managed to gum it together. I was greatly surprised. My father says it is a splendid likeness. It looks just about the same age as Mrs Nye, perhaps a little younger. . . . I can hardly believe it is my mother when I look at it. She seems so young, and yet here I am 19 years old. Well! Women are very deceptive in everything . . .'

At this time Fisher was facing his greatest testing time since he had entered the Navy, and was in need of letters of support from his family, as well as from Mrs Warden, who never quite fulfilled Fisher's demands as a correspondent. His commission as Lieutenant in the *Furious*, 'a horrid old tub', began on 13 June 1860, and one of Fisher's last preserved letters to Mrs Warden shows what life could be like in the service then under a fearful captain. Captain Oliver Jones was, Fisher wrote, 'an awful scoundrel. There has been one mutiny on board of her already through him, and he has very cunningly managed to get none but acting Lieutenants, in fact all the ward-room officers acting, so that he can do just what he likes with us to a certain extent, because he knows we are all young and don't want to risk a court-martial just after we have received our commissions . . .'

As an Admiral of the Fleet, Fisher's view of Oliver Jones had mellowed with age, but, even allowing for exaggeration, the picture of this relic from a more barbarous sea age, remains clearly etched:

'He was Satanic; yet I equally [with Admiral Hope] liked him, for, like Satan, he could disguise himself as an angel; and I believe I was the only officer he did not put under arrest. For some reason I got on with him, and he made me the navigating officer of the ship. He told me when I first came on board that he thought he had committed every crime under the sun except murder. I think he committed that crime while I was with him. He was a most fascinating man. He had such a charm, he was most accomplished, he was a splendid rider, a wonderful linguist, an expert navigator and a thorough seaman. He had the best cook, and the best wines ever afloat in the Navy, and was hospitable to an extreme. Almost daily he had a lot of us to dinner, but after dinner came hell! We dined with him in tail coat and epaulettes. After dinner he had sail drill, or preparing the ship for battle, and persecution then did its utmost.'[1]

During the fourteen months Fisher served under this firebrand, he added prodigiously to his knowledge of human nature, and how to manage it in its extreme forms. He also learnt much of the fine art of navigation, from the Gulf of Pechili in north China, where the *Furious* was frozen in the ice in winter, to the desert island, *en route* for England, on which Fisher was landing to carry out a survey.

[1] *Records*, 15–16.

Fisher was pining for home, and he heard with delight that the *Furious* had been chosen to bring to England a selection of presents from the Emperor of Japan to Queen Victoria. The passage took six months. On 20 August 1861 the old ship sailed into Portsmouth harbour. It was Fisher's first sight of the downs and green fields of southern England for five years. During this time he had grown to be a man, tough in physique and wise in the ways of the world and the service. He had proved his courage in battle. His judgement of men and women had grown shrewd, his self-confidence and his ambitions were already boundless. He had made few enemies, and they were of no consequence, and he had made many friends, including several Admirals and Captains. His ability, at the age of twenty, to endear himself to a commander of the calibre of Captain Jones was shown by the testimonial Fisher received from him when the *Furious* was paid off: 'As a sailor, an officer, a Navigator and a gentleman, I cannot praise him too highly'. It was a good enough summary after his first seven years service in the Royal Navy.

Chapter 2

PRELUDE TO GREATNESS

The rank of Lieutenant, Royal Navy, of which Fisher was so proud ('mind you don't get making a mistake', he had warned Mrs Warden, 'and address to J. A. Fisher, Esq., instead of *Lieut. J. A. Fisher*, R.N.'), had not been confirmed on his return to England. He had passed his examination only in seamanship. In the late summer of 1861 in the old hulk H.M.S. *Excellent*, the gunnery establishment at Portsmouth, he studied mathematics and gunnery with zeal and enthusiasm. He passed out with first-class certificates in both subjects, receiving the highest marks in mathematics of any officer that year, and gaining as a result the highly prized Beaufort Testimonial, an annual award in memory of the famous hydrographer, Admiral Sir Frederick Beaufort. So exceptional was his success that his commission as Lieutenant was back-dated some twelve months and in January 1862 he was appointed a gunnery staff officer in the *Excellent*.

This triumph was followed by an immediate setback. A new order intended to improve the standards of gunnery in the service made it necessary for every Lieutenant to submit himself to a six-months course at the Royal Naval College before qualifying as anything better than a third-class gunnery officer, future pay being determined by marks. As Admiral Bacon, his first biographer, wrote, 'This did not suit Fisher, for there was nothing third class about him; so he set to work daily after his duties were done, and devoted the evenings to study. In due course he applied for a special examination, which was granted; he then obtained a first-class certificate, and became a first-class Gunnery Lieutenant.'[1]

The additional 3s 6d a day was very welcome. Fisher was already developing sound financial judgement to offset his lack of the private means which were enjoyed by so many of his contemporaries. He

[1] *Bacon*, i, 26.

44

retained a good sense of balance about money all his life, and he was encouraged in this by the example of his father's hopeless improvidence and the ruinous effects extravagance produced among some of his friends. But there was never a hint of parsimony in the ordered care of his finances. Some years later, he wrote to his wife with characteristic generosity, 'I was thinking, darling, yesterday that if we gave away £18 5 0d a year in charity, which is just a shilling a day and 1/20 of my pay, and . . . keep a book and note down what we give away in pure charity, and at the end of the year, whatever this comes short of the £18 5s to send to some charity. I think we ought to give some stated sum, and this, I think, is the VERY LEAST that we ought to give . . .'

William Fisher's coffee plantations were still in a terrible state. Eighteen months earlier, he had written to his son in China, 'I have long wished to send you a trifle but have been so hard-pressed I could not. I have sent you a tenner which I hope will be of use to you . . . If you still require a *little* assistance let *me know*, but I am very hard-pressed with the other children.'[1] On hearing of his sons' success in his examinations William Fisher wrote on 14 January 1862 to say how pleased he was, and was '*sure* you will continue to prosper'.[2] Then, regretting that he had not sent him anything recently, he added that he was 'so distressed for money I don't know when it will end. I have no crop at all this year and my Estates will have cost £2,000 which is clear loss . . .'

Very little had gone right for William and Sophie in the past fourteen years since Jack had been sent home to England. Most of the coffee seasons had been poor ones, debts had mounted and babies had been born with inexorable regularity. All those who survived were sent home in turn: Alice and Lucy; the four brothers, Arthur and Frank, who became civil servants and returned to Ceylon; and Philip and Frederic William, who joined their eldest brother in the Navy. The eldest daughter, Alice, as a married woman, was charged with caring for her youngest brother from the age of four years. In this sort of way the Fishers contrived to be free of all their children in turn though, as Sophie lamented, it was 'cruel parting with them'.[3]

In spite of all his troubles, William Fisher remained vigorous and energetic until his death in 1866 after falling from a horse. In a letter to a friend in England in 1862 he wrote proudly, 'We are both wonderfully well considering I have been thirty-one years here and my wife twenty-four. I have not a grey hair on my head and can shoot and ride just as well as I ever could. Sophie is forty but very stout and young-looking.' But, inevitably it seems, he ends on a sombre note which

[1] Kilverstone MSS.   [2] *ibid.*   [3] *ibid.*

confirms his incapacity to cope with the mechanics of their life. 'I want [Sophie] to go home with Alice, but she won't and I shall never be able to go . . . it is hopeless.'[1]

It was never quite hopeless: Sophie, the manager, saw to that. Without her organizing power and fibre, total bankruptcy and ruin would have fallen on Fisher's parents. It was certainly a happy division of parental qualities which gave their first-born his father's physical robustness and tenacity, and his mother's will to survive and analytical sharpness of mind.

During 1862 Fisher prepared himself for the new responsibilities which must soon confront him. He applied himself earnestly to the art and practice of authority, and trained in public comportment as an officer, even to his voice and facial expression. '[He] was rather a terrifying examiner in practical gunnery,' one of his pupils later recalled. 'He used to stare at his victims without any expression on his face, and only by the movements of the pencil could it be guessed that dots and crosses were being registered with a consequent loss of numbers.' According to Bacon, he developed this assumed abstraction, which became one of his more notorious eccentricities. 'Whenever during a conversation he was analysing or digesting a remark, his lips parted slightly and his face assumed an expression of complete vacuity which was most disconcerting to anyone who wished to gather information as to how the remarks were affecting him.'[2] On the brisk walks he took for exercise on the downs behind Portsmouth harbour, almost his only recreation, he could be heard from a distance shouting orders to an absent crew in order to develop the carrying power and authority of his voice.

Fisher continued to make friends easily—too many of them, he used to say later, at a time when their usefulness provided the lie to his complaint. On leave and sometimes at week-ends he would take them to Catton Hall, or Lady Wilmot-Horton's London house in Arlington Street, Mayfair. Lady Wilmot-Horton not only continued to offer Jack Fisher her affection and a home, but had by this time 'adopted' his brothers Arthur, Frank and Frederic. After five years abroad, Fisher and his godmother had easily picked up their old relationship.

Before his next seagoing commission Fisher visited Paris for the first time, and wrote from the city to one of his aunts: 'I am very much pleased with Paris but I am exceedingly glad that I am not a Frenchman. From the highest to the lowest they are the most dirty, immoral people I have ever seen. My friend with whom I am staying is a

---

[1] Kilverstone MSS.   [2] *Bacon*, i, 26.

nephew of Marshal Baillaut who is at the head of the Emperor's household so I see lots of things which I should not have if I had been staying with someone else. I went the night before last to see some grand theatricals (amateur). The actors were all 'bigwigs', two princesses, a marchioness and counts no end . . . I enjoyed it very much . . .'[1]

During 1862 he acquired as high a reputation among his superiors in the *Excellent* as he had earned on the China Station. It is easy to see why. 'The Lords of the Admiralty,' a shipmate's story runs, 'were paying their annual visit to the ship, and during drill with guns, at which I was powder-boy, one of the Admirals was heard to remark to the others, "Is this Lieutenant Fisher as good a seaman as he is a gunnery man?" Lieutenant Fisher at once stepped forward and said, in my hearing, "My Lords, I am Lieutenant Fisher, just as good a seaman as a gunnery man." At which they each bowed their heads.'[2]

Opportunism as quick as this, added to an outstanding record, brought their just deserts, and in March 1863 Fisher was made Gunnery Lieutenant of the frigate *Warrior*. It was the most sought-after gunnery appointment in the Royal Navy. The *Warrior* was the cynosure of the whole service, and the new pride of the maritime-conscious British people.

The first of the major revolutions in naval *matériel*, which were to mark all Fisher's service life and dominate his own mind and activities, had begun in the previous decade as a result of the general introduction of steam power, and guns that were bigger, rifled and fired an explosive shell. By the middle of the century the days of 'the wooden walls' were numbered. The Crimean War and the hectic Anglo-French naval competition which followed it accelerated the demise of the wood two- and three-decker ship-of-the-line. Steam engines were fitted into sailing battleships, and two years before Fisher entered the Royal Navy, the Admiralty ordered their first steam two-decker, although masts and yards remained *de rigeur* for several more decades. Six years later the French created a sensation with the world's first ironclad frigate, the *Gloire*, whose hull was protected against shellfire by iron plate nearly five inches thick. A year later, in 1859, the British laid down their answer to the threatening new French fleet of 'unsinkable' ironclads. The *Warrior* went one better than the *Gloire*. She was an iron-hulled warship and not just an 'iron clad' wooden frigate like the *Gloire*. She was designed to overtake and overwhelm any other warship in the world, and she and her sister the *Black Prince* fulfilled every expectation of their designers. The *Warrior* could steam at the unprecedented speed of 14 knots, an even under canvas she was only marginally slower.

[1] Kilverstone MSS.   [2] *Bacon*, i, 27.

Her armament, disposed traditionally on either beam, consisted of twenty-six 68-pounders, four 70-pounders and ten immense breech-loading 110-pounders. The *Warrior* was the first in the long line of modern iron and steel battleships (though rated as a frigate she could blow any number of wooden battleships to smithereens) which culminated almost a century later in the giant Japanese *Yamato* and American *Missouri*.

During Fisher's three-and-a-half years as Gunnery Lieutenant of the *Warrior* he developed his newly acquired authority, learnt much of the art of handling guns as well as men, and sustained a remarkable double act of fierce disciplinarian on duty and light-hearted playboy and tireless conversationalist in the wardroom. For the first time he was able to exercise his zeal for reformation which over the next fifty years was to take heavy toll of reactionary methods and reactionary men. His heart-felt angry cry of 'Efficiency! *Efficiency!!* EFFICIENCY!!!' at any cost which later was to echo through every Admiralty office, every shore establishment, dockyard and coaling station, and from the engine room to the fore-top of every man-of-war in the Royal Navy, was first heard on the gun decks of the *Warrior* in the mid-1860s.

The *Warrior* was a 'crack' ship in every way, and unique in the service. The quality of her crew matched her fighting prowess. Her Captain was the Hon. Arthur Cochrane, a son of the famous Lord Dundonald, and her Commander was George Tryon, a fierce and brilliant officer. It was an enormously lively and colourful ship. The lower deck was highly disciplined but more than usually liable to extravagant behaviour ashore. After a mayoral reception in Liverpool, where the beer flowed too freely, Fisher could get his party back to the ship in decent order only by ordering them to link arms and march in sections of four to disguise their condition; 'and I got highly complimented for the magnificent way they marched back through the streets!!'[1]

The wardroom was equally lively. Here, recalled Fisher, 'they kindly spoilt me as if I was the Baby'; and for his part he was the inspiration of most of the frolics. 'There was a dear old grey-headed Paymaster, and a mature Doctor, and a still more mature Chaplain, quite a dear old Saint', wrote Fisher, referring to John de Vries, Surgeon Samuel Wells and The Rev. Robert Jackson. 'These, with other willing spirits, of a younger phase, I organized into a peripatetic band. The Parson used to play the coal scuttle, the Doctor the tongs and shovel, the dear old Paymaster used to do the cymbals with an old tin kettle. The other instruments we made ourselves out of brown paper, and we perambulated, doing our best. The Captain came out of his cabin door and asked

[1] *Memories*, 147.

the sentry what the noise was? We were all struck dumb by his voice, the skylight being open, and we were silent. The Sentry said: "It's only Mr Fisher, Sir!" so he shut the door! The Commander, Sir George Tryon, wasn't so nice! He sent down a message to say the Gunnery Lieutenant was "to stop that fooling!" '[2]

As Gunnery Lieutenant, Fisher established an excellent working relationship with his men, who respected him for his firmness and eagerness for efficiency and the way he joined them in their hardest and most unpleasant tasks, and not only coaling. They equally loved him for his gaiety and high spirits off duty. He was, in their eyes, 'a character' and a tough one at that. There was no quicker way to their hearts. One of his contemporaries later wrote of him at this time, 'He was a dear boy, so full of fun and humour, but at the same time so really dignified and strict on duty; the contrast was quite understood by his brother-officers and duly appreciated. As gunnery officer he was quite unique.'[1]

Everyone who witnessed the *Warrior*'s gunnery remembered it for the speed and accuracy Fisher brought to every drill. At Weymouth in April 1864 Giuseppe Garibaldi inspected the new ironclad, and Fisher later recounted in a letter to his Aunt Kate what happened when the great revolutionary leader came down to the gun-deck. '. . . we went to general quarters and commenced firing away like fun and went through all sorts of different evolutions with the guns; first we supposed the enemy on one bow and then on the other; in fact, the enemy was everywhere in the course of ten minutes. The men worked the guns splendidly. I never saw them moved quicker before. Garibaldi turned round to me and said "he was vary moch pleased indeed," and he afterwards said it was almost the finest thing he had seen in England.' Before leaving the ship, he told the ship's company 'that he had seen one of the things he had set his heart on seeing, and that was the *Warrior*. I had a good look at him', the ever-observant Fisher concluded his letter, 'for the Admiral made me go round with him everywhere to explain things he wanted to know about the guns, etc. I thought him looking very worn and done up. I don't wonder a bit at people being so enthusiastic about him, for he has such a noble face and at the same time such a very simple manner . . .'

A month earlier at Lisbon Admiral Sir Michael Seymour inspected the *Warrior* and afterwards told Fisher 'he had hardly ever in his life seen a ship in such splendid gunnery-order, and that he should bring my conduct to the notice of the Admiralty in consequence of which when we arrived home I got a special letter of thanks from the

[1] *Memories*, 147.   [2] *Bacon*, i, 30.

Admiralty'.[1] Such praise was rare from any Admiral, and from the fierce and highly critical Seymour almost without precedent.

As the Royal Navy's show ship, the *Warrior* was constantly on the move. In the early spring of 1864 she was at Madeira, Teneriffe and Gibraltar as well as Lisbon. The cruise was interrupted by a brief moment of alarm when Prussian aggression against Schleswig-Holstein created a threat of war, and the *Warrior* was ordered home. The crisis passed over and the cruise was completed according to programme. Everyone wanted to see the famous ironclad, and the taxpayers at home, too, were offered every opportunity of inspecting her. From Invergordon, Fisher wrote to his Aunt Kate: '. . . We have been having great fun at the different places we have called at and of course crowded with people but at Sunderland I was perfectly astonished at the number we had on board, 14,000 in one day on board this ship alone and there were 7,000 on board at the same time so you can imagine that we were rather crowded. The people are most hospitable to us everywhere, every night there is always a Ball or Dinner, or something of the kind . . . At Leith I went up to spend a day at Linlithgow at Sir James Hope's who was my great friend in China. He sent down to ask me to come up and spend a few days but I haven't time. We leave this on Tuesday morning for Kirkwall in the Orkneys and then Loch Swilly . . .'[2]

Besides adding to his reputation as an exceptionally efficient officer and taking him to so many ports in home and European waters, the cruises of the *Warrior* were indirectly responsible for Fisher's marriage, at the age of twenty-five. On a visit to Portsmouth with her mother to see her brothers, who were in the Navy, Katharine Delves Broughton met and fell in love with Lieutenant Fisher, who was a few months younger than she was. Fisher was charmed by the pretty dark young woman. He was also at the right age for marriage, and just had sufficient means to set up a home. He proposed to 'Kitty', and on 4 April 1866 John Arbuthnot Fisher married Frances Katharine Josephine Delves-Broughton. In the last years of his life Fisher wrote of his beloved Kitty, 'She married a "boy" Lieutenant, who was penniless and friendless, with the blood of the Plantagenets in her veins, and left him with a coronet and covered with his flag of Admiral of the Fleet at her death.'

Fisher was by no means friendless or penniless at this time. But this passage accurately represents the spirit of respectful humility with which Fisher entered into matrimony. They were married for fifty-two years. The affection and tenderness never died, and he did his best to avoid wounding her sensitive feelings. But especially in his time of fame and

[1] Kilverstone MSS.   [2] *ibid.*

greatness and in the full floodtide of his vitality, there were many other women in his life, and there were years of distress and anxiety for Kitty when she was made to feel conscious of her inferior intelligence and wit by her husband's attentions to some of the most beautiful and clever women of the day.

For the present, however, and for many years to come, Fisher's devotion was undivided, and Kitty offered him in abundance all that he needed. Katharine Delves Broughton had been brought up the daughter of the Rector of Bletchley in Buckinghamshire. Her religious training had been rigorous, and after her marriage she did much to reinforce Fisher's religious convictions. Some of their early correspondence has been preserved, and reveals the intensity of their religious devotion and the love they shared.

TO MRS J. A. FISHER

H.M.S. Ocean, at Amoy
December 4th, 1870

My darling Heart,
. . . My darling, if only I was back with you I should be so *very very* happy, but still I feel very grateful to God for having separated us, for it has made me feel much nearer to Him and it has also proved to me how dear and precious you are, my own dear wife, and that you are more to me than all the world besides. I read some lines in Ecclesiasticus the other morning which I feel to apply so entirely to myself: '*The beauty of a woman cheereth the countenance and man loveth nothing better . . .*'

December 9th

. . . I am so glad to be down at Hong Kong, as there is always Sacrament every Sunday at 8 a.m., to which I can go without interfering with my work in the ship, and I intend to go every Sunday without fail while we are here, for I so seldom get the chance anywhere else, and when very occasionally we have it on board there's always an unpleasant feeling about it, as there are seldom more than 3 or 4 take it, so that one is in a certain kind of way held up to a certain kind of unpleasant public observation . . .'

Your own most devoted husband,
J.F.

Soon after his marriage, Fisher received an appointment at Portsmouth, which allowed him to live ashore with his new wife for some three years. They rented a furnished house in the town and lived a life of domestic bliss and contentment, economy and sobriety. On Sundays they went twice to church. They were the apotheosis of middle class mid-Victorian wedded bliss; and here their first two children, Cecil and Beatrix, were born. This was a period of tranquillity and complete happiness for both of them.

By contrast with his married life ashore, Fisher's service life as First Lieutenant of the *Excellent* was eruptive and unpredictable. His lectures on gunnery and the duties of a gunnery Lieutenant were sprinkled with wit and memorable phrases and axioms. No one could ever forget a Fisher lecture. A young officer, who later, as Sir Arthur Knyvet Wilson, became First Sea Lord and an Admiral of the Fleet, remembered for all his life his first Fisher lecture at Portsmouth. 'The main feature was a narrative of the cunning devices he used in order to get the Commander to detail men for gunnery drills instead of employing them in cleaning, painting, and polishing the ship. His method, which was highly entertaining as recounted, consisted chiefly in the artful use of judicious flattery, at which he was a past master.'[1]

The gunnery school was concerned with all forms of weapons of sea warfare, and it was Fisher's good fortune as well as an event that was to influence powerfully his whole thinking on *matériel*, that an effective form of locomotive torpedo was invented while he was here. The sinking of men-of-war by striking at their hull below the waterline is almost as old as sea warfare. The use of explosives for this purpose had been used during the Napoleonic wars, and forms of drifting mines which could be exploded when they struck the side of an anchored warship were developed by a number of scientists, most notably the Americans Robert Fulton and Samuel Colt. A more dangerous weapon for the operator, the spar torpedo, by which an explosive charge was thrust against the side of a ship at the end of a long pole, had been used in the American Civil War. The most effective and destructive of all underwater weapons was conceived by an Austrian Navy officer, one Captain Lupius, in 1864. His self-propelled torpedo with a small charge of explosive in the nose, and fired by contact, did not function properly until development work was taken over by a British engineer, Robert Whitehead. Within two years Whitehead had transformed Lupuis's ineffectual weapon into the first real locomotive torpedo, propelled by compressed air and carrying a charge of eighteen pounds of dynamite. Its range was only 300 yards, its speed a mere six knots.

Fisher was one of the few officers in the Royal Navy to recognize the vast potential of this new weapon, and he threw himself with prophet-like enthusiasm into the conversion of his fellow officers to his new cult. Early in 1868, years before a Whitehead torpedo had even been seen in England and when Whitehead himself was still trying to achieve some reliability for his invention, Fisher published privately

[1] *Bacon*, i, 35.

A Short Treatise on Electricity and the Management of Torpedoes. In this he stated that the torpedo 'is destined to play a most important part in future wars, for the following reasons:

'I. Ships as at present constructed are powerless against its attacks, supposing them to get within its destructive area . . .

'II. The demoralizing effect on the men from the constant dread of sudden destruction . . .'

In the 1860s, when the gun was the sole arbiter in war at sea, and naval thinking had not developed the intellectual and scientific flexibility it was forced to acquire in the next century, the first of these prophecies is remarkable enough. But for an officer in his twenties, brought up since thirteen in the conservative traditionalism of the Royal Navy, his belief in the likely moral effectiveness of 'sudden destruction' from this primitive weapon showed uncanny percipience. Within fifty years Fisher was to witness the arteries of his country brought almost to a condition of thrombosis by the attacks of submarines against its merchantmen, and the greatest fleet of battleships the world had ever seen was steaming in constant anxiety and turning from the enemy at the height of battle for fear of the torpedo.

In June 1869 Fisher took over all the torpedo instruction work in the *Excellent*, and held the post for some six months before being again appointed to the China Station. This was a most unwelcome appointment, and the next three years were the least fruitful in Fisher's career. He had hoped for an Admiralty appointment in London, which would have combined the pleasures of domestic life with a position of greater influence and responsibility. From China he wrote sadly to Kitty in June, 1870, '. . . my own precious Kitty, I am *always always* thinking of you and feel it so very hard that we should be separated now just in the prime of our lives . . .' And a few months later, '. . . I had pictured to myself our living at Ditton [Long Ditton, near Kingston-on-Thames] for the next 5 years and my going up every day with Arthur [his younger brother] and coming down in the evening and always having Saturday afternoon and Sunday to ourselves, and, besides all this, the mere fact of being at the Admiralty gives one a great lift in the Service, as one gets to know all the bigwigs so intimately. I feel quite sure that it is a most horrid mistake being so far away from England—one either gets forgotten or else it's too far off to send for anyone even if a good billet does offer.' But later in the same letter he adds philosophically, '. . . I have been most extraordinarily lucky so far in everything, so I must expect a disappointment now and then . . .'

As Commander of the *Ocean*, a fine new ironclad, Fisher did not allow those at home entirely to forget his existence. Letters arrived from

China addressed to officers of influence at the Admiralty and elsewhere, filled with strictures and recommendations and the gleanings of his fertile mind.

Shortly after his arrival in China he wrote to the Captain of the *Excellent* his frank criticisms of the gunnery school. The nature of the letter confirms Fisher's forthrightness and the intimate terms of his relationship with his old chief. 'The great failing of the *Excellent*', ran his letter from the *Ocean*, 'is an aversion to change. I mean large changes. She has seldom led the way, and this is but natural. Everyone on board has so much to do that (unless they are enthusiasts) they only have time to keep up their work, whereas at Woolwich, at Shoebury, and at Chatham the Staff and the permanent committees which are always sitting at those places are so large that they never fail to remind me of the Athenians and strangers who spent their time in nothing else but either to tell or to hear some new thing.'

To this same officer, Captain Henry Boys, he enlarged at length on the folly of the Admiralty's dependence on the War Office 'for almost any species of warlike store, from a 35-ton gun down to a boarding pike and a common shovel'. And he cited, in characteristic light vein, which made the point so much more memorable, as an example of the Army's ignorance of all things naval, the Colonel of Cavalry 'who was appointed Controller of Stores to the Indian Navy, and some ship expended her main-yard as "carried away", so he sent down an order that whoever took it away was to bring it back directly!'

In 1871 papers, articles and treatises flowed from Fisher's pen in China, and none failed to find its mark back in England. There was an especially important privately printed pamphlet on *Naval Tactics* which 'seems to have been made a great deal of'. Each added one more stone to the rising edifice of his reputation. Bacon wrote that 'Fisher spent all his time on board the *Ocean*, working far into the night, at schemes for the improvement and modernizing of the Navy. He held that, if the Navy was to continue supreme upon the seas, it must no longer rely on the methods of Nelson's days, and that it must be reconstituted from top to bottom both as regards its personnel and *matériel*. Many of the reforms he effected in later days were first conceived during his service on board the *Ocean*.'[1]

In his letters to his wife, too, there are frequent references to the work he was accomplishing outside the normal duties of a ship's first officer. He tells her of his continuing experiments with torpedoes and of his *Addenda* to his earlier treatise on the subject. Then he writes to Kitty with special satisfaction when the Admiral sends him a specially

[1] *Bacon*, i, 46

complimentary letter, sending her a copy and telling her that she may
'show it if you like, unless you think it is too flattering'. He also adds
that he is thinking of sending another copy to Tryon, now promoted
Private Secretary to the First Lord, where he was confident its contents
would do him most good.

As usual, and with the same favourable consequences as before,
Fisher had no difficulty in attracting the attention of his Admiral.
This again brought its own special difficulties. There was jealousy
among his contemporaries, and his relations with his Captain became
uneasy for a time. Vice-Admiral Sir Henry Kellet was 'constantly saying
before Captain Hewett and a lot of people that as long as he has me
by him to take care of him,' wrote Fisher, 'he doesn't care what happens,
and he asks me confidentially about things he speaks to no one else
about at all . . .' The favouritism of which Fisher so warmly approved,
and later practised, could often lead also to personal embarrassment.

But Fisher was much too shrewd to allow poor relations with his
Captain to last for long and jeopardize this trying and critical period in
his career. Work, that great balm, deflected his irritation in a more
profitable direction—like improving every branch of the service, and
his own reputation at the same time.

In September 1871, Fisher had completed his sea time as a Commander, and could look forward at last to the end of his term in the Far East,
and eventually to his promotion to Captain, 'which I fear at present
rates will not be for five or six years . . .' The *Ocean* had not docked
since her completion, and she was in sore need of attention. The
journey was a long, tortuous and hazardous one, from Singapore to
Plymouth at four and a half knots in 164 days, by way of Zanzibar, and
the Cape of Good Hope and Sierra Leone. 'I am so longing for this
weary passage to be over,' he wrote to Kitty.

The most hazardous stage of the journey was off Madagascar, where
the ship struck a typhoon. The *Ocean*, though comparatively new, was a
compromise design, having been laid down as a wooden two-decker, and
converted to an ironclad while under construction. This was accomplished by securing over 1,700 tons of iron to her decks and sides, with
odd effects to her stability. Moreover, loss of stability in high seas had
only a few months before caused the sinking of the ironclad *Captain*,
with the loss of all but eighteen lives. When the typhoon struck, the
Ocean was soon rolling forty degress each way, and the iron plates
began to open out the ship's sides from the deck.

Fisher refused to accept that there was any danger to the ship,
and rose delightedly to the challenge. 'The seas were very high,'
he later wrote to Kitty, in a letter which in a few words of description

of himself in a crisis, reveals also courage, supreme officer-quality, and disarming immodesty. 'They washed two of our large boats away and broke in one side of the quarter-deck, and at one time the sea washed up to my waist in my cabin on the main deck, so you can imagine what a lot of water there was knocking about; but we were never in the least danger, although I think a few were in rather a fright. I lost two caps overboard and, worst of all, my silver ring, which you know, if we lived, was to have been yours when we had been married 25 years! Now it is all over I am rather glad that we have had this gale, although it's rather a nasty spirit that leads me to say it, but it gave me an opportunity of coming to the front again, and I think I did very well. Now, darling, you must give me a blowing-up for praising myself like this. She once rolled 41 degrees over to one side. I was up in the foretop at the time, helping to furl the fore-topsail, and it was as much as I could do to hold on . . .'

In his last letters to his wife he speculates keenly on his future appointment. He had many people to advise him and gave the matter exhaustive thought. When it became known that he was going back to the *Excellent* there was considerable surprise that he, a Commander whose record was so exceptional, and who could wield such influence in high quarters, should accept such an unexciting appointment. It appeared to be no step forward from his position three years earlier. But Fisher was more confident than ever that the torpedo marked an epochal step forward in naval weapons, and that he would benefit most valuably from a high reputation in this field. This time he was again in command of all torpedo instruction in the *Vernon*, the new school attached to the *Excellent*, and 'I am not going to do anything,' he told his wife, 'which takes me off the main line of the profession.'

Nor did Fisher allow himself to be forgotten, as if he were in some backwater of the Navy. 'He entered on his new work with a vigour which much impressed all who passed through the various courses. These included officers of Post-Captain's rank. One of the Captains who took the course records his surprise at the way Fisher inspired these rather dignified personages, making them pull oars like seamen, and handle the wet cables and heavy chain moorings as if once again they were midshipmen.'[1]

His lectures were convincing and memorable. Who could ever forget the name of the Daniell electric cell, or Fisher's passion for the Old Testament, after he had started his lecture by uncovering a picture on the wall of Daniel in the lions' den? It was quite impossible to evade the spell of enthusiasm Fisher cast over all his students, from junior

[1] *Bacon*, i, 50.

Lieutenants to aged Admirals. He loved to address his class thus: 'If you are a gunnery man, you must believe and teach that the world must be saved by gunnery, and will only be saved by gunnery. If you are a torpedo man, you must lecture and teach the same thing about torpedoes. But be in earnest, terribly in earnest. The man who doubts, or who is half-hearted, never does anything.'

The torpedo became for him a Cause and he spread it far and wide, inviting to the *Vernon* anyone who could draw attention to the work and help in the raising of the status of (and therefore the funds for) the torpedo. Politicians and journalists were attracted to Portsmouth, and Fisher treated them to fervent lectures and astonishing practical experiments and electrical tricks involving detonations at a distance by electrical charges. They loved it, and loved Fisher. But he gave offence, too, to those outside the Cause, those who were jealous of his popularity, and many more who thought it all rather vulgar and ostentatious. 'I remember one officer who came into the wardroom after one of these entertainments and said, "Is this a blooming circus? When I joined this ship I did not know I was going to Barnum's show!"'[1] This was only a mild foretaste of what was to come when Fisher acquired greater power and responsibility.

It says much in favour of the Admiralty at that time, when it is traditionally thought to have been so reactionary, that Fisher's qualities were rapidly recognized. On 3 October 1873 the First and Second Naval Lords visited the *Vernon* with the First Lord of the Admiralty, and were much impressed with all that they saw. The Second Naval Lord, Vice-Admiral Sir Walter Tarleton, wrote in his diary that evening: '. . . Had a most interesting lecture from Commander Fisher, a promising young officer, and witnessed several experiments. The result of my observations was that in my opinion the Torpedo has a great future before it and that mechanical training will in the near future be essential for officers. Made a note to speak to Goschen [First Lord] about young Fisher . . .'[2]

As a direct result of this visit, and of the high praise accorded to him by Admiral Kellett, Fisher was promoted a Captain in October 1874, at the exceptionally early age of thirty-three.

During the 1870s the potential greatness of John Arbuthnot Fisher was becoming increasingly recognized among the most senior officers of the service and at the Admiralty. It was now quite impossible to ignore him. If there had not been substance behind the self-advertisement, his value would not have been worth judging; and he would

[1] *Bacon*, i, 53   [2] *ibid.*

doubtless from time to time have been reprimanded for outrageous behaviour. But the young Captain in his first twenty years service had shown exceptional aptitude as a seaman, exceptional bravery in action, brilliance as a lecturer and an administrator, and uncanny skill at getting on with people of every rank and class. His driving ambition was immediately noted by all who met him. The daughter of one senior admiral wrote of her 'father's opinion of him often repeated: that he was bound for the "TOP", "One of the finest brains in the Navy"—and so on—"with an inexhaustible capacity for hard work." '[1]

During the second half of this decade he became the *protegé* of two of the most senior and powerful Admirals, Sir Astley Cooper-Key and Sir Geoffrey Phipps Hornby, future and past First Naval Lords. His continued success while serving under them ensured his next rise, this time to an eminence from which he was unlikely ever to be dislodged. By the early 1880s the summit was just in sight.

Between September 1876, when he left the *Excellent* and briefly went onto half pay, and January 1881, Fisher's time was shared mainly between the Mediterranean and North American stations. He began with a short period on special service in the Mediterranean, a 'capital opportunity' for 'picking up a little experience in fleet sailing' under Vice-Admiral the Hon. Sir James Drummond, C.-in-C. Mediterranean Fleet, at a time when war between Turkey and Russia appeared imminent and there was a strong likelihood of the British Navy becoming involved. Fisher's unique knowledge of torpedoes was especially valuable, and he was also consulted on the defences of Malta harbour in the event of war.

Fisher's first turn of duty in North America, a station which included the eastern seaboard of Canada and the West Indies, began with his appointment as Flag-Captain to Sir Astley Cooper-Key in the *Bellerephon* —or 'Old Billy' as the ship was affectionately nicknamed—a fine 7,500-ton battleship armed with some of the largest guns in the service. Admiral Cooper-Key had for long recognized Fisher's qualities. He had commanded the *Excellent* during Fisher's first period there as an instructor, and Fisher had often been invited to his home in the dockyard, where he had become close friends with Cooper-Key's wife.

Fisher's arrival as Flag-Captain 'caused something like consternation in the ship', one Midshipman wrote, 'for his reputation as a strict disciplinarian was well known. The state of the ship was undoubtedly slack . . . Captain Fisher was not long in letting his opinion be known. He fell the officers and crew in on the quarter-deck; and, having told them what he thought of the want of smartness and proficiency, said:

[1] *Bacon*, i, 59.

"Now I intend to give you 'hell' for three months, and if you have not come up to my standard in that time you'll have 'hell' for another three months." [1]

'He was as good as his word. We had drills and exercises all the time . . . and in three months the ship was as smart as any in the Service. Then the Captain, with characteristic energy and versatility, threw himself heart and soul into the amusements of the officers and men.'

For Fisher the first and most important amusement was dancing. At Halifax at this time he developed a boundless enthusiasm for this activity, which lasted all his life. He liked it for relaxation, for its rhythm and its simple musical form and for the opportunity it offered for being with women. Everybody else had to dance, too, and there were to be no exceptions. In case his partners might not match up to his high standards, or endure his pace, he took along with him one or two Midshipmen who were expected to dance with him. Bacon has written that 'he eventually went so far as to stop the leave of any midshipman who could not dance. This was the origin of what afterwards became the universal practice, that the gunroom officers danced on the quarter-deck while the band was playing during the dinner-time of the wardroom.' Sir Astley Cooper-Key's daughter was his most frequent partner. 'He would come to the schoolroom, or the verandah, or the lawn, it did not matter where,' she later recalled, 'and we would dance for any length of time to his own whistling! if no better orchestra was available . . .'[2]

When war with Russia again became imminent, and his Admiral was ordered to form a Particular Service Squadron, intended as a reinforcement to the Channel Fleet, Fisher accompanied him as Flag-Captain in the *Hercules*, an even larger and more modern battleship than the *Bellerephon*. Fisher's close association with Cooper-Key and his family ceased when the Admiral was made First Naval Lord, an appointment for which so many of Fisher's patrons seemed eventually to be destined.

Fisher was not for long without a sponsor, and a berth. Early in January 1879 he heard from the C.-in-C. of the Mediterranean Fleet that he could have command of a ship. 'I am much obliged to my lords,' wrote Admiral Phipps Hornby to Fisher, 'for appointing you to the *Pallas*, and I shall be very glad to see you here . . .'[3]

Again, it appeared at first sight to be a most inferior commission for an officer of Fisher's standing to accept. The *Pallas* was only a corvette, and a rotten old tub at that. But Fisher knew that there was more to the appointment than was immediately apparent. He had known Phipps Hornby for many years, and was well aware of the high

[1] *ibid*, i, 56.   [2] *ibid*., i, 59.   [3] Kilverstone MSS.

opinion in which the Admiral held him. For his part, Fisher 'simply adored' him. 'That great man was the finest Admiral afloat since Nelson,' he described him. '. . . There never lived a more noble character or a greater seaman. He was incomparable.'[1]

Fisher was immediately taken under the wing of this brilliant Admiral. A ship was sent down from Ismid, where the fleet lay at anchor, to Constantinople when Phipps Hornby heard of his arrival, and when it was discovered that the Captain's quarters in the *Pallas* were in no fit state for the new Commander, the Admiral asked him to come and live with him aboard his Flagship. Fisher's estimate of his C.-in-C. rose even higher when he observed him ('I was next ship to him always when at sea') carrying out evolutions. 'He was astounding. He would tell you what you were doing before you did it; and you couldn't say you weren't going to do it because you had put your helm over and the ship had begun to move the wrong way.'[2]

During the following six months Fisher was being groomed, under an incomparable master, for greater responsibilities in the Mediterranean. The training and experience continued, step by step, towards the culmination of what can conveniently be defined as the first half of his professional life.

He next served briefly as chairman of a committee working on a revised version of the *Gunnery Manual of the Fleet*, and followed this with some leave, before taking up an appointment again as Flag Captain to the C.-in-C. North American station on September 25, 1879.

This time Fisher had a brand new ship and crew to shake-down, a new and most valuable experience for him. The vessel was the *Northampton*, the last word in cruisers and carrying any number of innovations in her equipment. 'Shortly after commissioning,' wrote one of the cruiser's Lieutenants, 'the *Northampton* proceeded for a week's cruise in the Channel for trial of guns and to test the ship under sail. The amount of work put into that week was prodigious: steam trials under steam alone, trials under steam and sail, trials under sail alone, tacking, wearing, making and shortening sail, gun trials, general quarters, night quarters, searchlight tests, and frequent coaling ship.'[3] Once again Fisher threw himself with almost frenzied industry into the new task, and probably no man-of-war before or since has 'worked up' with such speed.

The tight and demanding régime in the *Northampton* did not cease with the arrival of the cruiser on her station. Fisher was confident that this was his last appointment as Flag-Captain, and that a ship of his own—an important ship—was likely soon to come his way. He was

[1] *Memories*, 142.   [2] *ibid*.   [3] *Bacon*, i, 64.

determined that this was to be a memorable commission, so that with its termination the record would show that he had brought the Flagship to its maximum efficiency. The reaction of the lower deck was, as always, magnificent, even idolatrous. Among the officers there were mixed feelings. He was, after all, a too colourful character for many of them, sometimes inconsistent, often mysterious, and certainly controversial. There were some who did not care for his eccentricities, and others who took time to accustom themselves to them. The unpredictability of the man was unsettling—blowing hot one minute, icy cold the next. It was all very troublesome.

Fisher's Commander was Commander Wilmot H. Fawkes, a conscientious and dutiful officer, by no means a stupid fellow but too slow to understand at first the Fisher formula for running a warship, and uncertain in many ways about his Captain. The letters this officer wrote home over a period of eight months from April 1880 until January 1881 reveal clearly the puzzlement many fellow officers of lesser intelligence experienced when faced for the first time with his ruthless and quixotic manner; and how affection and loyalty usually grew with familiarity.

'What strikes me most is a lack of system. I fancy Captain Fisher is a splendid man for each individual thing but does not stick to a routine enough to make things work easily and well . . . Captain Fisher has been very pleasant indeed to me and I think I shall get on very well with him . . .

'I am disappointed with him. Of course he must be wonderfully clever; but I don't admire him as an Officer. He gets into a state on deck and shouts himself instead of telling me what he wants done but I mean to take it all very coolly . . .

'Captain Fisher has quieted down very much and things are getting down well . . . he is more of a scientific man full of torpedoes and inventions and does not attend much to the details of a ship's organization. He is very friendly with me . . .

'The Captain is quite disgraceful. He danced nearly every dance with one young lady and every one but two with her last night . . .

'We have just had a very merry dinner to celebrate the first anniversary of commissioning. The Captain's health was proposed and he made a very good chaffing answer. I really think there is not a happier ship anywhere . . .

'We went down to an outer anchorage and did our firing and torpedo practice. In three days we made more runs with the Whitehead torpedo than the whole Mediterranean Fleet did in their practice which pleased the Captain very much. I have never had such a time of it . . . I have got on capitally with him, but he makes everything such a rush that one can't do things properly.'

Commander Fawkes's letter of 14 January 1881 gives the news which Fisher had long awaited—his own ship at last, and what a ship!

'Very sad news for the ship, but very good for Captain Fisher, has just arrived by telegram. He is appointed to the *Inflexible*, the new large ironclad. It is a *very* great compliment to him, as these ships are generally given to men very much senior to him.'[1]

It was, indeed, tremendous news. The *Inflexible* when she was commissioned was not only the newest, most powerful and largest warship in the Royal Navy but in the world. She was the wonder ship of her day, and any Captain in the service would have given his right arm for the chance to command her.

The Admiralty's announcement could not have been better timed to raise Fisher's spirits. He was feeling frustrated and ineffectual out on the North American station far from the seat of power. He even had time to read. He had been reading a life of Nelson, which had had an uplifting yet humbling effect on him. 'We all seem such puny, insignificant people after reading of Nelson's times. I quite despise myself.'[2] Then, a few days after writing this, he received the tragic news of the death of his brother Philip. Philip Fisher, his 22-year-old younger brother, had followed him into the service and was doing splendidly. His eldest brother was devoted to him. As a Lieutenant he had already attracted the attention of many influential people. It was Queen Victoria herself who had persuaded the Admiralty to give him an appointment in the training ship *Atalanta*. And now the ship had disappeared with all hands. Fisher was heartbroken, and he was still in a state of depression seven months later when the news of his appointment came through.

Fisher broke the news to his wife by letter, and hastened home.

TO MRS J. A. FISHER

H.M.S. Northampton
Antigua
January 14th, 1881

My own darling Heart,

You may fancy my joy this morning at the following telegram from the Admiralty . . . 'Lord Northbrook has selected Captain Fisher for the *Inflexible*. Send him home immediately, if you have no objection, and name a

---

[1] Kilverstone MSS.   [2] *Bacon*, i, 68.

successor.' The Admiral is, I think, very sorry at my going away, and so say all the officers, and I really think they all mean it.

I am going to go home by the next mail, which leaves Barbados on January 29 and gets to Plymouth on February 12th. I suppose I shall then go straight to London, and then to Portsmouth, and I think I may be able to get a few days leave to come over to you. But it's not a bit of use to decide anything till I get home, for I must be most careful in all I do, because they have paid me a most wonderful compliment, I think, and I am sure to be most awfully envied and watched, so I want to show that I put duty in the first place. So I hope, my loving heart, you will not mind stopping quiet at Wiesbaden till I am able to see my way clearly . . .

My very tenderest love to you all, and we must not forget to be most heartily thankful to God for this great prosperity. Goodbye, my best and most loving of wives.

Ever your devoted husband,
J.A.F.

Chapter 3

GUARDING QUEEN AND COUNTRY

Of the three wonder warships of his lifetime, Fisher was First Officer of one, Captain of the second and prime creator of the third, the *Dreadnought* of 1906. In the twenty years since the launch of the *Warrior*, the battleship had become increasingly uglier as the theoretical battle between the gun and armour plate intensified. The cult of the biggest gun and the thickest armour had reached its culmination in the Italian battleships *Duilio* and *Dandolo*, designed by the brilliant if undisciplined naval architect, Benedetto Brin. These two freaks carried four 100-ton guns mounted in a central citadel protected by plate up to $21\frac{1}{2}$ inches thick. Because of the low rate of fire of these monster guns, their battle value was not rated highly. But fighting ships as provocative as these could not go unanswered by the greatest naval power in the world. Britain's response was the *Inflexible*, a monster of nearly 12,000 tons, carrying even thicker armour plate than the Italian ships, and four 16-inch guns, the largest in the service. She was an even greater 'wonder ship' than the *Warrior*; and at once the most hideous and belligerent fighting ship in the world. She was also full of gadgetry, like ballast tanks to reduce rolling, and electric light, both of which were doubtful in their operation, and even dangerous. A final touch of the bizarre was provided by her masts and rigging. In spite of her bulk and tubbiness, and reliable engines which gave her a speed of over 14 knots, the *Inflexible* was fully rigged. 'The sails,' as Fisher later remarked, 'had as much effect upon her in a gale of wind as a fly would have on a hippopotamus in producing any movement.'[1]

During his brief period as Captain of this strange and wonderful vessel, Fisher continued to demonstrate his reforming ardour, consolidated his good relations with the Royal family, fought on land and sea

[1] *Records.* 212.

for the last time, gained the first of his many decorations, and almost died from dysentery.

The *Inflexible* was commissioned at Portsmouth on 5 July 1881, and at once Fisher entered into a running battle with the Admiral Superintendent of the Dockyard, Rear-Admiral the Hon. Fitzgerald Foley, 'an old fossil', as Fisher uncompromisingly described him. Fisher demanded, and was at first refused, among other items a navigating bridge, more water closets and incandescent lamps for the lighting of the ship. The first and second were considered unnecessary, the last dangerous. He followed his usual effectual procedure of going over the head of his superior to the real source of power, and soon orders arrived from the Admiralty for Admiral Foley stating that 'all Captain Fisher's requests were to be complied with'.[1]

The summer of 1881 was a demanding period for Fisher, and he had little time to see his wife and family, from whom he had for so long been separated, and who had established themselves in a little house in Southsea. The numerous innovations in the battleship required a lot of testing and adjustment. Her poor ventilation, for example, demanded the installation of fans and fresh air leads and cowls. Below decks, the ship contained so many tortuous passages and compartments that even after some time in which to familiarize themselves, the men 'used to lose their way altogether amidst the mazes of this iron labyrinth, and knew not what deck they were on, what compartment they were in, or whether they were walking forward or aft; so it occurred to the Captain that if he had to take his ship into action there would be pretty general confusion down below . . . '[2] Fisher solved this problem by painting the bulkheads and passages in different colours, and adding a direction code with arrows and symbols. 'He succeeded after several months of close personal supervision and attention in evolving order out of chaos, and rendered his ship a valuable fighting machine.'[3]

In October 1881 the *Inflexible* left England to join the Mediterranean Fleet, then under the command of Admiral Sir Frederick Seymour, a heavily-built, ponderous and pompous officer of the old school, who had deplored every advance in the service's *matériel* since the introduction of steam and the shell-firing gun. In spite of a particularly rough passage through the Bay of Biscay, the new battleship had been brought up to Fisher's standards of fighting efficiency by the time she joined the fleet. But ability to fight her guns did not feature at the head of Admiral Seymour's priorities. As one of Fisher's contemporaries

---

[1] *Bacon*, i, 76.
[2] Oscar Parkes, *British Battleships* (London, 1957), 257. (Hereafter cited as *Parkes*.)
[3] *ibid*.

wrote, 'When the Admiral's inspection took place but scant credit was given to the Captain and his Officers for all the pains and trouble they had taken to get their ship into fighting order, and as they could not cross topgallant and royal yards and shift topsails quite so smartly as other ships in the squadron, they found themselves but lightly thought of, and suffered under the cold shade of official displeasure.'[1] Fisher was incensed and determined to correct the situation, even though he deplored the prevailing emphasis on gymnastics aloft in a ship which could only be handicapped in battle by her masts and yards. Very soon he had his men shifting topsails a few seconds quicker than any other ship in the Fleet. 'Then she immediately rose from the depths of official displeasure to the highest pinnacle of fame—she acquired the proud title of "the smartest ship in the squadron" and nothing was good enough for her.'[2]

In 1882 the *Inflexible* was granted the honour of acting as guardship from 18 March to 15 April to Queen Victoria while she was on holiday at Mentone. This was an opportunity to make himself known to the Court which Fisher seized eagerly, and there were Royal inspections, illuminations and all manner of ceremonials. Fisher had met the Queen some four years earlier, and he had good reason to believe that she had approved of his manner and admired his professional qualities, for soon afterwards he had received a letter from a member of the Queen's household, which said that 'the Queen was speaking of you yesterday . . . [she] said she liked you and had a high opinion of you, and that you were much respected and looked up to in your profession, and so popular'.

Queen Victoria had had no special affection for the Royal Navy since the Admiralty had refused her request to make her late husband an Admiral of the Fleet. Fisher went some way towards wiping out the memory of this slight. The Queen and Fisher later became warm friends, and he had a standing invitation to stay at Osborne when she was there and he was in England. She found his charm irresistible, and respected the serious professionalism he displayed as an officer. With royalty he always had a marvellous talent for taking lighthearted banter to the very edge of that delicate boundary between respect and disrespect; and every member of every Royal family in Europe he met enjoyed laughing with him and watching him play this dangerous game. Marder cites a fine example of this skill: 'When Fisher was Admiral Superintendent at Portsmouth in 1891, and a French squadron visited the dockyard, the Queen impressed upon him the necessity for the exercise of his delicate form of courtesy at the Royal dinner party to the French

[1] *ibid.*   [2] *ibid.*

Admiral. Few people would have attempted facetiousness in the sovereign's presence, but Fisher replied: "Yes, your Majesty, I have arranged to kiss the French Admiral *on both cheecks!*" The Queen broke out into laughter.'

Before 1882 Fisher's relations with his sovereign had not yet developed to this degree of familiarity. The means by which they did so are partly revealed in a letter he wrote home to his wife in which he told her of the Queen's gift.

TO MRS J. A. FISHER

> *Mentone*
> *April 11th, 1882*

My *darling Heart*,

The Queen has sent me a beautiful large print of herself and a most lovely large photograph of the Princess, and a most kind letter from Sir H. Ponsonby begging me to consider them as remembrances of my time at Mentone guarding the Queen. To-morrow I go to take leave at the station at 10 o'clock, and then we go straight to Malta, reaching there Saturday or Sunday.

Now I must tell you of my evening at the Châlet. We were ushered into a little tiny room, which is the only dining-room and, after a little pause, the butler told Sir Henry Ponsonby in a whisper that the Queen was ready. . . When we went in, she stood in the middle of the room, Prince Henry of Prussia who you remember, on one side, and the Princess on the other, and Lady Churchill and Miss Baillie (to whom I have lost my heart, and the attachment is mutual!) stood quite on one side. Sir Henry Ponsonby bowed very low indeed, and said, 'Captain Fisher, Ma'am!' She bowed, then stepped forward two or three paces towards me and began talking in the most pleasant and friendly way. After three or four minutes, she turned towards the next one, the Consul at Genoa, . . . Then she came again towards me and asked me where I was going after she left, and whether we hadn't found it very rough here. Then she laughed very much when I reminded her of our all getting ashore in the *Lively* and running into the *Alberta*, and she said, 'Yes, and I had to send all my Admirals and Captains back in one of my own yachts, and I was waiting and waiting and waiting for you all to come and could not think what had happened.' She talked to me for about ten minutes, and then spoke to Prince Henry and afterwards to Sir Henry Ponsonby, a handsome, tall man, who remained half bent double all the time. . . . Then suddenly we saw the Queen bow to Sir Henry Ponsonby, who immediately flew to the door as if his whole future depended on getting to it rapidly. He opened it and then bowed to each of us. The Queen then bowed to each of us, and we bowed to her and backed out . . . Then we went into the little room we first went into and had to write our names in the Queen's birthday book, and I saw Sir Henry carefully put markers into each place, as if to show them in the morning . . .

> Ever your loving husband,
> *J.A.F.*

There is evidence of Fisher's increasing preoccupation with his health while he was in the Mediterranean. By the end of 1882 this was to be fully justified, but at the time when he was appointed Captain of the *Inflexible*, he appears at least from his photographs to be in the same condition of robust health he had always enjoyed. He was now forty-one years old, a touch overweight perhaps but not corpulent, but he was anxious about his diet and his lack of exercise now that he was, more than ever, confined to administrative work. The first twinges of gout affected him in the Mediterranean, and he was soon writing home to tell Kitty all about 'that horrible tingling pain in my legs when I get out of my bath'. He gave up wine and spirits entirely for a time, and reduced his smoking to two or three cigars a day, and took to reading books on gout and skin diseases. 'They all recommend the same things apparently: water only to drink, no potatoes, sugar, pastry or condiments . . . I am going to get the butcher to weigh me, as Parkes recommends that one should watch one's weight . . .'

Although Fisher did not for long remain a teetotaller, from this time he never drank heavily and was economical with his smoking. His interest in his health continued for the rest of his life, and he always enjoyed a good talk on medical matters and increasingly took the waters at Marienbad and other spas. Mild corpulence and stomach disorders were not unusual at this time, when most people with the means to do so ate too much and did not take enough exercise. But it is curious that Fisher, who rated the manly qualities so high, was so evidently fit himself, and had his mind engaged on so many other things, should become absorbed so readily in the state of his body. This is evidenced in the number of medical analogies in his letters. The health of his family also greatly interested him. 'I found out from one of these books', he writes to his wife, 'that Dorothy [his second daughter] requires cod-liver oil. If I remember right, she dislikes fat and has occasionally rough places on her face.'

For the following few weeks Fisher had no time to think about his own health or the health of his children. A crisis was developing in Egypt which was demanding the immediate attention of the Mediterranean Fleet. The nationalist anti-European elements in the country had found a champion in an Army officer, Arabi Pasha. Arabi repudiated the authority of the Khedive, who, he claimed, was no more than a tool of the oppressors. Under joint pressure from Britain and France, Arabi was briefly forced from power, but as a result of the vacillations of both French and British policy, he reinstated himself on 27 May as a military dictator. This event was followed by uprisings and the massacre of sixty-eight Europeans and the hurried departure of most French and English nationals. After the fall of their government, the French withdrew the naval units which had been lying at anchor as a threatening force during June and early July.

Meanwhile, Arabi was continuing to whip up nationalist sentiments and was preparing for British intervention by strengthening the defences and forts protecting Alexandria. British accusations were denied, and on 10 July Admiral Seymour was instructed to send an ultimatum to the Egyptians, demanding that all further work on the forts must cease and that they should be surrendered within twenty-four hours. The eight British battleships, among which the *Inflexible* was the largest, newest and much the most powerful, assembled preparatory to bombarding the forts and forcing their surrender. On the evening of 10 July the British fleet took up station at ranges from 1,000 to 3,750 yards from the forts and cleared for action.

On 30 June Fisher had written from Alexandria to his wife that she 'need not be the least bit anxious about a row out here. There is no chance of it in my opinion, because I feel sure the Egyptians will not fight . . . You need not have the least alarm about me, as I am bound to stick on board the *Inflexible*, and there is not the slightest prospect of my landing with the men . . . if all the forts in Alexandria could get all their guns together, they could not possibly hurt us, and I don't believe they will be able to reach us even with their heaviest guns . . .'

For once, all Fisher's predictions were proved false—or was he only trying to cheer and reassure his anxious Kitty?

'The morning broke fair and clear,' ran one account of the attack, 'with a smooth sea, and a light N.W. breeze, which, when the action began, carried the smoke in-shore, and obscured the target, making good shooting a little difficult.

'At 7 a.m., by order, the *Alexandra* fired the first shot at the battery near Fort Ada; and a signal for general action was hoisted in the *Invincible*, where the Commander-in-Chief still flew his flag. It was greeted with cheers. Indeed, throughout the action there seems to have been more noise and chaff on some of the British decks than would have been desirable, or even safe, had the enemy been a more serious one. The Egyptians replied quickly and pluckily, their officers not hesitating to leap upon the parapets in order to direct and encourage the gunners; and the guns' crews sticking manfully to their work in spite of the overpowering fire.'[1]

The effect of the firing of the *Inflexible*'s monster guns was shattering. It 'blew my cap off my head and nearly deafened me',[2] Fisher recounted; and at 7.15 a.m. noted that the forts were replying vigo-

[1] *Clowes*, vii, 328.   [2] *Records*, 62.

rously. 'Both shot and shell from the Lighthouse batteries passing over the ship, principally between the masts, the shells bursting over the ship . . . A glancing shot hit the port quarter near the waterline, causing a leak in the breadroom above the armoured deck.' Half an hour later, 'A 10-inch Palliser projectile from the 400-pounder gun at the lighthouse battery killed Mr Channon, Carpenter, and severely wounded Lieutenant Jackson (and two others) . . . .[1]

The British had not expected such stout and courageous resistance. The *Inflexible*'s upperworks and boats were badly knocked about, but mainly small, obsolete smoothbore Egyptian guns could not do serious military damage to the ironclads. Intermittent fire was continued for ten hours before the forts appeared to be silenced and overwhelmed. The *Inflexible*'s gunnery was first rate, but the damage inflicted by her guns was not as great as had been expected, mainly because insufficient suitable ammunition was available, and more than half the British projectiles failed to explode.

That night the *Inflexible*'s new electric searchlights were used to sweep the shoreline and intervening sea as a precaution against attack by torpedo and drifting mines, and on the following day her big guns were ordered to renew fire against one of the forts which was still showing signs of life until at last the white flag was raised on shore, and a small party was landed to occupy the forts.

The chief consequence of the bombardment was to strengthen Arabi Pasha's hold on his people, and cause an outbreak of looting and rioting in the city, and the destruction of European property. Arabi's army and a strong force of Bedouin tribesmen installed themselves outside the city. Admiral Seymour therefore decided to land a party of bluejackets and marines, and Fisher was appointed as their Commander.

Fisher accepted the command with enthusiasm, and the fact that Arabi's troops vastly outnumbered the British force and that it was a most hazardous operation only added spice to the challenge. Fisher himself almost became a casualty on the first night, after strongpoints had been set up about the city walls. 'About 1 a.m.,' one of his Sub-Lieutenants later reported, 'Captain Fisher proceeded to inspect our outposts beyond the Maharun Bay Gate. He arrived without warning, and so suddenly that one of the gun's crew fired at him with a revolver. I knocked up the man's arm and the bullet went over Fisher's head. He took no notice of the occurrence, but merely inspected the gun, etc. He then told the officer to expect an advance of a large number of Arabi's followers during the night, and that the post must be held at all costs, remarking, finally, in a jocular way, "You can't miss 'em.

[1] *Bacon*, i, 81.

You've only got to put in the ammunition and off it goes." Then he disappeared as silently as he came.'[1]

For three days and with a force of only some four hundred men, Fisher managed to give the impression that his strength was much greater than it was. These were 'the most anxious days ever spent in my life', and the busiest, too. There was no sleep for any of the officers. At the same time, Fisher and his old friend Captain Arthur Wilson, contrived an armoured train for reconnaissance, and mounted a 40-pounder gun on it. This was ingeniously constructed from some old sheets of steel found lying in a railway yard, and proved sensationally effective. This, the first-ever armoured train, attracted great attention, and was used long after a large army force arrived to relieve the pressure on Fisher's men. 'Our armoured train is in constant requisition,' Wilson wrote home, 'and judging from the number of Correspondents who come to see it, I think you will see full descriptions of it in the papers, and pictures as well in the illustrated ones. We go out every afternoon to see what Arabi is doing . . .'[2]

The successful defence of Alexandria and the construction and operation of the armoured train, with which Fisher was exclusively credited, brought his name for the first time before the British public. The newspapers were full of reports of his ingenuity and gallantry. Admiral Seymour and the Army Generals heaped praise on him, and the Queen caused her private secretary to send him a letter of congratulation:

TO CAPTAIN J. A. FISHER[3]

Windsor Castle
[?] July 1882

My dear Fisher,
    Though the Queen has already through the Admiralty conveyed her thanks and congratulations to the Fleet at Alexandria, Her Majesty desires me to assure you of the extreme interest with which she has followed the movements of the *Inflexible* during recent times, and, in Her Majesty's name, heartily to congratulate you, your officers and men on the successful issue of your action on the 11th . . .
    The Queen little thought how soon the splendid guardship at Mentone would be actively engaged, and trusts that the capabilities of the vessel have proved themselves equal to your expectations.
    May I also offer my sincere congratulations?

I remain, yours very sincerely,
Arthur Bigge

---

[1] *Bacon,* i, 84.

[2] Admiral Sir Edward E. Bradford, *Life of Admiral of the Fleet Sir Arthur Knyvet Wilson* (London, 1923), 71. (Hereafter cited as *Wilson.*)

[3] *Bacon,* i, 86.

Accompanying this letter was a private one from Sir Arthur telling Fisher how the Queen had spoken 'with particular warmth' about Fisher and his 'splendid ship'.

The Alexandria affair had not been an especially glorious one for the Royal Navy afloat. Eight of the best battleships had required all day to defeat some old-fashioned amateurishly constructed forts, and had expended a huge amount of ammunition to inflict very little damage. But ashore it had been a different story. And no one had contrived to gain greater credit from the Navy's activities than Fisher. When the Honours and Rewards list was published, his name appeared among those privileged few granted a c b. He was as delighted by this honour as he was distressed and angry at the omission of Arthur Wilson's name.[1]

These had been particularly anxious days for Fisher's wife. The bombardment and the subsequent naval operations had been widely and sensationally reported in the newspapers, and it appeared that Fisher was always at the point of greatest danger. Late in July she read that the officer in command of 'the ironclad train' had been badly wounded and had had his foot amputated. By this time Fisher was back on shipboard, but some weeks passed before he could reassure his wife. There was almost equal dismay at Windsor Castle, too.

At this time Fisher nearly did die, though without violence. Dysentery struck him on 22 August. It was an especially violent attack. The treatment was equally fierce, but so effective that for a time it appeared that he had been cured. 'The doctors say I have made a wonderful recovery,' he wrote to his wife on 29 August. 'I took 8 pills of ipecacuanha and opium every 4 hours for two days. The proper dose is *one* pill a day, but Sedgwick, having had a great experience of dysentery in the East Indies and China, had learnt by experience that the only way to cure dysentery is to poison the patient with ipecacuanha. The remedy was 50 times worse than the disease; the sickness was simply indescribable . . .'

Everyone was very kind, and letters poured in from friends. Admiral Seymour had all his cabins in the *Alexandra* made ready for the convalescent, and Fisher was also told that of course 'the *Inflexible* might go anywhere if I wished a change' if he preferred to remain with his ship.

Although confined to a sofa in his cabin during his convalescence, Fisher could not resist the temptation of working overtime. The

---

[1] The scrupulously honest Wilson replied, when asked 'whether the train is my invention or Fisher's': 'I am sure I cannot tell you, as almost every step has been the result of consultation between us.' (*Wilson*, 76.)

September heat off Port Said, where the Fleet remained on guard while the Army dealt with Arabi and successfully fought the battle of Tel-el-Kebir, was highly unsuitable for someone in his precarious physical condition. 'I have such a lot of back work to do in the way of writing that my heart sinks at the thought of it,' he wrote to Kitty on 11 September; and on the following day prepared a long and detailed report on the technical handicaps from which the *Inflexible* suffered by contrast with the Italian giant, *Dandolo*, advocating among other modifications, 'the stem taken off, 50 feet put on to her, a false keel of two feet given her . . .' in order that her speed might be increased by three knots.

Fisher left for Malta, but still he would not spare himself. A relapse was inevitable, and it occurred soon after his arrival at the island. This time he was much worse, and his doctors despaired of his life. When the First Lord, Lord Northbrook, received the news he sent Fisher a special signal begging him to come home. 'We can get many *Inflexibles*, but only one Jack Fisher,'[1] he concluded his appeal. Fisher refused. In spite of his unique reputation, shown by messages of sympathy from the Queen and the First Lord, he was worried that to give up his prized Command would be a bad setback for his career. He would also have to pay some £50 for his own passage home, and this was money he could not afford, nor was it offered to him by their Lordships, who could not imagine a senior officer being unable to find this paltry sum.

Ever increasing physical exhaustion caused a weakening of his will to stay with his ship.

Early in October he wrote to his wife:

TO MRS J. A. FISHER

Malta
October 9th, 1882

My darling Heart,
I am sorely tempted to come home, but I don't like leaving the ship, especially with all these new officers, and so much to be done on board, and besides that, I am decidedly better and in whatever way I came it would certainly be an expense, and I should all the time have an anxious mind. But it's very difficult to resist coming home with everyone recommending it, and the Admiralty makes it so very easy . . .

Your loving husband,
J.A.F.

It was a bitter decision to have to make, but Fisher at last yielded to the pleas. He was greatly encouraged and sustained, above all the

---

[1] *Bacon*, i, 89.

other messages of sympathy from the Queen, the Admiralty and his Commander-in-Chief, by a letter from the lower deck of the *Inflexible*, which became 'one of my most cherished possessions'. 'We trust shortly to see you again amongst us,' ran one passage of this letter, ' . . . and at the end may you receive your share of rewards and laurels, and your ship's company will then feel as proud and prouder than if it was bestowed on themselves.'

Fisher sailed for England on 9 November 1882. 'As I was being carried on board,' he wrote later, 'in a brief moment's consciousness I heard the Doctor say: "He'll never reach Gibraltar!" and then and there I determined I would live.'[1]

Everyone was most solicitous during Fisher's long winter convalescence, and when his condition had sufficiently improved the Queen invited him to stay at Osborne House. He had been ordered to wear 'tights and pumps', 'but I was let off with trousers on account of being an invalid'. His dress was the subject of a *risqué* joke on the first night at dinner. The incident confirmed that he had quite regained his spirits and his aplomb. He was sitting next to Lady Ely, who was 'a very nice old lady but talks very indistinctly', when the Queen saw them laughing. Asked to repeat his joke, Fisher said, seemingly undismayed by the impropriety of the subject, 'I was telling Lady Ely, Ma'am, that I had enough flannel round my tummy to go all round this room!'[2] Very few people at this time could have caused the Queen to join in the laughter.

Only the meals with the household at Osborne were rather demanding. For the rest of the time, Fisher was left to his own devices. On one day the Queen invited his wife and his eldest daughter Beatrix, then aged fifteen, to join the party at luncheon, and afterwards the family went out for a drive with Lady Ely. Fisher saw the Queen mainly before, during and after dinner, which took place at nine in the evening and 'is very soon over'. He watched eagerly for all the points of protocol, and the manner of the Queen herself. 'She talks to one a good deal more than I expected,' he wrote at the time. 'She is sometimes silent for a little time, preparing her next subject of conversation, and I believe the plan is to remain silent also. They say "Your Majesty" to her much more frequently than I was led to suppose. The Princess always sits next to her, and the most comfortable place is next to the Princess, as she is so very pleasant and helps on the conversation. The other folks at the table talked in a very low tone. I believe it's the custom, except those near the Queen.'

Just before Christmas 1882 Fisher was writing that 'I fear I shan't

---

[1] *Memories*, 157.   [2] *Bacon*, i, 94.

eat a dinner for the next year'. It is some measure of the success of his cure, and his physical resilience, that he was able to be at Osborne in March; and a month later accept a new active appointment.

Little more than two years had passed since he had taken up the command of the *Inflexible*. These were two of the most eventful years of his life. For the price of a dangerous illness and untold anxiety and and suffering, his reputation in both royal and service circles had risen greatly. He had also, for the first time, become nationally known. In an age which search the records of every minor action for heroic figures Fisher had acquired a moment of popular fame. The intervention of the armoured train, and the successful defence of Alexandria against 'Arabi's hordes' were events for countless and usually picturesque retellings in later years when Fisher anecdotes were all the rage.

Chapter 4

THE REFORMER AT WORK

With only one brief break during the next fourteen years, until he hoisted his flag as Commander-in-Chief for the first time in 1897, Fisher's employment was ashore. He was concerned almost entirely with the Navy's *matériel*, and especially with weapons. Directly in Portsmouth and in London, and indirectly through the service all over the world, the influence of his reforming energies was increasingly experienced. Outmoded customs and practices were cast aside, obsolete weapons were thrown on the scrap heap, sinecures were sacrificed with as much impunity as smooth-bore guns, and all around him inefficiency and waste, his most hated enemies, were stifled to death. In the tasks to which he put his hand during this period he accomplished great things. Personal ambition, a passionate love of his country, of his Queen, and the service, impelled him forward at a breathtaking pace. His vitality was prodigious, his lust for work insatiable. 'He was never the same man for two days together,' wrote one naval journalist who knew him intimately, 'but all that he did he did always wholeheartedly . . . [His mind] was never at rest. The story is told that he had two tablets by his bedside—one with a red pencil, which meant "urgent", and the other with a black pencil—and that in the night he would wake and make a note on one or other of the tablets or ask his wife to do so."[1]

A fellow officer who served under him for many years admired him equally for his speed and decisiveness on the one hand and the considered wisdom which preceded each step. 'Here was a man with a brain like a razor, quick in repartee and in his decisions, but backed up withal by constant ruminations of the essential details of his profession which provided a ready supply of ammunition in debate. One characteristic he possessed, very peculiar in the naval Service, was that he sought and

---

[1] Sir Archibald Hurd, *Who Goes There?* (London, 1942), 60–1. (Hereafter cited as *Hurd.*)

treasured the opinions of anyone he considered likely to have special knowledge on any naval subjects. This was a rare quality in those days . . . Rank is apt to carry with it an assumption of quasi-omniscience . . . This was not so with Fisher; he would willingly pump the brains of a midshipman dry if he found the boy had ideas of value [though he] . . . never pretended that his proposals came from his own brain alone.'[1]

A reformer of the first calibre was sorely needed in the Royal Navy in the 1880s and 1890s. The seaman by the very nature of his calling has always been conservative. The sense of insecurity endemic in a life of hazard in a hostile element sees to that. Change suggests the threat of increased danger. Other factors were at work to resist reform. Socially, Britain had ridden out the storms of revolution which had struck every European country in the past century; while at sea the nation had remained in almost unthreatened omnipotence since Trafalgar. This was also a bad time for the reformer. Only a handful of wise prophets who recognized the portents of Europe's threatening imbalances of power wanted him.

Fisher's arrival heralded discomfort, from the moment the door was opened and the chill draught rushed in. Nor, as he settled to his task, were his methods calculated to soften the blows. In the 1880s he began to make enemies at an unprecedented speed. Marder has written of him: 'His fondness for generalizations couched in picturesque epigrams, and unsupported by fact or argument, was not a trait which endeared him to many thinking elements in the Service. Fisher was too assertive in his likes and dislikes of others and could brook no opposition to his plans. In his zeal for the efficiency of the Navy he was no respecter of persons . . . [he] was, it must be confessed, indiscreet, harsh, abusive, revengeful and increasingly autocratic. In a word, he was a very hard person to get along with, if one did not happen to agree with him.'[2] Even his admirers were forced to accept that he was utterly ruthless when he thought it necessary. 'When the Service requires it Fisher is pitiless, cold and cruel,' wrote one. 'It is difficult for any English Naval Officer to be cruel, but cruelty is part of the surgery of the great reformer . . . There is undoubtedly a useful dash of the savage in Fisher's nature.'[3]

It is a measure of Fisher's strength and courage that he managed to

[1] Admiral Sir R. H. Bacon and Francis McMurtrie, *Modern Naval Strategy* (London, 1940), 185.
[2] Arthur J. Marder, *The Anatomy of Sea Power: British Naval Policy 1880–1905* (London, 1941), 394. (Hereafter cited as *British Naval Policy.*)
[3] *Pall Mall Gazete*, September 1904.

accomplish during the next three years, at a time when his health and vitality were at a low ebb, more than most officers could have done at the peak of their health. Dysentery is one of the most debilitating diseases. Fisher's experience of it was made worse by the complications that set in after the drastic treatment which saved his life. For several years after his return to England he was in almost constant discomfort and had to watch carefully what he ate and drank. Every physical and mental activity demanded twice as much from him as it had done before he was struck down.

The work began at Portsmouth, where he had entered the Navy thirty years before, and where he would haul down his flag for the last time twenty years hence. On 6 April 1883 he was given command of the *Excellent*, where he had already done such good work as a staff officer and instructor. 'What was called the "forty years' routine" was in full swing; practically nothing had been altered for forty years, since the *Excellent* had been made the Gunnery School. All the firing practices were carried out with old smooth-bore guns. The establishment was crowded with "dead-heads", i.e. pensioners who occupied accommodation to the exclusion of active service ratings, who should have been there for training. All the gunnery methods were antiquated; the whole place was in a state of Rip-van-Winkleism.'[1]

Fisher brought about a revolution in the *matériel* and methods in the *Excellent*. Against a strident chorus of complaints, he sent away the pensioners and replaced them with active service ratings, and modern quick-firing guns were installed. Under his command were two Lieutenants, John Rushworth Jellicoe and Percy Scott, who talked Fisher's language and closely matched his energy. Both were to achieve high honours and appointments under him in later years. Scott was a gunnery fanatic, who was already raising the ratio of 'hits' and devising all manner of gunnery improvements. While he was in the *Excellent* he proposed the creation of a new gunnery school on Whale Island, then no more than a dump of excavated mud. Fisher recognized the value of Scott's proposal, enlarged and elaborated it. Their joint plans led to the creation of a magnificent gunnery and torpedo school.

Among the officers passing through the *Excellent* during Fisher's brief period as its Captain was Prince George, the Prince of Wales's second son and the future King George V. This was a happy coincidence, and Fisher took full advantage of it, following his progress with special attention. On 8 October 1855 Prince George passed out and was promoted Lieutenant. Fisher reported to the young man's grandmother:

[1] *Bacon*, i, 94.

October 8th, 1885

Madam,

Having received your Majesty's commands through Sir Henry Ponsonby to write to your Majesty about Prince George, I have the honour to report that during his six months' stay on board the *Excellent* under my command his attention to his work and the manner in which he has performed all his duties has been all that your Majesty could desire. He has with great tact and good judgment and quite of his own accord declined many invitations kindly meant to give him pleasure, but which would have taken him too much from his work besides bringing him more prominently into public notice than your Majesty might have thought desirable under the circumstances.

His instructors have reported to me that his aptitude for the practical work of his profession is very good, and your Majesty may perhaps consider that this is the chief point, as it will not probably fall to his lot to write learned reports or make mathematical investigations. Quite incidentally, this morning I heard the remark made by one of his late mess-mates that it was a subject of general regret that Prince George had left the *Excellent*, and his pleasant and unassuming manner has been a matter of general notice.

Trusting your Majesty will pardon me if I have written at too great length.

I have the honour to be

Your Majesty's most humble and *grateful* servant and subject,

J. A. Fisher

Captain, H.M.S. *Excellent*

On the following day Fisher wrote privately to the Queen's secretary, explaining why the Prince had not quite come out top. 'Prince George only lost his first-class at pilotage by 20 marks. The yarn is that one of his examiners, an old salt-horse sailor, didn't think it would do to let him fancy he knew all about it . . .'[1]

Fisher made other associations and contacts between 1883 and 1885 which were to prove long-lasting and profitable on both sides. By 1884 he had already known for some time William Thomas Stead, the thirty-five-year-old fiery editor, the archetype of the late-Victorian sensational journalist. Until Stead's death in 1912, the two men worked together with mutual enthusiasm to achieve their ends. They were marvellous allies, and made many enemies. Fisher's admiration for Stead was boundless. He described him as 'one of the best friends I ever had and in my opinion the greatest of all journalists. Lord Morley once told me that he had never known the equal of W. T. Stead in his astounding gift of catching the popular feeling. He was absolute integrity and feared no man. I myself have heard him tackle a Prime

[1] John Gore, *King George V: a Personal Memoir* (London, 1941), 68.

Minister like a terrier a rat. I have known him go to a packed meeting and scathe the whole mob of them.'

One of Stead's closest confidants in the political and defence fields was the Hon. Reginald Brett, later Lord Esher, a brilliant, withdrawn figure, a plotter and schemer, a Machiavellian figure who preferred to work behind the scenes but numbered the highest in the land among his closest friends. From such unostentatious and seemingly innocuous appointments as Secretary to the Office of Works and Deputy-Governor of Windsor Castle, Esher wielded a more profound influence on affairs of defence up to the outbreak of the First World War than any other single man. In 1885 his association with Fisher was still a new one. It was to mature quickly before the heat of Stead's enthusiasm, and these three men—the relentless journalist, the back-room negotiator and *eminence grise*, and the reforming naval officer—were to work together with increasing intimacy in the years ahead, impelled by their different ambitions and common patriotism.

Stead amazed and amused them both. Brett admitted that he was 'wild and odd'; yet 'he is, I am confident, unswayed by any other motive than conviction';[1] while Fisher excused his eccentricities: 'Of course every genius has a strain of queerness.'[2]

Fisher and Brett together made a marvellous working partnership. 'It was curious how he and Esher seemed to hit it off together,' wrote the younger Ponsonby many years later, 'and I think the reason they got on so well was that they had the same type of mind. Both were very clever; both preferred to come in at the back door instead of the front; both had the early Italian type of mind. There was something tortuous about both of them,' but while Fisher loved a fight and was prepared to stand or fall by his measures, Esher was very susceptible to public opinion and shrank from any responsibility. I always think that Esher's strong point was that he never minded who got credit for any measure he devised so long as it was adopted by the authorities.'[3]

Together with H. O. Arnold-Forster, the student of military and naval affairs and later Secretary of State for War, this powerful triumvirate brought about the first of the 'naval panics' which resulted in successive strengthenings of the Navy against the increasing power of Russia, France, and finally Germany. Esher was secretary to the Secretary of State for War, and at this time still Reginald Brett; Stead was editor of the Liberal newspaper the *Pall Mall Gazette*; and Fisher

---

[1] Maurice V. Brett and Oliver, Viscount Esher, *Journal and Letters of Reginald, Viscount Esher* (London, 1934–8, 4 vols), i, 229. (Hereafter cited as *Esher*.)

[2] *Memories*, 263.

[3] Sir Frederick Ponsonby, *Recollections of Three Reigns* (London, 1951), 129. (Hereafter cited as *Ponsonby*.)

was still Captain of the *Excellent*, with sufficient duties and demands on his time to tax the resources of the fittest man.

Anxiety about the strength and condition of the Royal Navy had been revived by increased naval shipbuilding in France, Russian hostility towards India, and the opening of the race for African colonies. During 1884 Russian armies had crossed the frontier into Afghanistan, and one of their Generals had even declared that it was 'a political necessity for Russia to possess herself of India'.[1]

Agitation against the state of the Navy and against the Board of Admiralty was first stirred by Arnold-Forster, although there had been earlier public questioning about the service's strength during the spring of 1884. At some time during the summer Arnold-Forster suggested to Stead that the *Pall Mall Gazette* should publish a series of sensational revelations about the inadequate strength of the service, that Stead himself should write them, and that Arnold-Forster should make himself responsible for providing all the information on which the articles would be based. He also agreed to contribute a preliminary article under his own name in August. Stead, a campaigner by instinct and commercial persuasion, agreed to the plan, and either separately or together the two men made overtures, through Brett, to Fisher, the best qualified man in the service to give them what they needed.

The information was readily forthcoming. Fisher was anxious about many other aspects of the Royal Navy than gunnery and ordnance and torpedoes. Under the supposed authorship of 'One Who Knows the Facts', the first of Stead's 'The Truth about the Navy' articles appeared on 15 September 1884. This revelation and succeeding articles alleged that Britain was spending then less than in 1868, although since that date the country's wealth and trade had increased by 40 % and shipping by 30 %, that French warships and guns were superior to British, whose likely enemies were spending almost as much as were the British on their Navy, that British docks and bases were almost undefended, and the service was in sore need of more torpedo boats.

Every newspaper and periodical began discussing the state of the Navy, and for some weeks it displaced Egypt and the Soudan as the first topic of conversation. Scenting new shipbuilding orders, the armament barons raised the outcry an octave or two. 'It is surprising that so much apathy should be displayed regarding the unprotected state of our commerce,' proclaimed Sir William Armstrong at the Annual General Meeting of his company. 'There is at present a well-founded scare about the state of our Navy.'[2]

[1] *Parkes*, 329.   [2] *The Times*, 2 October, 1884.

Armstrong's judgement was correct. The government was made to feel distinctly uneasy by the widely-quoted articles. Henry Campbell-Bannerman, the Parliamentary and Financial Secretary to the Admiralty, who was not easily unsettled, wrote to Hugh C. E. Childers, the Chancellor of the Exchequer, on 2 October 1884:

'I am growing anxious to know what view the Cabinet is likely to take of the question which has been raised so loudly regarding the Navy. I wrote to Lord Northbrook [First Lord] last week, judging that although he is not to be troubled about ordinary Admiralty matters, he ought to be consulted on the general Party-question of naval policy which is now being discussed . . . and although I do not believe that the hysterical excitement of the *P.M. Gazette* extends far beyond London, there is sufficient interest and anxiety felt in the country to prevent the question being shelved and poohpooed . . .'[1]

Lord Northbrook was far removed from all these disturbances. ('I see that he has gone to Upper Egypt,' remarked Campbell-Bannerman.) He was in fact very preoccupied with the aftermath of the Arabi revolt. The Cabinet decided that this was no time for fussing with protocol. 'In those less spacious days Chancellors of the Exchequer fought desperate battles with Departments over a thousand pounds. But the Cabinet, as it turned out, was by this time thoroughly roused, and, without waiting for the First Lord's return, announced a naval programme requiring a supplementary estimate of £3,000,000.'[2]

When the first of Stead's articles was published Northbrook was in fact already *en route* back to England. On his arrival, and for some weeks after, he was subjected to fierce criticism, and was offered little support even by the responsible press. *The Times* was moderate in its opinion columns; but soon, in another column of the same newspaper, the Poet Laureate was adding his voice to the chorus of anxiety and accusation, and the first and third verses especially of Tennyson's poem addressed to Northbrook, were widely quoted.

> You—you—*if* you have fail'd to understand
> The Fleet of England is her all in all—
> On you will come the curse of all the land,
> If that Old England fall,
> Which Nelson left so great—

[1] J. A. Spender, *The Life of the Rt. Hon. Sir Henry Campbell-Bannerman* (London 1923, 2 vols), i, 53–4.
[2] *ibid.*

'You—you—who had the ordering of her Fleet,
If you have only compass'd her disgrace,
When all men starve, the wild mob's million feet
Will kick you from your place—
But then—too late, too late.[1]

Northbrook was in a vulnerable enough position without these threatening verses. In July 1884, before his departure for Egypt, he had made a speech which included the passage: 'The great difficulty the Admiralty would have to contend with if they were granted £3,000,000 or £4,000,000 tomorrow for the purpose referred to would be to decide how they should spend the money.' Even within its context, which referred to the increasing vulnerability 'of large ironclad ships', it was a dangerous enough statement; out of its context, as it was freely quoted by his opponents, it placed the First Lord in a very awkward position, from which he had the greatest difficulty in extricating himself.

In the Royal Navy the blame for the supposedly dangerously weak condition of the Fleet was directed more towards Admiral Sir Astley Cooper-Key, now the First Naval Lord. It was widely known that Fisher was behind the *Pall Mall Gazette* exposures; and that he also owed much to this Admiral for his earlier advancement, who had been his friend and supporter on the North Atlantic station and elsewhere. Now, it seemed, Fisher had turned on him. The degree of ruthlessness to which he would resort to achieve his ends came as a surprise to some of his contemporaries.

Cooper-Key was a moderate in all things and was a staunch advocate of gradualism. Sudden increases in armaments, he believed, only incited your potential foes to greater endeavours and arms races. He defended himself sturdily, but mainly ineffectually. On 2 December 1884 he wrote in a letter to Phipps Hornby, Commander-in-Chief Portsmouth, and Fisher's immediate superior: 'It is rumoured at Portsmouth that I am opposed to the increase in the Fleet—I wish to disabuse *your* mind on the subject. If you had seen what I had written, heard what I have said at the Board, you would know that I have been disturbed about the absurdly small sum the Government are asking for . . . I have scarcely slept for the last five nights, having been so worried about it.' Then in apparent contradiction to all this, a few lines further on he claimed, 'I have always deprecated asking for a very large sum for shipbuilding purposes—it will only induce other Nations to make another start . . .'[2] The Admiral did not resign for the present.

[1] *The Times*, 23 April, 1884.
[2] Vice-Admiral P. H. Colomb, *Memoirs of Admiral the Rt. Hon. Sir Astley Cooper-Key* (London, 1898), 451.

Fisher was quite unabashed by his action, and if there were suggestions that he was an informer, he disregarded them. Besides, he had the support of many senior officers, who shared his feeling that it was time to unseat the incompetent Cooper-Key—a fine man afloat, a weak man at a desk. All the same, he decided that a breath of sea air would be a refreshing experience, and at the same time refute any suggestions that he was an armchair Judas. Phipps Hornby was forming an Expeditionary Fleet for emergency war service in the Baltic against Russia, and Fisher temporarily left the *Excellent* in June 1885 to serve on the Admiral's staff in the battleship *Minotaur*.

The war scare blew over after many anxious months, the activities of the Baltic Expeditionary Fleet were limited to exercises, and Fisher returned to Portsmouth, refreshed by his experiences and content with the results of the press campaign, which had resulted in the expenditure of an additional three million pounds and the construction of two new battleships and thirteen cruisers.

The effects of Fisher's dysentery still lingered and were troublesome. He knew that he could never work at the peak of his form while they remained. 'When all the doctors failed to cure me,' he wrote later, 'I accidentally came across a lovely partner I used to waltz with, who begged me to go to Marienbad, in Bohemia. I did so, and in three weeks I was in robust health. It was the Pool of Bethesda, and this waltzing angel put me into it, for it really was a miracle, and I never again had a recurrence of my illness.'[1]

After this first visit in 1886, he visited Marienbad almost every year, sometimes alone, at other times with his family. It became 'beloved Marienbad'. This watering place, two thousand feet up in the Bohemian mountains and owned by a colony of monks, was a Mecca for him, and the annual pilgrimage a delight to which he eagerly looked forward. It combined many qualities. The waters renewed his health, the scenery refreshed his spirits, the company was not only pleasant—it was rich, important and influential. Marienbad provided the perfect setting for establishing contacts, sounding out opinions, and setting up campaigns. 'It's an ideal spot . . . At Marienbad I met some very celebrated men, and the place being so small I became great friends with them. If you are restricted to a Promenade only a few hundred yards long for two hours morning and evening, while you are drinking your water, you can't help knowing each other quite well . . . Russell (afterwards Chief Justice), Hawkins (afterwards Lord Brampton), the first Lord Burnham, Labouchere (of *Truth*), Yates (of the *World*), Lord Shand

[1] *Memories*, 157.

(a Scottish Judge), General Gallifet (famous in the Franco-Prussian War), Rumbold (Ambassador at Vienna), those were some of the original members . . . I almost think I knew Campbell-Bannerman the best. He was very delightful to talk to.'[1]

A gossipy letter home to his wife a few years after his first visit to Marienbad is evidence of the lighthearted pleasures the town offered, and of the contemporary preoccupation of the inmates with the hopeless struggle against overweight.

TO MRS J. A. FISHER

Grünnen Kreuz
Marienbad
August 9th, 1889

. . . I have seen the Grants, Mr Campbell-Bannerman, Colonel Eyre . . . Then there is an American, Mrs Moore, a very large, handsome woman, a great friend of the Prince of Wales at Cannes, so they say. I knew her a little last year. She told me Mrs Robertson wasn't coming, as she had found a secret for preserving her figure without it, and she, Mrs Moore, had found it out. You soak a towel in soda and water, wring it out dry, and wrap it round your 'tummy', and it is unfailing—brings you down. I will inquire further about this.

I had my wine-glass this morning of Kreuzbrünnen, and the water has not lost its chief characteristic. The whole town is now lit with the electric light, and a beautiful large open building on the promenade instead of the old smelly place that people walked in when it was wet. I had my breakfast at the dear old Dianahof. Both Mädchens welcomed me most cordially. The breakfast cost five and a half pence. I had a tremendous blow-out in the Stern last night—Wiener Schnitzel, spinach, Prague Schinken, Pilsener iced beer, and a Britannia cigar—two *'portions'* of fried Schinken! Anton has got the electric light in his dining-room, so you can now see what you are eating . . .

Now I must leave off, as it is dinner time. I will write more to-morrow. My very fondest love to you all. I do so wish you were all here. The weather is simply delicious and the air like champagne, the woods smelling so lovely of pine, and the footpaths as soft as velvet. This is paradise, but Eve is absent.

P.S. Gemischtes Kompot has currants and walnuts in it now—so good!

These visits to Marienbad strained Fisher's finances. As a Captain in the late 1880s his pay was no more than £660 a year, and from this he had, besides his always generous contributions to charity, to provide an allowance for his mother, and probably for other insolvent members of his family. But he was a careful spender, and took pride in his economies. At Marienbad 'I certainly did manage on very little, and it is wonderful what a lot you can get for your money if you think it over.

[1] *Records*, 30–1.

I got breakfast for tenpence, lunch for a shilling and dinner for eighteen-pence and barley water for nothing and a bed for three and sixpence . . . I did a three weeks' cure there, including the railway fare and every expense, for twenty-five pounds. I don't believe any Economist has ever beaten this. I preserve to this day the details of every day's expenditure, which I kept in a little pocket-book . . .'[1]

The evident success of Fisher's reforms as Captain of the *Excellent* soon led to greater responsibilities. He left Portsmouth dockyard again, and on 1 November 1886 was appointed Director of Naval Ordnance (DNO). This should have made him virtual dictator of all matters relating to the Royal Navy's guns, torpedoes and mines (he soon added 'and Torpedoes' to his title). But at this time the scope of the appointment was strictly limited as a result of one of the more deplorable outcomes of the Crimean War. The Army had gained control of the supply of guns and ammunition to the Navy as well as to its own service. For more than thirty years, when the advances in propellants, guns and projectiles had been greater than in the previous three centuries, the Navy remained dependent on the War Office for its ordnance. All money for naval guns and ammunition was included in the Army estimates, and at no time did the Navy know how much ammunition it would have to draw on in time of war; all that appeared certain was that the Army would get the lion's share. The most serious consequence of this extraordinary state of affairs was that the Royal Navy was far behind its rivals in gun development, and was still using primitive muzzle loaders. In a close fought action the expectation of life of British gun crews, who had to expose themselves every time the gun was loaded, was cruelly brief.

When Fisher sailed with Phipps Hornby to the Baltic during the Russian war scare in 1885 not one British battleship carried a breech-loading gun above 6-inch calibre; but all the Russian ships they were supposed to fight had replaced their old muzzle-loaders with modern breech-loading guns. 'It is difficult to realize how low our material has fallen,' wrote one of Fisher's contemporaries at this time. 'I had a few years before been employed slave-cruising on the east coast of Africa. The cartridges supplied for revolvers often would not go off, and if they did they burnt like squibs . . . owing to the pig-headed obstinacy of an Artillery General, the Navy, at that time and for many years afterwards, was armed with inefficient, inaccurate, and dangerous muzzle-loading guns, while every continental nation had breech-loaders. Nothing but an earthquake or a torpedo would disturb the equanimity of the Artillery General.'[2]

[1] *Records*, 35.   [2] *Bacon*, i, 98.

Fisher's manner of operation was not unlike that of an earthquake, and torpedoes were dear to his heart. Only he, it was believed, possessed the tenacity and ruthlessness (as well as the friends in high places) to end this army dominance. 'I came to the definite conclusion,' Fisher wrote, 'that the ordnance of the Fleet was in a very bad way, and the only remedy was to take the whole business from the War Office, who controlled the Sea Ordnance and the munitions of sea war. A very funny state of affairs!'[1]

Fisher had powerful allies in the Prime Minister, Lord Salisbury, and the First Lord. Northbrook had gone, and in his place was Lord George Hamilton. Fisher had the highest regard for Hamilton, and classed him with Lord Spencer as the two First Lords, among the thirteen under whom he served, who had the toughest jobs, 'because of the constitution of their respective Boards of Admiralty; and yet neither of them received the credit each of them deserved for his most successful administration. With both of them their tact was insurpassable . . . To both of these (I consider) great men I am very specially beholden.'[2]

Fisher had cause for gratitude to Hamilton, who had done so much for him and had been responsible for his appointments to Portsmouth, and as DNO.

For his part, the First Lord admired Fisher greatly, although with qualifications. He found him rather too fiery, too eruptive, too precipitate. 'Though he had great social gifts, Fisher was too volatile in his judgment and too assertive in his self-advertisement and in his likes and dislikes of others . . . ' he wrote in his memoirs. 'As an administrator and organiser he will rank very high, but he was not equally successful as a reformer. His absorption in the idea of the moment made his grip of the future very fitful. He had, however, such a fund of latent originality and resource and driving power that it was a real pleasure to work with him, and I shall always regard as amongst the most memorable of my experiences my long official association with this remarkable man . . . [He] was strong, ambitious and go-ahead, and he made a rare splash in naval and other circles. Right throughout his career he showed instincts of genius, but, like most men so gifted, he was changeable and inconsistent. He was an extraordinary hustler and a marvellous showman.'[3] Lord George Hamilton also judged Fisher 'an invaluable public servant' when controlled.

The First Lord's power of control may have been taxed during the

---

[1] *Records*, 54.   [2] *Memories*, 242.
[3] Rt. Hon. Lord George Hamilton, *Parliamentary Reminiscences and Reflections, 1886–1906* (London, 1922), 132–5.

long and exhausting meetings of the inter-departmental committee during late 1886 which decided the issue of the Navy's lifeblood. But it was largely thanks to Fisher's dogged persistence, rather than to the volatility of which Lord George Hamilton was to complain, that the Navy won their case.

The committee consisted of the Prime Minister, W. H. Smith, Secretary for War, Lord George Hamilton, Brigadier-General Henry James Alderson, Lord Salisbury's brother-in-law and Director of Ordnance at the War Office. 'It was really a very remarkably unpleasant time,' Fisher wrote of these meetings. 'I had an awful bad cold —much worse than General Alderson . . . and Lord Salisbury never asked after it, while he slobbered over Alderson. I just mention that as a straw indicating which way the wind blew. The result, after immense flagellations administered to the Director of Sea Ordnance, was that the whole business of munitions of war for the Navy was turned over to the Admiralty, "lock, stock and gun barrel, bob and sinker" . . .'[1]

But it took an unconscionable time for the transfer to be completed. The Army saw to that by delaying tactics which continued through to the fifth year of Fisher's own tenure of office at the Admiralty in 1909. But the principle had been established, and the most important transfers took effect immediately. In spite of his apparent disregard for Fisher's health, Lord Salisbury had noted approvingly his adeptness and perseverence as a committee man, and how he had contrived throughout the sittings to avoid making enemies with Lord Salisbury's own brother-in-law. This was to pay Fisher handsome dividends later in his career.

Another consequence of the meetings of the inter-departmental committee was to have results of a far-reaching though quite different nature. Now that the Director of Naval Ordnance was at last to have overall command of the design, development and construction of his own guns, Fisher began an intense and very useful association with the country's gun- and shell-makers. Among the closest of these was Josiah Vavasseur, the fifty-year-old technical director of William Armstrong Ltd, the gun and shipbuilding company on the Tyne at Newcastle. While Armstrong's partner, Sir Andrew Noble, was mainly a chemist and gun man, Vavasseur bent his skills towards gun mountings. Encouraged by Fisher's keen interest in *matériel* of every nature, Vavasseur created a device which absorbed the energy of recoil of a gun, and thus allowed a simpler and lighter form of gun mounting to be used. Fisher was in constant correspondence with Vavasseur during his period as DNO, and often visited the Armstrong Elswick works on the

---

[1] *Records*, 54–5.

banks of the Tyne. A warm friendship grew up between the two men, and Vavasseur, who was happily married but had no children of his own, stayed with the Fishers. The Fisher family in turn were invited to Vavasseur's Norfolk estate, Kilverstone Hall, Thetford. He took a special fancy to Fisher's son, Cecil, an eighteen-year-old youth in 1886. Seventeen years later, Vavasseur adopted Cecil as his heir, and the second Lord Fisher inherited the fortune and property of Vavasseur when he died, the only condition being that he and his heirs should use the name Vavasseur.

Fisher's periods of appointment as DNO (1 November 1886) and as Third Naval Lord, with a brief time as Admiral Superintendent of Portsmouth Dockyard in 1891, coincided with a vast number of *matériel* innovations and improvements, a number of which he personally encouraged and accelerated. In the field of ordnance, the theoretical combat with armour continued apace, and after the belated return to breech-loading heavy guns, advances in weight of penetrating power and muzzle velocity of the projectile quickly went ahead. The clumsy, slow-firing giant guns of the *Inflexible* were superseded in the mid-1890s by the more manageable 12-inch wire gun, firing a shell of 850 pounds which, in theory, could penetrate more than 3 feet of wrought iron at the gun's muzzle. The demand for improved machine-guns and quick-firing heavier weapons to drive off the new torpedo boats and destroyers, which were becoming ever larger and swifter and more numerous, resulted in the introduction of more effective weapons to minimize this threat to the battleship.

In Fisher's first year as DNO the remarkable advance in light artillery since he had entered the service some thirty-three years earlier was demonstrated at Portsmouth, where a new 4·7-inch quick-firer succeeded in firing ten rounds in less than fifty seconds. By the early 1890s, the torpedo had been developed from the innocuous Lupuis-Whitehead 'toy' to a menacing weapon with a speed of 30 knots, a range of some 1200 yards and carrying an explosive charge of some 200 pounds. The battleship had replied not only by fitting batteries of quick-firing guns but also by hoisting out thick steel nets, or 'crinolines', when at anchor and therefore most vulnerable. The potential danger of underwater mines had not yet been realized, but this further threat, and that of submarine boats, was already being discussed.

Shipbuilding remained at a low level during the late 1880s, in spite of the 'Northbrook programme', and it was not until Lord George Hamilton introduced the Naval Defence Act of 1889, with its great increment in all classes of warships, that the Navy could hope to replace some of its obsolete tonnage. By then auxiliary sail propulsion had at last been dispensed with, and the shape of the battleship, with two tall funnels amidships and twin turrets or open barbettes fore and aft had become standardized. In the Royal Navy, the period of the bizarre and experimental was over at last: the ironclad battleship had grown up.

Fisher followed all these *matériel* advances with compulsive interest and enthusiasm. It was a wonderfully exciting period and at the Admiralty and at Portsmouth he was at the heart of things. His period at Portsmouth coincided with the construction of the first of the new Naval Defence Act battleships, the *Royal Sovereign*. He determined to set an example of unprecedentedly swift construction in order to galvanize the sleepy dockyard staff into awareness of his arrival.

'The methods he used were peculiar to himself. One important official was hard to move out of his office. Fisher wanted him to visit, and supervise personally, the building sheds more often; but to this he demurred; so, one morning, Fisher sent him a note to tell him that he had heard that there was going to be a vacancy at Trincomalee, for which he was eligible. That was all! But according to all accounts that official was seen, within two minutes of receiving that note, sprinting down to the building sheds . . .'

Slow shipbuilding infuriated Fisher. 'If you build two ships in the same time as it formerly took to build one,' he would argue, 'then you want half the number of slips and half the plant; therefore you effect a great saving in capital outlay and depreciation; moreover, a ship gets into commission earlier, and your Fleet therefore is stronger; and instead of a ship being almost obsolete by the time she is commissioned, she is in the prime of her power.'[1]

'One way that he had of encouraging the workmen was to find out quietly from the charge hand the names of one or more of the men who were working on the *Royal Sovereign*. A little time afterwards he would pass one of them and say, 'that's right, Thomas Williamson, glad to see you digging out so well." "Good gracious me, the Admiral knows my name," the man would think, and the report went round the Yard that the Admiral knew the names of all the men. The net result of such craft and energy was that the *Royal Sovereign* was . . . built in just two years,.[2]

Repair and maintenance work was also speeded up at Portsmouth, and again Fisher was prepared to use unorthodox means to bring about greater efficiency. While at Portsmouth, he succeeded in reducing the

---

[1] *Bacon*, i, 104.   [2] *ibid.*

time required to hoist out and replace a battleship's heavy gun from two days to two hours, and his first step in accomplishing this was to order a table and chair to be placed on the barbette and for his lunch to be served. He then announced that it was his intention to remain there until the work had been completed.

Chapter 5

UPHEAVALS IN WHITEHALL

On 1 February 1892, Fisher was appointed Third Naval Lord and Controller of the Navy, a post he held for five-and-a-half years. The responsibilities were broad and exciting, and they perfectly matched his enthusiasms and skills. The Controller of the Navy possessed powers over all *matériel* aspects of the service, from the design, construction, maintenance and eventual scrapping of the largest ironclad battleship to, say, the condition of small arms ammunition at some remote overseas base. The post required tact, discrimination and incorruptibility, especially in dealing with armament companies and shipbuilders, a firm judiciousness in the introduction of almost anything that was new, and an overall understanding of strategy and the changing *matériel* needs of the service to conform with new threats or opportunities.

The *matériel* progress of this decade was one of the most eventful in naval history. There was a rapid advance in all fields, in gunnery and new processes in armour construction, and in the creation of altogether new types of warships, and in the introduction of new forms of propulsion. It was also a decade of great international anxiety. There was large-scale war in the Far East between the great Chinese Empire and Japan, the precocious new military power. In Africa, too, there were numerous uprisings, and several major revolts against Britain, one of which developed into a dangerous war. Britain was never remote from the threat of major war with one or other of the great powers. While relations with Russia for a time improved, they deteriorated badly with France. Relations with America, too, became embittered at the end of the decade.

While Britain remained, with her small volunteer Army, a negligible power on land, her Navy was still omnipotent. If its strength threatened to fall below the 'two-power standard', that is if the combined strength of the two next greatest navies came close to matching that of her own, there was a national outcry. The great conscript armies of France, Germany, Austria and Russia precluded the possibility of any successful attack by Britain on the continent of Europe, but Britain's own security depended on keeping open the trade lines to her overseas empire. These, and the defence of her possessions, could be guaranteed only by an all-powerful Navy. But any rich power with the inclination to do so was able at any time to challenge Britain's power at sea and build up a powerful naval force. Given determination, skill and the means to pay for it, anyone could build a Navy. It did not even have to be as big as Britain's; if it was nearly as powerful, by concentrating its strength it might overcome the Royal Navy piecemeal, or at least in suffering defeat, so weaken the power of Britain that she would be vulnerable to attack by others.

In this decade, by the Naval Act of 1898, Germany decided on just this provocative policy; and the most intense competition in naval history began.

For more than half of this decade, Fisher was responsible for the condition of the Navy, to ensure that it was adequate in numbers and efficient and battle-worthy to meet any old or new enemies. It was for Fisher a time of great accomplishments, achieved through constant controversy and even rancour, and at the price of a reputation for utter ruthlessness. He made many enemies, and among his old opponents the depths of bitterness against him increased with every rebuff which they suffered. For the first time, as a member of the Board of Admiralty, he was in constant touch with the political scene, and he came increasingly to depise it. For the first time he begins to express opinions on his opponents in a tone that was later to become feared and frequent: of Lord Salisbury's Chancellor of the Exchequer, Sir Michael Hicks Beach, he wrote that he was 'a perfect beast, without a single redeeming feature that I ever found'.[1] He was equally outspoken, and wrote in the warmest terms of affection, of those who fought on his side. Among these was Lord Spencer, his First Lord for the greater part of his time at the Admiralty, and his First Naval Lord, Admiral Sir Frederick Richards.

Of Lord Spencer, Fisher was to write that he 'was really a very magnificent man' with an exceptional gift for selection of men for responsibility, 'the biggest gift that a man in such a position can have, and the life, the fate of his country may depend upon him . . . His manners were superb. He satisfied that great description of what constitutes a gentleman: "He never hurt any man's feelings".'[2]

Fisher had an equal love and respect for Sir Frederick Richards, who saw him through so many difficult times. He and Fisher 'were on the

[1] *Records*, 51.   [2] *Memories*, 244.

very greatest terms of intimacy. He had a stubborn will, an unerring judgment, and an astounding disregard of all arguments. When anyone, seeking a compromise with him, offered him an alternative, he always took the alternative as well as the original proposal, and asked for both. However,' continued Fisher, 'he had one great incapacity. No one could write a more admirable concise minute; but he was as dumb as Moses. So I became his Aaron . . .'[1]

During the course of Fisher's second year in office as Controller, there occurred the third of the great 'naval scares' of the 1880s and 1890s. The first, set in motion by Stead's 'Truth about the Navy' articles, had led to the 'Northbrook Programme' of naval construction. The second had occurred in 1888–9, following a report that the Royal Navy had already lost its 'two-power standard' of superiority. The nation's alarm had resulted in an even larger appropriation for warship construction under the Naval Defence Act of 1889, which provided for no less than seventy ships at a cost of £21½ million, far beyond what the Board considered to be necessary, a veritable *embarras de richesse*.

Besides the modernization of dockyards and fleet bases, and the construction of numerous cruisers and smaller craft, the programme included the construction of ten of the largest battleships. Only one or two of these had actually been completed when the new wave of national alarm broke over the country in 1893, less than four years after the Navy had judged its appetite replete. The cause of the new crisis had political as well as technical origins. First of all, internationally 1893 was a most anxious year, and the French were proving exceptionally troublesome. Europe's new colonial enthusiasm, which had begun in 1884, was still undimmed; the competition especially between France, Germany and Britain was as keen as ever. There were certain unwritten rules in the colony game, and there was an unspecified limit to how much anyone should take at any one time, and how it was taken. When France decided to acquire Siam in the early part of 1893, and actually declared war on her intended victim in May, she broke nearly all the rules at once, and greatly alarmed and angered Britain. The 'Mekong' crisis was the result, and war between the two countries at one time appeared imminent. As always, both countries took a long and critical look at the strength of their Navies. For the British, this was an unfortunate time to do so. The effects of the Naval Defence Act had scarcely been felt, and there had just been an accident in the Mediterranean. The Commander-in-Chief was Tryon, Fisher's old Commander in the *Warrior*, and now a Vice-Admiral, K C B. Tryon had little respect or love for his second-in-command, Admiral Markham, and had ordered

[1] *Records*, 50–1.

an evolution to be performed which could result in a collision between the two battleships, *Victoria* and *Camperdown*, unless unusual initiative in his subordinate were exercised. It was not, with the result that the Flagship was rammed and sunk and Tryon and most of the Flagship's company drowned; while Markham's battleship was seriously damaged.

The scandal that followed was bad enough. Fisher himself, while blaming Tryon for making a dangerous signal, stated that if he were Markham 'I never could hold up my head again'. The loss to the Fleet of two of its most powerful battleships not only dangerously narrowed the gap between the strength of the British and French fleets during a critical period in Anglo-French relations, but by revealing the vulnerability of these 'monster ironclads' brought home to the public as well as the Board how by misadventure in peace or, say, by a few well-aimed torpedoes in war, an enemy might gain superiority in numbers. This was the price of *matériel* progress. Nelson had sailed into Villeneuve's line at Trafalgar in a Flagship already forty years old, and in 1805 the Royal Navy could call on some thirty first- and second-rates. In 1893 the *Royal Sovereign* class of battleship, completed at a total cost of nearly seven million pounds, were threatened by the pace of technical progress with obsolescence almost before they were even commissioned.

The ever-increasing cost and danger of naval armaments was recognized by all the great powers. To people of more pacific and more liberal persuasion, they appeared as an expensive folly which retarded social reforms in peace and increased the danger of war. For those responsible for the country's security, the only answer was to build battleships incorporating the most up-to-date advances in offensive and defensive power in batches, and in rapid succession before your rivals got in first. Fisher's own policy, which he loved to trot out, with many bangs on the table, was to

> Build few and build fast,
> Each one better than the last!

And, of course, in his judgement any other policy was criminal lunacy.

Press and service agitation against the inadequate funds available for the Navy built up during the summer and autumn of 1893, and in the House of Commons Lord George Hamilton, First Lord under the previous Ministry, moved on behalf of the Opposition the resolution 'That in the opinion of this House, it is necessary for the maintenance of the security of the Country and the continued protection of British interests and commerce, that a considerable addition should at once be made to the Navy.' This was strongly opposed by the Liberal government. The aged Gladstone, serving his fourth term as Prime Minister at the age of eighty-two, ventured 'to assure the House on the responsibility of the Government that neither the House nor the Country need entertain under the existing circumstances, the smallest apprehension as to the distinct supremacy of Great Britain'.

For a while the Cabinet seemed to be holding the line in support of the Prime Minister. The Chancellor of the Exchequer, Sir William Harcourt, whom Fisher described as 'a genial ruffian', at first supported him and infuriated Fisher by suggesting in the House that the Navy was quite content with its existing strength. There were hints, incited by Fisher, of resignations from the Board. Fisher responded in tempestuous vein, and rallied from all sides the Board's supporters. Among these was Austen Chamberlain, Joseph Chamberlain's eldest son, to whom he wrote:

TO AUSTEN CHAMBERLAIN

Admiralty, Whitehall
December 22nd, 1893

Strictly Private
Dear Mr Chamberlain,

In reply to your kind letter (and please excuse my strong language), Sir William Harcourt told an unmitigated lie when he said that the professional officers of the Admiralty were satisfied with the present condition of the Navy. We gave Lord Spencer to understand that unless Sir W. Harcourt explained we would resign. Sir W. Harcourt tried to wriggle out by private notes and messages, and Mr Campbell-Bannerman was sent to the Admiralty yesterday to endeavour to avoid a public statement by Sir W. Harcourt, but we would not have it and we were very loth to accept the statement he did make, but Lord Spencer was in such distress that out of pity for him we did not really like to rub his nose in it any harder. But Lord Spencer has, however, been given distinctly to understand that we don't intend to stand any repetition of such gross misrepresentation of our views, and further that we will not stand much longer delay in dealing with pressing naval requirements. Now let me ask you to thank your father for his splendid speech. I began a letter of thanks to you the moment I had read it, but then I thought I should only be bothering you and gave it up. . . .

It's an immense advantage to us that you and your father take an interest in the Navy.

Yours very truly,
J. A. Fisher

Lord Spencer was equally vehement in rejecting Harcourt's contention that the senior professional officers in the Navy were content with the present strength of the fleet. A colourful *précis* of the overture the drama that was to topple Gladstone was provided by Fisher himself many years later: 'The moment arrived when that magnificent old patriot, Lord Spencer, had to choose between fidelity to his life-long friend and leader, Mr Gladstone, and his faithfulness to his country. Sir Frederick Richards . . . had convinced him that a certain programme of shipbuilding was vitally and urgently necessary. Mr Gladstone would not have it. Sir Frederick Richards and myself, in quite a nice way, not quite point-blank, intimated that the Sea Lords would resign. (My bread and cheese was at stake, but I did it!) Lord Spencer threw in his lot with us, and conveyed the gentle likelihood to Mr Gladstone; whereupon Sir William Harcourt and Sir Henry Campbell-Bannerman were alternately turned on the three of us (Lord Spencer, Sir F. Richards and myself) sitting round a table in Lord Spencer's private room . . . But it was all no use. We got the ships and Mr Gladstone went.'[1]

Gladstone's last weeks in office were magnificently yet pathetically defiant. Political sagacity had diminished with senility to such a degree that he fought on long after his cause was doomed. He considered that the Board had 'got their knife' into him, that the members were 'mad! mad! mad! No statesman that ever lived,' he told his private secretary, Sir Algernon West, 'perhaps excepting Palmerston, would have given way.'

The Navy triumphed, and the end came for the greatest Liberal of all time, in a quixotic manner, which has been described so ably by Sir Philip Magnus:

'On 9 January 1894, Gladstone addressed his colleagues for nearly an hour with scarcely a pause in cabinet, but he convinced no-one, except the First Commissioner of Works, J. G. Shaw-Lefevre. Harcourt and Morley expressed sympathy with their chief, but both urged that Gladstone would be better advised to accept the estimates than to resign on that issue. Gladstone was so indignant that he moved his chair and turned his back on Harcourt. He said that he would resign if his colleagues so desired, and that he would base his reasons upon the state of his hearing and eyesight . . .

'Gladstone convinced himself that Sir William Harcourt's conversion to the policy of increased Naval Estimates was due to his being "charmed" with the idea of raising the money by means of a graduated death duty. The Prime Minister regarded that proposal with disgust, and described it as the "most radical measure of my lifetime". He added that he found it "too violent. It involves a great departure from the methods of political caution established in this country, where reforms,

---

[1] *Records*, 51–3.

particularly financial reforms, have always been considerate, and even tender". He considered that real estate deserved to be handled with especial tenderness, on the ground that it "has more of presumptive connexion with the discharge of duty than that which is ranked as personal."'

'Gladstone was impervious to argument . . .'[1] And late in February he wrote to the Queen telling her of his intention to resign his office.

And so it came about that the *matériel* appetite of the Royal Navy, inflamed by international competition, the heady scent of the more jingo-inclined press and the relentlessness of the Board of Admiralty was satisfied again at the cost of swingeing new taxes and the postponement of social reforms.

Fisher's influence in bringing this about was profound. He might despise the predatoriness of politics, contrasting it with the clean wind and salt air of life at sea, but when the security of his beloved Navy, his country and his own career were at stake, he could play the game as ruthlessly, dangerously and skilfully as the rest. Gladstone went, never to return, and Fisher got all that he wanted. The full Spencer programme of 8 December 1893 provided for seven battleships, thirty cruisers of various kinds and no fewer than 112 torpedo boats and destroyers, at a total cost of £31,000,000. This was later only mildly modified, and the great batch of battleships (nine in all, of the new and even more fearful *Majestic* class) were all laid down within the next sixteen months.

Fisher's own part in this formidable victory for national security was recognized when he was appointed a KCB on 26 May 1894.

A shipbuilding programme as immense as this seriously stretched the resources of the nation and resulted in industrial unrest. Shipbuilding, ordnance and steel workers in particular found their services in unusual demand and wisely claimed wage increases. These were not always met, and there were many disrupting and expensive strikes. The appropriation of orders for this vast fleet of new ships also brought with it many other problems for Fisher. The competition for the making of the guns was especially fierce, and there were many inspired accusations that the Controller's office was giving an unreasonable number of favours to Woolwich Arsenal, which in effect was a nationalized ordnance works. Competition, as always, was especially severe between the great armament works of Armstrong and Whitworth. In October 1894, when the first orders were being placed for the big ships under

---

[1] Philip Magnus, *Gladstone* (London, 1954), 417.

the Naval Defence Act, Fisher was under constant heavy pressure. Here he recounts to his First Lord some of his difficulties in dealing with Lord Rendel, a vice-chairman of Armstrongs, and the directors of Whitworth:

TO EARL SPENCER

Admiralty, Whitehall
October 22nd, 1894

Private
Dear Lord Spencer,

Lord Rendel spent over an hour with me on Friday last saying exactly, but at greater length, all that is contained in [his] letter to you. What he wanted was to get the order for 7 ships for Elswick instead of only 5, and he frankly told me Noble had sent him for that purpose. I asked him in reply whether five-sevenths of an order of over half a million was not a good share for Elswick? and that so far as I knew Whitworth's design was not a servile copy, nor indeed a copy at all, of Elswick design, and did he deliberately propose that a firm of the European eminence of Whitworth, who had succeeded admirably in producing efficient mountings for two existing battleships, were not to have any orders at all! Of course, he had nothing to say, but went off on what he called 'general principles.' I told him that the question had been decided as to the mountings for the 7 battleships and that there was no likelihood of any alteration in the decision, which had been arrived at after most careful consideration.

The Chairman and Directors of Whitworth have been here declaiming against Elswick. I suggest for your consideration not saying anything further to Lord Rendel till you come to town and see White and myself on this subject.

Yours very truly,
J. A. Fisher

Another letter to Lord Spencer, a few days later, highlights one more of the many burdens Fisher had to carry as Controller at a time of heavy naval expenditure, and the natural public interest that accompanied it. Even at this period of imperial power and wealth, self-denigration was a national occupation, and nothing infuriated Fisher more than its excercise against the Royal Navy's *matériel*. The *Pall Mall Gazette*, no longer under the editorship of W. T. Stead, had published what Fisher described as 'a tissue of misrepresentations about battleships as compared with the French'. Fisher continued to Lord Spencer: 'As *The Times* said the other day some people seem to experience a chastened pleasure in discrediting everything English . . . I suppose the *Pall Mall* goes on the principle that if you only throw enough mud some of it will stick!'[1]

[1] Fisher to Spencer, 29 October, 1894. Spencer MSS. Admiralty MSS.

The French were then building ingenious, unorthodox and utterly hideous battleships which, it could be and was argued, were superior to contemporary British ships. The Russians, too, had some fine naval architects, and their designs were causing anxiety in England. As the world's greatest trading nation, Britain was especially sensitive to the construction abroad of fast ships which might, as corsairs, repeat the successes of the French *guerre de course* of the Napoleonic wars. In the mid-1890s the Russians constructed a number of cruisers which were intended to be superior in speed and armament to any contemporary British cruisers, and to have exceptional endurance. Their target in war would clearly be British merchantmen. When details of the fast 10,900-ton *Rurik* arrived in London, there was great consternation, and she was seen 'as a roaring sea lion, going up and down the world devouring British traders, and slaughtering out of hand any British cruiser that might have the temerity to withstand her'.[1] Fisher consulted urgently with the Director of Naval Construction (DNC), William White, and the result was the designing of the *Powerful* and *Terrible*, magnificent and fast vessels with a speed of 21 knots and the size of battleships, which were really progenitors of Fisher's battle cruisers twelve years later.

But it was in the field of torpedo craft that Fisher wrought the greatest revolution of the decade. Torpedo boats had grown ever larger, faster and more numerous over the past fifteen years. Already they were having a profound effect on naval tactics and the design of the larger ships. Like David's sling against Goliath, the torpedo boat offered inferior naval powers the opportunity of delivering at small cost a series of blows at a great naval power which might bring about parity in capital ships. The danger of sudden destruction from a blow beneath the waterline, together with the ever-increasing cost of the largest ships, was already beginning to create the policy of caution and a preoccupation with preservation in naval fighting which was to reach its culmination in the First World War.

Once again it was concern at developments abroad that sounded the alarm. Until 1893 the chief defences at sea against the torpedo boat were the quick-firing guns of the big ships, and 'torpedo boat catchers'. But the catchers had proved a failure; they were too slow, clumsy and expensive. Then, within a few weeks of Fisher's appointment as Controller, Alfred Yarrow, one of the pioneer builders of light high speed launches and torpedo boats, returned from a visit to France and asked to see Fisher. While abroad he had learnt that the French Navy were constructing torpedo boats that would be faster than any projected

[1] *British Naval Policy*, 163.

by the Royal Navy. The French already had some 220 torpedo boats, a number of which could be transported by rail across the country and launched suddenly into the Mediterranean or from the Channel ports of Calais, Boulogne or Dunkerque, filling the sea like a sudden swarm of released bees. It was a nightmare prospect for any British Commander-in-Chief.

Fisher asked Yarrow for a formal report and a proposal for a new type of torpedo boat catcher that would be faster than anything the French were planning and also armed powerfully enough to destroy them. A number of specialized shipbuilders submitted plans, and after exhaustive discussions between the DNC, Fisher and the builders, the first boats of this new class were put in hand. A memorandum from Fisher dated 8 August 1892 re-designated the craft with typical inspiration, as 'torpedo boat destroyers'—because 'they will destroy French torpedo boats'. Yarrow's own first boat, *Havock*, a vessel of 240 tons, armed with a 12-pounder and three 6-pounder guns and carrying three 18-inch torpedo tubes, ran her trials in October 1893 and showed a speed of of over 26 knots, marginally below Fisher's minimum of 27 knots, but fast enough to overhaul anything the French had at the time. Yarrow's second destroyer, *Hornet*, made 28 knots, and so became the fastest vessel in the world.

Although the contemporary torpedo boats appeared diminutive beside them, these first destroyers were less than 200 feet long, and were little more than ultra-lightweight shells for their 3,500-horse-power engines and the coal to fuel them. They were wet and fearfully uncomfortable, with no fewer than twenty-eight men working almost elbow to elbow in the engine room. At high speed they developed appalling vibration and a defect appropriately named 'panting', the thin plates of the hull dangerously beating inwards and outwards in time with a vibration period. One report on a high-speed destroyer run stated that 'when hatches were closed the engine room temperature was unbearable, the hot coamings being a just cause for complaint as they would seriously injure naked feet'.[1]

In spite of these early defects and dangers, the first destroyers proved in exercises their capacity to deal with the torpedo threats from across the Channel, and many more were ordered by Fisher, even at the expense of deferring construction of the *Terrible* and *Powerful*, and compromising his happy relations with Yarrow. Without Yarrow's knowledge, Fisher arranged for copies of all Yarrow's detailed engine drawings to be distributed among this shipbuilder's competitors, together with contracts. Yarrow, pretending ignorance of how this

[1] Edgar J. March, *British Destroyers* (London, 1966), 26.

confidential and valuable information had leaked out, inserted advertisements in the press offering £200 reward for information leading to the discovery of the culprit. This brough the matter out into the open, and the Admiralty offered him compensation. Yarrow refused. He was fighting for a principle, he said. The Secretary to the Navy then climbed down and issued a statement acknowledging the debt owed to Yarrow for his pioneer work. Fisher remained unrepentant. He maintained that Admiralty contracts were so valuable to contractors, in terms of prestige, profits and consequent foreign orders, and that the Navy provided them with such valuable facilities as an experimental establishment, that any short-term losses were more than compensated for in the long term. In rather more ruthless terms, this meant 'If you do not care to work with other firms for the good of the Navy, then you will no longer be asked to tender.'

Fisher bore no grudge against Yarrow for his attack on Admiralty methods. Yarrow was a realist, too. However, the warmth of their relationship diminished, and it was not until they met by chance some time later in the corridors of the Admiralty and reminisced about their old dispute that complete trust between the two men was re-established. Later, Fisher was influential in ensuring that this brilliant designer was awarded a baronetcy.

None of Fisher's major accomplishments as Controller was completed without controversy. The introduction of water-tube boilers, of all technically mysterious things, aroused more wrath than any reform of the decade.

In the destroyer of 1893, Fisher, White and Yarrow between them had stolen a march on the French, Russians and Germans. It was a great coup. But in the field of boilers, the French led the way, and the Russians were not far behind. The water-tube, or small-tube, boiler had been introduced by Du Temple in France. In essence, it provided for a small instead of a large quantity of water to be heated in order to gain rapid pressure. 'A Fleet that is always ready to go to sea at an hour's notice is a splendid national life-preserver!' Fisher wrote. 'Here comes in the water-tube boiler; without previous notice or even an inkling, we have been ready in an hour with water-tube boiler ships. You can't exaggerate this!'[1]

Water-tube boilers also offered higher working pressures and saving of weight, and hence greater efficiency and economy. There was no doubt that they marked a great step forward. But in England they remained a suspect component. Three factors told against them. First, they gave a lot of initial trouble, which was also expensive. Secondly,

[1] *Bacon*, i, 167.

their general acceptance would mean that great firms would have to re-equip themselves with expensive new plant, which would displease their shareholders. And lastly, there was the old inborn suspicion among many senior officers, most of whom had entered the service when masts and yards were the first form of propulsion, that it would not work because it was new. 'It is sea-going human nature', Oscar Parkes, the naval historian, once wrote, 'patiently to suffer accustomed evils, but to be very intolerant of new difficulties; hence what might be only a trifling and remediable defect in a water-tube boiler would be regarded as outweighing all the long-standing troubles experienced with the older types.'[1]

However, when it was learned first that the French were using them in all their new big ships, and that the Russians had them in their new big cruisers, Fisher persuaded the Board that they must fit them in the *Powerful* and *Terrible* and the new battleships. The opposition remained fierce and implacable. Some early and expensive failures, and Fisher's uncompromising advocacy against reasonable as well as unreasonable argument, only hardened the will of his enemies.

The 'Battle of the Boilers' continued to rage after the return of the Conservatives under Lord Salisbury in 1895, when George Goschen replaced Lord Spencer as First Lord at the Admiralty. The trouble was that the Belleville water-tube which the Royal Navy was using had still not been brought to a state of reliability, partly because it was more complicated to maintain and insufficient engineers understood its working. Nor was the issue decided when Fisher himself left the Board in the summer of 1897, bequeathing the problem to his successor, his old friend Arthur Wilson. Goschen and Wilson were not of the same calibre as Spencer and Fisher, and to Fisher's exasperation Goschen at length yielded in the House of Commons by agreeing to set up a committee of enquiry. As a result, one of the most necessary of the engineering reforms was delayed, and there was a lapse of a decade between the time when the French first fitted this superior form of boiler to a big ship, and its wholehearted acceptance by the Royal Navy.

Some years later, when passions had cooled a few degrees, Fisher wrote more objectively to Goschen's successor: 'The whole pith of the matter in our difficulties with the water-tube boiler lies in the fact that we suddenly went to a pressure of 300 lbs. and the workmanship did not keep pace with the increase of pressure, hence tons and tons of water going unperceived up the funnel through an infinity of leaking joints. . . Surely we must expect great difficulties when we have

[1] *Parkes, 393.*

capsized everything. We have put the water where the fire used to be and put the fire where the water used to be, and some of us think everything ought all to go on just the same!'

But neither did Fisher ever forget the intensity of the fight, the rebuffs and temporary defeat he suffered and the means by which. his enemy overcame him. These added a new note of bitter cynicism to his judgement of all businessmen and politicians, and sharpened his suspicions of everyone and everything at Westminster when he returned to take up administrative powers again at Whitehall in the new century.

As a Flag Officer, a KCB, a man of affairs who numbered royalty, prime ministers, dukes and industrial magnates among his friends, it was generally assumed that he was rich. Very few people climbed to this eminence without a large private income. In fact Fisher's pay, which was almost all his income, was only £1,460 a year as a Vice-Admiral, to which he was promoted on 8 May 1896. Out of this he had to pay his expenses, support his own family and help to support at various times importunate relatives who could not or did not want to believe that he was a poor man. His mother, poor Sophie, had died in 1895, a crusty, lonely figure who lived humbly in London mainly on Fisher's allowance. This relieved him of one burden. But the offers of wonderful highly paid jobs from armament and shipbuilding companies became increasingly attractive, especially when he was feeling frustrated and bitter. Some of these offers he described as 'really beyond the dreams of avarice'. He received the first as long before as 1887 and almost took it. Lord George Hamilton appealed to his patriotism and helped to persuade him to turn it down. Fisher hated the discomfort of penury on the one hand, and the vulgarity of riches on the other. In moments of financial gloom he cheered himself by quoting Swift: 'If you want to know what God thinks of riches—look at the people he gives them to.'

During his long period at Whitehall Fisher worked long hours, starting always very early in the morning, returning home late and retiring early to bed, as was his custom all through his life. But he saw more of his own wife and children than at any other time, and he made a special point of allotting them a certain amount of his precious time. He loved them all and took a warm interest in all their activities. They were at this time still a united family. 'I hope, darling,' he once wrote to his wife, 'it may be said of us and our children what David said of Saul and Jonathan: *"Lovely and pleasant in our lives and not divided in our deaths"*.'

In 1895 Cecil left England to return to his duties in the Indian Civil Service, an appointment which he had taken up five years earlier. In the same year Fisher's eldest daughter, Beatrix, became engaged to Reginald Neeld, a naval Captain. It was also in 1895 that Fisher took his second daughter, Dorothy, to 'beloved Marienbad', and then on a tour of Switzerland and to Paris. It was a happy time for them and they shared many amusing adventures. As always, Fisher had to budget with extreme care. Between them, they stayed at Marienbad for three weeks on £24. This letter he wrote home to his wife gives evidence of a happy relationship as well as the rigours of second-class travel, evidently without sleeper—an unusual austerity for a Knighted Rear-Admiral who was *persona grata* with half the crowned heads of Europe.

TO LADY FISHER

Between Würzburg and Nuremberg
August 8th, 1895

Darling Heart,

We have had a most prosperous journey so far though several panics! . . . We had a fine crossing, though a number of people were seasick . . . We had an excellent lunch at Calais—roast chicken and Dorothy's favourite potato! . . . We kept on losing time the whole journey, till it seemed absolutely impossible for us to catch the train at Cologne, as I had been told it did not wait. This put us in an awful state, as we couldn't get our luggage because it was registered through to Eger, and we probably couldn't get a bed, and it involved no sleeping, also at Nuremberg again without luggage, so we didn't know what we should do. So you can imagine our joy when we steamed into Cologne, nearly an hour late, to find the train waiting for us, which one guard said it would and another it wouldn't.

Then we had another fright! Would they wait for the luggage? At last Dorothy saw it coming along, so we were delighted, but in her excitement she forgot the window was up and nearly forced her head through the glass. Last year a man was impaled this way and could not get his head one way or the other. Just as the train was moving off, alas, to our horror, we saw our luggage being taken away, apparently not room or time to take it. This meant being several days at Marienbad without our luggage! So I began making plans of telegrams to all the officials at every station on the line! We got an excellent carriage to sleep in between Cologne and Mainz, and we woke up quite refreshed, just before Mainz, where we had wash, shave, and breakfast. Just as we had got to our carriage for Aschaffenburg, Dorothy saw our luggage! Hurrah!!! I ran out to embrace it and waved my handkerchief on the platform.

Y.l.h. [Your loving husband]
J.F.

A non-conformist in so many ways, a compulsive reformer, a receptacle for new ideas in everything relating to the Navy, Fisher was a traditionalist in many of his tastes. He liked light, jolly music—it was better to dance to. He liked walking in the countryside, and simple pleasures. His views on 'abroad' and foreigners were in line with most of his contemporaries'. Most of the letters he wrote home during his long tour to show Dorothy something of Europe have survived, and reveal his distaste for most of the people and most of the places, except of course Marienbad, 'the only decent place I know abroad'. Geneva he found 'a most overrated place. They say it's the largest, finest, richest town in Switzerland! In my opinion, it's a very second-class place—not a decent shop in the whole place. It doesn't compare with Portsmouth in shops, nor is there any view equal to the sunset at Portsmouth, looking up at the old hulks up the harbour. Mont Blanc, the monarch of the Alps, is a fraud, and the lake does not come near Plymouth Sound for beauty. I've come to the conclusion that all these foreign places do not approach in beauty our English scenes . . .' Paris was scarcely more agreeable. 'I've seen nothing to beat Bond Street in any particular, and no such pretty faces as one meets in Bond Street . . .' And of the Invalides, 'What a tawdry arrangement it is!'

In his taste in art, too, Fisher was a traditionalist. His greatest fondness was for sentimental and warlike subjects. From Paris he wrote to Lady Fisher telling of his delight in 'military pictures the very best I have seen', of a piece of sculpture. ' "The Death of a Young Patriot," quite lovely'; and at Versailles 'a battle piece by de Neuville, perfectly splendid'. On the other hand he greatly enjoyed at Versailles 'the picture of the Dauphin hanging up in Marie Antoinette's bedroom, the very place she used to see it'; and 'such lovely sculpture' at the Luxembourg—'one, "Sleep" by Boucher, 2 children asleep in an armchair'.

The people outside Marienbad failed to appeal to him, either natives or other foreign tourists. In Paris 'the Americans swarm so everywhere that the whole place abroad is quite nauseous to me. Such vulgar brutes they all are, both men and women'. Later, when Cecil married one, Fisher developed a warm affection for the Americans; and when in later life he became increasingly weary of the English climate, he modified his views on 'abroad'—so long as it was sunny and the food and wines were cheap and good.

On 28 January 1896 Beatrix and Captain Neeld were married at St George's, Hanover Square, and two days later Fisher writes to her on their honeymoon:

TO MRS REGINALD A. NEELD

Admiralty, Whitehall
January 30th, 1896

Darling B.,
We were delighted to get letters last night from you and Reginald. I am not [to] say 'Reggie'! What's your opinion? . . . Everything was cleared away yesterday by the store, and the house is just the same as ever. A chestnut exploded in Ida's hand last night with a report like a champagne cork going off, and the pieces hitting her mouth has made it all swell up. It appears the cook never cut the end off before roasting. Remember that in your housekeeping!

No time for more, as I have to see Mr Goschen, who enquired a great deal about your marriage yesterday and begged me to send you his best wishes. Did you speak to the Duke of Hamilton? Dolly and Pam talked to him and I could only nod to him on account of the crowd. They say we had 500 people and that the church was much fuller than ever it is on a Sunday. I had a regular levée in my room yesterday here offering congratulations on the way the whole thing went off. They all say it was first-rate and splendidly organized, both at the church and the house. That's all Mr Maisey and Dolly! Old Fitzgerald is greatly delighted at your saying he had stopped Reginald's pay! Old Brent considers the only fault was that you and I walked up the aisle too quickly. Did you see Sir George and Lady Wellesley and old Denman, the Judge! Really, I must stop. WRITE SOON. Best love to Reginald.

Your loving father,
J.F.

Chapter 6

THE HAGUE PEACE CONFERENCE

It was with delight and relief, and the certainty that he would return again in a more senior capacity to the corridors of power, that Fisher learnt in December 1896 that he would be going to sea again and to hoist his own flag for the first time. His command was a station on which he had twice before served, the North America and West Indies. It was an ideal appointment for recuperation from the rigours of Whitehall. In the winter the squadron cruised the sunny West Indies, showing the flag, performing little ceremonies here and there, receiving governors and distinguished foreigners. When it became uncomfortably warm again, it was usual to steam north, up the American coast, to Halifax. There was an Admiralty House both at Halifax and at Bermuda, and while ashore Fisher lived in sublime comfort at one or the other with Lady Fisher. But this was not a period of convalescence or even relaxation for Fisher. Rather, this and the subsequent seagoing command in the Mediterranean could be likened to the brief moments required by one of his largest guns for recoil and reloading before the next detonation.

Fisher's Flagship was a 'one-off' curiosity, the product of a passing phase in his battleship design thinking. As Controller in 1892 he had persuaded the DNC, William White, that the future battleship should combine 'the lightest big gun and the biggest secondary gun' in a ship of modest dimensions. The result was the *Renown*, carrying a main armament of four guns of only 10-inch calibre, and ten 6-inch quickfirers. Fisher had a quite unjustified confidence in her, and regarded her as very much 'his' ship. The *Renown* served as his Flagship on two stations, and it is ironical that it was on her decks that much of his thinking was done which led to the construction a decade later of the *Dreadnought*, which, as the biggest battleship in the world combining the biggest big gun and the smallest secondary gun, was a complete design reversal.

It was fifteen years since Fisher had held a seagoing command. Much had happened to him in this time. He had acquired great power, he had fought battles, many of them bitter ones, and he had won most of them. He was a veteran warrior from the wars of administration who had not seen any fighting since he was a young man. He believed passionately in all his causes, believed in himself, and believed in the public figure which he had acquired. He enjoyed his reputation for unpredictable behaviour, for shocking for the sake of shocking, for hurling his weight about and doing everything at full pressure. He loved to cut a fierce and grandiloquent public figure. But this appointment offered him the opportunity to show that he was a real sailor, too, and not just a landlubber decision-maker; it gave him the chance to demonstrate the reality of the colourful national reputation he had acquired since he had taken his own armoured train out to meet Arabi's men. He was going to be a man of action again.

In addition, Fisher was a believer in rigid discipline, and he had learnt after forty-three years' service that wherever he arrived to take up an appointment in a new place he would be sure to discover, in some measure, inefficiency and slackness. Like any reformer, he enjoyed their discovery, and was a terror until they were eliminated. But at no time was he an easy Admiral to serve under, for the peace of mind of his subordinates ranked at the bottom of his priorities.

'I have still a vivid recollection of the awe which the "great man" inspired whilst on board; not that he did any of us any harm, but he had such a terrific face and jaw, rather like a tiger, and he prowled around with the steady rhythmical tread of a panther,' wrote one of his officers on the North American Station. 'The quarter-deck shook, and all hands shook with it. The word was passed from mouth to mouth when he came on deck. "Look out, here comes Jack." Everyone then stood terribly to attention, while the great one passed on and away.'[1]

Carelessness or forgetfulness infuriated him as much as disobedience to orders, and he did not hesitate to humiliate publicly officers who failed him. At Antigua in the West Indies on one cruise he ordered a review of all seamen ashore at 7 a.m. The order stated clearly that hats were to be worn. 'I did not notice this . . .' an officer in one of the ships later confessed. 'Fisher was furious, and as soon as he returned on board . . . he made a signal asking whose fault it was. I implored the Captain to say it was mine, but he said he was responsible for everything in the ship, and replied accordingly. Fisher signalled for the Captain to repair on board the Flagship, and again asked the same question by signal, to which I answered that it was mine. He then made

[1] *Bacon*, i, 116.

a long signal by flags placing me under arrest, and ordered all ships present to repeat it. The effect as a display of flags of all colours was beautiful, while I wondered what would happen next. There followed a letter ordering me to give my reasons in writing for directly disobeying the Commander-in-Chief's order. I replied that it was due to my carelessness and stupidity. There was nothing left for Fisher to do, and about an hour after, he made a signal releasing me from arrest . . .'[1]

Another officer has written of his 'drastic methods'. 'When an officer had committed himself, the saying used to be, "Will he go home in the *Alpha* or the *Beta?*"—the two regular passenger ships from Bermuda for England. As a rule, the delinquent had no choice.' But this same officer also wrote of the 'two sides to his character, which the sooner you recognized the better it was for you . . . If any of us were in trouble, or any of the youngsters were sick, he and Lady Fisher were the first to inquire about it, and when possible made Admiralty House our sanatorium; and a mighty pleasant hospital-house it was.

'He always had at heart the comfort of the officers and men under his command, and there were few among those who served under him who had not some good reason to be grateful to him.'[2] Others have written of his 'devotion and kindliness towards the younger officers and middies', and of his practice of inviting the Midshipmen in turn to spend a week-end at Admiralty House. 'These week-ends were a great joy to us, as he universally made one feel absolutely at home.' In the evenings he would relax completely, the port went round, 'repartee was bandied about, and Jacky used to go into convulsions of merriment and laughter'.

Fisher played the rôle of the patriarch off duty with the same enthusiasm as the part of the fierce and relentless Admiral on board his Flagship. But the competitive instinct was rarely absent, even in the ballroom or on the playing fields. At fifty-seven he was as enthusiastic a dancer as ever, and delighted in dancing faster and for longer than anyone else, whether his partner was female or male—it did not much matter. 'Towards the end of the evening,' one officer wrote, recalling an all-male dance, ' . . . the dancing became more spirited. Jacky was observed going with the best. For the last waltz he pulled me out, off we went, faster and faster, dashing about, whirling and whirling, till I felt something unusual must happen, for we were riding for a fall. The inevitable did happen. We caught our legs in another pair and rolled over and over in the scupperway of the *Renown's* quarter-deck. Everyone was convulsed with laughter, including the Admiral.' Regattas and sporting

[1] Admiral Sir Lewis Bayly, *Pull Together!* (London, 1939), 80–1.
[2] *Bacon*, i, 115.

events of all kinds helped to fill the working days of a peacetime squadron on a distant station, and Fisher enlivened every event with his partisanship. He hated to see the Flagship being beaten. 'We'll win next time, even if I have to play myself!' he would say if the *Renown* lost a match; and 'he has been seen running along the touch-line at Halifax shouting encouragement to the naval side'.[1]

Only two political events disturbed the calm waters of the Caribbean during Fisher's period as Commander-in-Chief. The first was the Fashoda crisis with France over the control of Egypt which again brought the two countries close to war. In the West Indies French naval strength was negligible, and did not require the presence of the *Renown*. He therefore decided to take his Flagship to join the Atlantic Fleet at Gibraltar to ensure that he did not miss any of the real fighting. Orthodoxy played no part in his war plans. While the less powerful units in his squadron dealt with the French possessions in the West Indies and Îles des Saintes and Miquelon, a landing party was to attack the French penal settlement of Devil's Island. There they would capture Dreyfus, and with the intention of rekindling the flames of domestic passion which had followed his conviction for treason, land him secretly in France 'and so weaken the Government and the prestige of the officers appointed to high command'.[2] It is doubtful if Fisher took his own plan very seriously; it is much more likely that this was one more of his favourite quixotic acts to emphasize to his subordinates the need for surprise and the unexpected in the conduct of war. It was the sort of shock tactic that he loved to prepare in the silence of his cabin before dawn. Certainly his own preparations were complete in good time. 'One ought not to wish for war, I suppose,' he wrote to a friend after the crisis had passed, 'but it was a pity it could not have come off just now, when I think we should have made rather a good job of it.'

Whatever Fisher's opinions may have been about American tourists abroad, he admired the American professional sailors and always felt a strong sense of union with them. This feeling was cemented during the Spanish-American war of 1898. Relations between the two countries had been uneasy ever since the Venezuelan frontier dispute of 1895, but America's first serious colonial war against Spain brought sympathy from Britain, alone among the major powers. The campaigns against Cuba and Puerto Rico demanded the presence of Fisher's squadron, and he heard with feelings of pleasure, and certainly of envy, of Admiral Sampson's defeat of the Spanish fleet in Santiago Bay. Fisher invited the American fleet to visit him at Bermuda on 4 July, and he did them proud. The *Renown*'s band played American patriotic airs as they

[1] *Bacon*, i, 115–20.　　　[2] *ibid.*, i, 119.

steamed in for the first time, it was said, since the war of 1812, and there was a banquet for the Admiral and his staff and senior officers at Admiralty House. Fisher proposed Admiral Sampson's health, and the health of the United States. 'He never said a word,' Fisher recalled later.' Presently one of his Officers went up and whispered something in his ear. I sent the wine round, and the Admiral then got up, and made the best speech I ever heard. All he said was: "It was a d—d fine old hen that hatched the American Eagle!" '[1]

Between the signing of peace between America and Spain in 1898 and the outbreak of the Boer War in 1899, there took place an unprecedented international conference at The Hague in Holland. During Fisher's lifetime, the likelihood of world war, and the degree of destruction and suffering it might bring about, had both multiplied many times over. New industrial processes, new and ever more diabolical weapons, new riches and materialism, new nationalism, a sharpening of competition at all levels and the need to find markets for the products of the factories of western Europe and North America; all these factors had led to a sense of insecurity throughout the world, to the amassing of armaments, and to the consequent crises that had scarred every decade since the Crimean War. The 'naval scares' in France and Britain were only one manifestation. The scale of naval rearmament was slight by comparison with the creation and upkeep of vast standing conscript armies by the European land powers. The fresh outbreak of competitive colonialism after 1884 had heightened the dangers, and at the same time deeply exercised the consciences of the now better educated masses of the western world. Especially in the 1890s it became more and more politically fashionable to question the rate and scale of rearmament. In Britain, Lord Salisbury was not alone in pleading for a reappraisal of policy, and prophecying a 'terrible effort of mutual destruction which will be fatal for Christian civilization'.

The call which finally brought the nations together round a conference table came from the most unexpected quarter, and from decidedly mixed motives. Russia's finances were in their usual depressed state, and Czar Nicholas II's ministers viewed with dismay the increasing size and improving equipment of the military machines of Germany, France and Austria. He knew that Russia could no longer keep pace without breaking her economy and fatally increasing the power of the revolutionary movements. The realism of Russia's Minister of War, General Alexei Kuropatkin, and the wisdom of Count Sergei Witte, both commended themselves to Czar Nicolas. He fancied himself in the part of the white peacemaker and eagerly looked forward to the

---

[1] *Memories*, 225.

surprise this performance would cause throughout the chanceries of Europe.

The Czar was not disappointed. The surprise was overwhelming. Cynicism followed hard on its heels, then anxiety. How could one fail to answer the call for peace without appearing as a warmonger? And yet those who were satisfied with the strength of their war machine saw the danger of their superiority being whittled away, and those who were busiest trying to catch up saw their efforts being frustrated. The vast wealth and influence of the armament barons were thrown into the battle to destroy the conference before it could begin. The Czar was forced to compromise. In place of a conference to discuss the outlawing of war, an agenda was drawn up which proposed a ban on the increase of arms for a fixed period and the prohibition of certain weapons. The invited nations, still consumed with doubts and distrust, accepted after much heartsearching, and it was agreed that the conference would take place at The Hague from 18 May to 29 June 1899.

The British delegation was to be headed by Sir Julian Pauncefote, the ambassador in Washington, 'a calm, heavy-set, unfussed dignitary who reminded people of a polar bear' and 'accomplished wonders of diplomacy by acting on the principle: "Never give way and never give offence".'[1] Among those supporting him was the late Speaker of the House of Commons, Sir Arthur Peel, and Sir Henry Howard, British Minister to The Hague. The Army was represented by a wiry intellectual soldier, Major-General Sir John Ardagh.

On 22 March 1899, while staying at Admiralty House, Bermuda, Fisher received a telegram from the First Lord with the unexpected news that he was to serve as British naval representative at the conference, and that at the end of the conference he was to take up the appointment as Commander-in-Chief of the Mediterranean Fleet, the premier seagoing command in the service.

'Of course,' wrote Fisher on hearing the news of the most important appointment of his professional life, 'I had no option but to accept', although it was likely to bring its own troubles and anxieties. 'What I fear will cause frightful envy and jealousy,' he wrote to his daughter Beatrix on 23 March, 'is my being brought home specially for this Peace Conference, when there are so many eligible at home, all senior to me, a mass of them!' And of the command that was to follow: ' . . . there's no mistake about it that the Mediterranean is *the* tip-top appointment of the Service, and, of course, if there's war, there's a peerage or Westminster Abbey. But it's pretty sure to be Westminster Abbey, I expect!' And he concluded with disarming humility, 'I shall

[1] Barbara Tuchman, *The Proud Tower* (London, 1966), 243–4.

try my best to make a good job of it and so hope I may be a success, but 'it's a tough job all the same! . . . The great joy is that we shall see you again.' In this letter to his daughter, and another of the same date to the Naval Secretary to the First Lord, Captain Wilmot H. Fawkes, Fisher could not resist referring to one of his favourite quotations, about the Italian Cardinal's answer when asked how he got on so well:

$$\text{'I never} \left\{ \begin{array}{l} \textit{refused} \\ \text{resigned} \\ \text{asked for} \end{array} \right\} \text{anything'}$$

Fisher was Lord Salisbury's personal choice as naval delegate. He had been deeply impressed by his skill and conduct at the meetings to decide the future fate of naval ordnance, and he was confident that Fisher would stubbornly resist any attempt to cripple the powers of the Royal Navy in war. His confidence was well-placed. Fisher hated war, and all the suffering and waste it would cause. But once it broke out, any question of humanizing it, as the conference was to consider, was in his mind illogical and ridiculous. 'You might as well talk of humanizing Hell!'[1] he exclaimed angrily, and in later years wrote: 'War has no amenities . . . It's like two Innocents playing singlestick; they agree, when they begin, not to hit hard, but it don't last long! Like fighting using only one fist against the other man with two; the other fist damn soon comes out! The Ancient who formulated that "All's fair in love and war" enunciated a great natural principle.

"War is the essence of violence"
"Moderation in War is imbecility."
"HIT FIRST. HIT HARD. KEEP ON HITTING." '

The setting of the first Hague Peace Conference perfectly matched the purity and serenity of the supposed ideals of those who convened it. It took place at the House in the Wood (*Huis ten Bosch*), the summer palace· of the House of Orange, which stood out in the country surrounded by gardens and lawns and whispering fountains. The spirit of the delegates' intentions scarcely matched up to this paradise. Cynicism and defeatism lay like a grey cloud over the château and the surrounding woodland. The German delegation was the most determined to fight against any *status quo* in the arms race. War with France less than thirty years before had brought great rewards, and since 1871 the empire had expanded almost beyond measure in wealth, power and national aggrandizement. Military arrogance was a marked, and

[1] *Bacon*, i, 121.

feared, national characteristic. Only the year before the first step had been taken in the challenge to wrest naval supremacy from Britain. Germany had most to lose and least to gain from any diminution in the arms race.

But there was no member even of the powerful German delegation able to match the British naval representative's scorching assault on the premise that the conduct of war could be 'civilized'. Five years after the conference broke up, the prominent author and journalist Harold Begbie, wrote of Fisher's impact on one of the sessions at which he spoke: 'The polite gentlemen at the House in the Wood were debating as to how war might be conducted with as little pain and inconvenience as possible, when Sir John broke in with the way in which he intended to fight his sea battles . . . Men sat listening with blanched faces, with horror in their eyes, and at the end a shudder ran round the circular yellow room.

'It was said to be the most dreadful and appalling picture of war ever drawn by a human mind. And this frightful and awful picture, which whitened the faces and froze the blood of all those soldiers and sailors, was drawn by an open frank-faced man, leaning back at ease in his chair, speaking quietly and pleasantly, with a straightforward smile in his round, boyish-looking eyes.'[1]

Stead, who was there to report the conference for the *Manchester Guardian*, wrote of Fisher that 'no man at The Hague was more popular than he'. It was not only that 'he was personally most gracious, put on no airs, and danced like a middy till all hours in the morning . . .' While 'he was a bit of a barbarian who talked like a savage at times, to the no small scandal of his colleagues',[2] he relieved the minds of many of these same delegates who were deeply concerned with their tortuous processes of thought on how to kill each item on the agenda in turn while avoiding accusations of chauvinism.

Fisher himself vehemently exclaimed over and over again, 'I am not for War, I am for Peace. That is why I am for a supreme Navy.' In Stead's autograph book he wrote, 'The supremacy of the British Navy is the best security for the peace of the world.' His sole object, he kept claiming, was for peace. 'What you call my truculence is all for peace. If you rub it in, both at home and abroad, that you are ready for instant war with every unit of your strength in the first line, and intend to be first in, and hit your enemy in the belly, and kick him when he is down, and boil your prisoners in oil (if you take any!), and torture his women and children, then people will keep clear of you . . .'

---

[1] Harold Begbie, *Master Workers* (London, 1905), 36–7. (Hereafter cited as *Begbie*.)
[2] *Bacon*, i, 121.

CONFÉRENCE
DE LA PAIX
LA HAYE 1899.
—◦|◦|◦—

This is the
Chinese Ambassador's
Signature and
rank which
he kindly write
down for me
while I was sitting
by his side at
the Conference as
he had just asked
me to do the same.

The English writing at
the bottom is also
his writing

大
清
欽
差
出
使
大
臣
工
部
侍
郎
楊
儒

yang yü
le ministre
de chine

J. a. Fisher
Aug. 1. 1899

The Chinese Ambassador's signature, annotated by Fisher.

On the day before the conference closed, Fisher received a reminder
of the heavy duties that lay ahead of him.

FROM EVAN MACGREGOR[1]

June 27th, 1899

Sir,

I am commanded by my Lords Commissioners of the Admiralty to acquaint
you that orders have been given for your flag to be hoisted on the 1st July in
H.M.S. *Renown*, as Commander-in-Chief of the Mediterranean Station,

[1] Permanent Secretary of the Admiralty. Lennoxlove MSS.

vice Admiral Sir John Hopkins, and to be struck at sunset of that day in consequence of your absence on duty as a member of the Peace Conference.

I am, Sir, Your obedient servant,
E. *MacGregor*

Fisher referred to his responsibilities in time of war in this new and supremely important command, after The Hague delegates had been discussing the immunity of coal-carrying merchantmen from seizure by the fleets of the belligerents. 'I listened to them,' Fisher told Stead on the way back from church on a beautiful Sunday morning, 'wondering that they could think any of their resolutions would be recognized in war. When I leave The Hague I go to take command of the Mediterranean Fleet. Suppose that war breaks out, and I am expecting to fight a new Trafalgar on the morrow. Some neutral colliers try to steam past us into the enemy's waters. If the enemy gets their coal into his bunkers, it may make all the difference in the coming fight. You tell me I must not seize these colliers. I tell you that nothing that you, or any power on earth, can say will stop me from sending them to the bottom, if I can in no other way keep their coal out of the enemy's hands; for to-morrow I am to fight the battle which will save or wreck the Empire. If I win it, I shall be far too big a man to be affected about protests about the neutral colliers; if I lose it, I shall go down with my ship into the deep and then protests will affect me still less.'[1]

Fisher's remarkable prescience was publicly demonstrated before the world for the first time at The Hague. He was already certain in his mind that in any future major war, civilians would no more be spared than they had been in the dark ages; that however many idealistic resolutions might be advanced in times of peace, the nature of a twentieth century war would be as cruel and relentless as the shocking picture he had drawn before the delegates. When the 'launching of projectiles from balloons' and the use of poisonous gas came up for discussion, Fisher knew and stated that these were the weapons of the future. Science, and the beastliness of man, ensured that. A new era of barbarism, Fisher was convinced, lay round the corner; and it was his country's duty to prepare for it.

The submarine, still in a primitive stage of development, was another weapon discussed at The Hague. Fisher not only already knew that it was the coming weapon of sea warfare, but that it would be used without restraint—just as the bombing of women and children and the use of poisonous gas would soon become a commonplace of total twentieth century war. (*'War is HELL!!!'*) The cruelty and ruthlessness of the First World War came as no surprise to Fisher.

[1] *Review of Reviews*, February, 1910.

Even as great a twentieth century prophet as Winston Churchill, writing as First Lord fourteen years later to Fisher in temporary retirement, had to confess that he was not convinced of Fisher's belief that German submarines would sink British merchantmen. 'I do not believe this would ever be done by a civilised Power,' he wrote to Fisher. 'If there were a nation vile enough to adopt systematically such methods, it would be justifiable and indeed necessary to employ the extreme resources of science against them: to spread pestilence, poison the water supply of great cities and, if convenient, proceed by the assassination of individuals. These are frankly unthinkable propositions . . .'[1]

When the delegates to the peace conference returned home, most could reflect with complete satisfaction that little had been accomplished except the drafting of an Arbitration Council, and the banning of expanding 'dum-dum' bullets and the dropping of projectiles from balloons. They carried with them the memory of many righteous pleas and long-winded speeches made by their fellow delegates. In the minds of these delegates, no one made a stronger impression than Fisher himself, and his picture of future warfare and how he would conduct it was often remembered in the years ahead.

A few weeks later the Boer War was to break out in South Africa, signalling the beginning of a long and dangerous period of world-wide Anglophobia. The wall of deterrence which held back Britain's enemies before she found new allies in the Far East and in Europe was a thin one. The first strongpoint was the British fleet, and the centre of the power of this fleet was in the Mediterranean. The fierce and relentless warrior, the new Horatio Nelson, whom the great diplomatists and service officers of the day had seen and listened to in wonder and awe at The Hague was then in command of this, the mightiest single concentration of power in the world. The man who had taken a leading part in the creation of this fleet and would lead it in battle would have to be defeated before his country and its empire could be destroyed. This was an uncomfortable proposition—so formidable indeed that no nation in their senses would take it on.

It was one of Lord Salisbury's shrewdest moves in his last ministry to show the world the nature of the man they would have to break if they took up arms against Great Britain. When the conference was over Fisher received proper recognition from Lord Salisbury. From the Foreign Office there arrived a message to say that the Prime Minister was 'greatly obliged to you for the important services you have rendered'.[2]

---

[1] Lennoxlove MSS.   [2] *ibid.*

Chapter 7

MEDITERRANEAN RENAISSANCE

Before Fisher left to take up his command in the Mediterranean, he suffered a grievous disappointment which was to influence his conduct and policy during his last seagoing command. It was known that Admiral Sir Frederick Richards was to retire as First Naval Lord in August 1899. The old Admiral had filled the post most competently during a difficult time. Of the man and his achievements, *The Times* wrote that he 'has stood at the helm of the Admiralty during a most critical and anxious period and has steered the ship with unrivalled fortitude, skill, and devotion to the national interests'.[1] There was no greater admirer among his colleagues than Fisher, who also saw himself as Richards's natural successor at the head of the Board. His selection by Salisbury as naval representative at The Hague increased his expectations. Fisher hoped that his Mediterranean appointment would be cancelled and that he would be invited back to Whitehall.

Instead, Admiral Lord Walter Kerr was selected in Fisher's place. It was not an inspired choice. Lord Walter Kerr was an undramatic character, sound and conservative, a fine seaman, but hardly adequate in an administrative capacity for the dangerous years that lay ahead for the Navy. Once before, when Fisher had aspired to an appointment, that time as Flag-Captain to the Mediterranean Flagship, Lord Walter Kerr had got in ahead of him. And now it had happened once more. Rank and influence again seemed to have counted above merit. An officer who was later to become Fisher's private secretary 'was told at the time that after the appointment was made known, Jacky shook his fist and said, "I will get there yet in spite of them".'[2]

Fisher went out to the Mediterranean in a dangerous frame of mind. During the 1890s, his ambition to reform the Navy had grown

[1] *The Times*, 24 August, 1899.
[2] 'Some recollections of Jacky Fisher', by Sir Charles Walker. Kilverstone MSS.

with every battle, with every success, and even with every defeat. He had accomplished much, especially in the fields of gunnery and *matériel*. But much more remained. His determination to reform every department and every activity of the Royal Navy acquired a new and anxious edge to it as a result of his dashed hopes of 1899. Only in his records was he nearing the end of his naval career. His energy remained boundless. He could work for as long hours as ever. But he was fifty-eight years old. He would be sixty-three, with only two active years ahead of him, on the retirement of the new First Naval Lord. For this reason alone, and never mind the enemies who grew year by year, there would be a strong prejudice against his succession to the highest post. Fisher realized that his only chance lay in publicly exposing the state of the stables, and his own suitability for the rôle of Hercules, so that no one could forget where he was now, and where he expected to be in 1904.

In the campaigns that he was planning even before he left England, he knew that he might at any moment go too far, and plummet over the abyss. It was a calculatedly risky policy; but the spectacular plunge to destruction was much more in the Fisher style of doing things than crawling down hesitantly, from foothold to foothold, ending up safely 'growing cabbages in some secluded village', as he had once humorously suggested for himself—though adding as a rider that 'I should have endeavoured that no such cabbages had been seen, even by the Queen of Sheba!'

The campaign of attack against Whitehall which Fisher determined to conduct from the Mediterranean was not to be carried out at the expense of his reforming programme for the fleet itself. Fisher had his priorities clearly in order, as always. His impact on the Navy's premier fleet was to be swift and impressive. That it was also to be intelligent was revealed within the first hours. His predecessor had already returned home through ill health, and his second-in-command was on manoeuvres in the western Mediterranean. Fisher did not take over at once, as he might well have done. He thought it more appropriate that the Rear-Admiral should complete the cruise, while he contented himself with the rôle of observer. His presence could not altogether be disregarded, however. Service custom called for each Captain to make an official visit to the new Commander-in-Chief, and for the Admiral formally to return each call. 'Fisher swept away this waste of time by directing all the Captains to assemble on board his Flagship at 10 a.m., and there he received them all together, the whole ceremony lasting only half an hour. He then called in turn, for three minutes only [instead of the customary half hour], on board each ship, so that all the official visits were ended and the conventions satisfied in a single day by 1 p.m.'[1]

Fisher's pace was bewildering for those unaccustomed to it. It extended to every department of activity in the fleet and his Flagship, where 'he gave dinners on the quarterdeck, one side being screened off for the purpose. After dinner he and his guests moved to the other side of the deck and a party of men, specially drilled, cleared and removed the tables. Crockery might be broken and glass suffer but three minutes was the time allowed for the deck to be cleared and the screen removed'.[2] This same officer recalled the degree to which Fisher demanded alertness and speed at all times. He 'gave us a tremendous hustle—we got out the torpedo net defence, cleared for action, then got out the bow anchor, went to fire quarters, deserted ship—that is, sent all the ship's company away in the boats as if the ship was sinking all in the space of two hours, and then he left us to replace the debris and get this ship again into a reasonable state'.

Surviving letters to his family confirm the state of 'hustle' which governed the conduct of the fleet during Fisher's time, and the delight he took in it all. To his son he wrote (5 October 1900): 'We have just finished some more exciting operations which all went off splendidly. We only had one collision between the torpedo craft which was wonderful considering forty vessels of all sorts were all dashing about at full speed with no lights, in every direction . . .'[3] The gunnery officer of the battleship *Caesar* has told how Fisher 'instead of cruising from port to port at ten knots' would 'steam at fifteen, practically full speed. With the reciprocating engines this was hard toil for engineer officers and stokers . . . The chief engineer . . . had to spend his time at sea in the engine room, coat off, sweating in the hot Mediterranean climate. It was all very well once in six months to do a full-speed trial, but to do one on every trip was surely unreasonable.'

'Fisher's critics, and he had many at home,' wrote one of his officers, 'asked questions about waste of coal, wear and tear of engines and so on. All very true; but efficiency was the watchword and answer. It was war we were preparing for, when high speeds would be essential; if high speed meant wear and tear and break-downs let us, said he, find it out in peace. Let our designers design engines, boilers and machinery that would stand the strain.'[4]

---

[1] *Bacon*, i, 126.

[2] Admiral Sir R. H. Bacon, *A Naval Scrapbook First Part*, 1877–1900 (London, 1925), (Hereafter cited as *Scrapbook*.)

[3] Kilverstone MSS.

[4] Admiral of the Fleet Lord Chatfield, *The Navy and Defence* (London, 1942–7, 2 vols), i, 36. (Hereafter cited as *Chatfield*.)

Speed and alertness, a quick and intelligent response to a crisis, were among the qualities Fisher most highly valued in his officers. This same officer, who later became Admiral of the Fleet Lord Chatfield, sometimes found himself with a torpedo officer ordered to inspect a ship's organization for battle. 'You are to think out how to test her fighting efficiency. You are to visit all her batteries and fire controls and give me your reports,' Fisher would order. Then he would 'think out ways to test the Captain's resources and imagination and quickness of thought. When the Captain was fully occupied superintending some order that the Commander-in-Chief had just told him to carry out, Fisher would suddenly say to him, "A torpedo has struck your ship on the starboard quarter", and then watch to see how he reacted and what orders he gave to cope with the emergency, how much in fact he was a master of his command.'[1]

In all the exercises and manoeuvres of the Mediterranean Fleet there was a strong emphasis on torpedo attack and defence. Fisher understood more than most of his contemporaries the very real threat to the fleet of a well-prepared torpedo attack. One of the first things he did after he arrived was to appoint a committee to prepare schemes for fleet manoeuvres. One of its members wrote of how he 'addressed us in his usual breezy style, and among other things he told us that he had just come from The Hague, where he had met some German Admirals who argued with him that our fleet was useless, as the Germans in wartime would sink the whole lot with their torpedo boats and destroyers. "Now," he said, "I have come out here and we will prove that this is all nonsense." '[2]

Over the following months he did just this, and enjoyed every minute of it. The evidence of his delight in high speed fleet evolutions and mock attacks is in the diaries and writings of those who served in the Mediterranean at this time, and in his own letters. On 17 June 1900 he writes to his married daughter, Beatrix: ' . . . We had the other day the Fleet in two parts going at each other and it was most exciting to see all the destroyers dashing out at 20 knots and gliding between the battleships to attack the enemy . . . '[3] This is accompanied by a detailed diagram showing how it was accomplished. Lady Fisher, too, received accounts of manoeuvres in all their technical detail, even if time was so short for him and many of his personal letters began 'I am most frightfully busy as usual . . .'

[1] *Chatfield*, i, 36.
[2] *Scrapbook.*
[3] Kilverstone MSS.

TO LADY FISHER

Lemnos
September 29th, 1900

Darling Heart,

. . . We finished the first part of our manoeuvres yesterday. They were quite splendid and everyone is delighted with themselves . . . It really all went first rate and was very realistic. Everything played into my hands to make it come off well. The only thing now is to look out that the 'foot of pride' does not come against me! We only had two collisions—with the destroyers—but a near shave, about 70 feet, between the *Royal Oak* and the *Ramillies* . . . It really was all most exciting and was as near war as it well could be. I never had any sleep for 48 hours, nor did anyone else, and not much rest for 4 days, so that we were all pretty well done for at the end. We had a final battle between the two parts of the Fleet, one against the other, all hands firing like mad, and it was a splendid sight . . . The destroyers all dashing about like mad in the middle of it all! and torpedoing everyone! It certainly is the best thing I have ever seen and the most realistic . . .

It was a pitch-dark night when we had the most exciting time, which added to the effect, and there was fighting going on all over the horizon, with destroyers chasing cruisers and other destroyers. I am immensely pleased with them all, as they all showed such good judgement and so much dash, and it was very ticklish work all the time . . .

Y.l.h.
J. A. Fisher

Within a year Fisher had entirely transformed the spirit, skill and fighting prowess of his fleet. He had good reason to be pleased with himself. The range of gunnery practice had risen from around 3,000 yards to 6,000 and even 7,000 yards. Second-rate officers were summarily dealt with and sent away, for Fisher knew that a first-rate replacement from home would eagerly answer the call from the premier fleet. One officer was 'guilty of dereliction of duty which might have been passed over by a supine Commander-in-Chief or punished with a reprimand. The delinquent was brought before his Admiral, who cheerfully assured him that if it were time of war he would have been court martialled and shot, but any way "you may go home tonight. I am sorry for your wife and children. The interview is at an end." '[1]

The *esprit de corps* of the officers and men soared. 'I cannot translate adequately into words,' wrote one officer of this time, 'the buoyant joy and relief that I felt when I found that at last I was serving under a master-mind, open to imbibe the latest ideas, however crude; and, moreover, under a man having the energy and influence to see new ideas carried out. It seems as if the Navy at last must be roused from

[1] *Pall Mall Gazette*, September, 1904.

its lethargic condition, that shortly it would arise and stretch itself, throw off old traditions and become a real live fighting service.'[1]

One of the first reasons for this great improvement in the enthusiasm of the fleet was Fisher's policy of close consultation on all matters with his specialist subordinates, especially junior officers whom he reckoned were less deeply influenced by old-fashioned notions. Even a Midshipman in one of his destroyers knew that his suggestions would be considered and perhaps approved. This was a novel and stimulating experience for officers who were accustomed to viewing their Commander-in-Chief as an aloof and somewhat alarming dictator.

Fearsome as it might be to sit in his presence, there was always the feeling of certainty that suggestions and confidences would be welcomed. By his firm and even ruthless discipline and his grandiose manner, Fisher retained the awesome power of his position, yet succeeded in introducing a sense of mutual co-operation and intimacy between the highest and the lowest. One Commander recalled how Fisher 'gave a big dinner and I was one of the guests. It was like dining with Royalty. After the King's health Fisher got up and went on deck. We had all been warned to sit still, then officers were sent for singly to go and talk with him. He sat on the Quarter deck with a chair beside his. When I went up he asked me a lot about the Navigating Branch and I had some views about it and told him them.'[2]

While Fisher's personal indulgences were restrained, and he continued to drink and smoke modestly, he enjoyed and improved on the luxuries that were a Commander-in-Chief's natural right. The decoration and furnishings of his day cabin resembled a suite at one of the grander hotels at Marienbad he had never been able to afford. His barge was said to be 'the envy of the German Emperor'. The *Renown* carried a special fore-top-gallant mast to ensure that his flag should fly higher than any other.

Life on a foreign station included many ritualistic social rounds and entertainments. With increasing time-saving mechanization, which began with the slow replacement of sail by steam power, it became more than ever necessary to fill the long periods between fleet manoeuvres and evolutions and occasional gunnery drill, with regattas, pulling races, shore-based sports and athletics, balls and parties and parades and receptions. The arrival of Fisher with his dramatic programme for increasing the efficiency and readiness for war of the Mediterranean diminished the social element. But it still flourished throughout the

---

[1] *Scrapbook.*

[2] Admiral Sir W. James, *A Great Seaman: The Life of Admiral of the Fleet Sir Henry F. Oliver* (London, 1956), 96–7. (Hereafter cited as *Oliver.*)

period of his appointment, for it was a basic ingredient of service life. Though much of it bored him, he enjoyed meeting the ambassadors, the sultans and pashas, the kings and queens, at the numerous ports at which his Flagship called during the year. The Commander-in-Chief was something of a potentate himself, the ruler of a very powerful floating state of many thousand subservient subjects. He was served and waited on, and lived in splendour. His wife and family lived in palace-like conditions in Admiralty House, Malta, or cruised the Mediterranean in the luxurious yacht *Surprise*, meeting the Flagship in beautiful secluded bays in the Aegean, off Tripoli or in the Bosphorus, at Sardinia or Venice. Poor as he might still be, and living on a pay of less than £1500 a year[1] and grateful for an unexpected £100 windfall from his son-in-law, Fisher by tradition and by the right of his position, lived in splendid luxury. In letters to his wife and children his preoccupation with mundane domestic detail blends inappropriately with accounts of royal social events. To his wife at Malta from Sardinia in the early summer of 1902, he writes:

TO LADY FISHER[2]

Sardinia
May 21,[?] 1902

Darling Heart,
  We got here this afternoon after a most successful passage, very fine weather . . . no end of tactics . . . and my face is all peeling from the sun and I never felt so thankful for anything as that elderflower water which fortunately I brought with me. It has a wonderful effect. *Mind you send me all my pocket handkerchiefs by the 'Surprise'* when Dorothy and Pamela come up. You will find about a dozen or so in my drawers and more at the wash . . .

Fondest love to you all,
J. A. F.

By contrast, Fisher writes to Beatrix from Suda Bay, 'We sail in a couple of hours . . . We have had no end of functions here. Banquets, luncheons, illuminations, etc. and I am very thankful it's all over! But it will begin again at Constantinople August 29th! Prince George who is High Commissioner of Crete is a most charming fellow, talks English perfectly and very fond of the English. He is devoted to Princess Victoria of Wales and I can't think why they don't let him marry her except that they are first cousins, but they allowed Princess Maude to marry her first cousin . . .'[3]

---

[1] His very considerable expenses were in part met by 'table money' of a further £1,642 per annum.
[2] Lennoxlove MSS.   [3] Kilverstone MSS.

Fisher's son Cecil had by now become a judge in the Indian Civil Service ('And gets £2,000 a year I believe,' his father proudly noted), and in his journeyings to and from India was of course included in the elaborate programmes Fisher arranged for all his family with as much care as those for visiting royalty and important persons.

TO CECIL FISHER[1]

> *Admiralty House*
> *Malta*
> *February 20th* [?] *1901*

Dearest Cec,

As usual I have been frightfully busy and not able to write to you sooner. It will be quite delightful your bringing out Beatrix. I enclose you your programme on a separate sheet which you can send to Beatrix, and Mother is most delighted at the thought of going home with you both. I rather hope that Beatrix and Reginald will come back with Mother. She is due at Venice on October 1st where she will find the *'Surprise'* waiting for her with D. and P. [Dorothy and Pamela], on board and they propose to stop at Venice a fortnight and then go somewhere else before returning to Malta on October 27th, which is the day I come back with the Fleet to Malta.

We are very busy with the preparations for the Duke of York and I have just been settling the details with the Governor. We are to have a Grand Procession through the streets, lined with sailors and soldiers. The Governor and I are to drive together in the first carriage, then the Duke and Duchess, then all the rest. I am going to send twelve vessels to meet the Ophir at Gibraltar as escort and vessels dodge out from the coast all along until he gets to Aden to take him the latest telegrams . . .

> Ever your loving Father,
> *J. Fisher*

But always the renaissance of the fighting qualities of the Mediterranean Fleet dominated Fisher's thoughts during his period of command. The culmination of his endeavours was the organization for the first time of joint manoeuvres with Britain's second most powerful naval force, the Channel Squadron, whose main base was at Gibraltar, and was intended in time of war to operate in the western approaches to the English Channel, in the Channel itself, and to support the Mediterranean Fleet should this be necessary. Fisher had always believed *'it to be a cardinal principle (that should never be departed from) that the Mediterranean Fleet should be kept constituted for instant war'*, and yet he knew that the most probable enemy during his period as Commander-in-Chief possessed the inestimable advantage of flexibility in deploying his forces; that the French with their central geographical position

[1] Kilverstone MSS

could strike without warning from Toulon, or into the Atlantic or the English Channel. As Fisher wrote to the Earl of Rosebery, the late Liberal Prime Minister, from Malta in May 1901, 'We are in a dangerous and a serious position in the Mediterranean (and I say this to you advisedly), because instead of seeking the French Fleet to bring it to action, I have got to seek reinforcements coming from England. The ancient and glorious rôle of the English Navy will be reversed: *the tables will be turned*; it will be the French Admiral from Toulon falling on the English Admiral in superior force or chasing him with malignant glee!'

The closest co-ordination of the Mediterranean Fleet with the Channel Squadron would be a crucial necessity in time of war, and yet no one before Fisher had thought of co-ordinating manoeuvres in peace time. His partner in these exercises was Rear-Admiral Arthur Wilson, the dour, dogged and experienced old friend and partner of the Egyptian armoured train days. The two Admirals met to discuss the exercises in detail off Lagos in Portugal. 'The two chief figures of this meeting . . . ' Wilson's biographer wrote, 'presented a remarkable contrast: [Wilson] self-restrained, reserved, silent and thoughtful, but watchful and attentive, with everything about him denoting a simplicity of life and habit; while Fisher loved to contrive a dramatic effect about everything he did.'[1]

The combined exercises fulfilled all Fisher's expectations, both dramatic and practical. 'We had a splendid day yesterday manoeuvring,' he wrote, '—the whole Fleet together, and it was a wonderful sight. A passing P. & O. liner stopped to see it . . . We had arranged it, of course, long before, and I had rehearsed it many times, so I felt pretty sure it would come off well when the time came to put such a mass of ships through it. *We just mount up to fifty vessels*, which is a big lot to work together.'[2]

Fisher's campaign against the Admiralty was tactically three-pronged, the direct assault, the flank attack from one side through his political allies, and from the other flank through his friends of the press. The first justification for the opening of hostilities was the condition of the Mediterranean Fleet. No Admiral since the beginning of time has been satisfied with the numbers of his ships, and few with the quality of his *matériel*. Even Nelson had cried out for more frigates. Fisher wanted many more of its contemporary equivalent, the cruiser; and many more destroyers, and battleships, too. He considered his Fleet dangerously inadequate, especially to fight off a joint challenge by the French from Toulon and Bizerta, and the Russians from the Black Sea; and he had every justification for his belief that the Mediterranean Fleet was all

[1] *Wilson*, 160.   [2] *Bacon*, i, 149.

that stood between his country, vulnerable and weakened by the Boer War, and the successful aggression of the great European land powers, not one of which could be counted on as a reliable friend. But Fisher operated on a much wider front than this, attacking foreign policy generally and especially as conducted by British ministers in the Levant; on training policy; on the inadequacies of most British *matériel*; and on the parsimony of the Treasury and even the wretched ineptitude of most senior politicians. Numbered among those to whom he looked for support (it was not always forthcoming) were James Thursfield of *The Times*, Joseph Chamberlain, the Earl of Rosebery and Earl Spencer, his old chief on the Board. While the tone of his writing was always extreme and even adjectivally outrageous, he tried to follow the principles of indirect persuasion through a third party as practised by his old ally, Lord Esher, rather than the methods of direct assault used by the Navy League and the sensational newspapers.

The trouble began in the early months of 1900 when Fisher began a long and sustained correspondence with Thursfield to acquaint him with the deficiencies of the Mediterranean Fleet. The war in South Africa was going badly, and cruisers had been withdrawn from the Mediterranean and other stations for patrolling the supply routes to the Cape. Fisher complained that the numbers of cruisers and destroyers under his command were 'criminally insufficient . . . if more destroyers are not obtained . . . we shall have the Boer War played over again at sea!' The lack of fibre of the Board against Fisher's *bête noire*, Hicks-Beach at the Treasury, were at the root of the trouble. 'I maintain the First Sea Lord ought to go before the Cabinet and say so much is essential for the fighting efficiency of the Navy,' Fisher wrote, 'and let the country know that the Cabinet take the responsibility of saying they know more about fighting Admiral Fournier than the First Sea Lord or the Commander-in-Chief of the Mediterranean! Who is going to be hung if we don't lick the French Fleet? Won't the Cabinet say, "We left all to the Admirals in command of our Fleets—we left them quite unfettered." Yes, but did they give the poor devils the tools they asked for to execute the required job?'

A new press ally who became one of Fisher's staunchest admirers volunteered support in the summer. He was Arnold White, a shrewd and industrious free-lance journalist who specialized in naval matters. In July he sent Fisher the proof of an article he had written supporting a strengthened Navy and prophesying that an early British naval defeat would be 'irretrievable, irreparable, eternal'. Fisher wrote back enthusiastically, and threw in for good measure the kernel of several of his beliefs as a kind of primer for a 'Support Fisher' campaign. 'Mr Barnes, the great Editor of *The Times*,' Fisher wrote in his best instructive vein, 'said "Repetition is the secret of Journalism." You must keep on telling the people the same things.' He summarized his view of politicians thus: 'The intense ignorance of the men at the head of affairs is what frightens and appals me! . . . Our curse is the parochial politician in Parliament and the ineptitude of our Foreign Office . . .'

It was at this time that Fisher's correspondents first noticed the capitalized injunction at the end of his letters to '*BURN!*' or '*DESTROY!*' them. It was one of his orders that seems rarely to have been obeyed. As Arnold White told Cecil Fisher many years later, 'Your father was different. His "burn and destroy" meant "publish as widely as possible, but don't give me away." '

In October 1900 Goschen retired as First Lord and was succeeded by William Waldegrave Palmer, the second Earl of Selborne and son-in-law of Lord Salisbury, with whom Fisher was to work in the closest association for many years. Fisher's regard for this young peer was always ambivalent. He greatly admired his qualities of patience and steadiness through all the problems of his administration, for many of which Fisher was responsible. After Fisher became First Sea Lord, he was able to write that 'never did any First Lord hold more warmly the hand of his principal than Lord Selborne held mine'. But his manner to Selborne was often hectoring and impatient, and he never considered him sufficiently stalwart in his combats, especially against the Treasury. For his part, Selborne recognized the genius in Fisher at once, and was quick to realize that one of his chief tasks while in office was to soften the impact of Fisher's blows and plead gently for discretion without diminishing the creative enthusiasm of this extraordinary man.

Fisher wrote to Thursfield shortly after Selborne's appointment and confided his fears for the future. ' . . . a strong hand is wanted at Headquarters and, *I say this to you in all confidence, the strong hand is not there now!* I fear the worst with such young men as Lord Selborne and Austen Chamberlain [Colonial Secretary], as opposed to Hicks-Beach, and the Army craze . . .'

When Selborne invited Fisher to write to him privately on any problems, Fisher seized the opportunity eagerly. He wrote frequently and fully, and at first with restraint, by his own standards. 'I am confident you will find [this correspondence] advantageous, and, if at times I express myself very strongly, I hope you will forgive me and kindly remember that I have the rope round my neck, and if we don't beat the French I shall be hung or shot like Admiral Byng! . . . *We want more ships of all classes*, with all their adjuncts in the shape of officers, men, etc. . . . in this year's estimates, *there is not a single destroyer to be built.*'

Fisher's massive dispute with Kerr soon featured in their correspondence. He made it clear to the First Lord that the Fleet was 'criminally deficient' in cruisers, destroyers and auxiliaries, but that 'My good friend Walter Kerr is kind enough to suggest in his last letter to me . . . that I may perhaps find myself in his place and will look foolish to find myself unable to meet these demands! I don't expect to find myself in his place, but you will see from this remark of his that my pertinacity in urging what I think to be imperatively necessary tends to place me at loggerheads with him . . .'

Fisher, with customary indiscretion, soon reported on his private correspondence with his First Lord to Thursfield, with some recommendations for future action. 'Lord Selborne writes me very excellent and clear-headed letters, and he seems to be bent on obtaining all we require; but I have no doubt a little "stiffening" from outside in the shape of one of those "do-your-duty-or-you'll-catch-it" leading articles in *The Times* will help him, along with that unmitigated cold-blooded rude brute Hicks-Beach, just about this time, when the Estimates are being roughed out in Cabinet meetings!' While of Kerr, Fisher wrote to Thursfield in two letters in January 1901: '*Between ourselves*, there's no question that we have missed in the last few years that clear, broad old back of Sir F. Richards set against the wall! It was no good politicians and Hicks-Beach arguing with him! And there's been a lamentable falling off in what I may call "ginger" and "enthusiasm" in Admiralty administration . . . *Very private*. I've just had a most discomposing letter from Walter Kerr, and I bless the wisdom of our ancestors in having a civilian First Lord, as Lord Selborne is far more alive to the great issues at stake than his chief naval adviser. *I say this to you quite privately* and I see the reason clearly! The civilian is not trammelled by the conservative habits and minute attention to unimportant details engendered by a long professional life, and he takes large views and his "perspective" is correct . . .'

Matters came to a head in that spring of 1901. The efforts of the Navy League, its president, Robert A. Yerburgh, and of the journalists in Fisher's confidence, to stir up public disquiet about the strength of Britain's first line of defence, produced the result Fisher was seeking.

TO ARNOLD WHITE

[*March 1901*]

Private
Dear Mr Arnold White,

I am anxious you and Mr Yerburgh should know that your joint endeavours have produced much more effect than either of you probably have any idea of, and I am most desirous you should both fully realize the great services you have both rendered.

Lord Selborne is bringing out (PRIVATE—*much against their will*) the First Sea Lord and the Director of Naval Intelligence to Malta next week *for no other purpose whatever* than to discuss and decide the questions you have both so ably and irresistibly pressed in your various letters and articles (though the ostensible reason is to see the new docks). Further, the Navy Estimates would not have been at the figure they are had it not been for the influence brought to bear from outside. Perhaps that money in the Estimates has not been allocated to the best advantage, but that is a matter I am going to fight with them.

. . . Such a thing as the First Lord, First Sea Lord, and Director of Naval Intelligence coming out to discuss such matters is unprecedented . . .

> Yours very truly,
> *J. A. Fisher*

This impressive party with its entourage duly arrived in Malta. Fisher subsequently wrote of 'our very heated discussion'. He got on badly with Captain Reginald Custance, the Director of Naval Intelligence (DNI) and it is probable that their subsequent enmity dated from this time. Neither was he reassured by the manner of Selborne and Kerr. His unfavourable view of Selborne at that time is evidenced in a letter to his old friend Lord Spencer, to whom he wrote, 'I hope I may live to see you again First Lord, being in my opinion *the best the Navy ever had!*' And he opened his heart in a long letter to Lord Rosebery:

TO THE EARL OF ROSEBERY

> *Malta*
> *May 22nd, 1901*

Private

Dear Lord Rosebery,

. . . We are in a dangerous and a serious position in the Mediterranean . . . Lord Selborne says, 'Trust us to send you ships *when the time comes.*' I don't trust them! . . . Believe me, *what we want is a more rigorous administration at the Admiralty. That is the root of the whole matter.* They are lost to a sense of proportion: they can see a pin but they can't see a mountain! because their eyes are fixed on the floor of petty details as to what coloured socks we shall wear and a new collar for an Admiral's full-dress coat! . . . I enclose for your private eyes a portion of a letter I wrote to Lord Selborne on his first taking office. Not one single thing has been done since that date, notwithstanding reiterated letters from me, until, like related in the second epistle to the Corinthians, the 10th Chapter and the 9th verse (I quote it because I know it by heart!), they say 'his letters are weighty and powerful, but (perhaps) his bodily presence is weak and his speech contemptible': let us go out to Malta and flatten him out! So, after getting on for nearly two years representing the inefficiency that may prove the death of the Empire, they come out—*three to one*—and there are fierce words, but again, to quote the Scripture: 'The words of the men of the Mediterranean were fiercer than the words of the Admiralty', and they were beaten all along the line! but delay goes on. Lord Selborne is attending to coaling stations; Lord Walter Kerr is attending to our socks and coats . . . As I have said before, the root of the matter is the want of a vigorous administration . . .

Yours very truly,
J. A. Fisher

Besides endangering his own career and chances of getting back to Whitehall, Fisher felt in the summer of 1901 that he had made no progress towards strengthening his Fleet after nearly two years on the station. Kerr, weak, incompetent, bedevilled by the claims of opposing factions, seemed to be as firmly planted in the First Naval Lord's chair as ever. While retaining an affection for the splendid seaman he had once served under, Fisher became more and more exasperated with his performance at Whitehall. Even if Kerr had wished to resign, Fisher was certain that he would not be allowed to go, for religious if not political reasons. Fisher knew him to be 'a slave to the Roman Catholic hierarchy', who would 'not be allowed to leave the Admiralty, however much he may wish it'. And to Arnold White he continued: 'He is a pervert and has all the antagonism of the pervert to the faith he has left! . . . In the Navy [the Roman Catholics'] one mainstay is Walter Kerr and they will make him die at his post!'

Fisher was fast becoming an exasperating and embarrassing figure to the Admiralty. Articles and leaders and letters were appearing with ever increasing frequency in the newspapers that were unmistakably inspired by him and disclosing information that could have originated only with a serving officer in the Mediterranean. When rebuked by Selborne, 'You seem to place no trust whatever in the Admiralty, Sir John!' Fisher claimed to have replied, '*No, I do not.* I know your intentions are good, but Hell is paved with good intentions.' Kerr's Naval Secretary wrote in June 1901 complaining of Fisher's lack of discretion, to which Fisher replied defiantly: 'I am sorry words and phrases of mine are quoted, as you mention, but with a large Fleet like this the Admiral cannot hide his views and opinions, and mine, as you know, are very strong . . .'

But there is also evidence that Fisher tried to restrain the enthusiasm of some of his press supporters. In a letter to Thursfield, headed VERY PRIVATE, he refers to a series of *Daily Mail* articles which had been a particular embarrassment to Fisher: 'I was assured by a mutual friend of the absolute trust that could be placed in Mr Yerborough and Mr White, and they, having asked me in confidence my views, I gave them freely, but *quite privately*, in view of their enthusiasm on behalf of the Navy.' Fisher evidently had more confidence in the discretion of Thursfield, for he then unfolds to him 'ABSOLUTELY BETWEEN OURSELVES' the new and highly secret plans for unifying the operations of the Channel Squadron and the Mediterranean Fleet in time of war—'*an immense result*' Fisher described it.

Fisher's greatest embarrassment was Lord Charles Beresford, compared with whom Fisher was a paragon of reticence. Some diabolical chance of fate had brought these two men together from their different backgrounds into the Royal Navy in the 1850s. For almost half a century the inevitability of the fearful explosion of their clash of wills and temperaments and ambitions had remained concealed as each progressed in his own way towards higher rank and responsibility and influence. In the Mediterranean the match was lighted to the fuse; when the detonation took place a few years later it was to split the Navy asunder and shatter both men.

The seeds of discord between John Arbuthnot Fisher and Charles William de la Poer Beresford lay in their temperaments, their upbringing and the deep social strata that separated them from birth. Beresford inherited wealth, self-assurance, good looks and a superb physique. His privileged status, his charm as well as his natural ability and fearless courage, brought him very close to the summit. 'Charlie B' had gone to school with the future Lord Rosebery and Lord George Hamilton, and his father inherited the title, among others, of Marquess of Waterford, Earl and Viscount of Tyrone. Concurrently with his rapid progress in the service, he became a Member of Parliament and a close friend of the Prince of Wales—so close that it was he who had been entrusted by the Prince, when threatened with blackmail over the Aylesford scandal, to deliver a challenge to a duel to Lord Randolph Churchill. Beresford became a member of the Marlborough House set, welcomed periods on half-pay so that he could hunt even more frequently and throw himself more ardently into the Season. Like so many of his rich and courageous contemporaries, Beresford was made for heroism. The urge for battle was thick in his good Irish blood, but the opportunities to express it were sadly few. His part in the bombardment of the Alexandria forts and the subsequent land campaign brought him even more attention than Fisher received, and this, with his extravagance, ostentatious eccentricity among the very grand and the very rich, ensured for him the love of the common people. He had been an admired national figure for more than twenty years.

Yet Beresford was no frivolous playboy. He worked hard for the good of the Navy. The lower deck loved him, and he had a marvellous capacity for gaining the loyalty of his officers. By 1899 he had reached the rank of Rear-Admiral, and was highly regarded as a seaman as well as an administrator. Many believed that he had at least as good a chance as Fisher of becoming the next First Naval Lord.

To appoint 'Charlie B' as second-in-command of the Mediterranean Fleet under Fisher was an excruciating decision by Goschen and the Board. Both were troublesome officers who were known to be strong —even violently strong—for reform. Beresford's reforming zeal had a streak of Irish cussedness about it; with the Navy, he lived in a condition of constant discontent, lit by patches of exasperation which blazed out with a disregard for logic, timing, and the feelings of others. In a peacetime service, governed by rigid protocol, suppression and discipline, it was natural to love a rebel, especially one as daring as this handsome, charming, arrogant, aristocratic Irishman: the vicarious excitement was irresistible.

Perhaps the Admiralty hoped that Fisher's and Beresford's seeds of discontent would cross-pollinate negatively. But nothing of this kind happened. It was much worse. Beresford instituted his own campaign in parallel, some have claimed in competition, with Fisher's own. This was partly Fisher's own fault. Almost from the beginning, he had decided to treat his second-in-command with great reserve, and consultation between the two Admirals was kept at a formal level.

In Lord Charles Beresford Fisher scented danger. They might both be reforming zealots intent on strengthening the Mediterranean Fleet, but Fisher did not fancy the idea of unifying their campaigns. To Fisher, Beresford was first a vainglorious naval officer intent on personal power for himself and the social advantages this would bring to his ambitious wife. Beresford was a dilettante and an elderly playboy. His parties were notorious for their extravagance and 'showiness'. Everyone had a fund of anecdotes about them, and talked about such wild affairs as his race with one of his Captains up the Rock of Gibraltar in their motor cars. Of course no one could deny 'Charlie B's' courage, or his seamanship, and most of all his popularity. But Fisher knew that Beresford could never have climbed as high as he had without his title, his background, his wealth and Royal influence. He also knew what a formidable contender he was in the race between them to be head of the Board of Admiralty. Fisher, the fighting patriot who had fought his way up 'without friends and without money', was determined that his own thunder from the Mediterranean must not be stolen. He was absolutely certain that the worst thing for the Navy and the nation was for Lord Charles Beresford to be the next First Naval Lord; and that only he himself could reform and reshape the Navy to the needs of the new century and the inevitable great war that lay ahead.

It is impossible accurately to put a date to the first onset of the trouble between Fisher and Beresford which later was to split the service asunder. Admiral of the Fleet Lord Chatfield traced the origins of the dispute to two incidents he witnessed when he served in the battleship *Caesar* with the Mediterranean Fleet. 'One forenoon,' wrote Chatfield in his memoirs, 'Lord Charles had sent his signalman ashore to the Corradino for signal exercises. He had not asked permission as he should have done by the station orders, an oversight and not a deliberate intention. The Fleet signal officer informed the Commander-in-Chief.

'"Make a signal to the *Ramillies* [Beresford's Flagship]," he said, '*Ramillies*' signalmen to return to their ship immediately. Report in writing why station order No. — has not been obeyed." To make such a signal to his second-in-command was unwise. The Fleet took in the signal and pricked up its ears. That evening Malta was talking of it. . . . There was a rift in the lute. But a storm was shortly to ensue compared to which this was but an April shower.

'A few months later the Fleet was returning to Malta at the end of the first summer cruise. Admiral Fisher always led in first in the *Renown*, and walked up to the "Barracca", a vantage point whence he could watch every ship come into the difficult and narrow harbour and turn round 180 degrees before securing bow and stern to her buoys. It was a fine test of the nerve and skill of their Captains. Rapidity in every task was the order of the day. Charles Beresford was a fine seaman and anxious that his division should be smarter than others. His Flag-Captain, unfortunately, was not one of the best ship-handlers. When the *Ramillies* came in, she had to secure to two buoys in Bighi Bay, the outer anchorage, a fairly easy task. He made a mess of it, got his ship stuck across the harbour and delayed the entrance of the second division. "Jacky" lost his temper and signalled to the second-in-command:

' "Your flagship is to proceed to sea and come in again in a seaman-like manner." '[1]

Lord Chatfield described this incident as 'a lamentable example of bad leadership'. Yet Fisher had never hesitated from publicly rebuking the most senior officers under his command if the misdemeanour warranted it: he judged that he got better results this way, and it was the results that counted above cordial relations.

[1] *Chatfield*, 41.

The relations between Fisher and his second-in-command survived such incidents, and at least on the surface even remained cordial. But Fisher continued to deplore Beresford's more crude and public methods of venting his views. On 27 June 1901, for example, Fisher wrote to Fawkes, who had been protesting at this public washing of dirty linen: 'I have told Beresford that the Government has got a majority of 130 and all the newspaper and magazine articles in the world won't have the slightest effect! So far as I am personally concerned, it will be of course obvious to you that I have nothing whatever to gain by kicking the shins of the Admiralty! so that the articles (of which, by the way, I have only seen a portion) are certainly not written in my interest! and only serve to aggravate instead of smoothing and facilitating . . .'

Throughout Fisher's Mediterranean appointment France was regarded as Britain's likeliest enemy, and all considerations and *matériel* calculations, all the war planning and manoeuvres, were based on this premise. It was the French Fleet at Toulon, under Vice-Admiral François Fournier, which would be the first object of attack, with the added threat of the Russian Fleet from the Black Sea always to be taken into account. Against the Russian threat, Fisher advocated developing better relations with Turkey, and he 'looked upon our handling of the Turkish problem with some disgust'. He got on well with the Sultan. When he took his Fleet near Constantinople he cultivated the friendship of the powerful Pashas and called on the Sultan. 'The Sultan received him most cordially, and was apparently much struck with him and his views. The Boer War was still in progress, and the Sultan was in some fear of the conflagration spreading to Europe, in which case he felt sure that Turkey would be thrown into the melting pot. Fisher's supreme confidence in his Fleet went a long way to reassure the old potentate.'[1]

Fisher's wise political prescience went beyond the need for Turkey's friendship, which would help to seal up the eastern Mediterranean from the Russians, while his Fleet dealt with the French. He believed that the enduring jealousy and enmity between Britain and France itself was unnecessary and undesirable, and that Britain must also ally herself with Russia. Already the coming German threat loomed large in Fisher's calculations for the future. The implications of Admiral Alfred von Tirpitz's naval acts of 1898 and 1900 were abundantly clear to Fisher. As early as November 1901, he was writing to Thursfield, 'Personally, I have always been an enthusiastic advocate for friendship and alliance with France. They never have and never will interfere with our trade. It's not their line and, really, we have no clashing of vital interests . . .

[1] *Bacon*, i. 146.

The Germans are our natural enemies everywhere!' Nine months later he wrote of the Germans to Arnold White that 'their interests everywhere clash with ours . . . If you turn to France—in absolutely nothing do we clash, *and never can clash.* We hate one another (or rather it is only they who hate us) because "Perfide Albion" is taught in their [French] nurseries . . . The French newspapers play the "perfide Albion" game because we are really the only nation they can insult with impunity! . . . I am perfectly convinced, if the matter was properly engineered, and the Press of both countries interested in the subject, we should have a vast change, and both enormously to the advantage of France and ourselves . . . Does the French nation realize, do you think, what the German Mercantile Marine in its advancing leaps and bounds means? It means another million of French soldiers required in the vicinity of Cherbourg, where a landing is easy . . .'

By 1901 there were a number among those responsible for the nation's foreign affairs who were beginning to recognize Britain's need for new allies both in the Far East and the Mediterranean in order to relieve the pressure on the Royal Navy and allow it to concentrate its strength more fully in home waters against the new German threat. But there was no other senior serving officer with Fisher's broad prophetic view.

This was one of the remarkable qualities Selborne recognized in Fisher when he paid his placating visit to Malta in 1901. It was to Selborne's vast credit that his judgement of Fisher's unique powers remained unprejudiced during the long and acrimonious exchanges between the Mediterranean and Whitehall that followed this visit; even the rigours of the parliamentary debate on the condition of the Mediterranean Fleet of 3 July 1901, which taxed all Selborne's powers of defence, and which was a direct consequence of Fisher's, and Beresford's, agitation.

Although Fisher had hinted several times to the Board that he would welcome a new shore appointment after three exacting years in the Mediterranean, he let it be known, to his family and closest supporters, that he had forfeited his chances of reaching the top. In this way he covered up for himself in case of failure, and impressed on them the purity of his motives in his campaign. But there were times when he felt he really had gone too far in his complaints and would not be forgiven. His relations with Kerr were at a low level. On one occasion Kerr had written: 'The C.-in-C. has a habit, noticeable in some of his communications, of indulging in strong phrases to emphasize his arguments such as "disastrous consequences," "imperative necessity," "immediate large increase," "I earnestly press," etc. These must be regarded as the outcome of impulse rather than of calm and deliberate judgment, and must not be taken too seriously . . . No one knows better than Sir John Fisher that the proposal of the Committee . . . is an impossibility under existing conditions, yet he calmly proposes it . . . Their Lordships have a right to expect something better than a demand for impossibilities from an officer holding the position of the C.-in-C. in the Mediterranean . . .'[1] These were strong words to an Admiral commanding the Navy's premier Fleet.

It was fortunate for the nation that Selborne took a broader and wiser view of Fisher's abilities. There was no question of Fisher displacing Kerr, inadequate though he might be. Kerr would have to serve his full term. But there is no doubt that this young earl was bent on Fisher succeeding Kerr and was determined to prepare the way for his promotion in 1904 when Kerr was due to retire. For his part, Fisher's ambitions were seemingly more modest—though who was to know that he did not still entertain some hope of reaching the office of the First Naval Lord, in spite of the storms he had created in the Mediterranean? Or perhaps because of them?

On 29 October 1901 Fisher wrote to Fawkes from Malta indicating that he would prefer to avoid another summer in the Mediterranean if this could be arranged, and quoting the precedent of Lord Alcester, who 'went from the Mediterranean to be Second Sea Lord'. Hopefully in a postscript, Fisher added, 'Having been ten years at the Admiralty, I think I could hit it off without treading on anyone's toes! . . . I think we've "dug-out" pretty well here since September 1899, and done our best to deserve their Lordships's favourable consideration!'

Fisher's wishes were met some three months later. He received the news from Selborne in a letter which strongly characterized the First Lord's regard for his turbulent, brilliant admiral: affectionate and admiring, yet still cautious and cautioning.

FROM THE EARL OF SELBORNE

Admiralty, Whitehall
[February 9th, 1902]
Private
My dear Admiral,[2]

. . . You have several times pressed me to relieve you in the Mediterranean before the combined manoeuvres came off with the double object of giving your successor the benefit of the experience, and of allowing you to see if you cannot grow better cabbages than anyone else in a secluded English village. I am now going to take you at your word, only instead of growing cabbages in the

---

[1] *British Naval Policy*, 400. [2] Promoted full Admiral, 2 Nov., 1901.

country, . . . I want you to take Admiral Douglas' place as Second Naval Lord. He goes to the North American Command.

I have received the King's permission to make you this offer, but in making it I want to make an observation or two to obviate any possibility of misunderstanding in the future. I much hope that you will come, because I believe there is a great deal to be done in connection with the personnel, and that we can do much together for the good of the Navy, but I make no promise as to your succeeding the present First Naval Lord when his time is up. I reserve complete freedom of choice of his successor for myself or my successor when the time comes.

My second point is that, if we ever differ, as in the natural course of events we probably occasionally shall, no one off the Board must ever know of our differences. Each member of the Board has his eventual remedy in resignation, a remedy which a wise man reserves for some special occasion only. But so long as we do not resign, our solidarity to the Service and world outside must be absolute.

I cannot state exactly yet the date* at which these changes should take place.

> Believe me, Yours sincerely,
> *Selborne*

*P.S. Conceivably it might not be till after the manoeuvres, but probably in May or June.

Fisher responded to the news with equal warmth. 'I think it shows an extraordinary Christian spirit on the part of Lord Selborne and the Admiralty to ask me to come and sit amongst them,' he wrote to his eldest daughter, 'after the way I have harassed them, blackguarded them, and persecuted them for the last three years! especially as nearly everything I have asked for has been given eventually, though strenuously opposed at first.'

Fisher's period as Commander-in-Chief of the Mediterranean Fleet had made him many enemies. The creation of an alert, efficient, battle-worthy Fleet out of the easygoing Fleet with its pride in polish and set evolutions which he had found in 1899, could not have been accomplished in such a short time without discomfiting many people of all ranks. There were some who would never forgive Fisher, from junior officers who suddenly found themselves despatched home, to sinecurists who were suddenly expected to work for their pay, and senior officers who simply did not hold with Fisher's unorthodox peremptoriness. Among these there were many who automatically allied themselves against him when internecine warfare later broke out in the Navy. There were many others, too, whose first-hand experience of Fisher's methods, especially his vindictive unforgivingness and his deliberate policy of favouritism, experienced their first feeling of uneasiness about him. These doubts were to harden later when the time came to choose sides.

Fisher might express his gratitude to the Admiralty for their 'extra-ordinary Christian spirit'; but only Lord Selborne deserved this. Ungenerously, Lord Walter Kerr failed to send the customary con-gratulations to Fisher at the termination of his command. This did not bode well for their future relations on the Board. Nor was any sort of message of appreciation received from the Foreign Office. Fisher noted cryptically to Arnold White 'that I have not seen or heard anything from Lord Lansdowne [Secretary of State for War] or any member of the Government, or received even the usual letter of thanks an Admiral receives on giving up a command. *Of course, it's pure absence of mind and unintentional, I feel sure . . .'*

But there were also those who recognized the debt the service and the country owed to Fisher for reviving the fighting strength and efficiency of the country's first line of defence, and for accomplishing this when the Mediterranean Fleet was most needed as a deterrent to European war. Fisher loved good brains, and especially in the Mediterranean he gathered about him a number of intellectually brilliant middle-rank officers like Jellicoe, Henry Jackson, and Reginald Bacon, with whom he loved to discuss every aspect of the theory and practice of naval warfare, from weapons and communications and ship design, to the management of battle fleets in action. These men became devoted disciples, and when war came they were selected for the most responsible commands.

Britain fought the South African uprising without a strong friend in the world. The Foreign Secretary may not have thought it appropriate to acknowledge the nation's debt to Fisher for doubling the efficiency of his Fleet and discouraging foreign aggression when almost the whole of the Army was busy five thousand miles away. But there were others prepared to offer their thanks. Sir Nicholas O'Conor, the British Ambassador in Constantinople, wrote privately to Fisher, 'I cannot let the moment pass without expressing to you my most sincere thanks for the cordial way in which you have been willing to give me any assistance during the term of your command. My object was to keep things as quiet as possible during the South African troubles, and that I could follow this policy without any fear that it would be put down to timidity was in great measure due to the state of efficiency to which you had brought the Fleet in the Mediterranean and to the fact that foreign powers knew and fully understood this.' Fisher's old friend, the Sultan of Turkey, added his own gratitude, and sent him a secret message 'implying that the efficiency of the Mediterranean Fleet had preserved the peace of the world during the Boer War . . .'[1]

[1] *Bacon*, i, 161.

Fisher's specific achievements in the Mediterranean were remembered, even by some of his future adversaries. Beresford himself claimed for Fisher that 'from a 12-knot Fleet with numerous breakdowns, he make a 15-knot Fleet without breakdowns'. He left behind him a Fleet experienced in long range gunnery and wireless telegraphy. The torpedo was now a respected weapon, for both offence and defence. Above all, he left behind him a body of fighting men who had been fired by his dynamism and educated by his example and the inspiring lectures he regularly gave to them.

The depths of the affection and loyalty of the main body of the Fleet were demonstrated during his last days of command in early June 1902. There were to be two big dinners, given by the officers, and by his second-in-command, and the governor of Malta organized a great banquet. Fisher had some doubts about the desirability of these events and succeeded in evading one of the dinners, but the second was 'followed by a dance on board the *Ramillies,* which last performance I shall thoroughly enjoy!'

Fisher's final departure from his Fleet, and the termination of his last seagoing command, was described in a letter to his son Cecil. It is a typical family letter, crisp and clear in its description, revealing the frankness of his prejudices, the pleasure in his successes, and the deep affection for his family which he retained all through his life.

TO CECIL FISHER

H.M.S. Renown, at sea
Off Rome
June 6th, 1902

Dearest Cis,

It has been an awful time saying 'goodbye,' and it was just as much as I could do to get through it. In fact, I didn't! for when Admiral Watson and Prince Louis came at the last to say 'goodbye,' I was simply speechless and I had to bolt! We went out 16 knots from Malta Harbour! which astonished them all and must have looked well, I think. Everything was propitious, the whole Fleet was there, and they cheered us to the echo! We fired a salute to the Governor as we were going out and that added to the spectacle. The Governor had ordered the troops to line the ramparts, but, as usual, they were all half an hour late, and we saw them all doubling up just as we were leaving the harbour! One does not wonder at South Africa when one sees every day the utter ineptitude of Military Officers! Half the year they are on leave and the other half of the year everything is left to the Sergeant-Major and the Non-Commissioned Officers!

We have had a very smooth passage so far. We stopped the *Renown* last night and sent a boat to *Surprise* to bring Mother, Beatrix, D. & P. to dinner here and to hear the band, so you may suppose how calm it was! . . . I've joined the Marlborough Club. The King ordered the Prince of Wales to propose me, and I was elected right off in consequence . . .

Ever your loving father,
J. A. Fisher

Chapter 8

SECOND FIDDLE

With the accession of King Edward VII in January 1901 there began a new and intense Royal interest in the senior service. King Edward VII was a real mariner-monarch. He loved the sea, and he loved yacht racing, at which he was most skilful. He had a real feeling for ships, knew a lot about them, and was fascinated by the special monastic and ritualistic life of the sailor. He also loved the Navy's uniform, and there was nothing he enjoyed more than pinning a new decoration on the breast of a naval officer.

The reign of Edward VII coincided with the most intense period of naval renaissance and competition Britain had ever experienced, and the sovereign was the Royal link between the Foreign Office, the Navy's Messiah, and the service itself. It was a happy state of affairs for the nation that the King possessed an equal enthusiasm for foreign policy, Sir John Fisher and the Navy his favourite Admiral administered for the greater part of the reign.

Fisher's relationship with King Edward VII was the most important of his career. Even when the old Queen was still alive, and while Fisher was still quite a junior Admiral, the two men had known and liked one another well. Their trusting friendship burst into full flower when Fisher became First Sea Lord and survived without fading to the end of Fisher's reign and to the King's death. Edward VII did not readily forgive those who crossed him, but such was the strength of their friendship that it survived many small misunderstandings and trivial disputes. On one occasion the King had set his heart on being rowed out in a grand pulling barge in the style of Henry VIII, to his Fleet at a naval review. Fisher was summoned to Buckingham Palace to discuss details of the arrangements, which he had in fact already settled. 'I found no Equerries in attendance,' Fisher wrote, 'no one about, and the King white with anger. "So!" he cried out to me, "I'm to go by such and such a train, am I? And I'm to embark at such and such a time, am I? And I'm to use your [powered] barge because it's a better barge than mine, is it? Look here, *am I King or are you?*" The upshot of the interview was that he threw the papers on the floor, with "Have it your own way!"'[1]

The King was always prepared to rebuke Fisher if he felt that he had really gone too far. 'Would you kindly leave off shaking your fist in my face?'[2] he is reported to have admonished him in the middle of some unrecorded tirade against an opponent, or perhaps while giving extra emphasis to his enthusiasm for a new scheme. Fisher has also recounted in his *Memories* two Edward VII anecdotes against himself. 'He used often to say to me at Big Functions: "Have I missed out anyone, do you think?" For he would go round in a most careful way to speak to all he should. Just then a certain Admiral approached—perhaps the biggest ass I ever met. The King shook hands with him and said something I thought quite unnecessarily loving to him: when he had gone he turned on me like a tiger and said: "You ought to be ashamed of yourself!" I humbly said, "What for?" "Why!" he replied, "when that man came up to me your face was perfectly demoniacal! Everyone saw it! And the poor fellow couldn't kick you back! You're First Sea Lord and he's a ruined man! You've no business to show your hate!" And the lovely thing was that then a man came up I knew the King did perfectly hate, and I'm blessed if he didn't smile on him and cuddle him as if he was his long-lost brother, and then he turned to me afterwards and said with joyful revenge, *"Well, did you see that?"*'

Equally light-hearted was Fisher's story of the beautiful woman. 'I was driving with him alone, and utterly carried away by my feelings, I suddenly stood up in the carriage and waved to a very beautiful woman who I thought was in America! The King was awfully angry, but I made it much worse by saying I had forgotten all about him! But he added, "Well! find out where she lives and let me know," and he gave her little child a sovereign and asked her to dinner, to my intense joy!'[3]

The most famous and ominous protest was the King's: 'Fisher, you must be mad!' when he had suggested to his King that the time had come to 'Copenhagen' the German Fleet in its bases without warning, as the Japanese had recently done to the Russian Far East Fleet.

These and other examples of a sudden flaring dispute between the two men confirm the unusual intimacy of their relationship. Lord Esher, who knew King and Admiral so well, commented that Edward VII 'thoroughly believed in [Fisher] as a great sailor and loved [him] as a

[1] *Memories*, 239   [2] *British Naval Policy*, 394   [3] *Memories*, 9.

man.'[1] André Maurois rightly claimed that the King 'liked Fisher's wildness of imagination, his respectful familiarity and brutal frankness'[2] The King's biographer, Sir Sidney Lee, has told how 'Fisher's vehemence in talk and his exuberant professions of loyalty to the Crown appealed to [him]'.[3]

Just as the King loved to be amused and stimulated by Fisher, he also relished giving Fisher pleasure and indulging, for example, his passionate love of dancing: when Fisher came to dinner at Windsor, an impromptu dance would take place in the crimson drawing room.

Fisher could never have survived the violent internecine warfare which lasted for the greater part of his time as First Sea Lord without the support and friendship of his monarch. Shortly before he became First Sea Lord Fisher reported the King reassuring him that 'so many people are jealous of me and fear me but HE *must look out for me*!'[4] Edward VII was as good as his word, although at times it seemed to Fisher that the King was the only powerful ally he had. Yet Fisher's enemies were impotent to break the chain forged between these two great men. With characteristic sagacity, Esher both encouraged Fisher's efforts to consolidate his friendship with the King before he became First Sea Lord, and foretold the enduring nature of their relations. Fisher had described to Esher how he had gone out in the Royal Yacht *Britannia* with the King 'and I was more or less alone with him for 5 solid hours! I once or twice got up to go, but he made me stop with him, so I rather hope what I said agreed with him!' Esher replied:

FROM VISCOUNT ESHER

The Roman Camp
Callander, N.B.
August 6th, 1904

My dear Admiral,

. . . What you say about your long talks with the King leaves me full of certainty that you have made lasting and final impressions. H.M. has two receptive plates in his mind. One retains lasting impressions. I have tested this over and over again. The other, only most fleeting ones. On the former are stamped his impression of *people* and their relative value. On the latter, of *things*, and these are apt to fade or be removed by later ones. But, and this is the essential point, if you can stamp your image on number one—which you have long since done—you can rely always on carrying your point, by an

[1] *Esher*, ii, 461.

[2] André Maurois, *Édouard VII et son Temps* (Paris, 1937), 271.

[3] Sir Sidney Lee, *King Edward VII* (London, 1927, 2 vols), ii, 328. (Hereafter cited as *Lee*.)

[4] Kilverstone MSS.

appeal to 'authority'—as the Catholics would say. The King will not go into details, for his life is too full for that, but he will always say to himself, 'Jack Fisher's view is so and so, and he is sure to be right.' I don't think you need trouble about H.M., for he will always back you . . .

Yours ever,
Esher

Although Selborne had sounded a note of caution in his letter inviting Fisher back to the Admiralty as Second Naval Lord and stated that there was no certainty that he would succeed Walter Kerr when the vacancy occurred in 1904, this already appeared inevitable to most knowledgeable people. His close friendship with the King was as well known as was Selborne's high regard for his powers. The post of Second Naval Lord was normally filled by a Rear-Admiral; Fisher was a full Admiral. This alone was significant. Moreover, his massive plans for the reform of all branches of the Navy had been the subject of the many lectures he had delivered to the officers of the Mediterranean Fleet. The sequence of future steps in Fisher's progress was almost predictable in June 1902 when he took up his new duties in Whitehall.

The traditional rôle of the Second Naval Lord was to supervise all matters relating to the Navy's personnel. But the power was not total, and Fisher was determined at once to increase the status of his department by gaining control of the appointment of all officers under the rank of Captain. It is said that he publicized the limitation of the Second Naval Lord's influence by walking the Admiralty corridors with a placard proclaiming 'I have no work' hung around his neck. Whether or not this is apocryphal, Selborne's appeal for discretion was already being disregarded. Nor was he seriously in need of work to occupy his time. He often began his prodigious correspondence soon after 4 a.m. His private secretary, Sir Charles Walker, wrote of this period: 'It was apparent from the first that he expected to be relieved of all routine work . . . He was the most amazing man at getting through work that I ever came across. I have seen him turn over the pages of a long report as fast as he could get hold of the leaves, and immediately write his opinion on the cover.'[1] Even during the second half of 1902, when he was preparing his plans for the complete transformation of the Navy's traditional training, he was keeping up a steady correspondence with Selborne, politicians and journalists, members of the Royal family and of his own family, on subjects ranging from Fleet tactics and the design of future warships, to the activities of his two still unmarried daughters and the Mediterranean political situation. He wrote his own letters at great speed in a large clear hand. He never

[1] 'Some Recollections of Jacky Fisher', by Sir Charles Walker. Kilverstone MSS.

seems to have dictated; the remainder of his correspondence he passed to Walker to answer.

There had been fundamental advances in every branch of the service since Fisher, half a century earlier, had leapt over that chair and drunk his glass of sherry as proof of his eligibility to serve as a cadet. But the education and training of the officers and men had failed to keep pace. This was something Fisher was determined to put right in the short time he had been allotted—if he was to take over supreme command in little more than two years time.

Fisher had abounding faith in the sea as a schoolroom, and in 'starting them young'. He wrote many letters on the subject addressed to Lord Knollys, King Edward's private secretary. These were really intended for the King's eyes, but when he was not actually writing to the King directly, he felt he could thus be more indiscreet and forthright. After his new scheme of entry and training had been introduced, he wrote to Knollys:

'Of all the systems of education ever devised by the wit of man, nothing approaches or can ever approach the education of the sea in giving self-reliance, fertility of resource, fearlessness of responsibility, and the power of initiative. These four great qualities are the habits of mind required for fighting people, for, as has been truly said, they are the four great Nelsonic attributes, and gales of wind, fog, the imminence of great danger, and the uncertainty of life from hour to hour (which uncertainty any night a collision may produce!), all of them conduce unconsciously to train the tender lad to become a brave and resourceful man.' But Fisher also knew that the old system of entry and training of officers and men was as obsolete as the *Victory* herself.

On 10 June 1902 he began work on his vast overhaul, and the devising of the new system which was to become known as the Selborne Scheme. Its very title hinted at its far-reaching nature and the disputes Fisher anticipated. He did not wish his name to be associated with it: he preferred his First Lord to receive the credit as well as the brickbats. There were going to be bigger troubles ahead after he had got through the Selborne Scheme, and he preferred to remain as far from the centre of controversy as possible, begging Arnold White, among other of his public supporters, not 'to mention my name in association with the scheme, as then the enemy would blaspheme at once'.

Fisher worked for the best part of three months on the spade work at the Admiralty. Late in August 1902 he was able to write to Selborne that he was 'getting on splendidly with all the investigations as to what is involved by the alterations in entry and training of officers and men, as set forth in the print, and hope to have every detail cut and dried by the time Parliament meets. Some of the obstacles', he continued, 'seemed gigantic at first, but "the mountains of the future are the molehills of the past!"'

Thus buoyed up by a characteristic aphorism, and driven forward by his love of the Royal Navy, his self-confidence and righteousness of his cause, as well as the certainty of support from the civil head of the Admiralty and the King, Fisher sailed out into the most dangerous waters he had yet encountered.

The reason why this was to be such a difficult passage lay in the deeply class-structured society which both split and held together the nation. Fisher disliked class distinction socially as he deplored it in the Navy because at heart he was a democrat and because it led to inefficiency and waste. His own humble origins and lack of private means, in a service still dominated by the well-born and rich, had brought about a curious ambivalence in Fisher's mind. He dearly loved to mix with the best people at Marienbad or Biarritz, to stay at the great homes, best of all at Balmoral or Windsor. These were the seats of power, and were important for this reason alone. But he was no exception to the prevailing fashion for social improvement. He delighted in the honours that were bestowed upon him. He was naturally pleased when his son later inherited Vavasseur's estate. He could even refer, with pride, to his own wife's rather obscure but ancient Plantagenet ancestry. He was a liberal by instinct, who deplored the vast profits made by the armament barons, yet hobnobbed with the Armstrongs and Nobles and was delighted when Cecil was 'adopted' by one of them, thus ensuring the financial independence of the family for the future. He was strongly opposed to the Boer War, while he was energetically and skilfully commanding Britain's first Fleet against those who might take advantage of it to attack his country. Fisher's determination to bring about a greater equality of opportunity in a service in which inequality was an almost unquestioned tradition was certain to bring wrath upon his head.

The strongest distinction in the Navy was between the engineer and executive officer, between what Michael Lewis in *The Navy of Britain* defines as those who 'make her go' and those who 'fight her'. Those who ran and maintained the first ships' engines were as unwelcome on board as the engines themselves. The year of the first permanent establishment of engineers was 1837. The engines and the 'greasers' were equally crude, dirty and noisy and not for another ten years was the first engineer specialist commissioned. Long after the sail as a useful source of power had been discarded, the distinction between the engineer and executive classes remained, and engineer officers were disparagingly referred to as 'engine drivers' and ate in their own mess, reputedly with their fingers. Matters improved in the last quarter of the century as the refinement of the engineers ran parallel with their engines, but not fast enough to satisfy the engineer officers, or the new and important engineering societies which supported their claims.

Fisher loved to recount the story of a chief engineer called Brown. 'Brown worried the First Lieutenant of a ship . . . to exasperation by telling him that he ranked before him when on shore or when going in to dinner. "Look here, Brown," said the First Lieutenant, "it don't matter what rank the Admiralty like to give you, and I don't care a damn whether you walk in to dinner before me or after me; but all I know, Brown, is that my Ma will never ask your Ma to tea!"'[1] While Fisher could laugh at this kind of story, he loathed the underlying implications. In a characteristic letter to Arnold White, defining freely the essence of his reform, he referred to an earlier schism which split the Navy:

'The old navigating class in the Navy, it was splendid, but dissatisfied, and unrecognized. They were extracted from a different social stratum and couldn't mix any more than oil and vinegar, and were kept in separate bottles all their time in the Service. But a magician arose and said, "Let's have no class distinctions! Enter them all as midshipmen, and those who show an aptitude for navigating they will take it up"; and the result has been splendid; and it's a matter of fact that fewer ships have been lost or grounded since this scheme came into maturity than ever known before in the history of the Navy. *So let it be with the Engineers.* Enter them as midshipmen in the Naval College at Dartmouth, put 'em all into the same bottle! And at a suitable time select those for engineering duties, give high special pay, higher than we now give to the Gunnery, or the Torpedo, or the Navigating Lieutenants, and you will then have no lack of Engineer officers of a higher calibre perhaps than at present.'[2]

Three years after it had been inaugurated, Fisher wrote of his common entry scheme:

'On the 25th of December, 1902, the new system of entry and training of officers for the Navy was inaugurated.

'The fundamental principles of this great reform are:—

(a) The common entry and training of officers of the three principal branches of the Service, viz., Combatant or Executive, Engineer, and Marine.

[1] *Bacon*, i, 186.   [2] *ibid.*, i, 187–8.

(*b*) The practical amalgamation of these three branches of officers.

(*c*) The recognition of the fact that the existence of the Navy depends on machinery, and that, therefore, all combatant officers must be Engineers.

(*d*) The adoption of the principle that the general education and training of all these officers must be completed before they go to sea, instead of, as heretofore, dragging on in a perfunctory manner during their service as midshipmen, to be finally completed by a short "cram" at Greenwich and Portsmouth.'[1]

Fisher was frequently accused by his enemies of a preoccupation with the *matériel* of the Navy, as well as of being impetuous, and as despising intellectual consideration in his reforms. This brief summary of his thoughts on naval education and training utterly refutes this suggestion:

'The rôle that a naval officer has to fulfil is a varied one; professional acquirements are of great importance, but many other qualities are essential. In distant parts of the globe he has to represent his nation; and is often called on to exhibit considerable diplomatic and social qualities. Essentially, therefore, his training should be broad and liberal; and everything with a narrowing tendency should be avoided. His hands require training as much as his brain; and constant and early contact with men is essential to encourage self-reliance and command. His training should be a practical one. Judgment, perception, and initiative should be fostered, and care taken to avoid such studies as tend to constrict or fetter these qualities.

'The general effect of education on character is not perhaps much studied; since success in specialities of learning carries with it qualities of character suitable to the prosecuting of those special duties. A profound study of mathematics or science carries with it habits of accuracy that are apt to stifle rapid judgment; and so it is with all educational subjects: some broaden; others, if too closely adhered to, tend to narrow it; but all have a direct influence on character.

'In the Navy the first object in view is to give an officer a good general education, so as to enable him to fill his station in life; next to supply him with knowledge of the theory and use of the ship on which he lives, and of the whole of its equipment; and, during the acquisition of this learning, to develop his aptness to command, and his initiative to its full extent, always taking care that theory is kept complementary to practice. Evidently the present-day and future naval officer must be a practical marine engineer; he lives in one vast machine; every day he

---

[1] *Records,* 156.

handles machinery; he must be fed on mechanism and learn its details. But, on the other hand, he is not required to be an engine designer. Normally he has to work and repair engines, not design them. At the same time he must be, above all things, a seaman, and possess that peculiar knowledge which only wind and sea, dark nights and mists, can give—that peculiar appreciation of sea conditions which is the overwhelming difference between the sea-going and shore-going sailor.'[1]

For the past thirty-five years officer cadets had received their first two years' training on board one of two old wooden hulks, the *Britannia* and *Hindustan*, where they learnt simple mathematics and French, navigation and practical seamanship. These old 'wooden walls' were never very satisfactory. They were damp, smelly and over-crowded. The boys' parents often complained. Under the Selborne Scheme all cadets went through the same training for two years at a new college Fisher planned to build at Osborne in the Isle of Wight. Edward VII hated his mother's house there and he was glad to present the stable block, which formed a part of the new buildings, and the adjoining land. This was followed by a further two years at another imposing new college being built high above the river at Dartmouth in Devonshire. The cadets entered at twelve-and-a-half to thirteen years instead of fourteen, after passing an interview and taking an examination. The young men's common training continued after passing out of Dartmouth, through the ranks of Midshipman and Sub-Lieutenant, in a training cruiser with the fleet. Only at about twenty-two years, as young Lieutenants, would a specialist element enter their training, and, according to individual choice, it would be completed in the engineering or marine branches, or gunnery, torpedo or navigation in the executive branch.

The preparation of the scheme in detail was an enormous undertaking. Fisher supervised it at all stages while continuing his regular duties as Second Naval Lord. It was a busy summer and autumn, and the work included a lot of controversy. At every meeting of the Board of Admiralty at which it was discussed, there was heated discussion. Relations with Walter Kerr became especially strained. 'I never knew that Admirals could be so rude to one another,'[2] Fisher exclaimed to his secretary after one particularly stormy meeting; to Cecil he wrote: 'I think the rest of my colleagues look on me as a sort of combined Robespierre and Gambetta.' As the time approached for the official announcement of its terms, Fisher made every effort to get the most

---

[1] *Bacon*, i, 188–9.   [2] *ibid.*, i, 179–80.

influential people on his side—press, politicians and royalty. The Prince of Wales, in a letter of warm praise, wrote, 'I call it a grand scheme and wish it every success.'

And later, when there were hints that one of the most important foundations of the scheme was going to be undermined, he supported Fisher.

FROM THE PRINCE OF WALES[1]

> *Frogmore House*
> *Windsor*
> *April 8th, 1904*

My dear Sir John,

I have just heard from a side wind that there is a proposal at the Admiralty (emanating no doubt from Professor Ewing) that the cadets should be given an *extra term* in the '*Britannia*'. This means six months added to the four years which according to the present scheme they are to spend at the two Colleges, Osborne and Dartmouth.

. . . an extra six months would be disastrous to the boys who would then be 16 to 17 years of age—high time in fact for them to be at sea getting in touch with the Service, taking command of men, learning responsibility and the hundred and one *practical* things which are so essential to the making of a good Naval officer . . .

> Believe me always most sincerely yours,
> *George*

Fisher's press supporters did stalwart work, too, that summer and autumn in preparing their readers for what was to come by conditioning their minds in advance to some of the more radical measures. So deeply had he inhaled Fisher's teaching and beliefs that Thursfield of *The Times* hardly had to be briefed. As early as 19 July 1902 he wrote a notable leading article for *The Times* calling for a reappraisal of the Navy's entry and training. 'Now the sea service,' he wrote, 'is from its very nature an almost incomparable school for the formation of character. It takes boys young, it subjects them from the very outset to the difficulties, dangers, and responsibilities of an arduous and exacting profession, it endows them with an experience, large for their years, of men, manners and circumstances, it enures them to habits of strict discipline, and it sobers them with early responsibilities of command . . . We may fairly express and hope that before further changes are initiated the problem will be boldly faced and considered as a whole. It will not be solved by piecemeal changes in the curriculum of *Britannia* . . .'

---

[1] Lennoxlove MSS.

The details of the Selborne Scheme were made known on Christmas Day 1902, and in spite of their warm commendation by such influential journalists as Thursfield and Arnold White, it was received with howls of dismay by 'the mandarins' and 'The Naval Rip Van Winkles' as Fisher dubbed them. The following day, Fisher wrote:

TO JAMES R. THURSFIELD

Admiralty, Whitehall
December 26th, 1902

Dear Thursfield,
. . . *Rest assured there will be no faltering at the Admiralty!* I wrote in chalk on one of my colleague's doors, '*Remember Lot's wife!*' No looking back now! and he has taken the hint! *They all know I should walk straight out of the Admiralty the moment we vacillate!* I need hardly say this is *entre nous.*

In haste ever yours,
J. A. Fisher

Your reasoning as to the course *The Times* should pursue is as excellent as your article on Xmas Day.

Yesterday Lord Spencer waited to see me to say it's the best and finest thing ever done by a Board of Admiralty, and he has written to Lord Selborne accordingly. He says a distinguished personage asked him to lead an attack on the scheme. He replied he would defend it with all his utmost strength! 'What!' said the great man, '*Are you going to defend our officers going down in the coal hole?*'

A few days later, Fisher told Thursfield of the twenty-four letters he had received from Captains and Commanders, 'THE VERY PICK OF THE SERVICE, in favour of the scheme'. He added, 'I prefer these twenty-four opinions of the coming Admirals, who are going to command our Fleets and administer the Admiralty, to any twenty-four Admirals now existing but who are passing away.'

The passion behind the attacks on the scheme today appears quite astonishing. But Fisher was cutting deep into the flesh of the country's social system. What he regarded as a necessary blood-letting, his opponents saw as a deep wound threatening the heart itself. No one in society, it was feared, would now permit their sons to enter the Navy when they would be obliged not only to study the infra dig subject of engineering, but to cover himself in grease and coal dust. Worst of all, he would be regarded as on an equal footing with the class from which the engineering officers had previously been drawn. There was a lot of talk about the Navy's going to pot, about its being a service of 'plumbers' and 'greasers'. Old vegetating Admirals painfully reached for their pens and wrote letters of protest to the Admiralty, the newspapers, and their influential friends in Whitehall.

Fisher did not believe that these attacks by 'the old fossils' needed to be taken very seriously. But younger serving officers publicly criticised the scheme, less on the social than on the practical level. Captains Berkeley Milne and Hedworth Lambton were among those who made thoughtful and reasoned criticisms. Even his old friend, Rear-Admiral Arthur Wilson, who now commanded the Channel Fleet, came out strongly against some of the proposals. From his Flagship he wrote to Rear-Admiral John Durnford, the Fourth Naval Lord, on the subject of the course for torpedo and gunnery Lieutenants: 'I cannot conceive how Fisher can advocate such a change. He must remember the conditions when he and I passed for Gunnery Lieutenants, when the mathematical course, such as it was, did come after the practical course, and everybody felt that it was entirely out of place . . . I sincerely hope the proposed change will not be made.'[1] In Durnford he had a sympathetic ear. The Fourth Naval Lord had been one of Fisher's strongest opponents throughout the preparation period of the Selborne Scheme.

Although Fisher had been influenced in his decision to introduce in the entry and training of officers what he described as the *Tria juncta in uno,* or 'the coalescing of all three branches', because of its success in the American Navy, it was not so easy to refute the charge that final proficiency in one of the three branches demanded the greater part of the young officer's attention from the time of his entry as a cadet. Not only was technology becoming increasingly complex; navigation and seamanship, too, were growing more elaborate with the introduction, for example, of wireless telegraphy and submarines. Surely, it could be reasonably argued, the era of the specialist had arrived with the new century and would grow with it. There was also the danger that the fighting capacity of the Fleet, the whole *raison d'être* of the service, might lose some of its priority with the new emphasis on engines and engineering.

In the light of what had gone before between them, and the bitterness of their later combats, it is surprising to find Beresford an enthusiastic supporter. 'The strongest opponents of the scheme will acknowledge that it is a brilliant and statesmanlike effort to grapple with a problem *upon the sound settlement of which the future efficiency of the British Navy depends* . . . I am of the opinion that the plan is one that has been thoroughly matured and well thought out, and I believe that when its details have been definitely settled it will make more complete the well-being,

[1] *Wilson,* 184.

contentment and efficiency of that Service on which the safety of the Empire absolutely depends.'[1]

Fisher was delighted with Beresford's long and favourable memorandum and liked to quote it in later years as proof of the friendship which still existed between them at this time.

The famous 'Fishpond' era, from which Beresford was to be the most notable absentee, really began with the publication of the Selborne Scheme. From the winter of 1902–3, in the Navy you were either in or out of the Fishpond. Those who were in, swam in a shoal behind the pilot Fisher, and basked in the warm glow of official approval. But woe betide those who did not conform! They found themselves threshing helplessly on the bank, from which they could never struggle back into the life-giving water. Captains Hedworth Lambton, Berkeley Milne, Reginald Custance and many more were never forgiven for their opposition to the scheme. Admiral George King-Hall later told how Captain George Egerton, a torpedo specialist, was summarily dealt with after a meeting at the Admiralty during the preparation of the scheme. 'Fisher beckoned him out of the Council Chamber and led him into his room, then shook his fist at him, and almost spat at him, saying:— "If you oppose my Education scheme I will crush you." Fisher was beside himself with rage—Egerton kept cool, and refused to be bullied into agreeing with Fisher, that Torpedo Lieutenants could be made in three months.'[2] Nor, according to Egerton, did Fisher forget this occasion after he became Commander-in-Chief, Portsmouth, when Egerton's life was made miserable as Captain of the torpedo training school, *Vernon*.

It is still not easy to give a just evaluation of the Selborne Scheme in the context of 1903. Like so many of Fisher's reforms, the manner and style in which it was introduced attracted many critics who might otherwise have been acquiescent. It can, on the one hand, be argued that a less precipitate introduction would have reduced the dissension among the members of the Board during its preparation and the antagonism in the service afterwards. On the other hand, the need for a complete reappraisal of entry and education was urgently needed, and as Fisher enjoyed reiterating on almost any occasion, 'Procrastination is the thief of time'. The implacable forcefulness with which he imposed his will on the Board not only caused bad feeling, it may even have induced obstinate resentment. After the Christmas announcement, the practice of his '3 Requisites for Success—Ruthless, Relentless, Remorseless (The 3 Rs)' may have actually weakened his case and made him more

---

[1] *Bacon*, i, 221–2.
[2] L. King-Hall, *Sea Saga* (London, 1935), 327. (Hereafter cited as *Sea Saga*.)

enemies than a conciliatory attitude would have created. But of course only his uncompromising nature and burning zeal and energy could have conceived and put into effect so rapidly one of the most important and urgently needed administrative advances the Royal Navy had ever undergone.[1]

The controversy did not die with the introduction of the scheme in September 1903. Both prejudice and reason nibbled away at its provisions over the years. The biggest amendment was the omission altogether of any reference to the Marine Branch, following a stout and prolonged counter-attack by the Royal Marines. As the years passed, fewer and fewer officers selected the engineering branch when the choice had to be made. As this developed with the increasing size of the Fleet, the scheme was threatened with breakdown. After only two years of operation, the Captain of the new college at Osborne, Rosslyn Wemyss, was reporting 'a tendency on the part of the parents of some of the cadets . . . to hope at least that their sons might never become Lieutenant (E), with no chance of commanding ships or fleets, and I have a suspicion that, for this reason, they have in some cases even discouraged their sons in their engineering studies'.[2] The result was that a form of 'conscription' for the engineering branch had to be introduced. In spite of this measure, and other 'watering down' processes, thoughtful opinion throughout the Navy judged the scheme a success over the following crucial ten years leading to the outbreak of war. Its two undeniable merits were that it produced a better and more fully educated naval officer, and a diminution of class prejudice in the service. Both led to greater efficiency, and this, as in all Fisher's reforms, had been his first aim.

More than a month before the announcement of the Selborne Scheme, the future events in his career had been settled in Fisher's mind, and moreover had been, as far as possible, officially blessed. In November 1902 there was still little likelihood that Lord Walter Kerr would resign before his time as First Naval Lord was up. Fisher's relations with the Board varied from cool to very poor. It seemed to him that it would be undesirable to continue to serve in Whitehall. As he wrote to his son, '[Selborne] admits that he can't expect me to play second fiddle here for 2 years after having played the first fiddle for so long.' Moreover,

[1] 'I first arrived at the Admiralty on June 10th last year, when at 10 minutes to 12 I said "How d'ye do" to Lord Selborne. At 5 minutes to 12 he gave me practically *carte blanche*, and at 12 I was read in at the Board, and five minutes after, I commenced operations in my room at the Admiralty in sending the first pages to the printer of the preamble of the new schemes of training, entry, etc. . . .' Fisher to Cecil Fisher, 10 April 1903.

[2] Wemyss to Fisher. Lennoxlove MSS.

he wanted to be close to the centre of operation of his new scheme when it began. From Portsmouth, he could supervise every stage of the construction and running of Osborne, still remain in touch with Whitehall and Westminster, and yet have time to formulate his great plans when he reached the position of supreme power. Moreover, he could ensure that his scheme would not be interfered with or diluted by another C.-in-C. who might be unsympathetic to it.

Fisher was now such a dominant figure in the service, that he could well afford to accept the apparent demotion the command of Portsmouth indicated.

TO CECIL FISHER

Admiralty, Whitehall
November 14th, 1902

Dearest Cis,

I've got through the biggest part of the big scheme I have been working on since June 10th last, and Lord Selborne seems very pleased; but I think the rest of my colleagues look on me as a sort of combined Robespierre and Gambetta!

VERY PRIVATE. I think it is quite decided that I go as Commander-in-Chief at Portsmouth . . .

Ever your loving father,
J. A. Fisher

Another three and a half months passed, during which the Selborne Scheme was hotly and publicly debated, before he knew for certain that Selborne's demands to the government had prevailed, and he would almost certainly succeed Walter Kerr in 1904.

TO THE EARL OF SELBORNE

Admiralty, Whitehall
March 5th, 1903

Private
Dear Lord Selborne,

I am greatly obliged by your kindness in letting me go to Portsmouth and shall, of course, keep strict silence, but I fear from time to time we shall see it so stated in the newspapers, as it is such a likely event to happen from my being next on the list. I feel very sorry not to take all the 'personnel' in hand before I go, simply because I think I could have made things much easier for my successor, and I should have left it with him in a more or less automatic condition. *Of course, I am very sorry to leave you,* but I honestly believe I can be of more service at Portsmouth as Commander-in-Chief than as Second Sea Lord, especially in view of inaugurating Osborne, new boys' and men's training, organization of barracks, and, above all, 'nucleus crews'. At all events, if all these things are not a success, I will do my best to make them miserable who prevent it! What makes me happy is that your motto will be *Vestigia nulla retrorsum*!

Yours very truly,
J. A. Fisher

I know you will believe how greatly I appreciate all your kindness to me.

During his last months at the Admiralty, while he continued to fight off the critics of the Selborne Scheme and at the same time ensure that Osborne would be completed in time for the first intake of cadets in the autumn, there were social and public events to be attended, all of which were important for keeping him in touch with the rich and the powerful.

Late in January 1903 he received one of his frequent invitations to stay at Windsor, and reported to Beatrix: 'I've had a splendid time here! I had over an hour's interview with the King before dinner who is most cordial then an hour with the Prince of Wales, equally friendly, and then half an hour with Lord Knollys who as we couldn't finish our conversation has asked me to dinner next week at the Cafe Royal to finish it up! After dinner the Queen talked to me for a long time and then for the rest of the evening I sat with the Princess of Wales and finished up again with the King and Prince of Wales and to bed at 1.30 A.M. and having been up at 4 A.M. I was pretty well done up! . . . Lady Eva Dugdale [Lady of the Bedchamber in the household of the Princess of Wales] came up to me to say good night and said: "No chance with you to-night, nothing but Kings and Queens for you!" '[1]

In July Fisher was at Marienbad, 'having a most splendid time', as he wrote to Beatrix, meeting inevitably a 'fabulously rich!' couple, a 'gold mine millionaire' and others in the oil business, one of whom offered him a post in Persia which would probably have paid him more in a year than he could have earned in a decade as a full Admiral. The next month he was up in Northumberland staying at the castle of Sir Andrew Noble, chairman of Armstrongs, who had recently offered him £10,000 a year to come and work for him.

At the Royal Academy dinner that year Fisher agreed to make one of his rare public speeches. The guests were formidable, the occasion splendid, and the speech a memorable success. The great were from all walks of life, from the Archbishop of Canterbury to the Lord Chancellor and Lord Chief Justice, to John Morley, Sir Ernest Cassel and the Prince of Wales. Fisher spoke without a note, and with what he called his 'exuberant verbosity'. After the formal opening, he said, 'Personally

[1] Kilverstone MSS

I have not the same pleasurable feelings on this occasion as I enjoyed last year when I had no speech to make. I remember quite well remarking to my neighbour, "How good the whitebait is, how excellent the champagne, and how jolly not to have to make a speech!" He glared at me and said, "I have got to make a speech, and the whitebait to me is *bête noire*, and the champagne is real pain." (Laughter.) He was so ready with this answer that I thought to myself, "You'll get through it all right," and, sure enough, he did, for he spoke thirty minutes by the clock without a check. (Laughter.) I'm going to give you three minutes. (Cries of "No.") Yes.'

Fisher gave them more than three minutes. There were some reminiscences of his early days at sea, followed by a brief and pungent summary of the changing face of warfare at sea. 'Look at the submarine boat and wireless telegraphy. When they are perfected, we do not know what a revolution will come about. In their inception they were the weapons of the weak. Now they loom large as the weapons of the strong. Will any Fleet be able to live in narrow waters? Is there the the slightest fear of invasion with them even for the most extreme pessimist? I might mention other subjects, but the great fact which I come to is that we are realizing, the Navy and the Admiralty are realizing, that on the British Navy rests the British Empire . . . I assure you that the Navy and the Admiralty recognize their responsibility. I think I may say that we now have a Board of Admiralty that is united, progressive, and determined—' and he continued amid cheers with a phrase both his enemies and friends were to quote again and again in the years ahead— 'and you may sleep quietly in your beds.'

Writing to Cecil the next day, Fisher told how 'shoals of them' came up to congratulate him afterwards. 'The Prince of Wales was very delighted and cheered me like anything,' Fisher reported, 'but I think he's rather partial to me.'[1]

[1] *ibid.*

Chapter 9

PRELUDE AT PORTSMOUTH

In the late summer of 1903, Fisher expected with confidence that he would be the Senior Naval Lord in little more than a year. As Second Naval Lord, he had launched the Osborne Scheme, sailed it into battle and warded off all boarders. It had been a twelve months period of vast accomplishment. Now the appointment as Port Admiral at Portsmouth offered a time for recovery and recuperation, perhaps even of contemplation, before taking up the burden of office and effecting the multitudinous reforms which he had planned for so long. But Fisher did not understand how to decelerate his activities. He was incapable of satisfying his appetite for work, which poured in on him in a giant tidal flow as if he were a bottomless reservoir.

The supervision of the construction of Osborne and the interviewing of the first candidates and the start of the new training would have filled the working hours of most officers. Fisher regarded this work as supremely important, but it did not interfere with a dozen other simultaneous tasks. In January 1903 he decreed that Osborne College must be designed and built in time for King Edward to open it on 4 August. The Admiralty contractor said it would take three years. Fisher had no patience for this sort of talk. An American building contractor, who had met and had been deeply impressed by Fisher years before when he was commanding the North American Squadron, was in England at the time. This American happened to call on Fisher who told him of his difficulties, and the contractor agreed to build the college by August. He succeeded, with a few days to spare. Fisher charmed and cajoled the brilliant Alfred Ewing into leaving his well-paid post at Cambridge and accept the new appointment as Director of Naval Education.

Many of Fisher's activities while Port Admiral took him away from Admiralty House, Portsmouth, on visits to Whitehall and to meetings with important and influential people. Less than a month after his term of appointment began on 31 August 1903, he was summoned to Balmoral to stay with the King and Queen as one of a party of distinguished guests, which included the King and Queen of Italy. Fisher derived much pleasure from these visits to Balmoral and they were of inestimable benefit to him. The importance which he attached to them is indicated by the letters he wrote to his family from the castle on this occasion.

He travelled up on the night train from King's Cross on 28 September, and drove the last eight-and-a-half miles along the River Dee behind 'two very fine horses which would suit us very well!' he told Lady Fisher. The King was out driving in his motor, and Fisher was shown to 'a lovely room with a bathroom and etcs. My servant tells me it's the best in the Castle and was specially ordered for me so I am being highly honoured . . .'[1] That night he sat next to the King at dinner 'and he talked to me the whole time and was so very cordial'.

On the following days there were deer drives, visits to local beauty spots, a lunch with the Princess of Wales at nearby Abergeldie Castle, and 'a Ball here which the King declares is on purpose for me', as he proudly wrote to Beatrix. The piper played opposite his bedroom window, which was next to the King's, at eight o'clock every morning, and there was a great deal of frivolous but witty chatter to fill the long hours between the great meals before he was allowed to retire to bed again in the early hours.

Fisher had not been invited to Balmoral for a week's heady entertainment. Edward VII was a much too wise, business-like and practical monarch to waste a week's work of his country's most industrious and valuable Admiral. The throne's influence on events was still very powerful in 1903. Fisher was well aware of this, and amid the elaborate rituals, events took place that underlined again the great wisdom of the Sovereign and his capacity for forwarding the claims to power of anyone in the field of defence he considered deserved it. The King was evidently determined that Fisher should succeed Walter Kerr as First Naval Lord. Fisher was certain of this after his first evening, when, as he wrote to Beatrix, 'he asked me with a merry twinkle in his eye how long I intended to stop at Portsmouth! I told him that, subject to the King's pleasure, I understood it was a three years' appointment!'[2]

Intense discussions on all matters of defence often followed dinner. The King 'has kept me pretty busy writing out various memoranda, which I hope won't get me into hot water later on,' Fisher wrote to his wife on 5 October, 'but His Majesty promises that no other eyes than

[1] Kilverstone MSS.   [2] *ibid.*

his own, the Prince of Wales, and Lord Knollys shall see them. He made a note on the last one yesterday in his blue pencil: *"These valuable papers are to be very carefully kept for future guidance. What a clear hand the Admiral does write"* . . .'

But the most important reason for the King's invitation was made clear on that first evening. The implications and the consequences were profound, for the nation's defence structure, and for Fisher himself.

As long before as 28 March 1903, at a dinner party at Buckingham Palace, Fisher had been approached informally by the King with an invitation to join a committee to reform the War Office. The idea had come as a complete surprise. 'I am not sure,' Fisher wrote the following day, 'whether it's wise to put my head in the Lion's Mouth! As probably they will murder me at the War Office like some of the Admirals would like to do now.'[1]

There is no evidence that the matter was discussed further until the visit to Balmoral. On this evening, six months later, the King put forward the proposition again, and on the following day, Fisher wrote to his wife, 'The King says he wants to put me on a Committee to put the War Office right. *Of course* this is *very secret*, so be careful to say nothing.'

A sailor—and as forthright, controversial and anti-Army sailor as Fisher—'to put the War Office right'! To some people it appeared as a lunatic idea, even if the Admiral was to be only one of a committee of three. For a different reason, some of his service friends believed it was an unwise step. One of his supporters wrote 'entreating me not to serve on proposed Committee, as he says it will cause endless ill-feeling and bitterness among the soldiers!'

The selection of Fisher by the King when he was at the height of his powers and on the brink of his greatest command was based on sound reasoning. The King shared with Esher, his most intimate adviser on defence matters, a very low regard both for the organization of the War Office and the administrative abilities of the senior officers, and a very high regard for Fisher's organizing and reforming powers.

As a result of the abysmal performance of the Army in the Boer War, a commission to enquire into its conduct had been set up. The majority report was suitably favourable; the minority report, for which Esher had been chiefly responsible, was critical, and after its publication Esher recommended to the King that he should head a committee of three to look deeper into the constitution and organization of the War Office. As the King and Esher were searching for a critically appraising eye, the choice was an eminently sensible one. Fisher regarded the Navy

[1] To Mrs Reginald Neeld, Kilverstone MSS.

as the 'First, second, third, fourth and fifth line of the nation's defence', and the home Army only 'as a projectile to be fired by the Navy!'

In Fisher's eyes the Army had blundered in the Crimea when he was still a boy, and blundered again a half century later. In between there had been little else but blunder. The Army was always struggling for greater funds, and every penny they got for their estimates was at the expense of the Navy. On 8 August 1902, Fisher had written to Arnold White on the subject of Army extravagance, 'When will the British public wake up? You would have thought the Boer War would have done it with its almost inconceivable military blunders, when our "Army of Lions led by Asses" were so needlessly slaughtered!' And shortly after his appointment to the committee, he wrote to Esher from Portsmouth, 'The military system is rotten to the very core! You want to begin *ab ovo*! The best of the Generals are even worse than the subalterns, because they are more hardened sinners!' The committee's findings promised to be stimulating!

The third member of the Committee was Colonel Sir George Clarke, Governor of Victoria, Australia, later secretary of the Committee of Imperial Defence, and already a critic of the Selborne Scheme, but rather surprisingly forgiven by Fisher for this sin. These three men, with a young and very able soldier, Lieutenant-Colonel Gerald Ellison, as secretary, made a formidable trio, and became known with mixed respect and fear as 'the dauntless three', and by Campbell-Bannerman as 'Damnable, Domineering and Dictatorial'; more formally as 'The Esher Committee'. Starting off in typical optimistic and ebullient mood and, quoting Kruger, Fisher claimed, 'We'll stagger humanity'. This was scarcely the case; but the results of the work of the committee were profound at the time and are to be seen in the defence structure of the country some seventy years later.

A lot of the spade work was accomplished by correspondence between Fisher at Portsmouth and Esher in London while Clarke was sailing back from Melbourne. Fisher's views of what the British home Army ought to be soon became clear in his letters to Esher at this time. He wanted a highly mobile, small striking force as an extension to the functions of the Navy. He wanted a force which could be landed rapidly and secretly by the Navy to create chaos behind the enemy lines.

In a light-hearted vein, but meaning every word of it, Fisher had referred briefly to his views on the Army in his Royal Academy speech six months earlier. 'We are different from continental nations,' he said, 'for no soldier of ours can go anywhere unless a sailor carries him on his back. I am not disparaging the Army! I am looking forward to them coming to sea with us again as they did in the old days. Why,

Nelson had three regiments of infantry with him at the battle of Cape St Vincent . . .'

As the committee began its work Fisher wrote:

TO VISCOUNT ESHER

Admiralty, Whitehall
November, 19th, 1903

Private
Dear Lord Esher,

. . . The Navy embarks it [the Army] and lands it where it can do most mischief! Thus, the Germans are ready to land a large military force on the Cotentin Peninsula in case of war with France, and my German military colleagues at The Hague Conference told me this comparatively small military force would have the effect of demobilizing half a million men, who would thus be taken away from the German frontier. They never know where the devil the brutes are going to land! Consequently, instead of our military manoeuvres being on Salisbury Plain and its vicinity (ineffectually apeing the vast Continental Armies!), we should be employing ourselves in joint naval and military manoeuvres, embarking 50,000 men at Portsmouth and landing them at Milford Haven or Bantry Bay! This would make the foreigners sit up! Fancy, in the Mediterranean Fleet we disembarked 12,000 men with guns in *19 minutes!* What do you think of that! and we should hurry up the soldiers! No doubt there will be good-natured chaff! Once we embarked 7,000 soldiers at Malta and took them round and landed them elsewhere for practice, and I remember having a complaint that the bluejackets said, 'Come on, you bloody lobsters! Wake up!' However, all the above *en passant* . . .

Yours truly,
J. A. Fisher

Because of his duties at Portsmouth, many of the Generals giving evidence to the committee travelled down there to see Fisher. They stayed at Admiralty House where they were properly entertained by Sir John and Lady Fisher, and this gave him the opportunity to show them and tell them what he was doing, and discuss his future plans. They were a trapped audience. It was impossible to resist the Admiral's boyish enthusiasm and charm, and Fisher certainly created many converts and supporters among the visiting military. At the same time, he recognized the vulnerability of his own position as a sailor putting the soldiers' house in order. 'I always explained to them,' Fisher wrote later, 'I was Lord Esher's facile dupe and Sir George Clarke's servile copyist, and thereby avoided odium personally.'[1]

On 17 December 1903 he wrote to Esher from Portsmouth: 'Another

---

[1] *Memories,* 165.

Military Nicodemus came to see me yesterday. I had never met him before! He occupies a high official position. He highly approved of you and me, "but he had never heard of the third member of the committee!" (How these Christians hate one another!) But the point of his remarks was the present system of Army Promotions, which he said was as iniquitous and baleful in its influence as could be possibly conceived . . .'

Fisher's close contact with the Army over the course of some three months confirmed his low opinion of the service as a whole, and most of those of senior rank who served in it. He found the amount of dry rot in the hierarchy appalling, and it was no wonder that they had nearly lost South Africa to a handful of Boer guerillas! The cult of the amateur flourished as fruitfully as ever. To the average officer it was a subsidiary occupation for gentlemen. The most insulting term you could use against a fellow officer was 'professional'. As Fisher wrote to Esher, 'They call Clarke "one of those d——d professional soldiers!" '

By January 1904 the main outline of the committee's proposals had been agreed between the three members, and Fisher and Esher were in correspondence about the selection of members of the proposed new Army Council.

The findings of the Esher Committee came in two related reports, which were sent to the Conservative Prime Minister, Arthur J. Balfour, on 11 January 1904. The first dealt with the recently formed Committee of Imperial Defence, which it was recommended should be enlarged to 'deal with the complex problems of Imperial defence' by the inclusion of permanent naval and military officers 'to obtain and collate information from the Admiralty, War Office, India Office, Colonial Office, and other Departments of State'. This important recommendation, which was accepted, represented an important step towards co-ordinating the nation's defences, which had previously worked almost entirely independently.

The second report dealt with the reorganization of the War Office, including the establishment of an Army Council based on Admiralty practice, the Chairman to be the Secretary of State for War, whose status in future would be similar to that of the First Lord of the Admiralty. It was an immensely complex report which affected almost every aspect of Army administration, and with the justification resting on new measures demanding new men. As Fisher wrote to Esher, 'We don't want dull dogs for this new scheme, we MUST have YOUTH and ENTHUSIASM, because, as you and Clarke know far better than I do, the whole military system is rotten from top to bottom (*more rotten at the top than the bottom*). And it is only by the agency of young and enthusiastic believers in the immense revolutions that must be carried out that our scheme can bear fruit.'[1]

The King and Balfour accepted the preliminary reports at once. But there were several aspects of the second full report with which the Prime Minister disagreed, and it looked for a time as if Fisher was not after all going to get his *totus porcus*, on which he had insisted from the beginning. Esher and Clarke showed signs of weakening; Fisher was determined to hold out for the whole reports or no reports.

TO CECIL FISHER

> *Travellers' Club*
> *Pall Mall, S.W.*
> *January 28th, 1904*

Dearest Cis,

Here I am 'tied by the leg' by the War Office Committee! I was to have gone back to Portsmouth to-day, but we have got a crisis on, having resigned unless our Report is swallowed whole! Of course, this is very private and you must never mention it, as it's rather a strong order to threaten the Cabinet as we have done. We sat yesterday for a long time with the Prime Minister and a special committee of the Cabinet who had been deputed to interview us, but we hung on like grim death to our own proposals, and I think we shall have our way. It's a great tax on one's time, but it's a very big business, so I don't regret it . . .

> Your loving father,
> *J. A. Fisher*

In the end Esher and Clarke held firm alongside Fisher, justifying their 'dauntless' reputation, and all but some very small and unimportant recommendations were accepted; and as a condition of Esher's acceptance of the presidency of the committee had been that everything recommended and agreed would be acted on at once, the Army's administrative structure was radically rebuilt over the next months.

Fisher did not allow matters to rest here. His direct contact with many Army officers had convinced him that the present system of military training was overdue for reconsideration on 'Osborne' lines. In a confidential letter to Lord Knollys (but of course intended for the King's eyes) in February 1904, he stated that it was his 'unalterable conviction that the real secret of military efficiency rests absolutely, wholly, and solely on the age of entry and system of training of the Officers of the Army, and on nothing else!' Referring to the Esher Committee findings, he added, 'We have evolved a most logical and lucid system for administering the Army, but Arnold-Forster [now Secretary of State for

---

[1] *Bacon*, i, 213.

War] will tell you we are actually at our wits' end to find in the whole of the British Army suitable officers to fill not only the few administrative posts in the new scheme but to the Military Commands . . . In the analogous case in the Navy there would be literally *hundreds* of suitable officers to select from!'

In the first years of the century, Fisher's earlier enthusiastic promotion of the torpedo as the naval weapon of the future derived further stimulus from its success at the outset of the Russo-Japanese war, when Japanese torpedo boats had crippled the Russian Fleet at anchor in Port Arthur in a surprise attack similar to the air assault on Pearl Harbour thirty-seven years later. The increasing reliability and destructive power of the torpedo had been matched by the speed and range of its carrier. In the late 1890s a new and more sinister torpedo carrier than the torpedo boat and destroyer had been effectively developed in the United States, and had already aroused enough anxiety for its inclusion on the agenda at The Hague Conference.

Experiments with submersible warships had been carried out from time to time since the days of Roman sea power, and the idea of attacking enemy vessels below the waterline was almost as old as naval warfare. The invention of a practical torpedo further stimulated inventive minds; an unseen submersible boat could extend the range of the torpedo to a theoretically unlimited extent. The most successful engineer working in this field was John P. Holland who produced in 1898 a submarine that was efficient and promising enough for the United States government to buy it for the Navy Department. It was a cigar-shaped vessel of 70 tons and could travel underwater at a speed of five knots. This 'Baby Holland' was followed by a much larger vessel with a range of several hundred miles, and carrying two torpedoes, which could be launched from beneath the water through a tube. The United States Navy ordered seven of these improved Hollands, and development in America went ahead at a great pace.

The British Navy could not afford to stand aside from this fearful new torpedo carrier, and arrangements were concluded for their manufacture in Britain under an exclusive licence. By 1904 five Hollands had been built by Vickers, and the first of an improved type, the A class, was entering service. Most senior naval officers viewed this new vessel with hostility or suspicion. Submarines were on the one hand criticized for their limited powers, being considered mainly for defence of harbours and anchorages and quite incapable of working at sea against a fleet; and, contradictorily, for being such a potential threat to the battleship, in which the country had invested more than any other two nations in the world, that to encourage its development was to hazard the country's security. Their powers were also considered a contravention of decent rules, like hitting a man below the belt. Arthur Wilson, by contrast with the enthusiastic advocacy of his friend Fisher, considered that the submarine was 'underhand, unfair, and damned un-English'. The early submariners were young, eager, adventurous men, who were rather looked down on by the established hierarchy of the Navy, like Fleet Air Arm pilots between the wars, and their efforts, especially on manoeuvres, to prove the effectiveness of their vessels, were deliberately underrated.

Fisher on the other hand loved these bold young submariners. In the autumn of 1903 he had witnessed the Navy's first flotilla at exercises off Portsmouth. He at once sat down and wrote a long and prophetic eulogy of this new class of fighting ship, and its weapon, the torpedo. 'This Whitehead torpedo,' he wrote, 'can be carried with facility in Submarine Boats, and it has now attained such a range and such accuracy . . . that even at two miles' range it possesses a greater ratio of power of vitally injuring a ship in the line of battle than does the most accurate gun . . . There is this immense fundamental difference between the automobile torpedo and the gun—the torpedo has no trajectory: it travels horizontally and hits below the water, so all its hits are vital hits; but not so the gun—only in a few places are gun hits vital, and those places are armoured.

'The submarine,' continued Fisher's memorandum, 'must revolutionise naval tactics for this simple reason—that the present battle formation of ships in a single line presents a target of such a length that the chances are altogether in favour of the Whitehead torpedo hitting some ship in the line even when projected from a distance of several miles.' The submarine, Fisher contended, affected the very roots of the country's defence system, even the Army's. 'Imagine even one Submarine Boat with a flock of transports in sight loaded each with two or three thousand troops! Imagine the effect of one such transport going to the bottom in a few seconds with its living freight!

'Even the bare thought makes invasion impossible! Fancy 100,000 helpless, huddled up troops afloat in frightened transports with these invisible demons known to be near.

'Death near—momentarily—sudden—awful—invisible—unavoidable! Nothing conceivable more demoralising!'[1]

From this time Fisher used all his powers to advance the claims of the submarine. He was later to be seriously criticized for publicly drawing attention to this new and frightful form of warfare. But for Fisher's

[1] *Records*, 177–8.

enthusiasm, it was claimed, Germany might never have built her own submarine Fleet.

Esher was one of the first to listen to his claims. 'If he is right,' Esher wrote in his journal, 'and his argument appears unanswerable, it is difficult to exaggerate the vast impending revolution in naval warfare and naval strategy that the submarine will accomplish.'[1]

Fisher acquired another early ally in the Prince of Wales. 'I am sure there is an enormous future for the Submarines,' he wrote to Fisher on 10 January 1904, 'so we ought to build more at once.'[2] A year earlier, Fisher had arranged for the appointment to the new post of inspecting Captain of submarine boats of one of his brightest disciples, who was also later to become his biographer, Captain Bacon.

Much of Fisher's time at Portsmouth was occupied in showing important and useful people round the dockyard and ships, demonstrating the latest weapons, taking them to sea on exercises, round the *Victory* and to the busy site of the future Osborne College across the Solent. Generals, Cabinet Ministers, Members of Parliament, newspaper editors and reporters, foreign statesmen, American naval officers— all of them were treated to an exhausting programme, were relentlessly lectured by the Admiral, and when they departed, were left in no doubt of their host's wisdom, enthusiasm and self-confidence. Each had been brushed, however lightly, with the Fisher creed. Such were his powers of conversion to his causes that nearly everyone was destined to become, in some measure, a Fisher supporter or ally during the long struggle for reform which lay ahead.

Fisher loved to welcome people to Admiralty House. When the King invited himself he was especially delighted. 'I can say I never more enjoyed such a visit,' he wrote.

The stay at Portsmouth had been arranged during Fisher's week at Balmoral in October.

TO CECIL FISHER[3]

Admiralty House,
Portsmouth
February 11th 1904

Dearest Cis,

I expect mother has told you all the news about the King coming. His Majesty is awfully keen about coming and I hope all may go off well but the weather is terribly bad. I sat next him at dinner at Lord Howe's.[4] He had evi-

---

[1] 'Notes from old Diaries', *National Review*, September 1918.
[2] Kilverstone MSS.   [3] *ibid.*
[4] Lord-in-Waiting to King Edward.

dently arranged this and talked to me the whole time. The night before I had dined at Lord Colebrooke's[1] to meet the Prince and Princess of Wales and he invited himself and all his family to stay from March 12th to March 19th. The same day I lunched with the Duke of Connaught and the Duchess and her daughters who said they wanted to come and stay! So if we're not bankrupted I shall be very much surprised! . . .

Your loving father,
J. A. Fisher

One of Fisher's most important tasks during this visit was to convert the King as enthusiastically as his son to the submarine. If this form of fighting ship was ever to shed its despised reputation among the majority of senior officers, then the support of the King was of first importance.

The subject of the submarine occupied so much of the King's time at Portsmouth that even his natural interest in anything relating to the Navy, and his renowned patience, were fully stretched. Ponsonby, who was there in his official capacity of assistant private secretary, has recounted how Fisher 'had explained the general principles on which the submarine worked and had outlined the various problems which had not yet been satisfactorily solved, so that the King knew a good deal before Captain Bacon . . . came to dinner, but he listened attentively to all Captain Bacon said when he practically repeated all that Fisher had told him. The following day we went on board a submarine and a very keen young officer showed us round. When he began at the beginning explaining things I felt inclined to say "We know all about that", but the King listened attentively a third time to these explanations and asked several questions as if he were hearing about the submarine for the first time.'[2]

On the social arrangements for entertaining his monarch, Fisher had still to learn that it was the royal prerogative to settle everything to his own wishes. 'I wasn't master in my own house,' Fisher noted sorrowfully. 'The King arranged who should come to dinner and himself arranged how everyone should sit at table; I never had a look in. Not only this, but he also had the cook up in the morning. She was absolutely the best cook I've ever known.' A few days after the King and Queen had left, the cook's absence was noted. 'One night I said to the butler at dinner, "This soup was never made by Mrs Baker; is she ill?" The butler replied, "No, Sir John, Mrs Baker isn't ill, she has been invited by His Majesty the King to stay at Buckingham Palace".'[3] But King Edward had not after all lured Mrs Baker away for ever. She returned shortly afterwards, and explained to Fisher that the King had suggested she might enjoy seeing how a 'Great State Dinner' was

[1] Lord-in-Waiting to King Edward.   [2] *Ponsonby*, 130.   [3] *Records*, 24–5.

managed. Fisher described this event as an example of the King's 'astounding aptitude of appealing to the hearts of both High and Low'.

Besides his inspection of a submarine, the King was taken across to the Isle of Wight to inspect Osborne College, and the convalescent home there. He was also taken down to the *Victory's* cockpit where Nelson had died. Lady Fisher had devoted herself to the task of restoring this to its original condition, and had got it ready in time for the royal visit.

Two of the three days at Portsmouth were fine for the royal party, and it was in every way a highly satisfactory visit, with the emphasis appropriately on the demonstration of the Navy's new technology. Besides the tour round the submarine, Captain Percy Scott, the Captain of H.M.S. *Excellent*, showed off his new method of rifle training, and there was an exciting mock attack by an armoured car mounting a Maxim gun.

FROM LORD KNOLLYS[1]

Buckingham Palace
22nd February, 1904

My dear Admiral,

I am desired by the King to write and thank you again for your hospitality.

His Majesty also desires me to express his great appreciation of all of the arrangements, which were excellent, and they reflect the greatest credit both on you and on those who worked under your orders.

I am very glad the visit was such a great success and went off so well. The King was evidently extremely pleased with and interested in everything.

Yours sincerely,
Knollys

The visit to Portsmouth of the Prince and Princess of Wales in March 1904 was longer, more eventful, and almost as important from Fisher's point of view. Manoeuvres in the English Channel, with simulated attacks by submarines, were arranged to coincide with the visit of the Prince, who was always eager to go to sea and loved to be reminded of his earlier and more active association with the service. The party embarked in the old cruiser *Mercury*, specially fitted out for the occasion. Her Captain wrote of the occasion: 'When we went out the weather was not smooth and the Princess and Lady Fisher did not embark. We cruised about with the Prince, his standard at the main and the Commander-in-Chief's flag at the fore. I had taken the Commander-in-Chief's Chief Yeoman and a signal staff from the *Victory* as I knew there would be much signalling. Once when some signal went foul and Fisher told me he did not think much of my signalmen and I told him that they were his own signal staff from *Victory*, the Prince said, "He rather got you there, Sir John".

'We had lunch in the wardroom—Pea Soup, Salt Pork and Plum Pudding to remind the Prince of his naval Service. I had got a specially selected joint of pork from the Superintendent of the Victualling Yard for the occasion.'[1]

The primitiveness and hazards of the submarine service had been recounted to Esher by Fisher a few days before the Prince's arrival. In a reference to the means employed to register the foulness of the air when submerged, and the gallantry of one particular commander Fisher had written: 'Yesterday all the mice died in their cages and two of his crew fainted, but the young Lieutenant of the submarine didn't seem to care a d—n whether they all died so long as he bagged the battleship he was after! . . . Another submarine had an explosion which made the interior *"hell"* for some seconds . . .' It was the commanding Lieutenant of this second submarine who took the Prince to sea a few days later, and instructed him in how to fire a torpedo.

'Everyone was averse from the Prince's going down,' wrote Esher to his son, 'but he *insisted*, and I think he was right. It will give a lift to the submarines—and being a sailor, why should he not take risks?' But Fisher, according to Esher, 'was jolly glad when he saw the heir to the Throne reappear'.[2]

Fisher's anxiety was justified a few days later when the Navy had its first submarine casualty, and there were no survivors. Immediately on his return to London the Prince of Wales received a full report on the disaster from Fisher.

TO THE PRINCE OF WALES

Admiralty House
Portsmouth
[*March 20th, 1904*]

Sir,

This is how the submarine was sunk. About noon on Friday the cruiser *Juno*, of the Home Fleet, was sighted in the offing. Submarine *No. 2* was given her direction and went after her, followed by submarine *No. 3*. Submarine *No. 2* got in a shot at *Juno* about two o'clock, but the torpedo missed her. This probably distracted *Juno's* attention, so *No. 3* submarine got unobserved within 400 yards of *Juno* and hit her with her torpedo. The head of the torpedo was smashed up and knocked off, and the body of the torpedo came up just as the King saw it when His Majesty witnessed precisely the same shot fired by the same submarine at the battleship *Colossus*. Well! Captain Bacon (not knowing

[1] *Oliver*, 105–6.   [2] *Esher*, ii, 49.

at the distance he was off what his young heroes were accomplishing) made a
signal to submarine *A1* (the big submarine in which the King and Your Royal
Highness and the Princess spent so much time in her internal regions) also
to attack the *Juno*, observing that Bacon did rightly what would be done in
war—sent a regular hornet's nest of submarines on to one part or one ship of the
enemy's Fleet, because he gets so distracted and flustered by all these infernal
brutes popping up from different directions that he hesitates which way to go,
and *'the ship that hesitates is lost,'* because the only escape from the submarine
is 'full speed ahead and helm hard over.'

I hope, Sir, this won't get into the *Daily Mail*, because it's the secret of the
manoeuvres! Well, Sir, to resume—submarine *A1* steered for the *Juno* far
off in the distance, and, poor fellow, I much fear her gallant Commander was
only looking at the enemy and didn't care a damn for anything or anybody else.
I am much afraid I might have done the same, so don't wish to throw a stone
at him; besides, it's the secret of war to be regardless of consequences, provided
you hit the enemy! At that moment the Castle Line steamer *Berwick Castle*,
from Southampton to Hamburg, was steering a course exactly at right angles
to submarine *A1* and was about 2 or 3 miles off, but, never having seen a
submarine in his life (he saw her $\frac{1}{4}$ of an hour before he struck her), her Captain thought it was a torpedo. His words are: 'He saw something.' Just before
she struck submarine *A1*, the *Berwick Castle* went full speed astern and put
his helm hard a starboard, but, alas, too late! . . .

Believe me, Sir, in very great haste, Your Royal Highness' obedient
servant,

J. A. Fisher

Although two months passed after the visit of the Prince and Princess
of Wales to Portsmouth before Fisher received formal confirmation
that he would succeed Walter Kerr as First Naval Lord, he continued
to busy himself with preparations in detail for his return to the Admiralty
during the spring and summer of 1904. Of first importance was the
appointment to senior commands of officers who were sympathetic
to his beliefs and plans; and the displacement of those who were already out of the 'Fishpond'.

Already in 1904 Fisher's unbalanced preoccupation with personalities,
which was later to become an obsession and his most criticized failing,
was making itself evident. Having been told by Selborne that he was to
be succeeded at Portsmouth by an officer he did not admire, Fisher let
the First Lord know that, in that case, he would remain at Portsmouth
and Selborne would have to look elsewhere for a new First Naval Lord.
King-Hall has recounted in his diary how one Captain caused Fisher
displeasure and lost his position as a result. Rear-Admiral Angus Mac-
Leod, as D N O, had not agreed with all Fisher's plans for reforming the
Navy's gunnery. In October 1903 he had been summoned to an inter-

view. 'You are trying to wreck my plans regarding gunnery,' Fisher had accused him. 'No, I am not,' he had replied, 'but as DNO it is my duty to express an opinion.' According to King-Hall, Fisher had then said, 'You know people talk of the three R's—my three R's are Ruthless, Relentless and Remorseless. Anyone who opposes me I crush, I crush.' MacLeod in reporting to King-Hall how he had lost his job, said that Fisher had 'got quite fierce, and glared'.[1] All this took place a year before Fisher returned to the Admiralty, when, according to MacLeod, 'the Admiralty is practically run by Fisher (though C.-in-C. at Portsmouth), Battenberg, and Tyrwhitt'.[2]

Prince Louis of Battenberg, a minor German prince who had married one of Queen Victoria's grandchildren and become an English naval officer, had for long swum comfortably in the deepest part of the Fishpond. Fisher had a sincere respect for him as a seaman and an administrator. He and the Prince of Wales were the two strongest bonds securing him to the palace. With Fisher back at the Admiralty, Prince Louis could be assured of the most intimate association with the Board, and a high place on it. Arrangements to this end were a subject of their warm and regular correspondence fifteen months before Fisher returned to Whitehall.

FROM PRINCE LOUIS OF BATTENBERG[3]

The Admiralty
July 17th, 1903

My Dear Admiral,

... I thank you most cordially for falling in so readily with my proposals. I am confident that I could be of some use to you in a squadron on Home Sea service like the cruiser squadron. Of course I should have loved going back to the dear old Mediterranean but there is another reason why I should go to the cruiser squadron in preference. It will look so much better if I move into the high office of Second Lord from an independent Command rather than from a very subordinate one—*Third* not Second in Command of Mediterranean.

... On 24.1.06 you must be made an Admiral of the Fleet, and a Peer a little later.

Hoping that you are getting much benefit,[4]

Ever yours very sincerely,
Battenberg

It was a curious element in Fisher's fight for power that he would often, half seriously, half teasingly, pretend that he had made so many enemies by his ruthlessness, relentlessness and remorselessness that he had destroyed all his chances of attaining his ends, and so compromised

[1] *Sea Saga*, 324. [2] Captain the Hon. Hugh Tyrwhitt, later Fisher's Naval Secretary.
[3] Kilverstone MSS. [4] Fisher was taking the cure at Marienbad.

himself with the forcible sweeps of his broom that he would soon find himself on half-pay. He was really searching for denials and reassurance. In spite of the seemingly unassailable position to which he had climbed by 1904, the honours which had been heaped upon him, the intimacy of his relationship with the most influential establishments in the country, Fisher had still not succeeded in casting aside the insecurity of the class and penury into which he had been born. He might be a formidable man, and all who knew him testify to the terror he could inspire when aroused. But he never in all his life experienced the absolute and uncompromising self-confidence and assurance of superiority which men like Beresford, and so many of his contemporaries, had inherited along with their titles and wealth. For Fisher, the warrior, everything had to be fought for; and a warrior not only enjoys the effect on others of his fierceness but likes to be told as often as possible how brave he is.

A surviving account of an interview with Fisher at Portsmouth by his Chief of Staff, a rich baronet, reveals in miniature the impression of formidable demeanour and arrogant ruthlessness he strived so successfully and consistently to present to those about him. Sir Robert Arbuthnot had been charged with repairing and making ready for the regular summer tourists H.M.S. *Victory*, which had been struck and damaged while at anchor at Portsmouth. Arbuthnot's report was placed in an envelope marked 'Sealed 6th January 1904' and 'To be sent to him [Fisher] if I die before he does'. Arbuthnot was killed at Jutland, four years before Fisher died in 1920.

'Went in to see Sir John Fisher, Commander-in-Chief at Portsmouth, in his office about 12.30. Found him writing and asked him if he wanted to see me about *Victory*. He said: "Yes" and got up and stood in front of fire.

'I asked him if we were to go into *Hercules*, and he said: "Yes on 15 Feb. without fail." I told him Admiral Superintendent not got the approval from Admiralty for defects to be taken in hand. He said he didn't care. He would give the approval himself—it had to be done by 15 Feb.

'No-one but three Chief Warrant Officers and twenty-one Privates were to live in the Victory. I pointed out that twenty-one men could not cope with the dirt brought on board by a thousand trippers on a wet Saturday in the summer. "Then tell off a working party to clean her." Then I said I should like to know what he was driving at, and is it all to be permanent? "Yes *permanent!*" "Always? Till I get up to Admiralty; than I'll alter it all! I'm not such a born idiot as to tell all those chaps at the Admiralty what I'm going to do before I go there. Lord Walter wrote to me only last week and said: 'My dear fellow, I haven't had a

letter from you or a report from Portsmouth for two and a half months.'
I replied: 'And you won't get any either!' The Admiralty are all a
lot of old women and bury their noses in their papers and think out
how wide a man's medal ribbon should be, and shut their eyes to what is
really going on in the world.

' "I tell you I had a man standing in this office a few days ago, who
has seen a Russian torpedo hitting a small target time after time at
3,000 yards and at 24 knots. We can only do 2,000 yards at 18 knots . . .
The Fleet Reserve is rotten to the core, and they keep asking me for a
report. Think I'm such a born fool as to tell them? When I get up there
I'll alter it all, and those who get in my way had better look out.

' "I've ruined about eight men in the last eighteen months, and I'll
ruin anyone else who tries to stop me."

'I laughed and said: "I hope you won't ruin me;" and he replied:
"I'd ruin my best friend if necessary for the Service. Mind you, Arbuthnot, I'm talking very confidentially to you and you mustn't give me
away." I said: "I think you can trust me, Sir," . . .'[1]

Fisher's pretended insistence that he had made so many enemies he
would be 'growing vegetables' before the year of 1904 was out was
stoutly and patiently denied by his supporters. 'As to your not coming
as s n l [Senior Naval Lord],' Battenberg once told him, 'that is
absurd. Your position in the Service and in this Country is now such
that no First Lord, Liberal or Conservative, would dream of taking
anyone but you. The King and the Prince of Wales moreover are determined about it.'[2]

This sort of message acted like a balm to Fisher's deep-seated insecurity. Even when Selborne told him officially in mid-May 1904 that
he was the next First Naval Lord, Fisher accepted only 'on the understanding I commenced work on October 21st (Trafalgar Day!)' and
with grave doubts that his 'relentlessness' would be tolerated for long.

A few weeks later, Esher, 'my best of friends!', was hearing of
Fisher's personal complaints about his pay, and about who he might be
expected to work with. 'The King told Selborne *straight* I would save
them millions, and they haggled at giving me a few hundreds! and
"Behold! this is in the House of Friends." (*See the prophet Jeremiah on
this topic!!!*)

'The Prime Minister, the Chancellor of the Exchequer, and the
First Lord of the Admiralty, all swearing eternal friendship to me and
see me d——d before they give me a shilling! and bring me up from the
plum of the Service at Portsmouth to penal servitude at the Admiralty

[1] Kilverstone MSS.   [2] *ibid.*

to suit their conveninece! on half the pay and double the work.[1] Such is life! *But please don't worry!* . . .'

Then a few days later, in the course of thanking Esher for his 'blessed confidence' in him in giving him the early news of Selborne's imminent retirement from the Admiralty, Fisher wrote to make clear with whom he was prepared and not prepared to work. 'I could not serve with Walter Long, so if he comes in I shall clear out, but Onslow I should love! I told the King last year at Balmoral that he was the man to succeed Selborne . . . Also, the other day at Marienbad I told him that the First Lord of the Admiralty should be a Peer, so as to give him more time than the House of Commons allows, and he quite agreed, so much so that he said to me how would Lord Tweedmouth do as First Lord on a change of Government, and I agreed with him. I've never met Walter Long, but am told that he is pestiferous and that we should not last together for a week, so I should be silly to start with him! . . .'

Fisher's suggestion to the King that he might be prepared to work under Tweedmouth was soon to be taken up. But meanwhile the responsibility for preparing the Admiralty to receive the first broadsides from Fisher in the autumn rested with the present First Lord. There were times during the summer when Selborne wondered whether the Admiralty could absorb the impact. Fisher's various postures between May and October 1904—the threatening utterances, the hints of withdrawal if everything was not just to his liking, the demands for heads to fall even before he was in command, the dark hints of the fearful revolution he was to perpetrate—all seemed like the elaborate evolutions of some savage war dance designed to instil courage in the warrior and fear in the enemy.

Moreover it succeeded in its object. Such was Fisher's reputation that Walter Kerr and his Naval Lords were relegated to a pale shadow of a Board, and Selborne was mainly occupied in dealing with Fisher. In June Fisher was writing, 'I am incubating like mad and Selborne keeps on hammering away at me to send him my views, but I have put him off . . .' Six weeks later Selborne knew no more of Fisher's plans.

TO VISCOUNT ESHER

Admiralty House
Portsmouth
Private   *July 28th, 1904*
Dear Esher,

. . . Selborne has been trying to draw me, but I have steadfastly declined to say a word or write a line before I am installed on Trafalgar Day! *One excep-*

[1] The pay of the C.-in-C. Portsmouth was £4,000 a year, the First Naval Lord £2,600.

tion! I drew up a scheme for the reorganization of the Admiralty and he has swallowed it whole and got the order in Council for it! *The new scheme gives me nothing to do!* It also resuscitates the old titles of *Sea Lords* dating from A.D. 1613, but which some silly ass 100 years ago altered to *Naval Lords*. Don't say a word of all this! As Evan MacGregor says Selborne is most anxious it should appear as HIS OWN scheme! . . .

I've got the preamble of my new scheme ready! It's 31 pages of foolscap! When finished at 4 p.m. on October 19, I will ask you kindly to read it!

Yours till death,
J.F.

By the beginning of August, Fisher was beginning to yield a little, if only because practical questions were involved. Hinting at the nature of one of his revolutions, he wrote to Selborne on 2 August begging him 'Not to take any step to lay down any fresh battleships, or that will in any way bind you to do so, until you have allowed me to set before you in detail in October next why we should hold our hands in the matter!'

Fisher had accepted the appointment as First Naval Lord 'on the understanding' he would take up his duties on Trafalgar Day; and until that day, *'our opening day'* as he whimsically referred to it, the First Lord would have to wait in suspense. So it seemed until early August 1904. But by the middle of the month Selborne decided to take the train to Portsmouth to consult. He 'was so cordial and responsive,' Fisher told Esher of this visit, 'that I made the plunge, and with *immense success*. He has swallowed it all whole, though I fully explained to him that, in accepting it all, he was writing himself down as a fool for not having done it all sooner! I sat him in an arm-chair in my office and shook my fist in his face for 2¼ hours without a check! "New measures demand new men," and he has agreed to all the new blood I want. Of course, everyone will say that I have "packed" the Admiralty with "my creatures"! (Very sorry, but I can't help it!)'

Fisher then divulged his plans to turn to his most important intimates. Esher, always his closest confidante, from November 1903 was kept apprised of them as they were conceived. Balfour, the Prime Minister, was 'lectured to' in August; and having decided in the same month that the King 'ought to know what is going on' Fisher wrote to Knollys with the notes he had used while talking to Balfour.

Fisher's press friends, too, were prepared for the October revolutions, although he gave no hint of the details even to those whose discretion he most trusted.

TO ARNOLD WHITE

Portsmouth
August 21st, 1904

Strictly Private
Dear Mr Arnold White,

. . . I am ready for the fray. It will be a case of *Athansius contra Mundum*. Very sorry for Mundum, as Athansius is going to win! Even you will want an extra whack of jam to swallow the powder! But I hope you will end with the best words I ever read, written by a pen that affords me my weekly solace in the *Sunday Sun*, and say of the new great scheme of reform which will emerge from the Admiralty like Minerva from the brain of Jupiter, full grown and armed against all objectors!

'Napoleonic in its audacity'.

'Cromwellian in its thoroughness.'

Ever yours,
J. A. Fisher

Burn this and *remember the oil!* I swear I'll boil you if you say another word!

In September Fisher made his annual visit to Germany and Austria to take the cure. Marienbad, his favourite spa, where he could also be sure of meeting the King, was prominent on the itinerary. On Fisher's last day the King, staying as the Duke of Lancaster in an effort at least to diminish the unfortunate publicity his presence always aroused,[1] sent his motor car to Fisher's hotel to collect him. They had an hour's talk in the morning, took luncheon together, and went for a drive in the afternoon. In the evening the King personally saw him off at the station. 'Nothing could possibly exceed his cordiality and friendliness,' Fisher commented.

On this occasion there was a special reason for the King's solicitous attention. It had been agreed between Selborne and the King that Fisher was to be appointed King Edward's principal naval A D C when he became First Naval Lord. Besides the honour, the £400 a year addition to his salary would be most welcome, and it would give him special privileged access to the King at any time. But it seemed as if it was not to be. 'I had a sort of presentiment that there was something amiss,' Fisher confided to Esher. In a sad letter Fisher recounted the event. 'He said he would have given anything for me to be his principal A D C on October 21st but on reflection he had come to the conclusion that it would do me harm as everyone would say it is the King's favouritism and that I'd got it for myself and he intended to make use of my not getting it to have my pay raised and he has written a very strong letter (which he read to me) to Selborne this afternoon. I told the King,'

[1] *Lee*, ii, 299.

THE ANNIVERSARY OF TRAFALGAR

Nelson (in Trafalgar Square):–'I was on my way down to lend them a hand myself, but if Jacky Fisher's taking on the job there's no need for me to be nervous, I'll get back on my pedestal.'

A *Daily Express* cartoon commemorating Fisher's appointment as First Sea Lord

Fisher continued, 'I regretted not having the honour of and pleasure of being his ADC but of course I bowed to His Majesty's opinion.'[1] As consolation, the King told Fisher that he was determined that he should be made an Admiral of the Fleet in January 1906, on Fisher's 65th birthday. But to Esher, Fisher wrote on 11 September 1904, 'I feel just a little bit bitter at not having it [i.e. the ADC]'.

There are hints that Esher took the matter up again with the King; it was in character for him to do so. If this was what happened, it was effective quickly, for in little more than three weeks time Fisher heard that the King had reversed his decision. Knollys told Fisher that he would be ADC after all. *'It all puzzles me beyond comprehension!'* Fisher commented to Esher.

On 21 October 1904, 99 years to the day after Fisher's great hero had fought his greatest battle and died in the ship, Fisher's flag was hauled down in the *Victory*. Fifty years and three months had passed since Fisher himself had joined the Flagship as a boy of thirteen. He had planned for months to enter the office of the First Sea Lord on that same day, and a number of celebratory events had been arranged. Instead, Fisher took up his duties a day earlier. It has never been satisfactorily explained why. It may have been forgetfulness, or unconscious impatience, or perversity. Whatever the reason, it was an entirely suitable piece of mistiming. Even a single extra day would be a help if he was to accomplish all his plans.

[1] Mutilated, but probably to Lady Fisher. Kilverstone MSS.

PART TWO

Chapter 1

THE MAN IN WHITEHALL

In October 1904 Admiral Sir John Fisher embodied in appearance, character and reputation the fighting strength of the richest nation and greatest empire in the world. His figure was thick-set rather than corpulent, thanks to the self-discipline he exercised in his eating and drinking, and his regular dieting following the invariable summer 'cure'. His eyes were quick and clever and wary. His full head of steel grey wiry hair, the absence of moustache, beard or side whiskers and the smooth skin of his face, made him appear much younger than his sixty-three years. 'Clad in a reefer jacket, his brown honest eyes peer out from his strong, peach-shaped countenance,' a journalist wrote of him, 'he seems almost boyish—from his portrait you could not guess his age as more than thirty-five.'[1] There was a touch of the Oriental both in the colour of his skin and the bone structure of his face, which led his enemies to spread the rumour that oriental blood flowed in his veins. Those who feared and hated him called him 'the yellow peril', while Beresford's favourite terms of abuse during the height of their duel were 'the Mulatto' and 'that damned Asiatic'.

TO ARNOLD WHITE

Admiralty,
Whitehall,
March 5th, 1906

My dear Friend,

My family are very much annoyed by the frequent allusions apparently made to my mother being a Cingalese princess or something of the sort. Kindly see the enclosed [newspaper cutting], and will you, if you are able, dispel the

[1] *Pall Mall Gazette*, September 1904.

illusion. Personally, I don't care, but as my relatives don't like it, I've promised to see if it can be denied. But I don't want to appear as if being troubled about it . . .

Ever yours,
J. A. Fisher

In repose or silent concentration his full lips curved down into an expression of supercilious distaste for the world with which he was at war; but as soon as he gladly broke into conversation his whole face was transformed and he at once resembled an intelligent schoolboy, eager to learn, eager to score a point, finding equal fun and stimulus in listening and talking. It was the joyousness and the driving power of his conversation, delivered in a softly-modulated and beautiful voice, and the pure smile of mischievous innocence that broke through again and again which made him so attractive, especially to women and to children, who always adored him. His persuasive charm was attested to by all who met him, even his most virulent antagonists. In serious debate he was an equally gifted talker, always enthusiastic and quick to change his line of argument and draw on his prodigious reserves of facts and records. He could cite precedents as readily as a barrister in full cry, and quote the Old Testament like an evangelist.

Spender wrote of him: 'His talk was racy, original, full of mother wit, and irradiated by a humour which was bracing and pungent as the salt of the sea itself . . . His spirits were unquenchable: when we asked him to dinner, it was as likely as not that he would come into the room dancing a hornpipe, and there seemed to be no company in which he was not absolutely at home. In all this he was absolutely unaffected and simple, without a trace of pose or affectation.'[1] When the ladies had left and the talk became earnest and masculine, or in his office in the Admiralty, the boundless vitality and eagerness of this social figure remained. '. . . we knew him,' Bacon has written, 'with his head thrown back, lips slightly parted, eyes a trifle vacant, as he listened to the thrust in controversy; then would come the sudden flash of animation, then the riposte, the flood of argument, the Biblical quotation punctuated by gesture and hammer-blows of the first on the hand; and in the end the talk invariably ended with a smile on the face of all who had been listening to him.'[2]

Fisher worked too long hours to lead the full and demanding social life of most of his contemporaries, but when it was obligatory or when he was on holiday at Marienbad or Carlsbad, or staying at Sandringham, Windsor or Balmoral, he threw himself into it with

---

[1] J. A. Spender, *Life, Journalism and Politics* (London, 1927, 2 vols), ii, 67.
[2] *Bacon*, i, 246.

youthful delight. He loved above all the company of pretty women. If they were gay and intelligent, so much the better. But they had to be able to dance—well, and for the whole night if necessary, no matter what their rank might be. His passion for dancing was undiminished. All his friends encouraged him to indulge in this recreation and enjoyed watching him waltz by the hour, and King Edward and Queen Alexandra always arranged the programme so that he had plenty of opportunity to dance in the evenings.

FROM SIR FREDERICK PONSONBY[1]

> *Sandringham*
> *January 16th, 1907*
>
> *My dear Admiral,*
> I was playing bridge last night within two feet of the band. Wagner was being played and the few musicians were sawing away as loud as they could. I was trying to play a difficult hand. The Queen was my partner. What I am pleased to call my brain was in a confused and addled condition partly owing to a heavy dinner but mostly owing to the deafening noise of the band.
> The band stopped and I collected my scattered senses but just as I was getting on, away went the band with a dreamy waltz. The Queen said, 'This is the waltz Sir John Fisher loves to dance to.'
> How can one play bridge?

Just before he died, Fisher recalled his meeting at Carlsbad many years before with the Czar's youngest sister, the Grand Duchess Olga, or 'Sunshine' as the Russians nicknamed her. The Prime Minister of Russia had told Fisher before he met her that 'she was a kind of lifebuoy because if you walked about with her you would not get bombed by an anarchist. All loved her.' Fisher continued: 'On my arrival at the hotel I found King Edward's Equerry waiting in the hall. I had written to tell the King, who was at Marienbad, in answer to his enquiry, as to the day I should arrive and what time; and he came over to Marienbad from Carlsbad. I went then and there and found him just finishing lunch with a peculiarly charming looking young lady, who turned out to be the Grand Duchess Olga, and her husband, the Grand Duke of Oldenburg, from whom happily she is now divorced (I didn't like the look of him at all). The King, having satisfied himself that I had had lunch, and he then smoking a cigar as big as a capstan bar, after talking of various things which interested him told me that his niece, the Grand Duchess Olga, did not know anyone in Carlsbad, and he relied on me to make her time there pleasant, so I promptly asked her if she could

1 Lennoxlove MSS.

waltz. She said she loved it, but she somehow never got the step properly, whereupon I asked the King if he had any objection to getting into the corner of the room while I moved the table and took the rugs up to give her Imperial Highness a lesson. He made some little difficulty at first, but eventually went into the corner; and when the lesson began he was quite pleased and clapped his hands and called out "Bravo!" The best waltz tune in the world is one of Moody and Sankey's hymns. I don't know whether Sankey originated the saying that he didn't see why the Devil should have all the good music. I don't by that implicate that the waltz was the devil's; but, without any doubt, there is a good deal of temptation in it, and when you get a good partner you cleave to her all the evening.

'This dancing lesson was unalloyed success, so I asked her to a dance the next night at the Savoy Hotel; and after some more words with the King I left, and walking down the stairs to go to my hotel, I thought to myself: "How on earth are you going to get up a dance when you don't know a soul in the place?" when who should I meet but a friend of mine—a Spanish Grandee, the Marquis de Villa Vieja, and he arranged what really turned out to be a ball, as he knew everybody, and I having some dear American friends at Marienbad I telegraphed them to come over and dine with the Grand Duchess and stay the night for the ball, and they did. When the dance had begun, and the Grand Duchess was proving quite equal to her lesson of the day before, suddenly an apparition of extraordinary grace and loveliness appeared at the door. Villa Vieja took on the Grand Duchess and I welcomed the beautiful Polish Countess and danced with her many waltzes running in spite of a hint I received that her husband was very jealous and a renowned duellist.'[1]

Fisher's relations with women were the subject of much speculation and sometimes of spiteful gossip when he became an even more important public and controversial figure. He was so transparently joyful in their company, so ready to admire them, and so eager—innocently but illadvisedly—to dance with the most beautiful woman of his choice for an entire evening, that he was often privately accused of indulging in a succession of affairs. An officer, perhaps recently reprimanded or otherwise out of favour, might at a service ball find himself deprived of the company of his beautiful young wife for a dozen dances. Or Fisher might be seen in deep and familiar conversation, broken by peals of laughter, with some beauty in the street or outside the Atheneum. He would wave and blow kisses to them from hansom cabs on the slightest acquaintance. His invariable success with them alone made him the subject of doubts, among both sexes. There is no shred of

[1] *Memories*, 232–3.

evidence that Fisher's relations with the numerous women who brushed against his life were anything but innocent. He was prepared to love them all, dance with them all, write them affectionate letters and address them in the most intimate terms, but the frequent attacks on his morals which he suffered over many years were almost certainly unjustified. Then in 1914 his name began to be linked with the Duchess of Hamilton, and a friendship developed with her and her family that strengthened and supported him before and after his wife's death. Fisher's affection for his wife endured all through these years. Katharine Fisher grew rather stout after her child-bearing years were over and remained a happy, uncomplicated woman, undividedly loyal to her husband, and a beloved mother to her children. The welfare and happiness of Pamela and Dorothy, who remained unmarried until they were thirty and thirty-five, was her main preoccupation. She was, wrote one who knew her well, 'a queen among women, with a dignity that I have never known to be excelled in anyone, imperturbability of temper and, above all, a kind and understanding heart'.[1]

During Fisher's first period as First Sea Lord, they remained a happily married pair. The timetable of his life meant that they saw little of one another at 16 Queen Anne's Gate, St James, where they lived. He arose usually between four and five o'clock when he made his way briefly to Westminster Abbey to pray and meditate, then briskly strode across St James's Park to the Admiralty. He would settle at his desk by six o'clock at the latest, and sometimes as early as 4.15 a.m., and get in three clear hours of work when the corridors were silent and he could be certain of peace. Here he would go speedily through his 'In' tray, perhaps making marginal notes in uncompromising terms, initialling documents, and writing letters with great rapidity in his round, clear hand. He rarely dictated, scribbled notes to his secretary indicating how letters should be answered, and distrusted and rarely used the telephone.

By nine o'clock Fisher reckoned that he had done more useful work than he could accomplish in the rest of the day. He walked home to a large cooked breakfast with his family, talked briefly to his wife and daughters, read the newspapers, and returned to the Admiralty when most people were arriving at their offices. Unless he had a luncheon appointment, he would have a glass of lemonade and a biscuit—and nothing more—in the middle of the day and returned home at about 7.30 in the evening. When he was not dining out, he would then bathe, change, take dinner with the family, read briefly afterwards, and retire to bed at about 9.30.

Hurd, 61.

But a day as First Sea Lord rarely worked out as uneventfully as this. Fisher had constant streams of visitors during the day, he was often out for a long lunch with politicians, editors, naval officers, or foreign dignitaries; and there were often social engagements in the evening. He was, moreover, often out of London, at country houses at weekends, visiting naval establishments, perhaps observing the firing trials of a new gun, or inspecting a new battleship under construction. In late middle age his zeal for work was as prodigious as ever. 'I've been doing 16 hours a day lately', he wrote proudly to his wife in November, 1904. Neither Lady Fisher nor his friends could keep him away from the Admiralty at week-ends. When King Edward heard from Lady Fisher at a Palace dinner that he was treating Sunday as a normal working day he wrote on the back of a menu, 'Admiral Sir John Fisher is to do *no* work on *Sundays*, not go near the Admiralty . . . By command. Edward R.' and ordered it to be passed to him.

Fisher's health on the whole stood up well to the strain of the long hours and unremitting battle, although every winter he was dogged by colds. A month after his return to Whitehall he was obliged to see the King's physician extraordinary, while his wife was away from London, and reported to her:

TO LADY FISHER

> *Admiralty,*
> *Whitehall*
> *November 18th, 1904*

Dearest Kitty,

I saw Sir Felix Semon, who was awfully kind and put all sorts of frightful things down my throat, and he says he will cure me in 24 hours! I saw him at 7 p.m., and he telephoned for some mixture and in ten minutes I had a dose, and I've hardly coughed since! It really is a wonder . . .

I've had a tremendous fight to-day and glad to say I won, but, of course, some very unpleasant quarters of an hour! However, I must expect that . . . I think this has been my hardest day. It's now 8:30 p.m., and it's the first moment since breakfast that I have ceased talking! . . .

> Y.l.h.
> J.F.

To his family he was a remote figure for most of the time, for they saw so little of him, he was away for so long and so often, and his activities were so important and so incomprehensible. To his son and daughters, he was a formidable figure for whom they felt affection and respect; but they little understood him. Except at meals almost their only opportunity for communicating with him was on walks. He would sometimes invite one or more of them to come for a walk. It would be a brisk affair. They walked far and fast and talked little. He never talked about his work to them; this, he considered, would be dull and meaningless for them. He would tell them about an interesting sermon which he had recently heard, or perhaps about a week-end with some politician or peer. He would ask them about their own lives, and talk about their health, a subject he always enjoyed discussing. The house at Queen Anne's Gate was run entirely to his own convenience—and on lines of extreme economy. One of his contemporaries has described how Fisher came to breakfast one morning 'and told the family to shift for themselves as he was going to shut the house and go to the Carlton for a fortnight. They all had to be gone next day and were busy telephoning to arrange visits to friends. It was a bit of discipline for the girls.'[1]

The religious influence in his life remained as strong as ever, although like so much else about him it became both simpler and more exaggerated as he aged. In his religious beliefs as in his professional beliefs and in his judgement of his fellow men, he tended to become more and more impatient with the half shades: it was as if time were so precious for all that he had to do that he had decided not to bother to mix the colours. He never stinted the time he was prepared to give to the worship of God, however. Rather, he spent more and more of his time in church or cathedral. But here again he tended to lose patience with the embellishments and procedures. By contrast with the early days of his marriage, and when he was serving on distant stations for long periods, there are few references to religion in the letters to his wife at this time. In 1871, when he was in the *Ocean* in the Far East, his frequent long letters were full of earnest religious analysis, with comments on his recent religious reading, as if he were searching for some elusive truth. Thirty years later, if there were still doubts he was silent about them. The Divinity was as deep, and as important to him as ever, but he now seemed obliged through lack of time to simplify the whole thing down and break loose from the narrow limits of dogma.

He was happy to go to church two or three times a day, and often did, but once in his pew he preferred to meditate in silence or listen to a good rousing sermon. His love of sermons became a part of the Fisher legend. On hearing that Fisher had listened to four sermons in one day, the Dean of Westminster warned that he might contract spiritual indigestion. Admiral Bacon shrewdly summed up Fisher's religious beliefs in later life:

'The strong religious convictions of his youth gradually...crystallized

[1] *Oliver*, 115.

around the fundamental truths of primitive Christian teaching. He appreciated a good sermon; but, even more than attending church services, he loved to sit and meditate in some church or cathedral, communing in solitude and silence. He was especially affected by the grandeur and solemnity of Westminster Abbey. Practically every day when in London he would spend some time in that Valhalla, finding a never-ceasing solace from the worries of his official life, wrapt in meditation and surrounded, in spirit, by the illustrious dead.

'He had a firm belief in Divine intervention in the affairs of this life; if he had doubts about justice in this world, he had none about matters being evened out in the next! "The Lord God of recompence will surely requite" was the thought with which he was wont to comfort himself, drawing from it almost Davidian consolation. He was convinced that the Day of Judgment would one day come along, and then the men, and the Society ladies who had laboured for their own friends under the cloak of working for the Navy, would get their just reward. Any desire he might have to strike down an enemy in this world was largely satisfied by remembering Dean Page Roberts's remark that "There was no Bankruptcy Act in Heaven, no ten shillings in the pound there; every moral debt had to be paid in full." His religion was in many respects a primitive and rugged religion; but it was all the more sincere for its directness. An ardent admirer of Joshua, David, and St Paul, as well as of Nelson, he firmly believed in the prayer, "O Lord, arise, and let thine enemies be scattered," being answered; but, at the same time, he believed in his countrymen doing their fair share of the scattering.'[1]

By the autumn of 1904 the scene had been set, the leading protagonists had taken their places, for the arms race that was to lead to world war ten years later. The naval competition between Britain and Germany, which was to become one of the chief causes as well as one of the chief results was already accelerating to a pace that made it a subject of international anxiety and speculation. For First Sea Lord the British had an Admiral who had always proudly boasted 'I have been fighting from my earliest youth!' and was at the age of sixty-three more than ever eager for battle. Few people in the higher counsels of the state could see as clearly as Fisher the likely course of the competition or were more certain of the inevitability of war with Germany; and certainly no one in the Navy could perceive with such clarity the shape of his own two campaigns which lay ahead, against Admiral Alfred von Tirpitz who had been in supreme command of the German naval

[1] *Bacon*, i, 231–2.

1. Sophie and William Fisher, Fisher's mother and father, in Ceylon, *circa* 1860

2. Lady Wilmot-Horton: 'She walks in beauty, like the night . . .'

Lieutenant John Arbuthnot
Fisher—age 19—in
command of the ship herewith!

3.
Fisher's annotation to a photograph
of himself, and H.M.S. *Coromandel*

4. Fisher's wife, Katharine Delves Broughton, shortly after her marriage

5. Fisher was promoted to the rank of Captain 30 October 1874, at the age of 33

6.
On 18 January 1881
Fisher was appointed
to command H.M.S.
Inflexible, the 'last word'
in battleship design, and
the biggest and most
powerful warship in the
Royal Navy

The armoured train
built to the designs of
Fisher and A. K. Wilson
for service against Arabi
Pasha

8. The Fisher family, *circa* 1890. L to R, J. A. F., Cecil, Dorothy. Lower: Beatrix, Pamela, and their mother

9.
Admiral's cabin, H.M.S. *Renown*. Fisher, as C-in-C Mediterranean Fleet, is in the centre, between a portrait of Queen Victoria and a painting of the Battle of Trafalgar

10. John Arbuthnot Fisher, First Sea Lord, 1904

11. Fisher's favourite First Lords,
the Earl of Selborne and
Reginald McKenna

12. Taking the waters. Fisher stating his case to the Hon. H. Lawson MP, editor *Daily Telegraph*, and Major-General Sir Ivor Herbert, MP

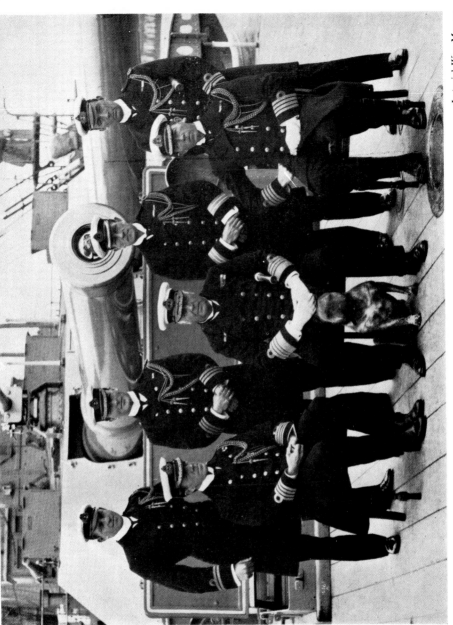

13.
Beresford and his Staff
at the height of the feud.
L to R, Flag-Lieutenant
Herbert Gibbs, Captain
F. C. D. Sturdee, Flag-
Commander Fawcett
Wray, Beresford, Fleet
Paymaster John Keys,
Flag-Captain Henry
Pelly, Lieutenant-Com-
mander Charles Roper

14. With Queen Alexandra

15.
A scrapbook fragment, annotated by Fisher. The occasion was the Royal visit to Russia in 1908

16. Fisher (right) with the Prince and Princess of Wales, later King George V and Queen Mary

17. H.M.S. *Dreadnought*, precursor of a new era of sea warfare

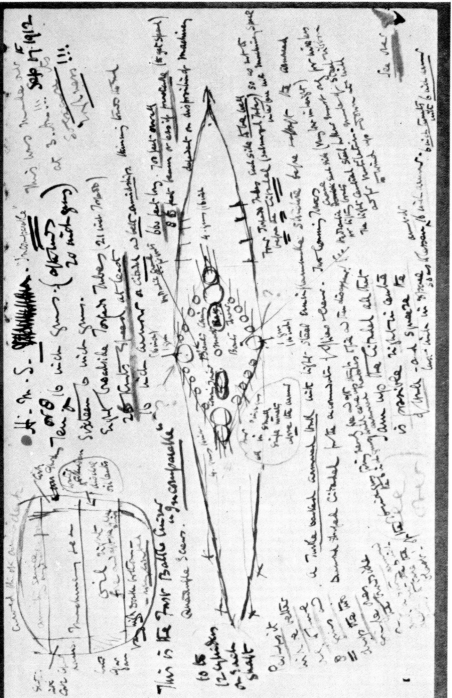

18. Fisher's restless fascination with the design of warships exemplified in a surviving drawing from the family papers.

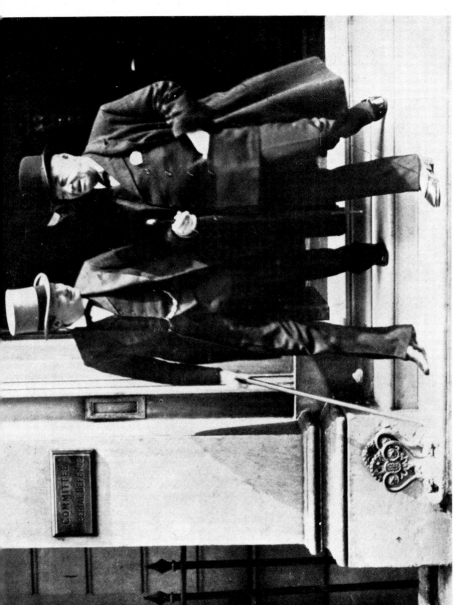

19.
The Master and Disciple: Winston Spencer Churchill and John Arbuthnot Fisher in earnest conversation after a meeting of the CID

20.
Fisher's Grand Fleet, at war with Germany and patrolling the North Sea

21. With Admiral Sir John Jellicoe

22. Nina, Duchess of Hamilton

23. Admiral of the Fleet Lord Fisher in 1917

24. *Above: En route* to Monte Carlo in 1920 with the Duchess of Hamilton
Below: The funeral procession in The Mall

renaissance as *Reichmarineamt* since 18 June 1897, and the reactionaries, the 'Bugginses', the curs and parasites who would struggle against every reform and hazard the outcome of the first contest by attempting to tie his right hand behind his back. Never in history had a fiercer or angrier officer entered the Admiralty to take over supreme command; and never had a First Sea Lord regarded the battles ahead with such evident relish.

And yet Fisher still possessed in as high a degree as ever the gentleness, kindness and thoughtfulness which had endeared him to women and children all his life, and to his shipmates as a young officer. Above all, the lower deck to a man loved him. Whatever divisions of opinion on his qualities there might have been in the past, and to an increasing degree in the future, among the officers in the service, 'Jack Tar' loved 'Jacky' Fisher, and always referred to him by his nickname. It was as simple as that. He loved his eccentric manner, his forthrightness, his style of dealing with both his seniors and his subordinates, his evident concern for their welfare, his strict and just discipline. There was no side to Jacky. To Jack Tar, he was that rare being, a democratic officer, one of them at heart.

His fitness for the tasks that lay ahead was beyond question. He had served at sea in almost every corner of the world, and he knew to a fine degree the qualities that made a good sea officer. He was probably better informed on the Navy's *matériel* needs than any other officer alive. His eyes missed nothing, and were those of a prophet. He understood and had acquired a very low opinion of the intelligence and integrity of the general run of those in power in high places. Yet he had developed a wonderful knack of bending their influence to his needs. He was on familiar terms with some of the most powerful figures in the land, and he could talk to, and delight with his wit and talent for narration and wide knowledge of the affairs of state and man, kings, prime ministers, foreign potentates and heads of state, newspaper barons, industrialists and beautiful and important women, all with equal facility. He was vain, but never boastful; and his vanity was in the innocent style of an actor or painter. He loved admiration, despised sycophancy, and derived endless delight from his popular image. His secretary once wrote that 'a medical man told him he had such a wonderful vitality that he "ought to have been twins." He was very fond of repeating this and one day he got the reply from a favourite commander, "What a mercy you were not! Just think of two of *you* in the Navy!" The idea made him chuckle.'[1] He loved to be thought 'a character' and something of a menace.

[1] 'Some Recollections of "Jacky" Fisher' by Charles Walker. Kilverstone MSS.

Fisher's industry and sense of dedication, too, were beyond question. His whole body and soul were consumed by his reform work and the struggles they brought with them. A writer who believed that Fisher 'has been learning to rule for sixten hours a day for fifty years', wrote a few days before he took up his duties: 'The world of a Naval Commander-in-Chief is crushing; but Admiral Fisher, who is never in a hurry, always gives the impression of tranquility and leisure, which is a restful contrast to the fussy importance of ordinary "busy" men . . . Sir John Fisher does his pen work with his own hand, and his output is greater than that of many a scribe in Fleet Street. Autographed letters carry greater weight than typewritten communications, and the iron constitution with which Fisher is endowed is worked at its top speed every hour of every day and every day of the year, and has helped him to make his opinions known to everyone whose influence is worth gaining.'[1]

The weaknesses which were eventually to prove his undoing were present for all to see in 1904—but only a few recognized the truth of them. Although he was so widely criticized it was mainly for the wrong reasons. Probably only Esher, who knew and understood him better than anyone, could recognize all the dangerous defects: the impatience and the weak boyish tendency to throw in the sponge if he did not get his way, all the way; the violent manner of expression which led him to over-state a case and suppress useful and constructive debate, and incense his opponents and tempt them, too, to overstate theirs, close their ears to the merits of Fisher's argument, and antagonize them; his readiness to make enemies; his reluctance to consult *after* his own mind had been made up; and finally and most seriously, his pride in his own excesses of temperament and demeanour. In 1904 the first lines in the self-caricature were already being drawn.

[1] *Pall Mall Gazette*, September 1904.

Chapter 2

'THE EDGE OF A PRECIPICE'[1]

The life and achievements of John Arbuthnot Fisher as First Sea Lord were shaped by the new realignments and new imbalances of national power which occurred around the turn of the century. France and Russia had for long been Britain's most likely foes, and naval calculations were based on the need for the Royal Navy to meet a combined attack by these two powers. The sustainment of the Royal Navy's 'two-power standard' was regarded as the first priority in the nation's defence planning. The threat by foreign rearmament to this two-to-one superiority had been the cause of the Navy 'scares' of 1888 and 1893.

By 1900 new dangers to Britain's security demanded new counter-measures. The building of three powerful Navies, by the USA, Japan and Germany, underlined the impossibility of Britannia ruling all the waves, everywhere, simultaneously, immense though her resources might be. In the Western Hemisphere political and naval predominance had already been yielded to the USA. Now Japan was building a substantial Navy which must soon outnumber British naval units in the Far East. But neither of these powers seriously threatened Britain. The direct threat, a dangerous and sinister one, was developing close to British territorial waters.

The 1898 German Navy Law provided for the construction of nineteen battleships and numerous smaller craft. It was, as one historian has recently defined it, 'no ordinary piece of military legislation. It began a new era. The emphasis in German military affairs shifted dramatically from the land to the sea. From April 1898 to August 1914, the Fleet, which the *Flottengesetz* of 1898 called into being, dominated Germany's international relations. After centuries of preoccupation

---

[1] '. . . I lunched with Jackie to-day and Francis Knollys at the Carlton. Jackie feels that he is standing on the edge of a precipice to which all great reformers are led, and over which they ultimately fall . . .'. Esher to his son, 3 January 1907. (*Esher*, ii, 215.)

with her land forces, Germany altered her defence priorities and now committed herself to a supreme effort to attain "standing" at sea with the dominant naval power of the day.'[1]

Britain's troubles in South Africa, and the resulting humiliations to Germany at sea, with British cruisers searching German merchantmen for contraband, helped von Tirpitz to get through the even more threatening Naval Act of 1900. Kaiser Wilhelm II announced in bellicose terms that he would make his Navy the equal to his Army. The challenge to the Royal Navy was too overt to be disregarded, especially when the nature of the ships became known and they were seen to have been designed for operation primarily in the Baltic and the North Sea.

Troubles in a part of the world remote from the North Sea helped Britain, by happy chance rather than by shrewd diplomacy, to take the first countermeasures against this threat. In the Far East Russian intransigence was causing as much worry to Britain as it was to that newly self-emancipated and newly powerful nation, Japan. In 1902 Japan and Britain came to terms and struck a useful bargain: if Britain would do her best to befriend France and restrain her from supporting her ally Russia, Japan would do all she could to counter Russian Far East aggrandizement, with Britain's support. Thus was formed the Anglo-Japanese Alliance, the first step to allow the greater concentration in home waters of Britain's scattered naval strength to meet the North Sea threat from Germany. As a result of Russian naval ineptitude, and the skill and courage and good luck of Japan's Navy, the Russians suffered a series of stunning naval defeats in 1904, and in 1905 virtual annihilation of her fleet at the Battle of Tsushima.

The cooling down of Anglo-French hostility was the most important diplomatic move in the new century. Fisher had for long advocated friendship with France, and Edward VII in 1903 and 1904 helped to prepare the ground for the *Entente Cordiale*. The main part of the Anglo-French ArbitrationTreaty was signed on 8 April 1904. Although the primary intention was to settle long-drawn-out colonial quarrels, it now became possible, and militarily advantageous, for Britain to redeploy her naval strength to meet the growing threat from Germany. The redeployment and the manner in which it was carried out, and the related improvement in efficiency in the service, were the causes of the conflicts which increasingly soured the Fisher régime and divided the Navy into two hostile groups.

Redeployment and concentration resulted in the reduction of status, responsibility and comfort of overseas appointments, in the prestige of

[1] Jonathan Steinberg, *Yesterday's Deterrent* (London, 1965), 201.

consuls who could no longer request the presence of a squadron of men-of-war to deal with recalcitrant natives or embellish a social occasion, and the loss of hundreds of related sinecures. None of this could be accomplished without causing protest and outrage in a service in which the compound of social routine and protocol on foreign stations had set into an almost indestructible mould. Fisher, armed with a pick and the muscular power to wield it effectively, could never hope to be loved for breaking it up.

The creation of an efficient, battle-worthy fighting force out of a mainly sleepy and self-contented group of officers and a mainly obsolete mass of fighting ships, brought much discontent, too, for scrapped ships meant scrapped appointments, from dockyard officials to Flag officers. The creation of controversial new fighting vessels brought about disaffection, too, as it always had done. Not long before, the discarding of masts and yards, and the introduction of iron-hulled ships, had caused outrage. New men-of-war demanded new tactics and battle practice. These were discomfiting enough anyway (gun firing meant stained paintwork and tarnished brass and generally shook things up), but Fisher's insistence on fighting efficiency and his intro- duction of new classes of fighting ships were very serious disturbances for conservative-minded officers.

New forms of entry into the service, new training and education, new and controversial ships and the wholesale destruction of old ships, new minor reforms in every department of the Navy, and above all the recall from foreign parts of numerous unnecessary ships, and the officers and men who manned them, and the creation of new fleets in home water were all acts calculated to bring disfavour onto the head of the man responsible for them. Fisher suffered the consequences, from anonymous abuse to virtual mutiny in high places, during his term of office. But it was the human results of the concentration on home waters of the Navy's most powerful Fleets which provided the catalyst for the greatest outcry, split the Navy from top to bottom, and broke up the 'band of brothers' spirit which had existed since the days of Horatio Nelson.

There were numerous Royal Navy squadrons in distant parts of the world because of the widespread nature of British interests, colonies and possessions, and because in the days of sail and slow communications there had to be adequate strength immediately available to deal with any trouble which might arise. Steam power, communication by cable and later by wireless, diminished and then eliminated the need for this multiplication of squadrons all over the world. But in 1904 nothing had been done to reduce the numbers of these ships, which were eating up money from the estimates every year and contributing nothing to the fighting efficiency of the Royal Navy where the country was most seriously threatened. Most of the ships were old and useless, and 'they could neither fight nor run away'. Fisher brought them home and scrapped them. The permanent South Atlantic, North America and Pacific squadrons were eliminated altogether. There was much outcry over these drastic measures, especially from old retired Admirals. Fisher's secretary one day 'asked him whether he ever saw anything of Sir Frederick Richards with whom at one time he had been very friendly. "Never", he said, "the old man thoroughly disapproves of me; at the Club not long ago he was heard to murmur, 'He may be a very clever fellow but he abolished Jamaica.' " '[1]

Many ruses were practised to evade or defer the orders to close down comfortable establishments and bring home comfortable ships. Even the major Fleets were affected. Admiral Sir Charles Drury, the C.-in-C. of the Mediterranean Fleet, found that he was losing his yacht. But he 'was a wily old man', wrote one of his subordinates, 'and he arranged for the *Hussar* to be attached to his Fleet as a dispatch vessel. Once he got us out to Malta our guns, all save two small ones for saluting purposes, and torpedo tubes were removed and the erstwhile gun boat was converted into a very fine yacht. Extra cabins were built . . . Furniture, fittings, carpets, and interior decorations were of the finest.'[2]

The withdrawal of aged gunboats and whole squadrons caused some alarm to local consuls. An earthquake in Jamaica and a mutiny among the military police in Zanzibar both occurred after the withdrawal of Royal Navy units which could have done useful service. The Colonial Office received complaints and Fisher was attacked in the press for failing in his duties.

TO JAMES R. THURSFIELD

Admiralty, Whitehall
January, 20th, 1907

Private
Dear Thursfield,

. . . I see the *Globe* has a leading article attacking the Admiralty for not having an ambulance corps of cruisers and gunboats distributed over the earthquake area of the globe! (That's not a joke!) The Navy Estimates would be a hundred millions if everyone had everything!

The funny thing is we get a most cordial and unaccustomed official letter from Lord Elgin thanking the Admiralty for sending two cruisers loaded with

[1] Sir Charles Walker, *Thirty-six Years at the Admiralty* (London, 1934), 52.
[2] J. M. Kenworthy, *Sailors, Statesmen and Others* (London, 1933), 35.

tents and provisions from Trinidad and Bermuda so very promptly and expeditiously! The *Globe* calmly suppresses these two cruisers, the *Indefatigable* and *Brilliant!* What a surpassing advantage it is to be able to lie freely!

Ever yours,
J. A. Fisher

Troubles in Turkey drew attention to the lack of adequate naval protection for British nationals. On 4 October 1906 Fisher wrote to the First Lord that colonial officers, consuls and ambassadors 'quite unduly magnify any want of Admiralty attention to their requests, but we cannot possibly get the Navy Estimates down to the figure which I think the House of Commons will insist upon sooner or later, unless we strictly confine our naval expenditure to *absolutely necessary services*, and it can be incontestably proved that any reasonable requirement of the Foreign Office or the Colonial Office has never been resisted by the Admiralty. Just by way of example, let me mention the second *stationnaire* at Constantinople, by Sir T. Sanderson, and by Lord Lansdowne. The Admiralty said *non possumus*, and here we have it not long ago from Sir E. Grey that we were right. That saved £15,000 a year, in the upkeep of a useless vessel for fighting purposes, but much more— it saved the deterioration of a fighting ship's crew . . .'.

Fisher was preparing for war, in home waters. He believed that it was inevitable, and that all the resources of the Navy must be deployed to meet the attack when it came. Elsewhere there must be efficient squadrons, organized for rapid concentration, to protect British trade and meet imperial responsibilities. His policy was widely propounded in the press by his journalist friends:

'On the 21st October, 1904, it was resolved that the venerable arrangements for the disposition of the Fleet then in force, which had lasted since 1812, should be brought up to date. The [old] arrangement pleased the Foreign Office and the Consuls' daughters, many of whom are extremely attractive girls who doted on the 1812 arrangement because, after all, there is no white male quite so agreeable as the British naval officer, whether he is a middy in his first commission or a retired Admiral, full of years and honours, who devotes a good deal of his life to attacks on the Admiralty. Though the old system of distribution was popular, there was one fatal mistake in it. For lawn tennis, waltzing, relief or distress, or ambulance work after an earthquake it was admirable; for war purposes it was useless, because the force was divided and subdivided and was largely composed of ships that could neither fight an enemy nor escape him. The change was made on the principle that Germany, not earthquakes, was the objective;

that Teutonic, not seismic, disturbances were the business of the Navy.'[1]

The end of the aged gunboat policy was at first unacceptable to people better informed than consul's daughters. The Prince of Wales had his first difference of opinion with Fisher on the subject.

FROM THE PRINCE OF WALES

York Cottage
Sandringham
November 10th, 1904

Private
My dear Sir John,

. . . If you are going to remove the squadron in the Pacific because the ships are obsolete, you ought to send some new ones to take their place, at least that is my opinion. I consider that this question is much more than a naval one and that the whole thing should be carefully considered from every point of view, and that the Colonial Secretary and Prime Minister should both be consulted, and also the Foreign Secretary. But no doubt you will bring it up before the Defence Committee. Forgive me for having brought up this question, but I feel rather strong on it, and, of course, it applies to the other squadrons you talked of removing . . .

Believe me, most sincerely yours,
George

It was the expensive misuse of naval resources which Fisher was determined to eliminate. Wastage of any kind affronted him, and from October 1904 he applied his 'three R's' to its elimination overseas. The wastage stemmed from many sources. Here he cites one perpetrated by the officer with whom conflict on far larger issues was shortly to break out:

'Lord Charles Beresford goes to Mexico on private business and sees the President. "In the course of conversation the Admiral mentioned that some British vessels were to visit American waters during the coming season, and the President signified with emphasis what satisfaction it would cause him were the vessels to pay a visit to Mexico."

'The British Minister therefore urges that a British squadron should visit Mexico, and the Foreign Office "hope that the Lords Commissioners may see their way to make arrangements for a visit".

'Luckily, Admiral Inglefield (with his squadron) happens to be in West Indian waters, and, therefore, it is not necessary to send the First Cruiser Squadron to Vera Cruz; but no one except the Admiralty takes any account of the cost in coal and wear and tear of engines in the

[1] *Bacon*, i, 300.

squadron steaming an extra 3,500 miles; nor, apparently, till Lord Charles suggests the idea, was any necessity seen for the visit.'[1]

The withdrawal of ships from remote stations abroad and the formation of efficient and homogenous squadrons which could if necessary rapidly join forces, was carried out in spite of doubts in high places and protests from many small colonies. The concentration of the great battle fleets in home waters had to be accomplished more slowly and more judiciously. However certain Fisher and the more realistic of his associates might be that the new German battle fleet was being built exclusively to challenge British naval omnipotence, it was politically undesirable to acerbate the situation by completing the redeployment hastily or ostentatiously. Referring to this policy, which was the direct cause of the public conflict with Beresford, the Admiralty in 1909 defended its position by claiming that a single Home Fleet 'could not have been created in 1904 without unduly straining the international political situation, and it was necessary to proceed with the utmost caution owing to the sensitive state of public opinion in Great Britain and Germany. The Admiralty claimed that they have arrived at the result aimed at comparatively unobtrusively, and without causing political complications, while the safety of the country has always been fully assured.'[2]

The sensitiveness of the situation was emphasized when in July 1905 Fisher ordered the Channel Fleet into the Baltic and North Sea for manoeuvres. 'Our drill ground should be our battle ground' was the phrase he coined and quoted to Julian Corbett the naval historian, but begging him not to repeat it, although 'I've taken means to have it whispered in the German Emperor's ear!' These manoeuvres on her doorstep caused dismay in Germany and were used by the German Navy League, the *Deutscher Flottenverein* formed in Berlin in 1898, to promote their demands for a stronger fleet.

Evidence of the phased concentration of naval strength in home waters was first seen in June 1905. The Battle of Tsushima (27–28 May) and the almost total elimination of Russian naval power, made it possible to withdraw all the five battleships from the China station. The C.-in-C., Admiral Sir Gerard Noel, was outraged, and Fisher witnessed the first 'fumes of anger exuding from these scandalized Admirals'.[3] It was only a mild foretaste of what was to come.

This incident also provided evidence of how slack was discipline and

[1] *Bacon*, i, 301–2.
[2] Committee of Imperial Defence Inquiry, 12 August 1909. Lennoxlove MSS.
[3] *Memories*, 246.

how weakened the power of the Board of Admiralty had become after a hundred years without a major war. Noel informed the First Lord that he did not think it wise that all his battleships should be taken from him, especially as the American Navy had three first-class battleships on the spot; it was an 'indignity to the C.-in-C.', he complained. The First Lord strongly rebuked him, told him to obey his orders and to address himself to the Board and not to the First Lord personally in future.[1] Noel never forgave Fisher; nor, no doubt, did many of his staff and senior officers on this remote station. This was only one small example of how speedily a reformer caused pain in a service stiffened in every limb by a century's inaction.

The protests became louder and much more widespread twenty months later. In October 1906 the Admiralty issued a memorandum entitled *The Home Fleet* which had as its theme the need to reduce the strength of the outlying Fleets, Britain's 'only potential foe now being Germany'.[2] The proposed new Home Fleet was to consist of three divisions, stationed at Devonport, Portsmouth and Sheerness. The Nore Division at Sheerness in the Thames estuary and nearest to Germany was to consist of six fully manned battleships. The other two divisions, with seven battleships between them, were to be manned by nucleus crews, a system for the more efficient manning of ships held in reserve which Fisher had foreshadowed two years earlier.[3] The Admiralty claimed that these nucleus crew ships could put to sea and engage an enemy within a few hours. The critics would have none of this. They contended that Fisher was withdrawing protection from the Empire by taking battleships away from the Channel, Atlantic and Mediterranean Fleets and scattering them, in a half ready condition, about the home ports. The Foreign Office at once expressed its alarm. The Under-Secretary of State for Foreign Affairs, Sir Charles Hardinge, wrote that 'It is childish to expect sane people to believe that ships with nucleus crews lying in home ports can be regarded as efficient items in a fleet . . . Also it can hardly be denied that the ships available for police duties abroad will be considerably reduced and British interest and policy will suffer for the sake of concentration in the Channel against a possible attack by Germany which even Fisher regards as a very remote eventuality.'[4]

This letter from the Foreign Office, which claimed more knowledge of naval policy than that of the First Sea Lord, who could well counter-

---

[1] See Arthur J. Marder, *From the Dreadnought to Scapa Flow* (London, 4 vols, 1961–9), i, 85. (Hereafter cited as *Marder*.)

[2] Admiralty MSS., cited *Marder*, i, 71.

[3] *Distribution and Mobilization of the Fleet*, a memorandum issued 6 December 1904.

[4] *Marder*, i, 73.

claim that he appreciated better than the Foreign Office the aggressive intentions of Germany, was addressed to Knollys. The King's secretary agreed, and argued that the nucleus crew fleet could never be as efficient as a fully manned fleet. 'To my mind this contention is contrary to common sense,' he wrote to Esher.

Esher, who missed nothing, and was as deeply involved in the inner workings of Britain's defence counsels as anyone, knew better than Knollys the reasons underlying Fisher's long term plans and the agonizing need to keep them secret, which meant that he must fight his enemies with one hand tied behind his back. On 21 December 1906, Fisher made one of his frequent visits to Esher's London residence at 2, Tilney Street. After he left Esher wrote to his son: 'I saw Jackie for 1½ hours this afternoon. He expounded for my benefit his strategical plans, especially in view of a hostile Germany. They are too secret to write down. He sits still under calumny, because to reply would necessarily entail revelation of our strength and the main strategical idea. In point of fact, our power is six times that of Germany at the given point of battle. He discussed with me his own position, and the difficulties raised by his enemies, and his danger from their animosity . . .'[1]

The Prince of Wales still did not fully understand the implications behind Fisher's new arrangements. He wrote anxiously to his father, and King Edward summoned Fisher to Buckingham Palace to read him extracts which revealed the Prince's 'deep anxiety as to the reported approaching re-arrangement by the Admiralty of the fighting disposition of the Fleet', and claimed that it 'was open to the gravest condemnation'. At the end of 'a very prolonged interview', Fisher convinced the King of the validity of his case, and was ordered to send the King's sailor son 'an exact repetition of all I had said'. This Fisher attempted to do in the following terms:

Our only probable enemy is Germany. Germany keeps her *whole* Fleet always concentrated within a few hours of England. We must therefore keep a Fleet twice as powerful concentrated within a few hours of Germany.

If we kept the Channel and Atlantic Fleets *always* in the English Channel (say in the vicinity of the Nore), this would meet the case, but this is neither feasible nor expedient, and if, when relations with foreign powers are strained, the Admiralty attempt to take the proper fighting precautions and move our Channel and Atlantic Fleets to their proper fighting position, then *at once* the Foreign Office and the Government veto it, and say such a step will precipitate war! This actually happened on the recent occasion of the German Government presenting an ultimatum to acquire a coaling station at Madeira, and the German Minister was ordered to leave Lisbon at 10 p.m. on a certain Sunday

[1] *Esher*, ii, 209–10.

night, and war was imminent, as Lord Lansdowne had told Portugal England would back her. The Board of Admiralty don't intend ever again to subject themselves to this risk, and they have decided to form a new Home Fleet always at home, with its Headquarters at the Nore and its cruising ground the North Sea.

('Your battle ground should be your drill ground,' said Nelson!)

The politicians and the diplomatists will not be the people the Public will hang if the British Navy fails to annihilate the whole German Fleet and gobble up every single one of those 842 German merchant steamers now daily on the ocean! *No*—it will be the Sea Lords! and as one distinguished retrograde Admiral, Sir Gerard Noel (who wants to build sailing men-of-war), told the King, I am to have the proud pre-eminence of Haman amongst the Sea Lords. I never have been able to ascertain how high Haman was hung, but it couldn't have been higher than Noel wishes me! and yet I patiently enjoy his receiving the high and important command of the Nore! If this isn't charity, I don't know what it is. I digress to make this remark to Your Royal Highness, as I am accused of relentless hate towards those who differ from me!

To return to the argument:—The only way to obtain this new 'Home Fleet' is by moving six battleships and four armoured cruisers from the Channel, Mediterranean, and Atlantic Fleets (observing that these 3 Fleets are 50 per cent stronger than the present political situation demands) and combining them with the best of the battleships and cruisers now in commission in Reserve, forming an '*Escadre d'Élite*,' backed up by the remainder of the ships in Reserve, as the Reserve or Second Division of this new Home Fleet. The whole of the torpedo craft (some 150 in number) and the whole of the submarines will be incorporated with this '*Escadre d'Élite*' of the Home Fleet, and their crews so increased as to be almost at full strength.

Admiral Bridgeman (about the best Admiral we have) is to be the Commander-in-Chief of this new Home Fleet, with his Headquarters at the Nore and his cruising ground the North Sea, where the fight will be! perhaps off Heligoland (which was won by the sword and given up by the pen!).

The Board of Admiralty have also decided to adopt a 'sliding scale' of nucleus crews—thus the most important vessels will have the largest nucleus crews, and the least important not perhaps more than a skeleton crew. For instance, the 'Royal Sovereign' class of battleship, almost obsolete and dangerous for the line of battle owing to their unarmed [unarmoured?] ends as against modern high explosive shell, will be relegated to the lowest scale of crew, whilst those required for the first brunt of war will be almost at concert pitch!

This new 'Home Fleet' thus called into being by Mr Balfour's famous 'stroke of the pen' almost admits of more seagoing work being given to the ships in Reserve, *together with the essential fighting training they do not now get in Battle Practice and other important Fleet Exercises.*

I beg you, Sir, to note especially the following facts:—By this new distribution of the Fleet *not a single ship will be paid off, nor is there the reduction of one single man serving on board ship, and the Fleet, AS A WHOLE, will have more sea work than at present,* but there is also this further advantage, of immense value, that if any ship in the Channel, Mediterranean, or Atlantic Fleets, has to be long absent from her cruising ground, on account of repairs, her place will be AT ONCE temporarily filled from the Home Fleet.

Pure party feeling solely dictates the present '*Press*' agitation. The Board of Admiralty and *no one else whatever* can be responsible for the distribution of the Fleet for War, and the Board is united and determined in their belief that they are acting for the good of the Navy and the safety of the Empire in this and every other step which has been taken. *Reduced Navy Estimates are no sign of reduced naval efficiency.* On the contrary, swollen Estimates engender parasites, both in men and ships, which hamper the fighting qualities of the Fleet. The pruning knife ain't pleasant for fossils and ineffectives, but it has to be used, and the tree is more vigorous for the loss of excrescences.

I am, Sir, Your Royal Highness's obedient servant,
J. A. Fisher

All this appears to have satisfied the Prince of Wales, who invited Fisher to lunch. Afterwards, Fisher was able to enjoy the pleasure of writing to Knollys: '*He is cordially in agreement with all the Admiralty are doing.* I was two hours with His Royal Highness . . .'

Sir Charles Hardinge persisted in his expression of doubts about the redistribution of the Fleets, and again the King was involved. The Foreign Office Memorandum Hardinge prepared was read by the King, and promptly refuted by Fisher in a letter to King Edward dated 3 November 1906. In the candid and forthright style in which Fisher now felt able to express himself to his Sovereign, he wrote: 'The absolute fact is that the Admiralty always knows better than the Foreign Office and more wisely than the Consuls when vessels are likely to be required, because the Naval officer on the spot is invariably a better and more reliable judge than the frightened or gunboat-desiring Consuls, who one and all pine for the prestige of the presence of a man-of-war within signalling distance of the consular flagstaff and for the consular salute of seven guns!

' . . . The statement on page 3 [of the memorandum] that the effective strength of the seagoing Fleets is being reduced to a dangerous minimum is absolutely erroneous, *for the exact contrary is the fact!* The real truth is we have enormously increased both our readiness for war and our *instant* fighting strength, but to give these fighting details would be simply suicidal, for, if circulated (however confidentially), they would be at the German Admiralty in a week.' Fisher then went on to quote to the King the statement made by the Foreign Secretary himself, Sir Edward Grey, that 'no department, *nor any one else* must question the steps taken by the Board of Admiralty in the disposition of the fighting units of the Fleet.'

The withdrawal of naval strength from overseas struck deeply at the roots of British national pride and the national sense of imperial responsibility. It smacked of cowardice, of leaving the colonies and dominions 'in the lurch'. This was one reason for the spontaneous outburst of protest. The Conservative press felt further impelled to attack Fisher and all his works, for political reasons. The Liberal government of Campbell-Bannerman had been formed in December 1905, and the Conservative newspapers were on a keen lookout for signs of supposed cowardice and weakness. Fisher provided them with a fine target. He was, they claimed, aiding and abetting the new government by practising false and dangerous economies; and they could point, too, to the reduction in warship building since Fisher had come to power.

From this time until Fisher's retirement more than three years later, the press divided itself almost as clearly over Fisher policy as did the Navy itself. Loyal to Fisher were most of the Liberal media, journalists and proprietors: the *Daily News*, the *Observer*, the *Westminster Gazette*, and J. L. Garvin, Arnold White, J. R. Thursfield, Archibald Hurd, J. A. Spender, Julian Corbett and W. T. Stead. In addition, Fisher could usually count on the invaluable support of the normally conservative newspapers, *The Times* and the *Daily Telegraph*. But Fisher could rarely rely on a favourable word in the *Daily Express* and *Daily Mail*, the *Morning Post*, *Spectator*, *Globe* and *Standard*; and never from naval journalists like H. W. Wilson, Spenser Wilkinson, and later, Beresford's old crony, Custance, who styled himself 'Barfleur' when he went on half-pay to take up the pen against the Admiralty.

To the dismay of his enemies, and of many uncommitted naval officers who succeeded in remaining outside the area of combat, Fisher continued even more intensely than before to encourage by all means, and feed with private information, the journalists supporting his cause, and to attack those who opposed his reforms. 'You've fired a fine broadside in the *Spectator* this week!' began a typical letter of encouragement to Arnold White (31 December 1906). 'Hit them between wind and water!'

The terms of abuse hurled by the members of the opposition party at Fisher—the 'Syndicate of Discontent' as he sometimes referred to them—were quite as extreme, and no one was as free with his language as the syndicate's self-appointed leader, Lord Charles Beresford.

Early in 1905 Beresford was a Vice-Admiral and Commander-in-Chief of the Atlantic Fleet, comprising eleven battleships and seven cruisers. Many years of good living had made him fat and awkward in his movements. At 59 he was still remarkably good-looking, and he had a full head of striking white hair. His charm and gaiety had in no way diminished and he possessed in as full measure as ever the talent for attracting women. The lower deck loved him. Many officers, too, were strongly attracted to him, but they tended to be of an inferior calibre to those who served close to, say, Arthur Wilson and to Fisher himself. Those who served close to Beresford and aided and abetted him during the years of strife numbered in their ranks a high proportion of officers who were clever, ambitious trouble-makers like Custance, or sycophantic officers of limited intellect. Among this second class were Fawcett Wray and Doveton Sturdee who committed disastrous errors of judgement in 1914. All failed to recognize the limitations of the man they admired for his social standing, audacity, spirit and genial manner. All these officers were looking forward with hopeful expectation to the day when their leader would succeed Fisher, or even displace him, as First Sea Lord, with favourable consequences for themselves.

Relations between Fisher and Beresford had remained quiescent since they had served together in the Mediterranean but this was only because Beresford had been on half-pay for much of the time, and had got back into Parliament again as member for Woolwich. Beresford was not at his best in the Chamber. He was not a good public speaker, and was worse still as a debater. His mind was not quick enough and he never understood the special subtle interplay of parliamentary debate. He boomed away inarticulately, repeating himself and boring the house with his poorly synchronized broadsides against the Navy's adminis-tration. The Speaker once broke into one of his interminable harangues, 'The noble Lord is not entitled to go into the whole condition of the Fleet in the Mediterranean.'

But such was Beresford's heroic popularity in the country, where he often made widely reported speeches attacking the administration of the Navy, that the Board was seriously embarrassed. Selborne and Kerr promoted him to Vice-Admiral, and appointed him to command the Channel Fleet. Beresford gave up his seat in Parliament and hoisted his flag as C.-in-C. on 17 April 1903. Beresford, temporarily silenced, gave his attention to improving the efficiency of his Fleet. He was at his best at sea and he handled his ships well.

By one of the curious chances of fate that marked the relations between the two Admirals, a disaster occurred, within hours of Fisher's assump-tion of office, which was to lead to an international crisis and a fresh outbreak of personal conflict. On the night of 21–22 October 1904, a Russian Fleet under the command of Vice-Admiral Zinovy Petrovitch Rozhestvensky, bound for the Far East war with Japan, steamed into the midst of a British trawler fleet in the North Sea. The Russians were in a highly nervous condition as a result of earlier Japanese victories and the dissemination of ridiculous rumours that the Japanese in concert with their British friends had dispatched torpedo boats in pursuit of them. The confused Admiral had ordered fire to be opened on the supposed Japanese men-of-war. A British trawler had been sunk, and there were a number of casualties. British outrage knew no bounds, and for some days there was a serious risk of war. 'What do you say to the wonderful behaviour of the Russian Baltic Fleet,' wrote the Prince of Wales to Fisher (24 October 1904), 'who attack and sink a harmless fishing fleet in the North Sea in the middle of the night. If they start like that I don't think they will ever reach their destination . . . And fancy none of the ships stopping to pick up the wounded, after they had found out their mistake . . .'

Instructions to meet the crisis were transmitted from the Admiralty, and Beresford, with his main Fleet at Gibraltar, was deeply involved in the crisis. Units from his Fleet shadowed the Russian ships as they made their way towards Spanish ports in search of coal and supplies, and his battleships were deployed to destroy the weak, confused and heterogeneous Russian squadrons.

The breach between the two powers was healed within a few days, but old wounds between the new First Sea Lord and the C.-in-C. of the Fleet deputed to deal with the Russians were reopened when Beresford was ordered to submit to the Admiralty the plans he had prepared. They included the following astonishing statement: 'Being quite satisfied with the excellence of the gunnery of the Channel Fleet I should only have engaged the Russians at Tangier (in the event of their refusing to proceed into Gibraltar) with four of my battleships, at a distance of from 5000 to 6000 yards. It appeared to me that this would only be chivalrous, under the circumstances. If the Russian ships had commenced to knock my ships about I would have engaged them with the whole 8 Channel Fleet Battleships . . .'[1]

The Admiralty was outraged by the conceit and the amateur sporting doctrine directing his policy. '[It] could not have been justified on any grounds, and least of all on those of sentiment. In warlike operations such considerations cannot be allowed to have any place, and in any situation similar to that referred to, their Lordships would expect and require you to make use of the whole of the force at your disposal.' Prince Louis, the DNI, commented, 'If this statement became public property, the taxpayers would probably enquire why they were paying for the other half [of the Fleet] . . .' And Fisher added angrily, 'Lord Nelson's dictum was "the greater your superiority over the enemy the better" and he was a chivalrous man!'[2]

---

[1] *British Naval Policy*, 440.   [2] *ibid.*, 441 n.

Beresford was due to haul down his flag on 7 March 1905, when his two year appointment terminated, and there were suggestions that he might take over command in the Mediterranean, a Fleet diminished in relative strength since the *Entente Cordiale* and Fisher's first redeployment which had followed its signature. Fisher determined to show his displeasure by relieving Beresford before his time was up, and the news that he was expected to relinquish his command a month earlier unfortunately reached Beresford first from his successor, Rear-Admiral Sir William May.

According to one witness, 'Beresford wrote back [to May] that he would be very glad to give him lunch or fight him, but he would not be superseded. Beresford then went up to see Lord Selborne, who said he could do nothing, but referred him to Fisher. Fisher said to Beresford that all arrangements had been made for May to relieve him on the earlier date, and that he wanted Beresford to come on a Committee. Beresford said he did not intend to be superseded, nor would he go on a Committee. Fisher then replied:—"Well, then, you will not go to the Mediterranean," upon which all the pent-up wrath of years between the two men broke out, and Beresford said: "You dare to threaten me, Jacky Fisher. Who are you? I only take my orders from the Board. If I have to haul my flag down on the 7th February, I will resign the Service, go down to Birmingham, get into the House and turn out both you and Selborne. What is more, I will go to the Mediterranean, and I will not go on a Committee." '[1]

It was probably Selborne who persuaded Fisher to cancel the order and let Beresford have his way. Better the Mediterranean than a seat in Parliament with its accompanying public tirades against the Board, especially during the crucial months ahead when the most controversial of Fisher's reforms would be effected. In March Fisher lost the wise and calming support of Selborne, who accepted the appointment of Governor-General of South Africa.

Three months later Beresford hoisted his flag as C.-in-C. Mediterranean Fleet, from which so recently Fisher, and Beresford as second-in-command, had separately bombarded an earlier Board with complaints and demands.

There now followed a wary and watchful interlude in the relations between the two Admirals. Fisher was due to retire when he reached the age of 65 in January 1906, and, encouraged by his supporters and especially by Lady Beresford, an ambitious socialite who dearly longed for her husband's promotion and all the power and pleasure in the London society world this appointment traditionally offered, Beresford

[1] *Sea Saga*, 326.

sustained his hopes of succeeding Fisher as First Sea Lord. In the meanwhile he enjoyed the pleasures of the Mediterranean and, as the self-
appointed leader of 'the Syndicate of Discontent', more quietly at first,
continued to attack the reforms and the authority of the Board. He
also continued to canvass the support of the press, and attempted to
undermine the loyalty to Fisher of officers as high-ranking and influential as Prince Louis and the Prince of Wales.

Beresford could not hope to carry out this campaign without the
knowledge of the Board. Not all those about him were loyal to his cause.
Among the disaffected was Reginald Bacon. Encouraged by Fisher,
Bacon wrote confidential letters from the Mediterranean which described in detail the activities of the 'Syndicate'.

FROM CAPTAIN REGINALD H. BACON

H.M.S. Irresistible
[off Corfu]
[April ?, 1906]

Secret
Dear Sir John,

The Prince of Wales arrived here on Monday [April 9th] and, of course,
we went on board to be received. He seized on me at once, and was full of the
opposition he had heard of in some quarters of the Navy to the new schemes
of reform and that the Navy was becoming full of cliques, which was bad, etc.,
etc.; that the senior officers might perhaps be more consulted and more carried
with the reforms—more diplomacy, etc., etc. Evidently, from what he said,
Admiral Moore, Admiral Poë, and probably the two Admirals here (Lord
Charles Beresford and Admiral Lambton) had been wailing and bemoaning
the schemes and their exclusion from consultation. He asked if I wrote to you
and whether I did not represent to you the Service feeling, etc., and, although
he still professed adherence to the reforms, he evidently has been badly 'got at'
by the opposition, and they have had a full chance of airing their grievances.
Well, he talked so much and, I must say, so fluently and so well, that I could
with difficulty get in a word. But I told him he must remember that the Navy
was ultra-conservative and hated reforms. He complained that the Admiralty
only issued the arguments on their side of the question and never those against.
But I pointed out that the Admiralty issued arguments on their side merely to
confute those produced against the scheme, and that he need have little fear
that the whole of the opposite side of the case was not put before the public by
Admirals Bridge, Custance, and Fitzgerald, or that the agitators in the active
service were at all shy in providing them with every argument against the
scheme. He was of opinion that somehow the scheme might have been introduced with less friction. But, I pointed out, it *had* to come in; there was bound
to be great opposition, and to have consulted the senior officers earlier would
have meant merely starting the opposition earlier, but that I did think it would

have been better to have issued a popular statement of the whole scheme to the Navy, and that I think should be done now.

Well, I went away and wrote a paper on the subject, and sent a copy to Commodore Tyrwhitt and asked him to get the Prince of Wales to read it, also to get me an interview with His Royal Highness, because after a couple of days' thought more potent arguments come to the mind than when a bolt from the blue is launched at you. Well, this time was not wasted, as last night I dined on board the Royal Yacht, and after dinner the King sent for me, and after talking about submarine boats His Majesty hinted that he had heard that there was considerable opposition, and asked whether the schemes could not have perhaps been launched with less friction, saying that, of course, he knew that the Navy was ultraconservative and hated reforms. Well, I simply gave him my paper in a condensed form. I am not a courtier, never was, and never will be, but I can talk straight, which I did, on the lines of the paper, and quoted the anecdote of the naval officers turning dishonest, etc., and told His Majesty straight out that what the Navy was suffering from was want of loyalty to the Admiralty among the Admirals afloat; that any scheme they did not approve of, although their knowledge could not compare with that of the Admiralty, instead of accepting loyally, some (of course, not all) thought they were justified in throwing discipline to the winds and agitating privately against their governing body, the Admiralty. I think the King agreed to this; at all events His Majesty seemed interested and acquiesced. I think both the King and the Prince of Wales cordially approve the reforms, but the opposition admirals have been shaking their heads and grieving, and naturally the Prince of Wales has been impressed, and mentioned this to the King. . . .

Yours very sincerely,
R.H. Bacon

Recognizing the acute threat to his power if Beresford won over the support of the Prince of Wales, Fisher wrote (15 April 1906) to the Prince as soon as he heard Bacon's news that Beresford had been working on him, especially on the subject of the Osborne Scheme, which continued to arouse deep passions in the service. 'Believe me, Sir', ran part of Fisher's letter, 'that every single item and detail of the New Scheme has been pondered over and worried threadbare to make it perfection, and it is absolutely certain to be a success, but there must be no tinkering and no compromise.' Citing three of Beresford's strongest supporters, Admirals Cyprian Bridge, Custance and C. C. Penrose FitzGerald, Fisher complained to the Prince that they 'won't go to Osborne and Dartmouth to see the actual education going on. They don't want to be converted!' As to Beresford, he had once been one of the strongest supporters of the scheme, and now he was 'writing *exactly opposite* to what he wrote two years ago. It is all in print.'

All Beresford's hopes of succeeding as First Sea Lord in 1906 were dashed by Fisher's promotion on 4 December 1905 to the rank of Admiral of the Fleet, which automatically gave him five more years of active service. Simultaneously he was awarded the Order of Merit. Beresford's expectations of receiving the appointment at the end of 1910, when he would be 64, were so slim that he was forced to the conclusion that now his only chance was effectively to discredit Fisher in order that he would be forced to resign. From this time he devoted all his resources, all the means in his power, to toppling his enemy.

In justice to the popular 'Charlie B.', it should be added that he and his supporters sincerely believed that Fisher's rule was undermining the strength of the Navy, and hazarding the security of Britain and the Empire. They believed that every one of his 'reforms' was either retrograde or actually dangerous, and they could cite in support of their claims that the Selborne Scheme, the scrapping policy, the withdrawal of units and squadrons from more distant waters and the concentration of the battle fleet in home waters, the nucleus crew policy, and the revolutionary new design of battleships and cruisers, were all highly controversial and were the subject of criticism from a wide range of professional opinion. Beresford remained an enormously popular officer, admired and renowned for his attacking spirit, his seamanship and his undeniable talent for attracting the devoted loyalty of most of those whom he commanded. He was certain that Fisher's régime was a pernicious influence in the service, that his past real value to the Royal Navy had been overwhelmed by personal aggrandizement and megalomania, that his methods of gaining and retaining power were unscrupulous; and in short that under his malevolent influence the Navy and the nation were hell-bent for disaster.

It was true that so urgently did Fisher consider the wholesale strengthening of the Navy, under the threat of German naval rearmament, that autocratic methods were essential for its completion in time. And there is no doubt that he relished the power he wielded as First Sea Lord and could not bear the idea of losing it. King Edward's confidence in his régime was never to waver for one instant. But the Prince of Wales was becoming increasingly uneasy about the effect of the drastic and rapid changes Fisher was imposing on naval policy, and his doubts were to increase, but on a discreet and muted level, in tune with the intensity of Beresford's open warfare. Prince Louis was equally concerned about the breakdown of 'the band of brothers spirit'. As early as 16 March 1905 he was writing to Sir George Clarke from Gibraltar, 'I do cordially agree with all you say, especially the fever which has seized hold of J. F. . . . also the senseless way in which he insults and alienates our senior men . . . However, he shall have my views in season and out of season, from high and low altitudes, now that he has asked for them.'[1]

The tragedy of the conflict which was now publicly breaking out between the two men was that they were both impelled, primarily but not to the exclusion of other motives, by patriotism and loyalty to the service. Intellectually, both men were well enough endowed to have sunk their differences. If their relationship had not been so prejudiced by their class origins, uncompromising obstinacy, and personal vaingloriousness, Beresford could have been persuaded, in the name of logic and national security, to accept the absolute necessity for the Navy to adopt, for example, the all-big-gun ship; and Fisher for his part could have listened to and learned from those who advocated a naval staff in place of the oligarchy which held the strings of power at the Admiralty until the arrival of Churchill after his own retirement. But by 1906 it was too late. Beresford's insubordination and Fisher's obsessional fear that he might be deposed by his powerful antagonist before his tasks were completed, had both travelled beyond the point of no return.

The seriousness with which Fisher viewed the subversive activities of Beresford in the Mediterranean is revealed in an ominous appeal to Lord Tweedmouth the First Lord who had replaced Cawdor, dated 24 April 1906 and marked 'Private and Confidential'.

'It is with extreme reluctance that I feel compelled in the interests of the Navy and the maintenance of its hitherto unquestioned discipline and loyalty to bring before the Board the unprecedented conduct of the Commander-in-Chief of the Mediterranean Fleet in publicly reflecting on the conduct of the Admiralty and in discrediting the policy of the Board and inciting those under his command to ridicule the decisions of the Board. I need not enumerate in detail the comparatively minor cases of improperly worded letters and telegrams questioning Admiralty decisions, which in times past would certainly have led to drastic action preventing any repetition of such conduct. Nor do I dwell on the extraordinary conduct of a Commander-in-Chief "canvassing the Captains under his command" as to whether or no they approved the policy of the Board of Admiralty . . .'

In November 1906 an immensely rich brother of Beresford's died in South Africa and left him a fortune. By any standards, Beresford was already a rich man, but wealth on this scale was the final weapon Beresford needed to complete his armoury. The vocal Conservative

[1] Colonel Lord Sydenham of Combe [Sir George Clarke] *My Working Life* (London 1927), 207. (Hereafter cited as *My Working Life*.)

aristocracy was already behind him, muttering slyly about Fisher's doubtful eastern origins, his womanizing, his vindictiveness against all who opposed his ambitions and his dangerously revolutionary tendencies. Even his close friendship with the King was credited to his sinister powers of influence. Worse, he was working hand-in-glove with the Liberal party, which was determined to pander to the working population at the expense of the nation's defences. With limitless money, Beresford could keep open house in Grosvenor Street, where, according to Fisher, he could 'do more with his chef than by talking'.

Coincidentally with Beresford's inheritance Fisher, with the intention of both placating and silencing his enemy, committed the greatest tactical error in their battle by authorizing his appointment as C.-in-C. of the Channel Fleet and Custance as his second-in-command. It was no more than a stop-gap remedy for this was a command which, in the next stage of the concentration of the battle fleets, must suffer serious loss of status and eventual extinction. It was as certain that 'Charlie B.' would fight to the last for the power of his squadrons as that Jacky Fisher would complete his redeployment against the ever-growing German threat. A shattering conflict was as inevitable as the coming naval war itself.

It began before Beresford hoisted his flag in the battleship *King Edward VII*. Beresford had been one of the most outspoken critics of the redistribution of the Fleet, which he saw as a dispersal rather than a concentration of the Navy's strength in home waters, with the responsibility shared between the Atlantic, Channel and Home Fleets. Beresford knew, when he accepted the command of the Channel Fleet, that in the event of war the other two Fleets would instantly be placed under his command, and that 'on the representations of the Commander-in-Chief of the Channel Fleet' to the Admiralty, joint exercises would take place in peace time. He knew that in war he would command a Fleet of 26 battleships and 16 armoured cruisers, a force more than twice as powerful as the entire German Fleet; and that this force was superior to the strength of the combined fleets before he took over command. Moreover, Fisher had taken the precaution of inviting him to the Admiralty to explain the situation and the proposed working arrangements between the three Fleets. These were shown to be favourable at least for the time being to Beresford's strength as C.-in-C. in war. Beresford approved, and an agreement was drawn up and initialled by the First Lord, Beresford and Fisher.

Of the meeting at which this apparent solution to all outstanding problems between the two Admirals had been reached, Fisher later commented to the Civil Lord of the Admiralty:

TO GEORGE LAMBERT

Admiralty, Whitehall
January 21st, 1907

Dear Lambert,

Your letter splendid! I had three hours with Beresford yesterday, and all is settled, and the Admiralty don't give in one inch to his demands, but I had as a preliminary to agree to three things:—

I. Lord C. Beresford is a greater man than Nelson.
II. No one knows anything about the art of naval war except Lord C. Beresford.
III. The Admiralty haven't done a single d——d thing right! . . .

J. A. Fisher

The real reason behind Beresford's wrath, which burst upon the Admiralty in an increasing tide during the spring and summer of 1907 in spite of this initialled agreement, was Fisher's evident intention to continue to add to the strength of the Nore division of the Home Fleet at the expense of the Channel Fleet until the imbalance of power must lead to the transfer of command to the east coast. This fully manned division was being developed first as a front-line deterrent against a surprise German attack against the east coast of England and the Thames estuary, and in the long term as the nucleus for a combined Home Fleet which would absorb both the Atlantic Fleet and Beresford's Channel Fleet. Although Fisher, for political reasons, had to continue to carry out this policy of concentration discreetly, its purpose became evident even to the Germans as the newest Dreadnought-type battleships and battle cruisers were attached to this Nore Division instead of to Beresford. While Beresford remained C.-in-C. of Britain's most powerful Fleet, he could still hold onto some hope of succeeding Fisher as First Sea Lord. But now he could perceive that his present power was being eaten away, and he ascribed this humiliation to the Machiavellian designs of his enemy.

In defending the nature of Beresford's attacks his own supporters were the first to point out that Fisher himself had for decades been one of the severest critics of Admiralty policy. Because he was now at the helm, Fisher could hardly complain because others were 'distracting the driver'; there was even a sort of rough justice in it. But Fisher had never expressed himself in the language used by Beresford, had never gone beyond the bounds of service courtesy, had never shown insubordination nor attempted to undermine the Board's authority by disseminating his subversive views among his subordinates. So petty and personal were some of the attacks that it was scarcely believable that they emanated from the 'Admiralissimo designate in the event of war'. As Marder has written, 'He criticized Admiralty policy, commented on Admiralty orders, and repeatedly addressed the Admiralty on many topics in a decidedly tactless and insubordinate manner quite without parallel in British naval history. His opinions of the Admiralty and of Fisher ("our dangerous lunatic") were known to every officer and man in his fleet.'[1] Within a few weeks of taking over command and of initialling the agreement which settled the relative rôles of the Channel and Home Fleets, Beresford was describing the latter, in a memorandum to the Admiralty (13 May 1907), as a 'fraud upon the public and a danger to the Empire'. And yet only three weeks earlier he had written from his Flagship to Fisher in the most conciliatory vein, 'There is not the slightest chance of any friction between me and you, or between me and anyone else. When the friction begins, I am off. If a senior and a junior have a row, the junior is wrong under any conceivable condition, or discipline could not go on. As long as I am here I will do my best to make the Admiralty policy a success.'

The transparent hypocrisy of this utterance was evidenced without delay. The attacks continued, and their violence increased. Fisher determined to be rid of him, and submitted to the First Lord a summary of the position between himself as First Sea Lord and Beresford as C.-in-C. of the nation's premier Fleet.

Never had Fisher been in greater need of the firmness, decisiveness and wisdom of Selborne. But Selborne had gone, and Cawdor had not lasted long enough to play himself in. Since December 1905 the office of First Lord had been held by the second Earl of Tweedmouth, an uncle of Winston Churchill, who was an able enough administrator but quite incapable of withstanding the violent storms of controversy under which his period of appointment was to suffer. His policy towards trouble, when only the firmest action could save the Navy from a long period of debilitating internecine warfare, was to hush it up as far as possible, and then procrastinate.

FROM THE EARL OF TWEEDMOUTH

Admiralty, Whitehall
June 8th, 1907

My dear Sir John,
I have very carefully read through the papers you gave me on Wednesday, and I must say I should regret that in their present form they should be circulated to the Board. No one is more alive to the objections which can be taken to much of the attitude taken up by Lord Charles Beresford and to his methods of action. I know him to be ambitious, self-advertising and gassy in his talk,

---

[1] *Marder*, i, 91.

but we all knew those bad qualities of his, and no one better than you, when you very wisely recommended his and Sir Reginald Custance's appointments. You and we then considered that some serious disadvantages were outweighed by the advantages which were to be gained by their good qualities and their record of services in the past.

Lord Charles has especially a large share of the good qualities. He is cheerful, active, zealous in the Service, and his power of attracting and enlisting the sympathies, abilities and affection of officers and men alike who are placed under him is remarkable. The fleet in the Mediterranean was got and left in a high state of efficiency.

These being the facts, it seems to be a pity to lodge a formal and so unqualified attack against him, which, if accepted, must almost forbid his continued employment. . . .

I am the last person in the world to abrogate one iota of the supremacy of the Board of Admiralty, but I do think we sometimes are inclined to consider our own views to be infallible and are not ready enough to give consideration to the views of others who may disagree with us but who still give us ideas and information which can be turned to great use.

Believe me, Ever sincerely yours,
Tweedmouth

There were numbers of experienced and sagacious senior officers in the service who could have offered the Board valuable 'ideas and information', and Fisher was as eager as he had been in the old days to listen to them. But it was certain that Beresford was not numbered among them. The Admiral whom Tweedmouth described as 'active, zealous in the Service' had greatly deteriorated, even since his days in the Mediterranean. The wild Irish sportsman, the fearless and dashing officer so beloved of the British public for many years past, this personification of Imperial sea power, had rapidly decayed into a gouty, erratic, idiosyncratic and short-tempered Admiral, who would have been regarded as a buffoon ripe for satiric caricature but for the rank and responsibility he held in the service and in society, and his grandiose deportment.

A Sub-Lieutenant serving in Beresford's Flagship recalled how spit-'n-polish and the cult of the C.-in-C.'s personality, were classed far above fighting efficiency under Beresford. 'Everything centred round the person of the Admiral, and ceremonial had become almost an obsession with him. Every time that he showed his head above the coaming of his hatch, the Officer-of-the-Watch was required to call the Quarter Deck to attention, and everyone remained stricken into immobility until the well-known and slightly nasal voice graciously commanded: "Carry on Mr Officer-of-the-Watch." . . . My principal recollection of those days is, accordingly, unending pipings, callings

to attention, and buglings. Hurried dashes to and fro from the battery
. . . to my post by the gangway, interspersed with anxious darts from
one side of the quarterdeck to the other to see that all was in order with
the boats at the lower booms, and that their boat-keepers maintained
their upright attitude as they sat in them . . . Our occupation—whilst
I served in her—was principally a processional career round the ports
of the British Isles, varied by a few stately and somewhat hackneyed
steam tactics . . . I do not recollect that any very serious problems of
war were either attempted or solved.'[1]

The decline in the powers of Beresford to the figure of absurdity
he had become by 1907 was aptly symbolized by his bulldog Kora, an
overfed animal who lolloped about the spotless decks of the Flagship,
followed by an attendant with dustpan, brush and cloth to clear up her
messes. Beresford lavished equal affection on his motor car, which was
taken everywhere, along with its marine driver. One of the Flagship's
Midshipmen recalled how it 'was stowed on the booms amidships, being
hoisted in and out with special slings by the main derrick and taken
ashore in the launch. Wherever we went he used it, means of getting it
out of the launch being devised in the most remote places.' This same
officer also remembered how, when they were in Irish waters, 'the Old
Man often went fishing, usually accompanied by a lieutenant, myself
and sometimes another midshipman, our job being to get flies out of
weeds or bushes and disentangle knots. The coxswain and two of the
galley's crew followed with lunch-baskets, landing-nets, rugs and
other gear—and the inevitable Kora . . . On Sunday two midshipmen
were always asked to breakfast: we had to appear in the fore cabin at
two minutes to eight and sit on each side of him, whilst he told a string
of Irish stories, which it was best to greet with loud laughter.'[2]

Beresford's yacht *Surprise* followed the Channel Fleet almost everywhere, usually with Lady Charles as the honoured passenger. 'She was
an astonishing looking woman, very much made up. The Admiral, who
was on the quarterdeck watching the barge approaching through his
telescope, once turned to me,' recalled this Midshipman, 'and said:
"Here comes my little ship with a new coat of paint." '

This, then, was the man who was attempting to oust Fisher and was
accusing the Admiralty in ever more strident tones that he had not
sufficient ships to meet the threat of war with Germany, that there were
no proper war plans in existence and that the Board's new dispositions
were a blunder.

[1] Lionel Dawson, *Gone for a Sailor* (London, 1936), 131–2.
[2] Captain the Hon. V. Wyndham-Quin, cited Captain Geoffrey Bennett, *Charlie B.*
(London, 1968), 283. (Hereafter cited as *Charlie B.*)

Tweedmouth, fearful of the effects of a showdown, succeeded in persuading Fisher to tone down his memorandum, which was circulated to the Board in the following terms:

'This Memorandum has become necessary for the information and consideration of the Board of Admiralty in view of the fact that the present Commander-in-Chief of the Channel Fleet . . . has taken up a position of antagonism both to the policy and to the administrative arrangements of the Board of Admiralty . . . He has forwarded his own plan of campaign against Germany, which involves, notwithstanding the enormous preponderance of the British Navy, the employment of more battleships, cruisers and co. and co., than the British Navy possesses . . .

'Further, in official conversation, Lord C. Beresford has spoken of our naval position being such that "The Empire is in jeopardy", and his Chief-of-Staff (Captain Sturdee) has stated his opinion that we are "living over a live mine" . . .

'The truth is that such language on the part of L.C.B., and C.S., besides being insubordinate, is perfectly preposterous, and when used, as it freely is, in general conversation, it is also most baneful in its effects on the personnel of the Fleet in fostering a spirit of disloyalty towards the Admiralty. It is certainly a great blow to discipline that such disloyalty should be overlooked . . .'[1]

Meanwhile, Beresford continued his attacks. On 14 June 1907 his letter to the Admiralty reiterated his beliefs:

'In my opinion [ran part of it], if Germany was to undertake sudden hostilities with her naval forces perfectly organized in all details for a definite plan of campaign, including a landing party and a raiding party, Germany would have a considerable chance of succeeding; or, anyway, inflicting most crushing reverses at the initial stages of hostilities, in the present totally unprepared states of the Home and Channel Fleets in regard to the preparation and organization for war.'

Scenting that the dispute between his Board and Beresford must soon become public property, Tweedmouth ordered Beresford to the Admiralty for a three-way conversation with Fisher in an attempt to clear the air. This astonishing confrontation took place on 5 July. The verbatim report (see Appendix 1) reveals Beresford's inarticulateness and his dependence on his staff for the comparative intelligibility of his written messages. Tweedmouth and Fisher were conciliatory, like

---

[1] Robinson Papers, vol. 1. Admiralty MSS.

two uncles warily joining forces to deal with a difficult and dangerous child. Beresford expressed surprise that he should have been thought insubordinate, and repeated his earnest desire to maintain the most friendly relations with the Board. For his part, Fisher felt that little had come out of the conversations, but that he should attempt to maintain the spirit of supposed friendliness for as long as possible. He therefore followed up the meeting with a letter evidently worded for the eyes of Custance and other of Beresford's closest supporters, who would certainly be shown it.

TO ADMIRAL LORD CHARLES BERESFORD

Admiralty, Whitehall
July 6th, 1907

My dear Beresford,

You said yesterday you had heard of my saying things of you, but I hope you will take my assurance as I took yours on this point—that we have both to complain of liars trying to make mischief. I am most anxious to be as cordial in our relations as in the warmest days of our friendship. I remember Ormonde saying when we were in the Mediterranean—how the mischief makers tried to make out we were not friends. Nor do I forget how you have stood by me against the whole army of fossils in the past.

Ever yours,
J. A. Fisher

Beresford got all that he had demanded in additional ships, and he was able to send a telegram to Custance saying that he had brought the Admiralty to heel. To Fisher he replied with patronizing familiarity, 'The Admiralty evidently sees my points, and are doing what they can to meet my views, on those questions that I think weak, for defence of Home waters. They have given me what I asked for, and made it possible to have a Fleet ready in all its component parts and units for instant action. I can now make out a plan of campaign.' (Alongside this Fisher later wrote, 'We have never had it!') Beresford's letter continued, 'The only difference of importance that I see in my request and Admiralty offer is in three more unarmoured cruisers, a very important unit and one that should always be together, and a unit we are certainly weak in. I hope the Lord Commissioners of the Admiralty will give me the three extra . . .' And against this Fisher was to margin, 'The very day after getting all he asks for, he asks for three more.'

It soon became clear that Tweedmouth had failed to bring about any kind of armistice between the two most important and antagonistic officers in the Navy. One incident followed another throughout the

[1] *ibid.*

summer, and innocent officers who had not been involved in the dispute became drawn in. Among these was Vice-Admiral Francis Bridgeman, the C.-in-C. of the ever-growing Home Fleet. Beresford seized every opportunity to attack the conduct of Bridgeman, who had discreetly remained clear of the Fishpond and the Beresfordites. In October 1907 there were joint exercises between the Channel, Home and Atlantic Fleets under the command of Beresford. After they were over, Beresford strongly criticized the management of Bridgeman's destroyers and asserted in a memorandum (11 November 1907) circulated throughout the Fleets that they were not properly trained. The Admiralty ordered the withdrawal of the memorandum and the deletion of this reflection on Bridgeman's competence.

A second and simultaneous running battle concerned the rumours of the Admiralty's proposal to remove several of Beresford's most valuable officers, including Captain Doveton Sturdee, his Chief of Staff, and Custance himself. Beresford saw this as a calculated attempt by Fisher to break up the hard core of the Admiralty's opposition. 'It has come to my notice,' he wrote to the Admiralty on 12 November 1907, 'that a feeling has arisen in the Service that it is prejudicial to an officer's career to be personally connected with me on Service matters. This may not be a fact, but the impression I know exists . . . The removal . . . cannot help me to add to the efficiency of the Fleet. It may not have been intended, but it most certainly has the appearance of a wish to handicap and hamper me in carrying out the responsibilities connected with by far the most important appointment within the Empire.'[1] The degree of Beresford's insubordination and fury was revealed in another paragraph in which he charged that, 'The ordinary etiquette, civilities, and courteous dealings which officers of high and distinguished command have hitherto so markedly received from the Admiralty have been entirely absent in my case.'

The Admiralty was able to explain that Beresford had not got his facts quite right, that there was no intention of removing Custance, and it was Beresford himself who had been urging that Sturdee should be promoted. Moreover, as the Admiralty had been at pains to point out to him before, 'the responsibility for the Naval defence of the Empire, whether in Home waters or elsewhere, rests with the Board of Admiralty', and not with a single Admiral; and 'it becomes increasingly difficult for [the Board] in their correspondence with you to avoid overstepping the usual limits of official reserve while you continue to employ language which has no parallel within their experience as coming from a subordinate addressed to the Board of Admiralty'.[2]

[1] *Marder*, i, 96.   [2] *ibid.*

A cause of equal fury to Beresford was the behaviour of certain other of his senior officers who were unsympathetic to his attacks against the Navy's administration. Prominent among them was Rear-Admiral Percy Scott who had for four months past commanded Beresford's First Cruiser Squadron. Scott was a strong Fisher supporter. He was also a gunnery fiend, an innovator, a fiery officer who spoke his mind all too readily. These were characteristics certain to endear any officer to Fisher. But Scott had also revolutionized naval gunnery, and at a time when 'spit 'n polish' ruled and too much gunnery spoilt it, had made himself singularly unpopular with Fisher's 'old fossils'. By new techniques and by obliging his officers to concentrate their attentions on gunnery, he raised the average of hits made by his ships from a general average of 30% throughout the Fleet to 80%. Fisher had created a new post especially for him, that of Inspector of Target Practice, which he had filled admirably.

Beresford had always dearly loved the social ceremonials in which a major Fleet had to partake. When he heard that Kaiser Wilhelm II was to inspect his Fleet at Spithead on 8 November 1907 he was delighted, and accordingly ordered his ships to Portland at the beginning of the month to be freshly painted. Percy Scott had for long nursed the gravest suspicions about the value of frequently painting ships. 'The state of the paintwork was the one and only idea', he wrote of the Mediterranean Fleet in 1896. 'The quarter's allowance of ammunition had to be expended somehow, and the custom throughout the Navy was to make a signal, "Spread for target practice—expend a quarter's ammunition, and rejoin my flag at such and such a time." '[1]

Scott was characteristically engaged in gunnery exercises when he received the order that they were to repair to Portland. One of his Captains asked if he might continue, to which Scott replied, 'Paintwork appears to be more in demand than gunnery, so you had better come in, in time to make yourself look pretty by the 8th instant.'

This inexcusably provocative signal began 'the paintwork affair' which was to lead to the Fisher-Beresford feud becoming known to the nation at large. Beresford heard about the signal a few days later and was outraged. He ordered Scott to his Flagship and publicly dressed him down before a large and embarrassed audience. 'I heard enough,' one office recalled, 'to know that Lord Charles, white with suppressed anger, was sparing his subordinate nothing.'[2] But that was not all. Beresford next took the vindictive and unprecedented step of sending a

---

[1] Admiral Sir Percy Scott, *Fifty Years in the Royal Navy* (London, 1919), 73–4. (Hereafter cited as *Scott.*)

[2] Captain Lionel Dawson, *Flotillas* (London, 1933), 61.

general message informing the whole Fleet of what had happened, describing Scott's signal as 'contemptuous in tone and insubordinate in character' and ordering the two cruisers concerned to expunge it from their signal logs.

A *Punch* cartoon illustrating the dispute between Lord Charles Beresford and Rea-Admiral Percy Scott—'the paintwork affair'.

This public crucifixion of an officer who had done so much to improve the efficiency of the Navy's gunnery was quickly and critically noted by the press. Beresford was attacked by journalists who had often been critical of Fisher in the past. Beresford asked the Admiralty to refute their accusations, and the Board refused. Nor would the Board agree to the dismissal of Scott, although they wrote him a letter of 'grave disapprobation', which was later circulated to the Fleet. Scott offered his apologies, Beresford refused them, and further humiliated him by ostentatiously omitting his name from all invitations to functions attended by his fellow officers. The First Cruiser Squadron was banished to Bantry Bay, a highly uncongenial place in winter.

At this point, the notorious editor of *John Bull*, Horatio Bottomley, who was renowned for his acute nose for a public scandal, stepped in with 'A Grave Indictment of Lord Charles Beresford' which denounced Beresford's 'swelled head' and claimed that he was not fit to succeed to the post of First Sea Lord to which he had so long aspired. A copy of the issue of *John Bull* containing this blistering attack found its way in a sealed envelope to every officer in the Channel Fleet. Whatever small measure of discretion Beresford still retained was now cast to the winds, and he wrote to Sir Edward Carson that it was 'one of the most determined, audacious, treacherous and cowardly attacks on me, inspired by the gentleman from Ceylon'.[1] More effectively, Beresford redoubled his efforts to gather vocal support from his Conservative supporters in Parliament in favour of instituting an enquiry into the conduct of the Board of Admiralty; which would amount to a public arraignment of Fisher.

Fisher steamed back into the exploding broadsides, drawing on all his reserves. There was, for example, a two-hour lunch at the Ritz with his new ally, the brilliant and ambitious Winston Churchill, on which Fisher reported to his old and stalwart ally, Esher, 'He is very keen to fight on my behalf and is simply boiling with fury at Beresford and Co . . .' A 'Most Confidential' memorandum arrived from King Edward: 'I trust that Board of Admiralty will consider most seriously C.B.'s outrageous conduct, which if tolerated undermines all discipline in the R.N. I trust (to use your own words) "Serious action" will be taken!'[2] On 23 January Fisher hastened to the Foreign Office.

TO SIR EDWARD GREY

January 23rd, 1908

Private
Dear Sir Edward,

It was most kind of you to see me this morning. Of course I didn't say half of what is imperative should be known to you before the Cabinet takes the (in my opinion) most fatal step of intervening and enquiring into the purely expert matter of naval strategy and detailed war plans. As I said, the mere fact of such an investigation or enquiry, however secret, would be *prima-facie* evidence of the Cabinet being disquieted and shaken in its confidence in the Board of Admiralty generally and the First Sea Lord in particular, as he is the Member of the Board specially charged with the organization for war. No

[1] *Charlie B.* 292.   [2] Lennoxlove MSS.

officer under the Board of Admiralty—*no matter who*—has any other duty whatever except to obey orders, and it is simply unprecedented in the history of the British Navy what has occurred in regard to Lord C. Beresford interviewing Members of the Cabinet and indicting the Board of Admiralty as failing in its duty. . . . This present tampering with mutiny (for it is nothing else) is dealing a deadly blow at the discipline of the Navy in shaking the confidence of the Navy in the firmness and strength of the Board of Admiralty . . .

Are the Cabinet going to decide which is right—Sir A. Wilson, who wants the British Battle Fleet far removed from the North Sea, or Lord Charles Beresford, who wants it there? I venture to say to you with all the emphasis at my command and with the deepest respect for the authority of the Cabinet: 'If you have any doubts, get rid of the Admiralty and get fresh members in whom you have implicit confidence; but for God's sake have no Aulic Council for directing the War Policy of the British Navy.'

I will gladly disappear if I am in any way an embarrassment to the Government. BUT WHILE I AM WHERE I AM, I must press for Lord Charles Beresford obeying orders instead of wanting to give them. Never has such forbearance been shown as to him. The extracts from official correspondence I send herewith will make this plain.

Yours very truly,
J. A. Fisher

Then there was lunch with the leader of the last Conservative government, Arthur Balfour, who warned him that 'Beresford was holding forth "in every drawing-room in London" against the Admiralty'. Balfour next invited Captain Charles L. Ottley, the DNI, to lunch to ensure that this officer was properly supporting his chief. A torrent of hand-written letters poured from the home and the office of the First Sea Lord, heavy with underlinings and exclamation marks and suitably warlike Old Testament quotations, addressed to friends, to serving and retired officers, to past and future First Lords, to politicians, hostesses, newspaper proprietors and journalists, all loaded with invective against Beresford and calling for support against the threat to the Board's work of reform, redeployment and rearmament.

Many other powerful people rallied voluntarily to Fisher's support.

TO ARNOLD WHITE

16, Queen Anne's Gate, S.W.
February 23rd, 1908

Private
My dear Arnold White,

What a very wicked world this! F. E. Smith, M.P., asked me to meet Carson, Rufus Isaacs, Simon, M.P., and another whose name I forget, as being sympathetic and friendly, and certainly they all behaved so. I said but little,

H

as they were all so full of talk, and remained alone afterwards with F. E. Smith to discuss what we had at heart. I heard afterwards that Carson had been interviewed by Beresford to take up his case in the House of Commons. I mentioned this to Lady Londonderry, and she said, 'Well, you never know what one Irishman won't do for another.' Apropos of my saying that I thought Balfour would object to his doing so, I went for a walk with Balfour last night, and from what he quite spontaneously and unnecessarily said to me, I fancy he will see me through anything; *but please keep this private*. He apparently had heard fully about all the intrigues against me. I think I had better not open my mouth . . .

J. F.

'Why should any patriot wish to upset Jackie?' asked Esher in his journal. 'Only the old-fashioned fogey, the personal foe, or the political wrecker would want to destroy him.'[1]

All these categories were steadying their line against Fisher. There were also others, more influential and powerful and intelligent, who were yielding to their doubts about the Fisher régime. The Prince of Wales was now on a steady course from Fisher to Beresford. Although the Prince was obliged by his relative position to the Crown and a natural sense of decorum from openly expressing himself, Beresford knew that he had him, and the Prince's memorandum on 'the policing of the seas', casting doubts on Fisher's policy of concentration, had clearly confirmed this.

Beresford worked hard to find favour with the King again—with both on his side he must surely prevail! 'One evening,' reported Ponsonby, 'he gave me forty minutes breezy conversation on the Navy, presumably hoping I should pass on to the King what he said. He always began by saying "I wish to keep all argument impersonal", but after a short time he forgot and went on, "If it were not for that damned fellow Fisher". The whole of his conversations was impregnated with a hatred of Fisher, whom he accuses of having poisoned him with the King.'[2] Beresford's veritable bombardment of the King with letters did not help his cause much, either. The King just showed them to Fisher. 'I suggested to His Majesty,' Fisher later told Knollys, 'that the reply thereto should be "that the King feels quite assured that the Board of Admiralty will do all that is right in the matters he mentions." . . . As the King most truly said, "His overweening vanity and love of notoriety are simply intolerable."'

But many others, from less lofty heights, came down in support of Beresford. R. B. Haldane, defence expert and since 1905 Secretary of State for War, supported an enquiry. Most of the Admirals stood

<hr>

[1] *Esher*, ii, 276.   [2] *Ponsonby*, 132.

aloof or supported Beresford, who went on leave and fought back with even greater determination, going so far as to sham illness 'in order to coax Cabinet Ministers and other potential supporters to his bedside!' As Esher commented to Knollys, 'Imagine interviewing Beresford in a night cap, with Lady Charles holding his hand on the far side of the bed. What a picture of Naval efficiency and domestic bliss.'[1]

Fisher was the temporary victor. Scott remained as Commander of the First Cruiser Squadron, and in February 1908 the Prime Minister promised Fisher that there would be no enquiry into Admiralty policy, an assurance that was repeated when Asquith succeeded to the Premiership in April. In addition, with the new government Fisher acquired a new First Lord. Reginald McKenna was as inflexible as Tweedmouth had been vacillating and weak. He was young and vigorous and loyal. He got on marvellously with Fisher, and supported him unfailingly through the deeply troubled months when they worked together.

On McKenna's assumption of office, Fisher briefed him rapidly and plainly on the state of affairs with Beresford.

TO REGINALD MCKENNA

Admiralty, Whitehall
April 16th, 1908

Dear Mr McKenna,

I think I ought to explain to you at once what the Admiralty position *is*, *always has been*, and *must ever remain*, if discipline is to be maintained and the authority of the Board of Admiralty preserved—and that is, that there must be no cavilling at or criticizing of their orders by officers on active service afloat, and more especially by those in high command; . . . If complete confidence cannot be given to the Sea Lords, they ought to be changed, but there is an end of all things if, taking the instance you gave me, Lord C. Beresford is to dictate to the Admiralty what particular destroyers he should have, or what should be the constitution of his Fleet: 'Se soumettre ou se démettre' —that's the plain answer to give him; or, as Mr John Burns put it more graphically:

> *'The Quarterdeck and Silence*
> or *Westminster and Gas,'*

as Beresford threatens to go into Parliament and make it hot for the Admiralty!

I think my colleagues will tell you that it is unprecedented the lengths to which Lord Charles Beresford has been permitted (I think, wrongly) to flout the Admiralty; but I have subjected my strong personal convictions to the judgment of others, and having gone so far I think it's wisdom to wait now till the autumn, when probably matters will arrange themselves. In the meantime I am confident, from what you have kindly said, that you will give no encouragement to Lord Charles Beresford that he will receive any sort of

[1] *Marder*, i, 100.

countenance in his disloyal, and what I may even term insubordinate, conduct towards the Admiralty because a new First Lord has arrived. . . .

Yours very truly,
J. A. Fisher

But by the Spring of 1908 the schism in the Navy had become a national scandal, and the public's appetite for news of the conflict encouraged the newspapers to keep it constantly before their attemtion. Not that there was much difficulty in finding fodder. There was another searing row in the Channel Fleet between Beresford and Scott, who had by then been ordered to communicate with his superior only in writing. With Scott's concurrence, his Flagship refused to obey a signal from Beresford which he considered would bring about a fatal collision. Beresford demanded a court-martial this time, and McKenna, on behalf of the Board, refused. Beresford blasted back at Whitehall: 'It is difficult to believe that the Board can fully understand the injury to the discipline, not only of the Channel Fleet, but of the Navy as a whole, which must result if open and flagrant disloyalty is allowed to pass . . .'[1]

Shortly before this, at a levée in May, Beresford turned his back on Fisher and his proferred hand in full view of the King and cabinet ministers.

Clearly, things could not continue like this. On 8 July *The Times* let it be known that Beresford should resign or be silent, '. . . so long as he holds his present position he is not free to let it be known, whether by his action or by his demeanour, either to his Fleet or to the world at large, that his attitude towards the Board of Admiralty is one of scant respect for its authority and avowed dissent from its policy'. A few days later Esher wrote in exasperation to Knollys begging him to persuade the King to intervene. 'No one, except the King,' he wrote (12 August 1908) 'can put an end to this stupid feud. I have long believed that the King by sending for Fisher and Beresford, and making them shake hands *in his presence*, and promise *him* that they will have done with this quarrel, both in public and in private, would earn and obtain the fervent applause of the whole country . . . From all I know of the circumstances, I am sure the King would not find the task beyond his powers. Will you think it over?'[1]

But the King did not feel able to act as a peacemaker, Beresford's attacks continued without restraint, and McKenna knew that the time had come when Beresford must be dismissed or the whole structure of the Navy would be fatally cracked. The matter had first been discussed at a meeting of the Board in January and referred to several times since.

[1] *Marder*, i, 102.
[1] *Esher*, ii, 328.

Now McKenna went to talk to Asquith about it. Unmindful of the fact that the row was the subject of common and warmly savoured gossip in every pub and club in the land, Asquith and his Cabinet flinched from permitting the dismissal of Beresford because of the political difficulties they were already in over the Navy estimates, and for fear that the public washing of dirty linen might cause the Liberal Party as well as the Navy irreparable harm. They were fearful of the explosion of wrath that would be heard throughout the land, from droves of old Admirals to society ladies who had adored Charlie B. for half a century and powerful Conservative aristocrats and politicians, which his dismissal might detonate. They recalled how much noise he had made in Parliament last time. Since then relations with Germany had greatly deteriorated, and the points of attack had extended in a great number of controversial naval fields—from the danger of invasion to the creation of revolutionary and highly controversial types of fighting ships. Deliberately to provoke further discord at this time required a calibre of courage which Asquith did not possess.

Asquith had greatly overestimated Beresford's power to make mischief. In the eyes of the general public, Beresford was no longer the lovable, dashing, eccentric who knew how to handle a pretty woman as well as a fresh mare. He had publicly humiliated in the most cowardly manner a subordinate—and, as it was soon to turn out, broken Percy Scott's career by persuading McKenna not to re-employ him after February 1909. Clever Bottomley had had his finger on the public pulse when he delivered his slashing attack on Beresford. For the present, the common man had had enough of Lord Charles Beresford, even if a growing body of intelligent opinion wanted to get rid of both the antagonists and start afresh.

Periodically throughout the summer of 1908 McKenna tried to persuade the Government to agree to Beresford's dismissal, but the 'blue funkers' as Fisher despisingly referred to them, would not comply. McKenna's struggle, like everything to do with the Beresford–Fisher fight, was not altogether a private one. There was free speculation on the ebb and flow of the tide of battle. On several occasions it was rumoured that Beresford had been sacked, and in August *The Times* printed the news as if it were official. Beresford read the report, and with understandable acerbity wrote to McKenna (8 August): 'Having read in *The Times* and other papers "that I am to be relieved at the date named" (March '09—after only 2 years) . . . I beg that I may be informed, as I have my private arrangements to consider . . .'[1] It was another false report, McKenna regretfully reassured him.

[1] Bonar Law Papers, Beaverbrook Library.

But in December 1908, McKenna, Fisher and the Board at last got their troublemaker out of the way. The dismissal was carried out with what politeness the Admiralty still retained, and the announcement was worded diplomatically to give as little offence as possible. The reason given was that the redeployment in home waters was to be accelerated, and the long-term plan to absorb the Channel Fleet into the Home Fleet was to be put forward by twelve months. So from March 1909 there would be no Channel Fleet to command, and Beresford was ordered to haul down his flag on the 24th. To diminish the sting of the blow, further, Bridgeman's appointment as C.-in-C. of the Home Fleet was similarly terminated a year earlier, and he was replaced by Admiral May.

Fourteen months had passed since the Board had first expressed its wish to dismiss Beresford. The weakness of Tweedmouth, and the subsequent delay and procrastination by Asquith and his Cabinet, were to prove fatal to Fisher, for the delay in this dismissal had caused the barometer of public opinion to swing round again in favour of Beresford. If he was such a menace and such a villain why had he not been thrown out months ago? The Admiralty must be afraid, or were hiding something—that was the common view. Bacon believed that, 'Had the authority of the Board of Admiralty been upheld by the Cabinet when Lord Charles first commenced his unfortunate campaign, and had the proper action been taken of superseding him in his command, the Prime Minister would not have been confronted with a difficult situation . . . It seemed to the ordinary person to be obvious that, had the Admiralty been in the right, Lord Charles would have been promptly dealt with; the apparent disinclination of that body to do so was interpreted as evidence that the Admiralty feared to take any action that might lead to the exposure of administrative failure.'[1] King Edward, always wise and percipient in his understanding of human motives, believed that the wrong decision had been made at the wrong time. For months he had been pressing for the dismissal of the Admiral whose 'outrageous conduct' was threatening the Navy's discipline. Now he was afraid that Beresford 'will make a disturbance and give trouble and annoyance'.[2]

The added burden of the long drawn out battle on top of the responsibilities of his office during the most critical years of the Navy's preparations for the inevitable war with Germany was beginning to prove too much even for Fisher's rugged constitution and will power. His friends began to notice the change.

[1] *Bacon*, ii, 50.
[2] *Marder*, i, 104.

FROM ARNOLD WHITE[1]

Windmill Cottage,
Farnham Common,
Bucks
November 15th, 1908

Dear Sir John Fisher,

You looked weary and heavy laden on Friday as if soul-oxygen were required. Very strong men are often misunderstood by their nearest friends who wrongly imagine that being steel in nerves they don't need sympathy. Spenser Wilkinson told me lately that the only chance of saving the country was getting rid of Sir John Fisher, and your departure is more desired than Paradise by a good many . . .

The *mob* is fickle but not the *people* who always remain faithful to a silent worker. Your great intimacy with the King curiously enough militates against you, as Beresford's quarrel with the Court helps him, for the same reason that Wilkes was a hero of the mob. The public dearly love a man who is against the powers-that-be, especially if he is a Lord: and C.B. works this for all he is worth . . .

Do take a stand-easy whenever you can, *because the best of your life is before you.*

I am, Yours ever,
Arnold White

For all his fierce and powerful demeanour, for all his claims that his skin was like that of a rhinoceros, 'and all the envenomed darts don't pierce it!', Fisher suffered excruciatingly from all the attacks that came in from every quarter. His last twelve months as First Sea Lord were to be the most agonizing of his career. As he mentioned to a friend, 'When I retire I shall write my reminiscences. I shall call them "Hell. By One Who Has Been There".'

When Beresford hauled down his flag for the last time at Portsmouth and came ashore, a cheering crowd met him on the Hard. The C.-in-C. Portsmouth, Admiral Sir Arthur Dalrymple Fanshawe, lent him his carriage to drive to the station. All the way he was followed by hurrahs, and mothers held up their children to see their hero, and Midshipmen ran alongside the carriage. At the station the departure of his train was delayed by the crowds who overran the lines. It was the same at Waterloo, where the great gathering threw their hats in the air and cheered and cheered. Beresford was delighted and deeply moved. When he returned home he read of himself in the *Standard*: 'Because he has fearlessly told the truth, he has been dismissed by Mr McKenna. There is the whole situation in a sentence.'

The events of that day alone were enough to encourage Beresford to reopen his campaign and to believe that, with two years on the active list still to run, he might yet displace his enemy. Even before his dis-

[1] Lennoxlove MSS.

missal he had been busily engaged in mounting a last stand that might yet turn the tide. One of the most important and effective weapons he helped to create in order to bring about this end was an organization called the Imperial Maritime League. The support of a wide number of influential people was canvassed, and rousing 'patriotic' meetings were held up and down the country. Fisher acquired a card of invitation to one of these meetings, and after underlining in red ink its heading 'God and my Country', sent it to McKenna with a note, 'This will make you shake in your shoes!' It announced that there was to be 'A Public demonstration against the passing of our Naval supremacy and the dismissal of Lord Charles Beresford from the command of the Channel Fleet will be held at the Hampstead Conservatoire on Wednesday March 3rd at 8.30 p.m.' The list of speakers and an announcement of 'Music and Singing' was followed by the appeal: 'All patriotic men and women are entreated to attend. Admission Free.'[1]

Beresford gained much popular support from these meetings of the new League, but he was not as selective as he should have been in choosing the names of prominent persons to be circularized.

FROM LORD REDESDALE[2]
                                            Batsford Park,
                                            Moreton-in-the-Marsh
                                            November 17th, 1908

My dear Fisher,
    It may amuse you to see my answer to these gentlemen's circular which I enclose in case you should have not seen it.
                                            Yours ever,
                                            Redesdale

Redesdale's reply stated that he had 'no reason for changing the opinion' he had expressed in a former letter replying to an earlier invitation to join. He also enclosed for Fisher a copy of this letter, which ran: 'You have honoured me with an invitation to join a League which considers itself to be capable of teaching the Board of Admiralty (with Sir John Fisher as their Chief Adviser) their business. Until further advised as to your superiority to that distinguished officer, I prefer putting my trust in him.'

The League also unfortunately approached Esher for support. His reply was crisp and characteristic. 'You ask me to join a body of persons, all actuated no doubt by honourable and patriotic motives, who are engaged in promoting a scheme designed to overturn one of the Prime Minister's principal colleagues and a Board of Admiralty nominated by him.

<hr>

[1] Lennoxlove MSS.   [2] *ibid.*

'For it is obvious that a public enquiry into the state of the Navy such as you desire to form, would indicate a want of confidence in the present Board of Admiralty, which might make the retention of office by the Board impossible . . .

'When I looked at the list of names of those who had joined the Council or Committee, I confess to having been struck by the absence from it of any great Naval authority or indeed any authority whatever upon questions of Naval or Imperial Defence.'

Esher also added to his first draft, but subsequently omitted: 'What harm is there, gentlemen, and would it not be more straightforward, if the admission were boldly made, that the object of the "Maritime League" is to upset Sir John Fisher, and the Naval policy for which all the world knows he must bear the chief responsibility . . .

'Then we know exactly where we are.'[1]

A week after his triumphant return to London Beresford was back in action, addressing to Asquith a letter (2 April) which attacked the administration of the Admiralty on two vital fronts, the redeployment of the fleets in home waters, which had led to the diminution and then termination of the power of his own command; and the lack of the proper means of developing the scientific preparation of war plans.

In spite of the great fund of public sympathy Beresford was now enjoying and the support of several of the popular newspapers, he could never alone have made Fisher's régime the subject of an official enquiry. Unfortunately for Fisher and McKenna the premature termination of Beresford's appointment coincided with a sudden new crisis in the naval arms race which had been running without respite and at an increasing tempo ever since Fisher had taken office. Asquith suddenly found himself under such strong political pressure that he was forced to appoint a committee of enquiry into the administration of the Navy. Whatever its finding might be, we shall see later this was a massive victory for Beresford. It was also a fearful blow and humiliation to Fisher.

'Imagine what a state of affairs,' he wrote in fury to Esher, 'when a meeting of Naval Officers on the active list in a room in Grosvenor Street is able to coerce the Cabinet and force the strongest Board of Admiralty to totter to its fall! . . . The country must indeed be in a bad way if so governed!'

So the devil at last had his reward! An ageing, powerful and wealthy, patriotic but outrageously insubordinate, Admiral had succeeded in bringing his First Sea Lord publicly to the bar—and to the very brink of the precipice over which, as Fisher had feared, he must ultimately fall.

[1] Robinson Papers, vol. 1. Admiralty MSS.

Chapter 3

'ONE KIND OF SPLASH': THE DREADNOUGHT

The most public of Fisher's controversial reforms, and the one by which he was to be most remembered, was his *matériel* revolution wrought by the creation of H.M.S. *Dreadnought*. Here was something tangible—all 18,000 tons of impressive steel—for denigration or praise. The merits and demerits of the Selborne Scheme or the nucleus crew policy or the redeployment of the Navy's battle Fleets could be argued over *ad infinitum* and fill endless columns of type in *The Times* or the *Naval & Military Record*. But from 3 October 1906 when she first steamed out of Portsmouth harbour, the *Dreadnought* was there for all the world to see: the most magnificent and provocative weapon of war ever devised by man.

By the end of the nineteenth century the constructors of the world's battleships were having a hard time keeping pace with the irresistible advance of science and technology, which had thrown defence counsels into a confusion not to be exceeded until the explosion of the first atomic bomb in 1945. New guns, new propellents, new shells, new optical equipment; stronger armour plate and improved forms of ship construction; and above all the increasing menace of the underwater mine and torpedo—these were among the numerous factors the designer and the naval theorist had to consider in planning the future form of what was still regarded as the ultimate weapon of war at sea, the battleship.

The first difficulty was the absence of any experience from which lessons could be drawn. Except for actions like Lissa and Navarino and the small-scale annihilations of the Sino-Japanese war of 1894–5 and the Spanish-American war of 1898, the design of battleships relied largely on theory and argument. But as the size, range, reliability and destructive power of the torpedo rapidly increased in the 1880s and

1890s, it became—as Fisher had long before predicted—the most feared weapon and the dominant influence in battleship design.

Before the turn of the century it was already clear that in action the battleship must shy farther away from its opponent for fear of the crippling underwater blow. Increasing battle range demanded two things: both bigger guns and higher speed to achieve the desired range and out-manoeuvre the enemy. From the basic simplicity and single calibre armament of Benedetto Brin's *Dandolo* and *Duilio* and Nathaniel Barnaby's *Inflexible,* the battleship had turned into an ugly hybrid seemingly intended for destroying anything from a torpedo boat to a protected or armoured cruiser or another battleship, at ranges from a few hundred yards to five or six miles. To cover all these contingencies, she might carry (like the American *Kansas* class) guns of 12-inch, 8-inch, 7-inch, and 3-inch calibre. The provision of ammunition for all these weapons presented a fearfully complicated problem, and any sort of fire control in battle, with all the interference from blast and smoke, with the different speeds of loading and firing, with the shells' varying trajectory in flight and size of 'splash' when they exploded in the water, must become a nightmare.

In the 1890s the scientist provided the sailor with smokeless powder and new guns and shells and propellants so that he could hit the enemy at some 8,000 yards. Yet firing practice was normally carried out at ranges little greater than those at which Trafalgar had been fought, until in the late 1890s, first the French, then the Italians, Germans and Americans, suddenly discovered that they could hit the target almost as accurately at 5,000 yards as they could at 1,000 yards, and thus greatly diminish the risks of receiving damage from enemy torpedo attacks. The British Navy was slow to follow. As C.-in-C. of the Mediterranean Fleet, Fisher learnt of the exceptional range at which the French were firing and took steps to emulate them. Utilizing the unique experience of Captain Percy Scott, Fisher in 1899 instituted long range gunnery practice at 6,000 yards. The difficulties of spotting the splashes with guns of different calibres firing simultaneously at once became apparent. As Marder has written, 'Only by firing salvos with several big guns of the same calibre could there be one kind of splash to show where the shots were falling'[1]—as 'shorts' or 'overs'. The firing of the smaller guns merely confused the observer aloft; moreover, the chances of making a hit with the smaller guns decreased with the increasing range made necessary by the torpedo threat, and the damage they were likely to inflict was diminishing with the increasing powers of resistance of new steel armour plate.

[1] *British Naval Policy*, 527.

With the opening of the new century, it was becoming more and more evident that a dramatic new development in battleship design was imminent, and that it would take the shape of a vessel of the largest practicable displacement and the highest practicable speed, carrying guns of only the largest calibre for destroying its own kind, supported by small weapons for driving off the torpedo carriers.

While still in the Mediterranean, Fisher often discussed the battle-ships he would one day build with the Chief Constructor at Malta dockyard, Mr W. H. Gard, a most shrewd and articulate authority on warship design. How nearly they approached in their discussions the all-big-gun *Dreadnought* design as settled in 1905 is not known. But there is little doubt that the minds of these two men were working along roughly parallel lines with those of the undisputed inspirer of H.M.S. *Dreadnought*, Colonel Vittorio Cuniberti, Constructor to the Italian Navy.

Cuniberti had already gained wide renown as the designer of a class of very fast light battleships which were ideal for Italian needs, when he published a long article in the 1903 edition of *Jane's Fighting Ships* entitled 'An Ideal Warship for the British Navy'. Cuniberti began by demolishing all arguments in favour of a mixed calibre armament because of waste and inefficiency, and envisaged for the Royal Navy a vessel of 17,000 tons with a very high speed of 24 knots, abundant ammunition, protective armour plate 12-inches thick, and no less than twelve 12-inch guns. As no other battleship at this time carried more than four guns of this calibre, Cuniberti could reasonably claim that his imaginary battleship could sweep the seas of all opposition:

'Secure in her exuberant protection with her twelve guns ready, she would swiftly descend on her adversary and pour in a terrible converging fire at the belt.

'Having disposed of her first antagonist, she would at once proceed to attack another, and almost untouched, to despatch yet another . . .'

With the advantage of hindsight, it may seem curious that it took such a long time for the steam-and-steel battleship to reach its ultimate form and specification as laid down by Cuniberti. Two drawbacks, which were later cited again and again by Fisher's detractors, were the increased cost of this super-battleship and the fact that it made obsolete not only the enemy's battleships, but all its owner's existing fleet. In fact, anyone building a fleet of these super-battleships would start from scratch with the rest of the world.

The publication of this article coincided with Fisher's period as C.-in-C. Portsmouth when so many schemes and reforms were germinating in his mind before he achieved supreme power in Whitehall. Among the subjects he studied and discussed were the new warship needs of the Navy to face the German threat. The battleship theme predominated, especially as rumours were rife that the United States, Japan, Russia and Germany were already contemplating entirely new designs. There were exchanges of views with Armstrongs, the big Tyneside ship-builders and gun-makers, and on 12 March 1904 Fisher told Arnold White that the chairman, Sir Andrew Noble, 'came all the way from Newcastle to see me yesterday about a new design for a battleship that will "stagger humanity" . . .'

Discussions between Armstrongs and Fisher at Portsmouth continued through the summer, Armstrongs favouring their new 10-inch gun over Cuniberti's recommended 12-inch.

FROM SIR ANDREW NOBLE[1]

August 21, 1904

MY DEAR ADMIRAL,—I ONLY last week completed a variety of designs in which your principles are practically followed.

Excluding machine guns, there are only two calibres in my type of new battleship. The main armament consists of 14 or 16 10-inch guns, and the secondary armament of 12 or possibly 16 4-inch guns.

I prefer the armament to be all 10-inch guns. They are nearly as powerful as the 12-inch, and you can have far more of them.

Looking at the great use now being made of torpedo vessels I think it well to, substitute the 4-inch for the smaller gun, 12-pr., they now carry. The projectile of the 4-inch gun is much more formidable, and its high explosive shell would put a decisive end to any torpedo vessel. There ought to be no difficulty in detonating small shell if proper means are used, and the Explosives Committee had a most successful day at Ridsdale and Silloth a fortnight ago. I shall send you some photos of the results if you care to see them.

Meanwhile, Fisher had convened an informal committee which included Gard, now Manager of the Constructive Department at Portsmouth dockyard, and Alexander Gracie of a rival firm to Armstrongs, the Fairfield Shipbuilding and Engineering Company. Between them, and while Fisher was simultaneously preparing the groundwork for many more of his reforms, they drafted out a sketch design for Britain's first all-big-gun battleship. In accordance with Armstrongs' recommendation, Fisher held out for a larger number of 10-inch guns. Then on 10 August 1904, the first major engagement between modern

[1] Lieut.-Commander P. K. Kemp (Ed.), *The Papers of Admiral Lord Fisher* (2 vols, London, 1960–4), i, 31. (Hereafter cited as *Fisher Papers.*)

battleships occurred in the Far East. The action between the Japanese and Russians off Round Island, when there was accurate firing at a range as high as 5,000 yards, and the Russian Admiral and all his staff were killed by a single Japanese 12-inch shell, seemed to confirm beyond doubt that only the largest gun could be considered for future battleships.

During that busy summer of 1904, Fisher was in frequent communication with Selborne, and told him of his intention to set up a Committee on New Designs as soon as possible after he took office in order to draw up plans not only for new battleships, but for armoured cruisers and torpedo craft, too. By November, when Fisher had shown how the pace of activity in all departments of the Admiralty could be accelerated, the most revolutionary battleship of all time was well past its generic stage. The members of the Committee on Designs had been selected by December, and they included such illustrious names as Philip Watts, Director of Naval Construction, Lord Kelvin, R. E. Froude of the Admiralty Experimental Works, Gard, and Sir John Thornycroft, with Fisher himself acting as chairman. On the service side, the cream of Fisher's intellectuals were represented, including Prince Louis of Battenberg, John Rushworth Jellicoe, Reginald Bacon, Captain Henry B. Jackson, and the brilliant commander of the torpedo and submarine flotillas, Rear-Admiral Alfred Winsloe. By February, this committee had produced its first progress report, which included a detailed specification of the *Dreadnought* (see Appendix 2). It fell little short of Cuniberti's ideal. There were to be ten instead of twelve 12-inch guns, but as three of the five twin-gun turrets were disposed on the centre line, the battleship could deliver as heavy a broadside, as well as fore and aft fire, as Cuniberti's. Displacement was just short of 18,000 tons, the main armour belt was 11 inches thick and speed 21 knots, 2 knots faster than the fastest battleship then in service.

The first and most evident characteristic of the *Dreadnought* was of course the armament: ten in place of the customary four 12-inch guns, with nothing smaller except a scattering of twenty-seven 12-pounders to ward off torpedo craft. But hidden deep inside the vessel's formidable and aggressive-looking exterior there was to be propelling machinery which was equally novel and which was to silence any doubts that this was a man-of-war which set entirely new standards. For the *Dreadnought* was to be powered by turbines instead of reciprocating engines, a type of machinery which had been used only in torpedo craft.

The main reason why Fisher had had so much trouble in improving the high speed cruising efficiency of the Mediterranean Fleet could be traced to the reciprocating engines of all the big ships under his command.

The working temperatures of pistons and bearings and numerous other moving parts had to be watched constantly. Reciprocating engines were inefficient, noisy, heavy, occupied a great amount of space and consumed a great deal of fuel. 'When steaming at full speed in a man-of-war fitted with reciprocating engines, the engine-room was always a glorified snipe marsh: water lay on the floor-plates and was splashed about everywhere; the officers often were clad in oilskins to avoid being wetted to the skin. The water was necessary to keep the bearings cool. Further, the noise was deafening; so much so that telephones were useless and even voice-pipes were of doubtful value.'[1] A battleship's steam turbine, by contrast and on a vast scale, was like an electric motor beside a car's internal combustion engine. 'In the *Dreadnought*,' wrote the ship's first commander, 'when steaming at full speed, it was only possible to tell that the engines were working, and not stopped, by looking at certain gauges. The whole engine-room was as clean and dry as if the ship was lying at anchor, and not the faintest hum could be heard.'[2] Turbines were shortly to propel the *Dreadnought*, without fuss, without anxiety and almost without vibration clear across the Atlantic at a speed of 17 knots—an achievement far beyond the powers of any other battleship in the world.

Fisher and his committee had one last surprise trick up their sleeve; and it was to have as profound an effect on the deadly international game that was about to be played as the epochal characteristics of the ship herself. The *Dreadnought*'s keel plate was laid on 2 October 1905, she was launched on 10 February 1906, and went to sea one year and one day after she was begun. Such speed of construction was unprecedented.

Fisher used several reasons to justify the speed and the secrecy with which the *Dreadnought* was built. He argued that if the Royal Navy was to make obsolete almost overnight its numerically superior battle Fleet, then it must gain for Britain as great a lead as possible. Thus the lessons learnt secretly from this prototype could be applied to her successors while Germany was still reeling from the blow. Nor, claimed Fisher, could the moral effect on Britain's chief rival be denied, for in one year the Royal Navy had set new standards and gained the equivalent of at least three mixed armament pre-Dreadnought battleships.

But there can be no doubt that Fisher relished every element of the theatrical in the design and construction of the *Dreadnought*, and judged that her sudden revelation on the stage of the world's armouries would not only put the fear of God into the enemy, but also at least temporarily silence 'the packs of yapping hounds' at home who would be snapping at his heels about his past and future reforms.

[1] *Bacon*, i, 263.   [2] *ibid.*

Fisher stage-managed the building of the *Dreadnought* with consummate skill. The secrecy was less to deny her details to Britain's rivals (the American Navy had publicly ordered its own all-big-gun battleships before the *Dreadnought* was laid down and the British ship was therefore hardly likely to retain a mixed armament) than to excite speculation. The most experienced and adroit public relations organization operating today could not have matched Fisher's skill in keeping his wonder ship in the headlines during the period of her building. Never had Fisher's cordial relations with the most important naval journalists paid off so successfully. Even Lieutenant Carlyon Bellairs, the journalist and member of parliament who was unsympathetic to Fisher and was later to become one of his most implacable foes, was consumed with curiosity, and wrote (5 November 1906) to Fisher before the ship was launched, 'I feel a sort of fractional propriety in the *Dreadnought*, for I have always advocated the big gun battleship. I am ready to praise your *Dreadnought* up to the skies as soon as the details are ready for publication.'[1]

Five days later the launching of the *Dreadnought* took place at Portsmouth. For Fisher it was a momentous and glorious occasion, unsurpassed in all his naval career, to which he could look back with satisfaction during the distasteful combats that still lay ahead. A huge crowd, and the press of the world, were present, and Fisher had managed to persuade King Edward to perform the ceremony. Fisher had gone over the arrangements for the day time and again to ensure that there could be no hitch. 'The launch is fixed in my memory,' wrote one journalist, 'because when it came to singing the seamen's hymn "For those in peril on the Sea", Fisher shared a hymn-sheet with His Majesty. I could not believe that another was not available. It struck me that the First Sea Lord had possibly taken care that it should not be offered to King Edward, so that they might sing together.'[2]

Although soon to be overtaken in fighting power by her successors, and regarded as obsolescent by the time war broke out, the *Dreadnought* was a remarkable success for Philip Watts, her designer, especially considering the speed at which she was conceived and built. But the short time she was on the stocks had important consequences. Fisher knew, and had planned from the beginning, that this speed of building would be regarded by the Germans as an intimidating act. The sudden new lead he had gained for the Royal Navy would result in Germany either intensifying her own efforts, or throwing in the sponge—an unlikely alternative. In the event, the *Dreadnought*, by the timing and manner of her appearance, by her ostentatiously evident power, by her

[1] Robinson Papers, vol. 1. Admiralty MSS.   [2] *Hurd*, 75.

warlike name even, was the greatest single cause of increasing German rivalry at sea, and the vessel must therefore bear a measure of responsibility for the outbreak of war eight years later. In German eyes, Fisher and his *Dreadnought* together represented not only the most formidable barrier to legitimate expansionist aspirations, but also the fear of a surprise British preventive war, which many Germans felt acutely right up to 1914.

A further and unexpected result of the speed of the *Dreadnought's* construction was its later use as an argument against accelerating battleship programmes in Britain because it seemed that shipyards could, in an emergency, always catch up with German shipbuilders. It was not generally known that Fisher had appropriated guns and mountings, which normally governed the time it took to build a battleship, from pre-Dreadnoughts already under construction. He also assembled much other material at Portsmouth before the ship was begun.

If the building of the *Dreadnought* was a spectacular rush job, her specification aroused opposition among pacifists, thoughtful liberals, service and lay experts who doubted her fighting value or the trend she was setting, and all those many people in the Navy, in society and journalism who were hostile to all the works of Fisher anyway.

Beresford was one of a number of Admirals who had been kept informed of the *Dreadnought's* plans and were sometimes consulted by Fisher over problems. By this means many senior serving officers who might otherwise later have voiced their criticism were forced to remain silent. Fisher, by eliciting Beresford's general agreement to the design nine months before her keel was laid down, deprived him of a weapon which he could have wielded destructively in their later battles.

The most powerful argument used by Fisher's critics was that it was wrong policy for the nation possessing overwhelming power at sea and the greatest shipbuilding capacity to pioneer new types of fighting ships; that traditionally it was Britain's rôle to allow others to experiment, and then herself improve in quality and surpass in numbers. As clever a man as Sir George Clarke considered that 'the "Dreadnought policy" evolved at a time when our naval preponderance in battleships was overwhelming, appeared to be dangerously misconceived and I did all that was possible to cause it to be re-considered . . . I believe it is now generally recognised that a great mistake was made... Of the *Dreadnought*, which I inspected at Portsmouth, I formed a poor impression,' continued Clarke, who entered in his diary the note that 'She is full of mistakes due to inordinate hurry and want of study.' Sir Frederick Richards wrote (3 May 1907) to Clarke from his seat of retirement: 'It has not hitherto been the practice of the British Admiralty, in international competition in shipbuilding, to take any such action as has been adopted in the case of that ship . . . Now we start a great and expensive advertisement . . . The waste of millions on docks for these creatures has yet to be discounted—but enough.'[1]

There were valid criticisms of the general and detail design of the *Dreadnought*. She was slow to respond to the helm, and her turret arrangement, which eschewed the superimposition already favoured by the Americans, was wasteful of space, displacement and money. It was also a great folly (later to be repeated) to place the foremast abaft the fore funnel. 'On one occasion,' Percy Scott later recalled, 'after the look-out man had gone aloft, the ship steamed at a high speed against a headwind, so that the mast near the top of the funnel got almost red hot. The result was that the look-out man could not come down for his meals, and it was necessary to hoist food up to him by the signal halyards which had luckily not been burned through.'[2]

The distinguished American historian and thinker, Admiral A. T. Mahan, led the school which held that 'Budgets not being illimitable in size, there results between numbers and individual cost of ship an opposition, in the adjustment of which, as in that between speed and offensive power, there should be no compromise.'[3] Bigger ships meant fewer ships, and thus, argued Mahan, the temporary loss of a single unit when coaling or in dock, or the permanent loss in combat, was therefore the more serious.

Fisher responded with customary violence to every criticism of his beloved *Dreadnought*. Of Mahan, he wrote (5 October 1906) to Tweedmouth, '. . . as a Yankee officer told me lately, he is *passé*, and has become a second Brassey and equally a bore! The advocates of small battleships and low speed have been so often pulverized . . . that it's wonderful how they can ever get anyone to print such nonsense.' When Admiral Sir Cyprian Bridge read a paper before the Institute of Naval Architects suggesting that moderate increases of speed are no use after an action, and that small battleships are more valuable than large ones, Fisher replied: 'Speed is the main factor in forcing an action, and speed is always of potential value strategically, and we fail to see how anyone can discount its worth . . . Speed can never be put into a ship after she has once been built. Want of speed in a single ship handicaps every Fleet she may be attached to for twenty years to come! Twenty years of evil may result from listening to faddists.'[4]

---

[1] *My Working Life*, 209. [2] *Scott*, 263.
[3] 'The Battle of the Sea of Japan' in *Proceedings of the U.S. Naval Institute*, June 1906.
[4] Tweedmouth Papers, vol. 3, no. 8. Admiralty MSS.

Although other factors contributed to the Japanese success in the battle off Round Island and the annihilation of Tsu-Shima in May 1905, Fisher could reasonably cite speed as one of the most important. 'At the opening [of Tsu-Shima] . . . the Japanese Fleet,' Fisher claimed, 'due to skilful handling, held a commanding position, giving a concentration of fire on the heads of the Russian lines. Had they not possessed superior speed, the Japanese would rapidly have lost this advantage, as the Russians turned away to starboard and compelled the Japanese to move along a circle of larger radius; their greater speed enabled the Japanese to maintain their advantage and so continue the concentration of fire on the Russian van until so much damage had been inflicted that the Russians lost all order and were crushed.'[1]

Nothing more strongly influenced Fisher in favour of speed above all qualities, even those of protection and armament, than the result of the Russo-Japanese war. Dearly as he loved the *Dreadnought*, the armoured cruisers which were the second class of ship considered by the Committee on Designs, were even closer to his heart. The new armoured cruisers, a class of warship introduced by the French Navy as commerce raiding cruisers and too fast to be caught by battleships, were intended to be as radical a step forward over their predecessors as the *Dreadnought* was over existing battleships. Again the armament was to be 12-inch guns, and nothing else except anti-torpedo weapons, and like her battleship cousin, the speed was to be far above that of any other cruiser in the world.

Committee discussions on the exact specification of this super armoured cruiser lasted a long time. Some members favoured using the 9·2-inch gun, a very satisfactory weapon with a high rate of fire, but throwing a projectile of less than half the weight of the 12-inch. Fisher argued for the larger size, and got his way. According to his own account, he went further than this. He had by now become so enamoured of the new armoured cruiser design that he wanted nothing else, envisaging a battle fleet of 12-inch gunned cruisers capable of outgunning and of outpacing by a wide margin any enemy they might confront. Nothing in the world would be able to catch them, and they would extricate themselves from any tight corner without difficulty. Writing to Arnold White, Fisher contended, 'It's no use one or two knots superiority of speed—a dirty bottom brings that down! It's a d——d big six or seven knots surplus that does the trick! THEN you can fight HOW you like, WHEN you like, and WHERE you like!' When Fisher proposed that only large armoured cruisers should be laid down, he lost by one vote in the committee—a fortunate result

[1] *Records*, 111.

for the Royal Navy considering how seriously they were to suffer as a class when opposed by German battleships and stronger German battle cruisers.

The first batch of battle cruisers, the 'I' class *Invincible, Indomitable* and *Inflexible,* were laid down after the *Dreadnought* was completed, and partly because they were for the first years of their lives called 'large armoured cruisers' rather than by the later term 'battle cruisers' and partly because the *Dreadnought* herself stole most of their thunder, they did not for a time arouse such controversy. Only later did their formidable and splendid characteristics impress themselves on the public. In appearance, at high speed, they were the very summation of power and ferocity at sea—long, lean and superbly handsome, with huge bow waves piling up from their stems as they cut through the water at 25 knots, and black smoke pouring from their three funnels. The power to deliver the swift and deadly blow was unmatched by any other warship afloat, their speed being at least six knots higher than that of the fastest battleship and their heavy gun broadside 50 % heavier. Only a few voices were raised to express disquiet at their armour protection, which on the main belt was only 6 inches thick, no more than that of the armoured cruisers they superseded.

But Fisher would listen to no word of criticism of his 'greyhounds of the sea', his 'New Testament ships', his 'hares to catch tortoises'. The Committee on Designs called them 'battleships in disguise', and members individually praised them enthusiastically, even if they were not prepared to forego the battleship entirely. Bacon envisaged the battle cruisers forming 'a fast light squadron to supplement the battleships in action, and worry the ships in the van and rear of the enemy's line', and to 'assist in a general action by engaging some of the enemy's ships which were already fighting our battleships.'[1] Others contended that they could fight in the line alongside battleships; or that their first rôle would be to hunt down enemy raiders. The committee claimed yet another mission for the battle cruiser, 'to overtake and keep touch with a fleeing battle fleet, and possibly bring it to bay by the wounding which her 12-inch guns are capable of at 7 miles or more . . .'[2]

The trouble with this hybrid man-of-war was that its supposed functions were never thoroughly thought out in peace time. Although they justified themselves as commerce raider destroyers and invoked a marvellous sense of self-confidence in those who served in them and with them, they suffered for lack of a properly defined rôle in war. The Germans felt obliged to follow the British lead, and sensibly

---

[1] *Bacon*, i, 256.   [2] *Fisher Papers*, i, 221.

built stronger, better protected ships which could survive a worse hammering than British battleships. The Japanese, too, followed suit, but for several years the American Navy remained loyal to at least a part of the Mahan belief and built only slow battleships of modest displacement.

Both the *Dreadnought* and her faster consorts rapidly proved their unique qualities of power and speed in trials which were partly secret, and improved vessels of the same general type were laid down in numbers and at intervals as political policy and estimates permitted. Inevitably, the Dreadnought battleships and battle cruisers grew larger, the gun calibres were increased and their disposition improved.

Until the appearance of the *Dreadnought* in 1906, Germany had small chance of matching the strength of the greatest naval power in the world; and Fisher could rightly claim that 'for 12 months past not a single battleship has been laid down in Europe, and this simply and solely owing to the dramatic appearance of the "Dreadnought", which upset all the calculations in Foreign Admiralties . . .'[1] Now it was not beyond the bounds of possibility that if Germany was prepared to expend the money and materials, she could in a few years build a battle fleet that could equal or even surpass that of Britain. For this reason, the technical controversy over the revolutionary types of warship with which Fisher planned to re-equip the fleet rapidly diminished in importance by contrast with the bitter political combats at home, and the more fearful rivalry with the German Navy, in which Fisher now became embroiled.

[1] *Records*, 101.

Chapter 4

THE FIGHT ON TWO FRONTS

The *Dreadnought* was one of the first and most important landmarks in the long, ever-widening channel of Anglo-German naval rivalry which led to open warfare less than a decade after the battleship was laid down. The rate at which her successors and their German counterparts left the slipways marked the tragic passage along the swiftly flowing current to catastrophe. Hopeful but futile efforts were made by pacifist influences on both sides to halt the tide, and the vast cost of these two growing armadas led to internal political conflicts in both countries in which the naval leaders became deeply involved. The historical evidence of the massed fleets that confronted one another across the North Sea in 1914 was the proof of how successful Admirals Sir John Fisher and Alfred von Tirpitz had been in their handling of the political side of their tasks, although their fleets could never have come into being without the enthusiastic support of politicians and statesmen, most of the press, the naval pressure groups, and finally the majority of the British and German people—for there can be no doubt that the incitement of mutual fear led to nearly everyone *wanting* these vast navies.

It was significant and ominous that Fisher's arrival at Whitehall in October 1904 coincided with, as well as contributing to, a marked decline in Anglo-German relations, which had never fully recovered from the antagonisms set up by the Boer War. Fisher's conviction that German naval expansion was aimed at Britain and Britain alone had come to be accepted by the Admiralty, the Foreign Office, many senior statesmen, and increasingly by King Edward himself, who in 1905 'considered that the folly of his German nephew portended war'.[1] Selborne was certain that 'the new German fleet . . . is designed for a possible conflict with the British fleet'.[2]

---

[1] Philip Magnus, *King Edward VII* (London, 1964), 341.　　[2] *Marder*, i, 107.

On the German side, the concentration of British sea power in the North Sea and the formation of the Home Fleet, had already been noted anxiously by the German Admiralty, and the nature of the threat was gradually made known to the public by newspaper articles and the publication of books prophesying future conflict. Graf von Reventlow contributed articles to the *Tägliche Rumbschau* and the *Hamburger Nachrichten*. One headed 'The English Menace' is typical: 'It is remarkable with what indifference, in spite of all the occurrences of the last few years, the new ordering of the English Fleet . . . has been received here. We have grown accustomed, indeed, to being threatened by England in word and deed, and to being regarded as "Germania delenda". Two years ago already the whole English Press recognized the then reorganization, or shifting of the centre of power to the North Sea, as directed against Germany . . .

'Let anyone take the map and notice on it the English Naval Stations and the strength appointed to them; it will show very clearly that it is a strategic offensive position as regards Germany, or, in other words, a menace . . .'[1]

'Who would be so immoral as to bring on the horrors of war?' asked the *Staatsburger Zeitung* (25 October 1906) ironically. '"No," said the Britons . . . and they do so by . . . building "Dreadnoughts". Very modestly now follows, under the idyllic title of Home Fleet, the concentration of English Naval Forces against us . . . to get ready and clear for sailing on a Viking raid. One fine day when the Home Fleet is ready to put out to sea the Britons will find some grounds or other for being filled with prodigious indignation against us, and then in the name of morality will run out at full speed . . .'[2]

A pamphlet entitled *Are Our Hansa Towns in Danger?* in which an imaginary future war resulted in the destruction of the German Fleet and the capture of Heligoland, had a wide sale, 'and the lesson derived is that the building programme should be accelerated and increased so that the desired thirty-eight battleships may be available as soon as possible'.[3] An instant best-seller was a book entitled *Der Weltkrieg: Deutsche Träume*, which more cheerfully foretold a Franco-German-Russian coalition resulting in the invasion and defeat of England and the destruction of the Royal Navy at Flushing.

Many 'scare' books of this *genre* were published in Germany and Britain and all owed much to their prototype, *The Riddle of the Sands*

---

[1] Quoted in 'German Views of the Home Fleet', a report by the British Naval Attaché in Berlin, 14 November 1906. Robinson Papers, vol. 1. Admiralty MSS.

[2] *ibid.*

[3] *ibid.* Quoted in memo. Ottley to Fisher, 4 December 1906.

by Erskine Childers (1903), although none matched this book's distinction and verisimilitude—and capacity to instil fear in the reader.

A further sharpening of mutual hostility was ground by the failure of King Edward's state visit to Kiel in June 1905, and the arrival by the King's invitation of a German squadron at Plymouth a few weeks later. There was nothing uncivil about the German reception of the British officers; equally there was no warmth or friendliness, and the professional efficiency of the German Fleet was noted with disquiet by the guests. Relations between the officers were no happier at Plymouth in July and British newspapers were distinctly cool.

Fisher's presence in the office of the First Sea Lord did not help the situation. His forthright pugnacity at The Hague Peace Conference four years earlier, where he had preached hell-fire and total warfare without restraint; his formidable reputation as C.-in-C. of the Mediterranean Fleet; his widely proclaimed belief in 'the three R's'; and his blunt, aggressive appearance, all marked him as a most dangerous antagonist.

Throughout the first year of Fisher's term of office evidence of the extent of British hostility to German naval expansion accumulated at the German Admiralty. The Kaiser, von Tirpitz and the German Navy League could cite anti-German articles in newspapers ranging from the disreputable class, through professional journals like the *Army and Navy Gazette*, to *The Times*, and what the Kaiser called 'scandalous articles' by J. L. Garvin ('Calchas') in the militant newspaper, the *Observer*. From this time there grew a genuine fear in Germany that Britain planned a sudden naval attack without a declaration of war. Germans were frequently reminded of the surrender of the Danish Fleet at Copenhagen in peacetime to Admiral James Gambier in 1807 following a surprise attack; nor was it easy to forget the successful results of the recent Japanese night assault on the Russian Fleet at Port Arthur without a declaration. It was unlikely that news of Fisher's proposal to King Edward, made soon after Fisher's appointment as First Sea Lord, that the Royal Navy should 'Copenhagen' the German Fleet, ever reached Germany; nor the King's reported response, 'My God, Fisher, you must be mad!' But the threat, made by Arthur Lee, the Civil Lord of the Admiralty, on 3 February 1905, that the Royal Navy 'would get its blow in first, before the other side had time even to read in the papers that war had been declared', was widely and angrily reported in Germany.

The Kaiser was certain that it was Fisher's intention to order a surprise attack. According to Alfred Beit, the powerful South African industrialist, the Kaiser had told him that 'England wanted war: not the King—nor perhaps the Government; but influential people like Sir John Fisher!' Beit, who had recently talked to Fisher while taking the cure with him at Carlsbad, had attempted to disabuse the Kaiser, without success. 'He [Fisher] thinks it is the hour for the attack,' replied the Kaiser, 'and I am not blaming him. I quite understand his point of view; but we too are prepared, and if it comes to war the result will depend upon the weight you carry into action—namely, a good conscience, and I have that.'[1]

Esher related this conversation to Fisher, but privately took seriously Fisher's threats to attack. In February 1906 Esher wrote to Clarke about the unlikelihood of the Germans getting in a surprise blow against England. 'There is far more risk of J.F. taking the initiative and precipitating war.

'I don't think he will do so, but the chances are more likely that we shall take the fatal step too soon than too late . . .'[2]

It is hardly surprising that Fisher's intentions on the question of a surprise attack on Kiel and a preventive war were misunderstood, even by such ardent admirers of his qualities as Esher and Selborne. It was his practice, derived from years of command at sea, to indulge in intellectual exercises to meet any set of hypothetical strategical and tactical circumstances. His manner of expression was also invariably extravagant, and increasingly so as he became older and his battles fiercer. Finally, there was his mischievous delight in exaggerating his own ferocity. These characteristics had led him into false and sometimes awkward positions in the past; but never before into such deep water as this. He was not in the least contrite, but he regretted what he had said to the King. Fisher was not 'mad', as King Edward had suggested; but he seriously, and increasingly, lacked self-discipline. He knew that an unprovoked onslaught on the German Fleet would be as unacceptable to the service as it would be to the country, and would alienate Britain from the rest of the civilized world. Fisher would no more order a peacetime attack on Kiel or Wilhelmshaven than he would (as he had once light-heartedly advocated) hit his enemy in the belly, kick him when he was down, and boil his prisoners in oil '(*if you take any!*)'

Fisher hated war. 'He was a man of peace and it was his conviction that war was the greatest idiocy of life.'[3] He used every means to introduce into the minds of his country's enemies that he was a frightful warmonger, but became worried when his inflammatory threats were taken seriously at home, especially by his friends. Summoned to

[1] *Bacon*, ii, 72.   [2] *Esher*, ii, 144.   [3] *Marder*, i, 112.

Fisher's office (17 December 1906) while on leave from Germany, the British naval attaché reported on German feelings towards him.

'He asked me if it was true they considered he wanted to fight them in Germany and where they had the story from,' wrote Commander Philip Dumas. 'I told him, which I thought gratified him enormously, that he was looked on in Germany as our most important man and that he was pushing on for a war. He asked if I had ever heard of any such remark directly traceable to him and I told him "No," which he seized on at once and said, "I know the King wants to see you. Mind you let him know that, and manage to tell him somehow." He then went on to discuss such a war and said he had once told Balfour that a Bismarck in England would arrange it as a matter of true policy, but as for saying that he wanted it, nothing was further from the truth and he defied anyone to fasten such a remark on him.'[1]

The day in October 1906 when the *Dreadnought* went to sea, and her magnificent profile was reproduced all over the world, brought Anglo-German relations to a new low level. Throughout the year the Germans had made every effort through their contacts in Britain to obtain the fullest information on the ship, and their British counterparts anxiously searched for news of German building plans. It was inevitable that Germany should follow suit, but would she build bigger than the *Dreadnought*? And what was her armament and how was it disposed, what was her speed, her protection, her endurance?

The most likely person to find out was Dumas, a superbly inquisitive and dogged naval attaché. Germany had been about to lay down a new class of battleship, reportedly with a broadside of six 11-inch guns, when the nature of Britain's new vessel was learned. As Fisher proudly claimed, all work came to a standstill for many months while further news was awaited; and when it was received, it took many more months to draw up new plans and order and manufacture the material.

Three months before the *Dreadnought* went to sea, Dumas was at Schichau's yard at Elbing, where he 'picked up many little useful items of information, among others that they would be laying down a large new battleship in the autumn . . .'[2] The British Admiralty wanted more precise information than this, and over the following months Dumas did his best to provide it, as his diaries indicate:

September 7th 1906
Started at 9.15 for the [Krupp's] works and had quite the most bewildering forenoon I have ever passed and it was quite evident to me that by showing me multitudinous details they wished to prevent me remember-

---

[1] Dumas Papers.   [2] *ibid.*

ing anything. I was, moreover, not allowed to take any notes so it was altogether maddening . . .

September 10th, 1906 (Wilhelmshaven)
After lunch set out and paid my official call but saw no-one except the dockyard Admiral's Flag-lieutenant, who I found studying an apocryphal plan of the *Dreadnought*.

September 11th, 1906
. . . Astonished to find the slip on which they are going to build the battleship here will not be ready till April and can only put down their slowness to a desire to see and copy the *Dreadnought*.

December 5th, 1906
A frantic letter from Ottley[1] saying he hears a rumour that Germany is already building her new ships behind screens at Kiel and will I go and look . . .

June 14th, 1907
. . . I found a note from Bashford saying he had been told officially that none of the vessels of the 1906–7 programme had yet been laid down . . .

June 20th, 1907
. . . A long and very dreary journey to Kiel where however in five minutes I had paid for the cost of my trip by seeing the state of preparedness of E. and Ersatz Baden. [Two Dreadnought-type battleships].

May 19th, 1908
. . . Bashford to see me with a photograph of the *Nassau* just after launching. It is not of much use but I think I can detect the position of all her guns . . . [2]

As an official begetter of information, Dumas was warmly welcomed on his leaves in London, and was ordered in turn to the Admiralty, Foreign Office, and Buckingham Palace. He was always interviewed closely by Fisher, and King Edward, too, liked to have the latest information:

December 20th, 1906
. . . Into the same room as before, H.M. coming in from his bedroom door in the opposite corner at the same moment. He immediately shook hands and led the way to two armchairs by the fire and told me to sit down and asked how I was and how long was it since last we met.

---

[1] Captain Charles Ottley, Director of Naval Intelligence.   [2] Dumas Papers.

He then went on to say that he had read my very interesting letters and was pleased with them and asked me innumerable questions about the ships building; when the new ones would be commenced; was it true the slips were delaying them; what I thought the armament was to be; what would be the probable whole cost to Germany of the transitions to the bigger ship type; would the canal require widening; what would be the cost. To sum all this up I said the whole cost of harbour and canal works would not be far off twelve million pounds. He looked astonished and said, 'Oh, a great sum.' . . . [1]

In referring to the Kiel Canal, King Edward touched on an especially raw spot for the German Admiralty, and one of the most provocative consequences of the *Dreadnought*. The 60-miles-long Kiel Canal, linking the Baltic with the North Sea and completed in 1895 was the master key to the communications of the German Fleet, allowing it to proceed from one sea to the other, through a series of locks, in a matter of ten hours, instead of taking the long and difficult journey through the Skaggerack. Its width was sufficient for a pre-Dreadnought battleship, but inadequate for the greater displacement demanded by a battleship to match the gunpower of the *Dreadnought* herself.

There is no evidence that this strategical blow to the rival Navy was considered when plans were drawn up for the *Dreadnought* by the Committee on Designs in 1905, but it is inconceivable that it was not, at an early stage, noted with satisfaction. After she went to sea, Fisher frequently crowed about the crippling effect the need to build bigger ships caused to the German Navy. Reminiscing about this time many years later, Fisher recalled a further oblique consequence, which his wily mind is likely to have played on when the plans for the *Dreadnought* were drawn up:

'If the German Navy followed suit . . . it meant a new Kiel Canal and many millions sterling more to dredge their harbours, and their approaches! And, by the way, this enabled thirty-three [British] pre-Dreadnought battleships to become available for fighting Germany which were previously incapacitated by their heavy draught of water! Rather Machiavellian!'[2]

Certainly within a month of the battleship's first public appearance, the Admiralty was anxiously enquiring about German plans for the canal; and as early as 13 November 1906, Mr A. Sartori, the British Consul at Kiel, was able to confirm rumours to Dumas. 'I have pleasure

---

[1] Dumas Papers.   [2] 'Lord Fisher on the Navy', *The Times*, 10 September 1919.

in informing you,' he wrote, 'that to my certain knowledge a thorough widening of the canal is intended. It is not known here what the figures will be, but I believe they will not be much less than double the size of the present breadth. Further, two new locks at each end are intended, considerably bigger than the present ones in every respect . . . and a general widening of the canal in order to do away with the heavy curves.'[1]

From this and subsequent information, Fisher was able to calculate not only the likely cost but also the likely time the rebuilding would occupy, and make one of his more accurate and astonishing forecasts. Eight years was the minimum time; and he further considered that the Germans would get their harvest in before going to war: hostilities would therefore break out in September or October of 1914. He subsequently amended the date to a Bank Holiday in 1914—and Britain went to war with Germany on August 4.

From time to time in British naval history the term 'two-power standard' had been used by the Admiralty as a convenient measure by which the minimum requirements of the fleet could be calculated. It dated back to the French wars, when Britain's security depended on her Navy matching the combined strength of France and Spain. There were times during the nineteenth century when the standard was in jeopardy, and naval 'scares' required its reaffirmation. The great re-alignments of power at the turn of the century—the Anglo-Japanese Alliance, the *Entente Cordiale*, the elimination of the Russian Fleet in 1905, and the growing menace of German naval rearmament—all demanded a reconsideration of the standard. Fisher saw to this as soon as he reached the Admiralty and appointed a committee presided over by Prince Louis. This committee decided that the most likely combinations of future foes were Russia and Germany on the one hand, France and Russia on the other. The Committee had also to consider the very real danger that after a successful war against two of these powers, Britain in a greatly weakened condition might be attacked by a third power. To meet this contingency the two-power standard was amended to 'two plus ten-per-cent', at least in capital ships. This was reaffirmed by a second committee's findings in February 1905.

But such was the pace of events that by the end of the year all this long-term planning was already obsolete. The Japanese had disposed of the Russian Fleet, and themselves emerged as a major naval power. America, already showing anxiety about the future control of the Pacific, was fast expanding her own Fleet. The Moroccan crisis, when Germany claimed to have 'great and growing interests' in that country

[1] Robinson Papers, vol. 1. Admiralty MSS.

as a taunt and challenge to the *entente*, instead had sealed many of the last breaches in Anglo-French relations. And it had become manifestly evident even to the strongest opponents of Teutophobia that Germany meant business at sea.

The year 1906 marked the final surrender of the Admiralty to the need to base its strength on the shifting sands of alliances. It was, too, the year of the demise of insular isolation. From the last months of 1906, the process begun by the Japanese Alliance of 1902 was complete. A Liberal Government, committed to public welfare including an expensive old age pension scheme, was in power (December 1905) and was determined not to risk its political future by piling up excessive armaments now that the country was no longer standing alone and there was only one likely enemy. Henceforward the Royal Navy would have to base its demands on the growing strength of Germany, and later of Austria, too.

Fisher was forced to trim his sails to the new Liberal winds blowing through Whitehall and accept the situation, as well as the weakness of his new First Lord, Tweedmouth. Besides, he was so fully occupied in proclaiming the unique powers of destruction of his new battleship that 1906 was a bad year to fight the Cabinet over next year's programme. Tweedmouth's Conservative predecessor, Cawdor, had laid down an annual programme of four big ships—Dreadnought battleships and battle cruisers—to meet the German threat and replace the British battleships made obsolete by the introduction of the all-big-gun ship. Campbell-Bannerman's Liberal Government at first accepted this inheritance and the estimates providing for them were approved by Parliament in March 1906. Then, like other governments which have come to power on promises of welfare for the masses, it had to make economies in its defence commitments. On 12 July Tweedmouth agreed, on behalf of the Board of Admiralty, to accept a 50 % cut in capital ship construction in the 1907–8 estimates, although the number could be increased from two to three if the second Hague Peace Conference, planned to take place the following year, failed to reach an agreement for the mutual reduction of armaments.

When the reduction was announced in Parliament on 27 July 1906, there were cries of outrage from the Conservative opposition. 'What possible confidence could the country have in its naval advisers?' demanded one member. 'Surely the Government owed some more adequate reasons than had yet been given for such great reductions.' (Opposition cheers.)[1] The Navy League was dismayed, and the militant and Conservative press attacked Fisher, Tweedmouth, the

[1] *The Times*, 28 July 1906.

Board, and Campbell-Bannerman's Government for cowardice. 'Lord Tweedmouth and Mr Robertson, having tasted blood in their reduction of this year's estimates', wrote *The Globe* (21 September 1906), 'are about to strike a blow at the vital efficiency of the Navy. But what are we to think of the naval officers on the Admiralty Board, men who cannot plead the blindness and ignorance of their civilian colleagues? No one knows better than Sir John Fisher the real nature and the inevitable consequences of those acts to which he is a consenting party. And we are not speaking at random when we assert that more than any one man, the responsibility and the guilt for those reductions lies at this door.'

Rumours began to circulate that Germany was answering this British reduction by a great increase, and a statement from Germany that her own Dreadnoughts would be bigger and more heavily armed than the *Dreadnought* herself added further fuel to the fire of 'the blue funk school'[1] as Fisher's supporters termed the Board's detractors.

Again Fisher was handicapped by his inability, for security reasons, to divulge the true statistical superiority of the *Dreadnought*, the fact that the three supposed armoured cruisers under construction were infinitely more powerful than any German battleship, and that the Germans were in a state of confused indecision about the nature of their own ships, made known by Dumas's confidential reports. On his annual leave, Fisher wrote in exasperation to Tweedmouth:

TO THE EARL OF TWEEDMOUTH

Levico
September 26th, 1906

Secret and Private

'Party,' as usual, has come before 'patriotism,' and I have it on undoubted authority that a skilfully organized 'Fleet Street' conspiracy is endeavouring to excite the British Public to believe *three* things:—

I. British naval supremacy is endagered by the Admiralty shipbuilding policy.

II. The repairs of ships are so in arrear that the fighting efficiency of the Fleet is being sacrificed.

III. That the present damnable and effete First Sea Lord must be got rid of.

Well, in regard to I and II, I've given certain leading facts and statements upon which to found a complete answer, based on considerations which I will briefly enumerate presently, and I propose that at the psychological moment a public statement should be made, and cause the earth to open and

---

[1] 'Did you invent the name of the "Blue Funk School" for those who oppose the "Blue Water School"? *It's splendid!*' Fisher to Arnold White, October 1906. The 'Blue Water School' represented those whose defence beliefs rested on a powerful Navy.

swallow up Korah, Dathan, Abiram, and all their company, who are represented by the *National Review*, the *Daily Mail*, and that pestilent young ass who represents King's Lynn [Carlyon Bellairs]. A calm and studied statement verified by accompanying facts can prove two things:—

(*a*) In dropping the one Dreadnought this year we are only doing what has been done in the preceding two years (and *more also*) by the late Government. That is to say, the foreign shipbuilding not having made the advances stated in foreign official statements, we were not justified in spending the money for the sole reason that Parliament had generously voted it.

(*b*) Also, our curtailed shipbuilding policy is so enormously in advance of our requirements (*at present*) that it's simply stupid to talk of the loss of our naval supremacy.

1 Dreadnought built;
3 to be laid down this year;
3 next year (because the Hague Conference will be futile);
3 'Invincibles' building, which vessels (*in my opinion*) *superior* to
— Dreadnoughts
10 Dreadnoughts practically built or building in two years!!!

What is there to touch this in foreign shipbuilding programmes?

Again (*and this requires to be most prominently and emphatically reiterated, ad nauseam*): 'The consistent policy of the Board of Admiralty since October 21, 1904, is to have a *yearly* programme only. *"Sufficient unto the year is the shipbuilding thereof."* We are not going to be frightened by foreign 'paper programmes' (the bogey of agitators!). But when foreigners, and especially Germans, actually build, *then* we will double!! But no houses of cards for us! Our present margin of superiority over Germany (*our only possible foe for years*) is so great as to render it absurd in the extreme to talk of anything endangering our naval supremacy, *even if we stopped all shipbuilding altogether*!!!

Anxiety lest King Edward might be having doubts about the reductions and the Board's rule, impelled Fisher to write again to Tweedmouth, who was staying with the King at Balmoral, to underline any explanation the First Lord had already given to the King.

TO THE EARL OF TWEEDMOUTH

Levico
October 5th, 1906

Dear Lord Tweedmouth,

Your second letter from Balmoral has just reached me, and I can only say that when you told His Majesty that nothing rash had ever been done or was contemplated, and that the case for Admiralty policy was unanswerably strong and only a continuity of that pursued since October 21st, 1904, *you were stating to His Majesty the exact and literal truth*! When Lord Selborne informed me on

May 14th, 1904, that the King had been pleased to approve my appointment as First Sea Lord, I had a long interview with Lord Selborne (as Lord Knollys is aware—for I had serious doubts as to the acceptance of the post, and consulted him before seeing Lord Selborne), and I put before him every single one of the Reforms that have already been carried out, those still in progress, and those yet to come, and I told Lord Selborne and Lord Knollys that all these Reforms were based on years of careful consideration and discussion with the best brains of the Service. I am writing all this at length so as to disabuse the King, when next you may have the opportunity of waiting on His Majesty, that the vulgar error has even a grain of truth in it that the Reforms introduced during the last two years are in any way piecemeal or haphazard. *On the contrary*, EVERY SINGLE ITEM IS PART OF ONE HARMONIOUS WHOLE! . . . in accordance with custom I know you will be sure to send the King the full and detailed account he wishes for, as regards the nucleus crews and any readjustment in the strength of our Squadrons.

The time is not yet ripe for this. We sent very confidentially to the Commanders-in-Chief what the Board had in view, and invited them to offer any remarks before we issued the final orders officially and publicly, and evidently some of these officers have broken faith with the Admiralty, and have been writing privately to the King or those who have told His Majesty, as mentioned in your last letter, or else those officers are writing entirely in the dark as to what is being arranged for.

As I ventured to put it to Lord Cawdor on a similar occasion of fright, is it likely, with such a Board of Admiralty as we have, that any steps would be suggested that would imperil our naval strength, and for ever ruin our reputations? Every conceivable motive exists for the Sea Lords to go in for big Estimates, and it has been a strange feature (AS SIR EVAN MACGREGOR WILL VERIFY TO YOU) that the political and civil pressure has been against economy in the Estimates, and Lord Selborne wouldn't take the saving that was prepared for him, and afterwards we had to press for the reduction that was made in the following year also. But I consider we should be grossly guilty if we spend one farthing more than necessary, and I am certain you share this view. I am busy preparing the various notes that will be of service to you in meeting any and every possible criticism . . . A very well-informed friend writes to me (and it is confirmed from other sources) that public opinion utterly repudiates any want of confidence in the Admiralty . . .

Personally, I am absolutely delighted with and revel in hostile criticism. I know nothing more intensely gratifying than placarding your enemy as a fool, which all the present criticism so easily admits of! Forgive me for troubling you with so much.

Our position in every little particular is magnificently splendid.

Yours truly,
J. A. Fisher

For the greater part of 1907 Fisher was content to match the political need of the Liberal Government for naval economy. By the end of the year there would be six Dreadnought battleships built or building, and one more was due to be laid down in 1908. In addition, all three of the first battle cruisers would be completed before the end of 1908. There appeared every likelihood that the Royal Navy would have ten Dreadnoughts before Germany got her first two, S.M.S. *Nassau* and *Westfalen,* laid down in the summer of 1907. Fisher wrote joyfully to his King, who wanted his views on a recently published book critical of Admiralty policy called *Germany's Swelled Head* by Dr Emil Reich.

TO KING EDWARD

Molveno
October 4th, 1907

Sir,

With my humble duty to Your Majesty, I have just received Reich's book from Davidson with Your Majesty's commands to me to submit my remarks thereon from a naval point of view.

On naval points the book is one unmitigated mass of misrepresentations, not redeemed by even *one* particle of truth! In March this year *it is an absolute fact* that Germany had not laid down a single Dreadnought, nor had she commenced building a single big ship for 18 months (*Germany has been paralysed by the Dreadnought!*) The more the German Admiralty looked into her qualities, the more convinced they became that they must follow suit, and the more convinced they were that the whole of their existing Battle Fleet was utterly useless *because utterly wanting in gun power!* (Half of their whole Battle Fleet are only equal to our armoured cruisers!) The German Admiralty wrestled with the Dreadnought problem for 18 months and did nothing. *Why?* Because it meant spending 12½ millions sterling on widening and deepening the Kiel Canal and in dredging all their harbours and all the approaches to their harbours, because if they did not do so it would be no use building German Dreadnoughts, because they couldn't float anywhere in the harbours of Germany! *But there was another reason never yet made public.* Our *existing* battleships of the latest type draw too much water to get close into the German waters, but the German Admiralty is going (is *obliged*) to spend 12½ millions sterling to allow our existing ships to go and fight them! It was a Machiavellian interference of Providence on our behalf that brought about the evolution of the *Dreadnought!*

To return to Mr Reich. As I mentioned just now to Your Majesty, he makes the flesh creep of the British Public at page 78 *et sequitur* by saying what the Germans *are going to do.* He doesn't say what *they* have *not* done and what *we* have done!

England has 7 Dreadnoughts and 3 'Invincibles' (in my opinion better than Dreadnoughts), total—10 Dreadnoughts built and building, *while Germany in March last had not begun one!* even if in May last a German Dreadnought had been commenced! You will see, Sir, from this *one fact* alone what a liar Mr

Reich is! Again, at page 86, he makes out the Germans are stronger in torpedo craft, etc. 'As a protection against the possible attacks of such a German force, Great Britain maintains in the North Sea only 24 fully commissioned destroyers.' What are the facts as stated in an *Admiralty official document* dated August 22nd, 1907? 'We have 123 destroyers and 40 submarines; the Germans have 48 destroyers and *one submarine*.' The whole of our destroyers and submarines are *absolutely efficient and ready for instant battle* and are fully manned (except a portion of the destroyers which have 4/5ths of their crew), and they are all constantly being exercised.

But there is one more private piece of information for Your Majesty alone. Admiral Tirpitz (the German Minister of Marine) has privately stated in a secret paper that the English Navy is *now* four times stronger than the German Navy! *And we are going to keep the British Navy at that strength . . .*

I have the honour to be

Your Majesty's humble servant,
J. A. Fisher

A month later Fisher was assuring his listeners at the Lord Mayor's banquet that they could still sleep quiet in their beds. Fisher claimed proudly at the end of his life that he had made only four public speeches. This was a pity, for he was a superb orator—articulate, witty, entertaining and informative. He lashed out at his critics in a jovial spirit, and reassured all those who had entertained any doubts about the administration, and the fighting process, of the Royal Navy. The Fleet was *'nulli secundus'*, he told his audience. 'The gunnery efficiency of the Fleet has surpassed all records—it is unparalleled—and I am lost in admiration at the splendid unity of spirit and determination . . . our object has been the fighting efficiency of the Fleet and its instant readiness for war; and we have got it . . . So I turn to all of you and I turn to my countrymen and I say—Sleep quiet in your beds (laughter and cheers), and do not be disturbed by these bogies—invasion and otherwise—which are being periodically resuscitated by all sorts of leagues . . .'

By the end of the year Fisher was regretting his outspoken expressions of satisfaction at the state of the Navy. There were powerful Radical elements in the Liberal party—among them the anti-militarists Lloyd George, Winston Churchill, Lewis Harcourt, John Morley and Herbert Asquith—who were especially deeply committed to public welfare and actually wanted to *reduce* the defence estimates. This group, backed by radical Liberal organs like the *Nation* and the *Manchester Guardian*, listened to Fisher's proud claims of the Navy's omnipotence: if they could all sleep sound in their beds, then now was the time to switch some of the nation's wealth from battleships to slums.

Then on 18 November 1907 there was published in Berlin the ominous news that Germany was accelerating her naval building plans. The increase amounted to 25 % in battleships over the next five years, and there were to be no fewer than five additional battle cruisers, giving the German Navy within ten years an armada of nearly sixty Dreadnoughts. Such naval power was far beyond anything Britain had considered necessary for her own needs; it was certainly greatly in excess of what Germany could require for the defence of her short coastline and her world trade, and as a deterrent to British aggression. It was the final, conclusive evidence that Germany, the greatest land power in Europe, was determined to oust Britain from her leading rank at sea. This must eventually spell the end of the British Empire, and even of British independence.

Today it appears extraordinary that the acute danger was not at once recognized by all shades of political persuasion. There was a great deal of alarm, of course. The Navy League was outraged and demanded an immediate rush programme of shipbuilding. All the Conservative press sounded out in a chorus of anxiety, and the militant Liberals were equally anxious about the country's long-term security. But the Government had set its heart and political reputation on a reduction in the Navy estimates. The Board proposed a comparatively modest building programme of one battleship, one battle cruiser, half a dozen light cruisers, sixteen destroyers and some submarines. This was only an interim programme in preparation for a heavy increase that would be inevitable the following year, unless the Germans relented. But Campbell-Bannerman's Cabinet would have none of it. Tweedmouth was informed that there would have to be a cut of £1,340,000. This meant that the one battleship would have to be dropped.

Fisher and the rest of the Board were outraged. 'With the full knowledge and absolute certainty (now afforded by the German programme just issued) of having to commence a larger battleship programme in 1909–10,' ran part of their report to Tweedmouth, 'it would be most unbusinesslike, and indeed disastrous to close down the armour plate industry of this country by the entire cessation of battleship building. It would be similarly disastrous to abruptly stop the manufacture of heavy gun mountings, which the omission of the battleships would also involve . . . Anyhow, it would be on all grounds quite inadmissable to omit the one battleship in next year's programme, and indeed severe criticism must be expected at our not commencing two battleships.'[1]

[1] 'Report to the First Lord on the Navy Estimates, 1908–9, by the Sea Lords, 2 December 1907'. Lennoxlove MSS.

Tweedmouth began his fight with the Cabinet in January 1908, and the contest lasted on and off for some three weeks. Fisher rose up in wrath and stormed in, threatening his own resignation and that of the rest of the Board if they were forced to yield. Lewis Harcourt, an intimate friend and supporter of Beresford, suggested that the alternative to the resignation of the Board was the resignation of a number of members of the Cabinet. If we go, Fisher suggested, you might find it difficult to find any officers ready to take our place. Harcourt jumped at the opportunity of putting forward the claims of Beresford: he was quite certain this Admiral would be prepared to step into Fisher's place. According to Marder, Lloyd George repeated Harcourt's suggestion at a dinner party the same evening, and claimed that Beresford was prepared to knock £2,000,000 off the estimates if he should be made First Sea Lord. 'Fisher retorted that Beresford would "sell" the Government in three months, and he reasserted that the irreducible minimum had been reached. The next morning Lloyd George attended a meeting of the Board. The estimates were gone over microscopically; the Board decided to stand by its guns. Fisher then had the Parliamentary Secretary see Campbell-Bannerman and carefully explain each vote and the impossibility of further cuts. The Prime Minister was convinced and decided that the Navy estimates were to stand . . . Fisher was satisfied.'[1]

The great body of navalists, the Conservative Party and the militant press were not satisfied. 'Is Britain going to surrender her maritime supremacy to provide old-age pensions?' demanded the *Daily Mail*. Nor was that lurking watchdog of Britain's defence, Lord Esher, satisfied. As always moving in mysterious ways, but on this occasion making one of his rare public appearances, Esher published in *The Times* (6 February) his answer to the invitation to join the Beresford-inspired Imperial Maritime League (see above p. 232). In it he wrote to the League, 'You say "the general position is that by economies introduced for the purpose of securing money for social reform the efficiency of the Navy as a fighting force has been most dangerously reduced." I suppose you honestly think Sir John Fisher and the Sea Lords have lent themselves to so indefensible an enterprise.

'If I could believe this, I should be glad to see Sir John Fisher and his colleagues meet the fate of Admiral Byng.' Esher told how he had been let into some of Fisher's secret plans while he was serving as C.-in-C. Portsmouth, and none of them made any provision for the Navy to make sacrifices for social reforms. The nation, Esher suggested, could

[1] *Marder*, i, 138.

rely on Fisher; and 'there is not a man in Germany, from the Emperor downwards, who would not welcome the fall of Sir John Fisher'.

The effect of this letter was more devastating and favourable for Britain's defence interests than even Esher could have anticipated. A most astonishing thing happened. The Kaiser read it and at once sat down to write a rebuttal, in the form of a nine-page-long letter personally to Tweedmouth in his own handwriting. In it the Kaiser trotted out the old and by now very unconvincing claim that German naval rearmament was not aimed at wresting the trident from Britain and that it was purely defensive. Esher's suggestion that the Kaiser and all his people would like to see an end to Fisher's rule was 'a piece of unmitigated balderdash'. Tweedmouth was amazed when he received this personal letter from the sovereign of an unfriendly foreign power, especially at such a critical time. He was also greatly flattered and could not resist showing it to his friends. This was indiscreet enough, but he then wrote a private eptly, giving the Kaiser prior information on the Estimates which had rno yet been published, and telling only the Foreign Secretary of his intention.

There was a brief lull before the press seized hold of this exquisitely spicy piece of gossip. *The Times* was first off the mark. 'If there was any doubt before about the meaning of German naval expansion,' ran a leader, 'none can remain after an attempt of this kind to influence the Ministe responsible for our Navy in a direction favourable tor German interest . . .' The other newspapers attacked Tweedmouth for his indiscretion, and the First Lord's attempt to justify himself in the House of Lords on 9 March was a hapless business. Tweedmouth was not well and was to die of a cerebral haemorrhage a year later.

Esher's letter to *The Times* had three results favourable to Fisher's cause, and to the cause of British defence. Beresford's fleeting opportunity of succeeding Fisher was lost, and Fisher acquired a strong First Lord in place of the weak and ailing Tweedmouth. Esher himself described the third and most important result in his journal for 14 March 1908:

' . . . the event of the past few days has been the success of A. J. B. [Arthur Balfour] in drawing from Asquith [deputising for Campbell-Bannerman as Prime Minister] a declaration about the Navy, which never would have been obtained but for the Kaiser's letter. The net result of that famous epistle has been to force the Government to give a pledge that in the next three years they will lay down ships enough to ensure our superiority. So good has come out of evil, if evil it was . . .'[1]

---

[1] *Esher*, ii, 295.

Esher's letter to *The Times* and its consequences marked the turning point in British defence policy in the years leading to 1914. The Liberals were forced to reappraise their idealistic intentions and face the reality of Germany's threat to Britain's power at sea. There remained ahead severe contests with the anti-militant wing of the party, led by Murray Macdonald in the House, and Lloyd George and Winston Churchill in the Government. But it was now clear that the nation would never yield its lead in Dreadnoughts, although the margin of superiority was so narrow when war did come, that it is impossible to over-emphasize the importance of the events of February and March 1908.

Esher found the loss of *grise* to his *eminence* distasteful and recognized the risks he had taken, including the danger of losing the King's support.

Fisher recognized at once the value to himself of the episode. 'You never did a friend a better service than you did me by that letter,' he wrote to Esher (25 March), 'and personally I regret nothing, not even for your sake, as it was a splendidly composed letter and the German Emperor and *The Times* between them have raised it into a classic!'

The King was greatly put out by Esher's seeming indiscretion.

KING EDWARD TO VISCOUNT ESHER[1]

Buckingham Palace
February 19th.

The King thanks Lord Esher for his letter of the 19th which he received this evening.

He deeply regrets the publication of the letter which Lord Esher wrote to the Navy League,[2] as the remarks about Sir John Fisher were very unfortunate, and though Lord Esher wished to do Sir John a good turn, the King is afraid the reverse is the result.

The allusion also to the German Emperor was likewise very unfortunate, and has, the King knows, caused him great annoyance. The next time the King sees Lord Esher, he will point out to him how injudicious were the remarks which he made as to Sir John Fisher having told him of the future plans of Sir John when the latter was still Commander-in-Chief at Portsmouth.

Edward R. and I.

Fisher hastened to make the peace:

TO VISCOUNT ESHER

Admiralty, Whitehall
February 20th, 1908

Secret
My beloved Friend,

I had a good long time with the King. He began in violence against you, but

[1] *Esher*, ii, 287–8.   [2] The King meant the Maritime League.

I pointed out to him that I was the culprit, not YOU, because I it was who showed you all the plans, etc., at Portsmouth, and also it was out of PURE FRIENDSHIP to ME that you wrote the letter, and the end bit about the German Emperor, etc., as true as gospel! So it was rather lovely, *and he is sweet!* He said, 'Well, what right had you to make plans at Portsmouth when you didn't know whether you were going to be First Sea Lord?' I think if you don't see him for a few days, it will be as ever you were. I said, 'Well, Sir, it *was* a good letter, wasn't it?' He said, 'Of course it was, because he is a most able man'! That dear blessed Francis [Knollys] is a real trump in standing by his friends.

No time for more.

Yours ever,
J. F.

I really do feel guilty, as I told the King, in being the real culprit.

Esher felt no sense of guilt. He answered Fisher's thanks and congratulations (March 25):

'I shall never, and have never, regretted that letter.

'It was well worth all this bother (not very much of that) to have done anything however little for the Navy.

'I shall always believe that we were then at the parting of the ways.

'The Nation was on its trial. The struggle is far from over yet . . .'[1]

On the occasion of the 'sacking' of his First Lord, Fisher wrote (11 April 1908) to the King that he was 'very sorry indeed for Lord Tweedmouth' who would 'feel it bitterly'. But the Navy required a fitter and stronger figure for the struggles that Esher had predicted. The years 1908 and 1909 were the most strenuous and agonizing in all Fisher's long career. His past reforms—the Selborne Scheme, the policy on scrapping and nucleus crews, the introduction of the all-big-gun battleship—continued to suffer sustained attacks from his critics. It was not only what he had accomplished, but his manner of accomplishing his reforms, which gathered increasingly hostile critics. The intemperance of his language did his cause no good. From his policy of bestowing power on those who agreed with him and supported him there grew rancour and bitter dismay among those who were deprived or superseded. His supporters tended to be intellectuals who, more often than not, came from the less socially influential families.

'Many officers acquired merit by supporting his half-baked reforms, and not a few ruined their Service careers by refusing to bow the knee to Baal,'[2] was a typical comment made later by one of his critics. A

---

[1] *Esher*, ii, 298.
[2] Vice-Admiral K. G. B. Dewar, *The Navy from Within* (London, 1939), 242.

future First Sea Lord was numbered among those who 'refused to bow'. Wemyss, the late Captain of Osborne, had for long had his eyes on the post of Naval Secretary. Fisher offered it to him, but according to Wemyss's biographer, 'adding that such an appointment would be a gross job, since there were many senior men to him who ought to be preferred, while plainly intimating that the price he would have to pay would be absolute subserviency to his views. Wemyss indignantly refused to accept the post under such conditions, though it was the one he most coveted at the time, and from that day on there was no more communication of any sort between the two men . . .'[1]

Incidents of this kind added fuel to the fires of fury in a service whose structure was supported by the sturdy pillars of conservativism. In spite of all the reforming efforts of recent years, time-honoured and predictable customs were too comfortably arranged and too deep-seated to be eradicated quickly. The 'Band of Brothers' spirit which had sustained the service through a century of almost total war inactivity was a precious creed, and the belief that Fisher was engaged in the profane act of breaking it up and causing widespread dissension was growing month by month. His feud with Beresford was, in service eyes, evidence of this. In 1908 the contest was reaching its climax, and was the greatest of all burdens Fisher was bearing. Again and again he refers to it in his letters at this time, evidence that the man had become an obsession. Renewed strength was given to Beresford's crusade by the seeming indifference of Fisher and the Board to the new German scare. On top of all his 'half-baked reforms' 'the mulatto', it seemed, was siding with the pacifists and placing his country in peril.

It is true that there was an apparent ambivalence in Fisher's response to Germany's accelerated naval construction. This stemmed from his absolute confidence in the Navy, reformed and redeployed in four years of his rule, to meet and defeat the foe at any time. He believed passionately in the absolute *matériel* superiority of the Royal Navy over the German Navy. An early convert to the magic of statistics, he could with long-practised deftness produce the figures to prove that the total weight of broadside, or the proved rate of fire, or the economical cruising speed, of the British Battle Fleet was superior to Germany's by so-much per cent.

But Fisher was also acutely conscious of the responsibilities of holding the senior appointment at a time of unprecedented scientific and technical progress. He had seen the torpedo transform the rôle of the battleship, and the strategy and tactics of naval warfare: by 1908 Arthur

[1] Lady Wester Wemyss, *The Life and Letters of Lord Wester of Wemyss* (London, 1935), 99.

Wilson and he were in agreement 'against the Battle Fleet being anywhere near the North Sea' in war because of the torpedo and mine
danger. In the same year he was making plans for a battleship, a vast
super-Dreadnought of over 20,000 tons armed with a new secret gun
of 13·5-inch calibre, that would make obsolete the *Dreadnought* herself—
after just two years! Thus his axiom 'Build few and build fast . . .' was
proved once again. In 1908 even newer technological revolutions appeared imminent. It was likely, he argued, that the product of the new
German programme would be as obsolete in 1910 as the ships of their
1900 programme were today. 'By 1910 Dreadnoughts may be out of
date . . ." made helpless by the submarine.

Then what of air power? Might not this be another 'vast impending
revolution'? His prophetic vision was already spying out this new threat
to the battle fleet. The Germans were experimenting a year before,
he had heard. Dumas had written how, when he was out playing golf,
'A German dirigible balloon came over our heads (one of the first
journeys it has made) and I took copious notes . . .'[1]

Fisher also had at his fingertips the data on the gun and gun-mounting
capacity of German armament firms. These figures and other information provided by Dumas showed that the situation was well in hand,
even though it had been worth the fight, and the threats of resignation,
to get the two big ships for this year. The Kiel Canal widening alone
was proving a prodigious undertaking, and Germany's short sea coast
offered only two acceptable harbours; nor was Germany's special steel
armour plate capacity anywhere near Britain's.

All this, and much more of a reassuring nature, the Board knew;
and Fisher could say nothing publicly to defend himself against his
assailants. By the end of 1908 it really did seem to Fisher that he had
few friends in the world—only supporters close to him in the service,
a scattering of devoted editors and journalists, and King Edward himself, whose faith in his friend continued unwaveringly. It was the knowledge of the King's support in all he did that most sustained Fisher
during these two years of unremitting toil and assault from those who
hated him and all his works—this and the certainty that the lower deck,
'the knife-and-fork-less', and the common people, were behind him.

The depth of the affection Fisher felt for the few who retained their
loyalty to him when it seemed that all society, most of the politicians,
most of Fleet Street, and so many of his old friends in the service had
turned against him, is movingly expressed in a letter he wrote to Arnold
White during the worst troubles of 1908, warning him of the danger
to which he was exposing himself.

[1] Diary 27 August 1907. Dumas Papers

TO ARNOLD WHITE

16, *Queen Anne's Gate, S.W.*
February 17th, 1908

Private
My Dear Friend,

I know full well what you have done for me and what you have hazarded for me and what you have forgone for me. I know it all! I know also that at the base of it all is the sincere and *well-founded* belief that it is for the public good you have acted as you have, and so that you don't care a brass farthing what anyone says or does to vilify you. But now I say to you (*with knowledge of what is going on*) that Beresford, being full of money as well as of malignancy, will seize any opportunity of a libel action, and you can't afford it, nor can I afford to help you. I don't know the wiles of libel. I only write this to warn you, as I could never forgive myself if you got beat by money and I had not tried beforehand to guard you against it.

Yours ever,
J.F.

Yet one more attack had to be endured and fought off. There had never been much love between Fisher and the Army, and his conviction that the Army was inefficiently administered by a lot of old muddlers was widely known. The problems aroused by the danger of invasion of Britain were as old as the Navy itself, and the bogey had been raised during every Anglo-French crisis of the nineteenth century from the time when the Grand Army's encampments could be seen from the cliffs of Dover. As recently as 1903 when the invasion problem had been discussed by the Defence Committee the assumed enemy was France. It was in the interests of the Army, and their share of the nation's defence budgets, to resuscitate this supposed danger from time to time after Germany replaced France as a potential enemy. The army's case for a possible future invasion rested on the risk of a surprise attack across the North Sea by as many as 100,000 or even 150,000 men—a 'bolt-from-the-blue'. The leader of the bolt-from-the-blue school was the elderly, active and highly respected Field Marshal Lord Roberts, who resigned from the Committee of Imperial Defence in 1905 to campaign for conscription and a stronger Army—which must threaten future Navy estimates.

Fisher, as natural leader of the 'blue-water' school, violently refuted the possibility of a bolt from the blue, which was a reflection on the 'instant readiness' of the Fleet. Small raids there might be; but a successful mass invasion was utterly impossible, because the Royal Navy would smash it long before it reached British shores. To Fisher and his supporters, the bolt-from-the-blue school was synonymous with the blue funk school, or, as the great Lord St Vincent[1] had described them, 'the old women of both sexes'. 'That great sailor,' wrote Fisher, 'when asked his opinion about invasion, replied that, being a military question, he hesitated to express an opinion. All he knew was that they could not come by sea!'[2]

Besides being a national extravagance, a large conscript Army was certain to be drawn into a full-scale Continental land war, a defence development Fisher dreaded, however strongly the French might press for it. The Continental ways of the nineteenth and eighteenth centuries had shown how nations could be debilitated and a generation of young men destroyed by great land battles. A large conscript standing Army, besides constituting an unbearable financial burden for the nation, at the expense of the Navy, suggested however indirectly that the Navy's strength could again be dispersed about the world and be used in conjunction with the Army for renewed Imperialist aggression. Thus the blue-water school found itself supported by the anti-militant anti-Imperialist Liberal press—strange bedfellows indeed!

Since the concentration of the Fleet in home waters against the only likely enemy was the cornerstone of Fisher's strategy; since anything that tended to diminish the relative status of the Royal Navy at once became the target for every broadside he could bring to bear; since he despised the Army anyway, Fisher's reaction to a carefully planned invasion scare at the end of 1907 was predictably violent.

The scare was set off simultaneously by a wide range of Fisher's opponents, including Lord Roberts himself, Colonel Charles A'Court Repington, military correspondent of *The Times*, Lord Brassey, the elderly editor of the *Naval Annual* and an old antagonist, and was supported by elements of the Conservative press, in voices ranging from the strident to the dignified yet deeply alarmed.

Fisher prepared his counter-attack in his usual thorough way. He had long ago considered the invasion problem from every aspect, and was certain, for example, that it would be impossible for the Germans to mobilize and embark a large force without the Admiralty's knowledge. But he wanted evidence to support his conviction on this and other points.

TO CAPTAIN PHILIP DUMAS (*in Berlin*)[3]

Admiralty, Whitehall
January 8th, 1908

Dear Dumas,

Colonel Repington . . . who is assisting Lord Roberts on the National

---

[1] John Jervis, First Lord 1801–4.   [2] Robinson Papers, vol. 1. Admiralty MSS.
[3] Dumas Papers.

Defence League and frightening the Country out of its wits by an imminent German invasion of England, has placed before the Defence Committee, with the connivance of Lord Roberts, that a Naval Surprise is not only possible but likely and that without any period of strained relations and without any warning whatsoever or any information leaking out, that 70,000 to 100,000 German troops could be embarked and leave in thirty-six hours from the German Emperor's order being given. They lay their whole case on the basis of a Naval Surprise and admit that in view of the strength of our Fleet an invasion is otherwise an impossibility. The question I ask you is whether you think it conceivable that no sort of rumours or indication of this great embarkation of German troops should not reach us for, say, twenty-four hours. Haag, the Vice-Consul at Bremerhaven, says it is absolutely impossible. The daily commercial interchange of communication if stopped or tampered with would at once indicate something amiss. Thirteen thousand telegrams a day come to London from Hamburg alone. Let us fully admit the tonnage is available and always sufficient but the mere fact of stopping steamers sailing on their ordinary dates and the absolute dead stoppage of all commercial and passenger traffic would, it seems to me, be instantly reflected across all frontiers and thus become known to us at once. What Repington asserts is that this huge mass of vessels containing such a German Army could leave Hamburg in thirty-six hours from the date of the order being given without England knowing anything of it. Please think it all over and send me a letter which could be placed before the Defence Committee.

Yours very truly,
J. A. Fisher

Dumas was able to oblige Fisher with the required ammunition, and von Tirpitz himself was able further to support the blue-water case a few weeks later, when in conversation with Dumas (3 February 1908) he referred to 'all the nonsense about invasion lately written in England. Out of the 30,000 military officers in Germany one might expect that one or two sheep-headed lieutenants might write such rubbish,'[1] yet he was informed that Lord Roberts was gravely bringing it forward in England as possible and probable. It was incredible to Tirpitz that a great soldier and statesman for whom he had always had the greatest respect could believe in such a thing. So far as he knew it was impossible for them to even embark such numbers as, say, 100,000 men, and none should know better what it meant than the English, and, in view of our sea forces, quite impossible that they should be disembarked on the other side. Even Napoleon had found it impossible when only twenty miles off . . . To carry out an invasion two things were absolutely necessary. First to land an amply sufficient number of troops and secondly to maintain the lines of communication.

[1] Dumas Papers.

'I have spoken of 100,000 men but that number would be wholly useless in England even if we had no Army there to oppose them.' Under circumstances of invasion it was certain that a million semi-trained soldiers would spring up like magic and in that connection he would advise Dumas to think over and study the German halt before Paris in 1870 . . .

Ponsonby's definition of 'semi-trained soldiers', however, was not flattering. Like Fisher, who called them the 'bows-and-arrows' brigade, he had no time for Roberts's new village rifle ranges and voluntary part-time military training. Ponsonby represented the Buckingham Palace view when he wrote of the invasion scare. 'My point is, if we are not safe from invasion, then make us so. Spend money on submarines, destroyers, etc., but don't waste money on an armed mob. You might as well arm all the caretakers in London houses instead of supplying them with a police force. Why wait till the enemy has landed?'

Fisher loved this exposition, and after adding an exclamation point and some underlinings, quoted it to the Prince of Wales, who found it 'most sound'. The Prince also wrote (24 October 1907) to Fisher that he was 'certainly convinced no invasion or raid could be successful in our days'.

However, the invasion agitation continued through the winter and well into 1908, greatly irritating Fisher and occupying much of his time. Even Esher, whose loyalty to Fisher and belief in his methods were beginning to waver, nagged away. 'A nation that believes itself secure,' he wrote to his old friend, 'all history teaches is doomed.

' . . . An invasion scare is the mill of god which grinds you out a Navy of Dreadnoughts, and keeps the British people war-like in spirit.

'So do not be scornful, and sit not with Pharisees!'[1]

Winston Churchill, Under-Secretary of State for the Colonies and still at the beginning of his turbulent friendship with Fisher,[2] was already developing a deep interest in defence matters and could not resist offering his advice, too. On 19 January 1908 he wrote: 'I think, however, you should face more squarely the one unique operation which falls in the third or intermediate category of half-raid half-invasion attack. Would it or would it not be worth while to sacrifice 60,000 men for the pleasure of burning London to the ground? Would it

---

[1] *Esher*, ii, 249.

[2] 'Winston said he felt a great fellow-feeling with me, as I always painted with a big brush . . .' (January 1907). 'Fell desperately in love with Winston Churchill. I think he's quite the nicest fellow I ever met and such a quick brain that it's a delight to talk to him . . .' (April 1907).

or would it not be possible to accomplish this, if it were thought worth while? This is to my mind the only doubtful point, and all other descents in the United Kingdom remote from the capital would be purely irrelevant operations from a military point of view and would only confer upon the British Government an immense excession [*sic*] of resisting power through the resulting infuriation of the whole people. I do not suggest that the destruction of London would be decisive; but it would be a staggering blow at the commencement of a long war.' As an afterthought, Churchill added: 'I would hang the people who did it.'[1]

Beresford, of course, inevitably reached out for a hand-hold on the beating stick and became involved. To Fisher's disgust, a sub-committee of the CID with Asquith presiding had met (27 November 1907) to consider the invasion problem. Both sides retired to draw up their cases, and Fisher called in the support of the best of the blue-water school intellectuals, including Julian Corbett. Of Repington's determination to call Beresford as a witness, Fisher wrote to Corbett that it was 'a scandal impossible to tolerate but a splendid platform for Beresford to resign on!' Corbett, whose advice throughout this acrimonious invasion controversy was invaluable, commented drily: 'Their reason for calling C.B. is admittedly that they regard the strategical disposition affirmed by the Admiralty as faulty in detail. I cannot see how, therefore, you can consent to his being called without admitting that the CID has the right to review the naval strategy of the Board.'

In the event the bolt-from-the-blue school were foiled in their attempt to stir the water even muddier by calling Beresford, whose hatred of Fisher and distrust of the whole Board were now notorious. Even without his presence the meetings of the committee were punctuated by sharp outbursts between the spokesmen for the two services. But the blue-water school proved the victors when the committee's report was published at last in October 1908, although it recommended that the Home Defence Army should be large enough to deal not only with small scale lightning raids but also to act as a deterrent against an invasion of 70,000 enemy troops. An invasion on this scale, however, could not hope to evade the Fleet, stated the committee—thus putting an end for the time being to the bolt-from-the-blue risk. Moreover, 'so long as our naval supremacy is assured against any reasonably probable combination of Powers, invasion is impracticable'; and 'if we permanently lose command of the sea, whatever may the strength

[1] Lennoxlove MSS.

and organization of the Home force, the subjection of the country to the enemy is inevitable'.[1]

Still the critics were not satisfied, and the rumblings of discontent continued right through to the spring of 1909—by which time they were almost inaudible to Fisher, such was the volume of the new cannonade.

[1] *Marder*, i, 350.

Chapter 5

'BLACK TREACHERY'[1]

'It is a hard fact,' Marder has written, 'that Fisher's idea of war direction was absolutely incompatible with the idea of a General Staff and the idea of a working agreement with the War Office on the major problems of imperial defence. Fisher (and Sir Arthur Wilson) believed that war plans must be prepared in the greatest secrecy by the First Sea Lord alone, kept to himself, and divulged to the Army only on the outbreak of war.' He regarded even a naval staff as of very limited value. 'A Naval War Staff at the Admiralty,' he once commented, 'is a very excellent organization for cutting out and arranging foreign newspaper clippings . . . the mischief of a Naval War Staff is peculiar to the Navy. I understand it is quite different in the Army—I don't know. The mischief to the Navy is that the very ablest of our Officers, both young and old, get attracted by the brainy work and by the shore-going appointment.'[2]

This comment suggests that Fisher was acting the bluff seaman, and was a believer in 'doing not thinking', rather than the ardent admirer of his own intellectual supporters.

But the volumes of *Naval Necessities*[3] on which his reforms were based alone testify to his own deep intellectual powers. His understanding of history on the one hand, his prophetic imagination on the other, marked him as exceptional at 'the brainy work' which he sometimes affected to despise. The success of the Naval War College at Portsmouth gave him enormous satisfaction and he followed its fortunes with interest to the end. During the closing months of his administration he established a Navy War Council to consider war plans and strategic problems.

---

[1] 'We are going to win all right, as I don't think *they* will face the consequences of the Board of Admiralty resigning. There is black treachery besides unspeakable weakness.' Fisher to Knollys, 18 February 1909.

[2] *Memories*, 108–9.   [3] See *Fisher Papers*.

In spite of the great progress to encourage the intellectual in a service which traditionally placed seamanship at the top of the necessary qualities and brains and imagination at the bottom; in spite of Fisher's own evident intellectual prowess; and in spite of his own clear grasp of the *matériel*, strategical and tactical problems of the Navy, it was his reluctance to set up a properly constituted naval staff (as the Army had done) for which he was most strongly attacked. His stand on this subject was one of the chief contributory causes of his downfall.

At the end of the nineteenth century the Army was as greatly in need of the services of a major reformer as the Navy. It was the Army's misfortune to fight first, in South Africa, and demonstrates its incompetence and inefficiency to all the world. Fisher was not in the least surprised, and soon derived vast satisfaction from his inclusion with Esher and Clarke on the Esher Committee: 'How I got there is still a mystery; but it was a great enjoyment . . .' The appointment of a permanent Committee of Imperial Defence (cid), which included the C.-in-C. of the Army, the First Naval Lord and the directors of military and naval intelligence, followed in March 1903. Although Fisher regularly attended its meetings when he became First Sea Lord, these contacts with the military only further hardened his belief in the low calibre of the military mind, and he implacably opposed any 'interference' by the cid in purely naval affairs. Nor did he ever offer the committee any hint of naval plans in the event of war.

For R. B. Haldane, Secretary of State for War (1905–12), he held the lowest opinion. 'The vulgar error of Lord Haldane and others, who are always talking about "clear thinking" and such-like twaddle, is that they do not realise that the Army is absolutely different from the Navy . . . The Navy is always at war, because it is always fighting winds and waves and fog. The Navy is ready for an absolute instant blow; it has nothing to do with strategic railways, lines of communication, or bridging rivers, or crossing mountains, or the time of the year . . . No! the ocean is limitless and unobstructed; and the Fleet, each ship manned, gunned, provisioned and fuelled, ready to fight within five minutes.'[1] Haldane, that 'soapy Jesuit', continued to advocate a naval war staff, even proposed a Ministry of Defence, and worst of all backed Beresford when the confrontation between the two Admirals reached its climax.

Fisher remained undeterred in his opposition to a naval war staff by the plea of two of his closest and cleverest confederates. Corbett deeply regretted his failure to convert Fisher. Esher, more outspoken and an older and more intimate friend, sometimes took Fisher seriously

---

[1] *Memories*, 104.

to task for his failure not only to create a naval staff but also to support more enthusiastically the Defence Committee. It was weakening for the country, the Navy, and for Fisher himself in his struggles with his naval opponents. In the early days of the Beresford feud, he wrote (4 February 1907) to Fisher:

'. . . *You* have shown mistrust and dislike of the Defence Committee instead of converting it to your uses. In my humble judgment you have made a mistake. During the past week or so, the forces ranged against each other have been Fisher versus Beresford. They should have been Fisher plus Defence Committee plus Cabinet versus Beresford, and the odds would have been overwhelming . . .'

Fisher seems to have been taken aback by these sharp words, and according to Knollys the 'letter to Jacky has terrified him'.[1]

Six months later, when Balfour was recommending that the CID should investigate the invasion problem and Fisher was demonstrating his outrage at such a proposal, Esher again took Fisher to task—'giving him a bit of my mind',[2] as he described (24 August 1907) his action to his son.

'What on earth do you mean by maintaining that a paper written by Mr Balfour for the *Defence Committee* is "purely an Admiralty business"? and talking of an "irresponsible sub-committee"?

'(*a*) Mr Balfour's original memorandum was a Defence Committee paper, and his speech in the House of Commons was *based upon* it, and not upon any Admiralty decision.

'(*b*) The Committee for Imperial Defence, of which the *Prime Minister* is the Chief, and its sub-committees, *if appointed by the Prime Minister*, are every bit as "responsible" as the Board of Admiralty, of which the *First Sea Lord* is the Chief . . .

'The Admiralty will have to recognise, as the War Office has recognised, that the Defence Committee is a new factor in our administrative system . . .'[3]

Fisher replied, unrepentant, in his best puckish schoolboy style.

TO VISCOUNT ESHER[4]

Carlsbad
September 8th, 1907

My beloved E.,

I quite expected to get 'slated' by you and *I've got it.* Also I fully expected you would have your wicked way and *you've got it!*

Yours ever,
J. A. Fisher

[1] *Esher*, ii, 219–20.   [2] *ibid.*, 247.   [3] *ibid.*, 247–8.   [4] *ibid.*, 248.

While enormously admiring him, Fisher was also well aware of Esher's ambivalence and his talent for self-delusion when it came to manipulating arguments to suit his case. In diametric contradiction to his fierce antagonism to Fisher's secrecy on his war plans, he wrote (14 January 1906) to his son, as if quoting Fisher himself: 'Of course he [Fisher] . . . is very reticent about Naval plans, and rightly so. For them [the Navy], no preparation is required. The Navy is always on a war footing, and a telegram can send a Fleet to the other end of the earth . . .'[1]

A later and widely accepted reason for Fisher's reluctance to set up a Naval War staff was expressed ten years after his death by the late Taprell Dorling ('Taffrail'):

'Immersed in the technicalities of his profession—the great reforms, his redistribution of the fleet, the creation of new ship and weapons—he literally had no time to devote himself to a profound study as to how the Navy could best be used as an instrument of war. No war plan that existed in his brain had ever been considered in all its aspects or worked out. It was repugnant to him to delegate powers to others, and that comparatively junior officers, in a considered staff opinion, should voice their opinions as to the conduct of war. He preferred to do his own thinking. Therefore no War Staff worthy of the name existed.'[2]

This seemingly neat summary was riddled with false judgments and statements. Fisher, in the course of his six-day weeks (and most of Sunday, in spite of the King's ban) and working from around 4.30 a.m. to 7 p.m., had time for everything that related to the efficiency of the Navy—and its efficiency in time of war rose far to the sky above anything else in the scale of priorities. His powers of delegation were prodigious, and celebrated at the Admiralty, where he even delegated the authority to falsify his signature on what he regarded as trivia. Anyone who would not accept delegated responsibilities was soon out— and those who did got their just reward. 'When I left the Admiralty at 8 p.m., prior to some approaching Grand Manoeuvres, I left it to my friend Flint, one of the Higher Division Clerks, to mobilize the fleet by a wireless message from the roof of the Admiralty. And the deciding circumstances having arisen, he did it off his own bat at 2 a.m.'[3] And of course the views of 'comparatively junior officers' (so long as they were clever) were the life blood of all his reforms and strategical thinking.

With all his extravagant style of manner and expression, Fisher

---

[1] *Esher*, ii, 134–5.
[2] Captain Taprell Dorling, *Men o' War* (London, 1929), 256.   [3] *Memories*, 110.

was essentially a man of his word. When he claimed that 'I had my
[war] plan in minute detail and was absolutely sure of its unqualified
success', he was surely stating a fact. But 'I would not divulge my plan;
and I never did to a living soul, as no plan, however perfect, can ever be
completed successfully unless the man who formed it carries it out.'[1]

Fisher's most formidable and almost fatal error of judgement was to
depart from this principle. When he was forced to resign, the case for a
naval war staff and a First Sea Lord who would enthusiastically work
with it, at once became overwhelming. Instead, Fisher saw to it that the
strings of dictatorial powers were handed over to the officer he most
desired to replace him, who was also as dead-set against consultation
on war plans as Fisher himself, but lacked his predecessor's genius for
war. The appointment of Sir Arthur Wilson as First Sea Lord, almost
at the point of a pistol held by Fisher, was the greatest administrative
catastrophe suffered by the Royal Navy in this century. As that brilliant
intellectual and judge of men, Captain Herbert Richmond, wrote in his
diary at the time, deploring Fisher's failure to set up a Naval Staff:
'He is a genius, and a genius may do things not within the compass of an
ordinary man: but his predecessors have not been, nor may his
successors be geniuses.'

Wilson himself was full of self-doubt, as Fisher told one of his
friends, who reported, 'Had I hypnotised him [Fisher] I could not have
obtained a more outspoken statement on current affairs'. 'I will tell
you how Wilson was got,' said Fisher. '. . . I said [to McKenna] there
is only one man in the country who can do it—the King. McKenna went
off to the King with a brief as to why Wilson was necessary. The King
sent for Wilson to Sandringham and the King told me himself the
curious nature of the interview. Sir Arthur Wilson reluctantly consented
but he said to the King, "Only once, Sir, have I asked a favour of anybody
since I entered the Navy and that was of Sir John Fisher, who, when he
was about to lay down the appointment of Controller of the Navy,
Fisher had already arranged for his successor but he cancelled the
arrangement and secured the appointment of me. I assure you, Sir, that
I was absolutely the worst Controller the Navy has ever had and if I
am to succeed Fisher again I may probably become the worst Sea
Lord in the annals of the Navy." Thus the matter was arranged.'[2]
Wilson's worst fears were to be realized.

Unfailingly during his term of office as First Sea Lord, Fisher
continued to take his summer leave at Marienbad, Carlsbad or some

---

[1] 'Lord Fisher on the Navy', *The Times*, 11 September 1919.
[2] Unidentified letter, 18 November 1909. Lennoxlove MSS.

other spa. There, for three or four weeks, he restored his body by adhering to strict diets and taking the waters. Fisher did not allow these holidays to interfere with his work. Papers arrived daily from the Admiralty and were answered promptly. His correspondence was as vast as ever. From Sienna where he stayed briefly in 1909 he noted that the post was late because of the rain. 'It's not good for the cure to have a busy mind,' he wrote to Knollys from Carlsbad one year— and continued with a long letter examining the current situation with Beresford, and followed this with another to Esher deploring the efforts of the *Nation* to reduce Navy expenditure, and discoursing on the Russian situation. Letters about fleet manoeuvres, about shipbuilding plans, about relations with Turkey, and a hundred other subjects poured from his pen.

Fisher derived the deepest pleasure from these summer leaves, revelling in the warm weather and the scenery. Especially at Marienbad, where Fisher usually stayed at the Grünes Kreuz next door to the Hotel Weimar, the *Kreuzbrunnen* offered as rich opportunities for useful conversation as it had when Fisher had first gone there as a Captain. Here he might be seen on colder days dressed in a long unbelted overcoat with concealed buttons, a wide-brimmed trilby hat, and spats, with an umbrella under one arm and the inevitable glass of water in his other hand, walking up and down with his head inclined towards his companion—perhaps Campbell-Bannerman while he was still Prime Minister, or Lloyd George, or Alexander Petrovitch Izvolsky, the Russian Foreign Secretary, or Sir Ivor Herbert or Sir Rufus Isaacs. On the *Kreuzbrunnen* Fisher revived old friendships and made new ones, and ensured the success of his plans while he secured the health of his body for one more year of trial.

Not only his allies but also Fisher's future foes were to be found in numbers at Marienbad and Carlsbad each year, besides the Germans who 'used to cross themselves at sight of the old sailor, whom they regarded as Germany's greatest enemy'. Von Tirpitz himself would often be there, instantly recognizable by his famous twin-spiked beard and bald domed head; and like Fisher accompanied by his own circle of powerful associates. There is no record that these two Admirals, the helmsmen set on their collision courses, ever met, and the diplomatic courtesies of the time, and the alert tactfulness of hotel staffs, could have ensured that this would not occur.

Other future antagonists were often at the spa, among them the Austrian emperor, with whom Fisher was on friendly terms. Another guest taking the cure recalled how Fisher 'sometimes acted the part of *miles gloriosus* and reproached the Emperor Francis Joseph for not managing to repress the naval ambitions of his ally, Wilhelm II'.[1]

But of course, above the statesmen and politicans, the wealthy industrialists and men of affairs, above even the beautiful women with whom he waltzed in the evenings, it was the company of his King Fisher sought most keenly at Marienbad. They would be seen together at the railway station when perhaps one left or the other arrived, on long drives through the hills, lingering over a long lunch at the King's hotel. They were on such evidently close terms that when Fisher's troubles worsened in the summer of 1908, Knollys stepped tactfully in

TO REGINALD MCKENNA   *August 11th, 1908*
  Dear Mr McKenna,
  . . . Knollys telephoned the night before last that the King directed him to come and see me about Beresford, and I saw him for an hour yesterday. Beresford had again intimated he was going to resign. I told Knollys I didn't believe it. Knollys confessed he didn't either. The signal incident is being resurrected by Beresford to implicate me as the communicator to *The Times*, and the King wanted Knollys to find out all about it. Also all the Dukes and Duchesses being worked up by Beresford and attacking the King, so much so that His Majesty thought it wise not to see me personally, as he had wished to, and Knollys was to explain this. So I said I wouldn't go to Carlsbad and the King couldn't come over to lunch with me, as he usually does, or write me to stay with him at Marienbad, as he usually does! However, I was to go and see His Majesty off at the station, which I did, and he quite spoilt it all by being more cordial than ever, and we had quite a long conversation, with Metternich glaring at us. The Princess Victoria sent for me *à la* Nicodemus and said all much the same as Knollys . . .

Yours truly,
J. A. Fisher

There were many other opportunities for Fisher to be with his beloved Sovereign, from state visits to foreign lands when King Edward would demand his company, to long week-ends at Balmoral—or just occasional chats: 'The King sent for me yesterday—a wet afternoon and he wanted someone to talk to.' Fisher especially enjoyed the Royal visit to Spain in April 1907. He and Churchill joined the King at Biarritz. 'Sir John Fisher and Winston Churchill arrived here a few days ago,' the King noted in his diary, 'and they are most amusing together. I call them the "chatterers".'[2]

But first a personal matter had to be discussed, for the exceptionally

[1] Sigmund Münz, *King Edward VII at Marienbad* (London, 1934), 121.
[2] *Lee*, ii, 534.

close relationship between the King and his First Sea Lord was still causing unfavourable gossip, inspired by Fisher's envious enemies. 'When I met the King on arrival,' Fisher told Esher, 'he said I was to be sure and see him as he had something serious to say to me. I suppose I was with him more than an hour, and he was as cordial and friendly as ever; and this was the serious thing—"that I was Jekyll and Hyde! *Jekyll* in being successful at my work at the Admiralty—but *Hyde* as a failure in Society! That I talked too freely and was reported to say (which of course is a lie) that the King would see me through anything! That it was bad for me and bad for him as being a Constitutional Monarch; if the Prime Minister gave me my congé, he couldn't resist it, &c., &c."... I told the King that if I had never mentioned His Majesty's name in my life, precisely the same thing would be said out of sheer envy of His Majesty being kindly disposed, and it could not be hid that the King had backed up the First Sea Lord against all kinds of opposition—As a matter of fact I *never* do go into Society and only dine out when I'm worried to meet the King ... Well he left that (having unburdened his mind) and smoked a cigar as big as a capstan bar for really a good hour afterwards, talking of everything from China to Peru ... But I did venture one humble remark to the King: "Has anyone ever been able to mention to Your Majesty one single little item that has failed in the whole multitude of reforms introduced in the last $3\frac{1}{2}$ years?" No! he said. No one had! So I left it there ... If the Angel Gabriel were in my place he would be falsely accused! I'm only surprised that the King hasn't been told worse things—perhaps he has!...'[1]

Relations between the King and his Admiral continued as warmly as ever after this episode, and Fisher proceeded with the Royal party to Cartagena, and later to Italy to visit the King.

The Royal visit Fisher most enjoyed was the one to Reval to visit the Czar and his senior ministers in 1908. 'This last ten days the happiest I ever spent!' he noted afterwards. It contained all the elements that always most delighted him, from politically momentous conversations to banquests and balls to which Fisher was able to contribute his own brand of flippant gaiety, and dance and flirt with beautiful women— especially the Czar's younger sister, the Grand Duchess Olga, with whom he had enjoyed that delirious night's dancing at Carlsbad.

In a postscript to a letter to J. A. Spender's wife (28 May 1908), Fisher wrote: 'The King has sweetly asked me to go to Russia with him, which is lovely, as the Queen has telegraphed for that Grand Duchess I am in love with to come and meet me.'

[1] *Memories*, 184–5.

The visit started off badly, with the Royal Yacht meeting exceptionally stormy seas *en route*.

TO LADY FISHER

H.M. Yacht Victoria & Albert
[June 7th, 1908]

Dearest Kitty,

A King's Messenger goes at 3 p.m., so I send this by him. We had a horrible knocking about in the North Sea. Every one ill from the King downwards. I wasn't actually sick, but a horrible sick headache, which was worse. The Queen lay on deck like a corpse! amd Princess Victoria beckoned me to her (when I went on deck in a quiet interval) and said she had been continuously sick and could not keep down a biscuit. Everything in my cabin went mad. The armchair went head over heels through the door and the teapot and milk jug emptied themselves on to my hairbrushes, and everything upset.

The Kiel Canal is quite lovely. The King sent for me to sit with him while he had his breakfast (he usually does this) and we talked away of everything. Now it's church and I must stop . . .

I did wish myself on dry land yesterday! I look with horror to the trip back across the North Sea and would like to come back by train . . .

Y.l.h.
J.F.

Fisher described with a schoolboy's relish the evening of the great banquet and ball, and the renewal of his friendship with the equally ebullient Grand Duchess. '. . . there was quite an affectionate meeting, and we danced the "merry Widow" waltz . . . with such effect as to make the Empress of Russia laugh. They told me she had not laughed for two years. At the banquet preceding the dance the Grand Duchess and I, I regret to say, made such a disturbance in our mutual jokes that King Edward called out to me that I must try to remember that it was not the Midshipmen's Mess; and my dear Duchess thought I should be sent to Siberia or somewhere . . .'[1]

Fisher was evidently not exaggerating his leading rôle in the social proceedings, and was a highly popular figure. 'What a very nice time we spent at Reval, wasn't it?' wrote Fisher's favourite Grand Duchess shortly after the return to England of the Royal party. 'All our gentlemen—ministers, admirals and generals—were delighted with you, as you brought such an amount of frolic and jollity into their midst. They couldn't get over it and spoke about you and your dancing, anecdotes, etc., without end. I told them even if they tried their very

[1] *Memories*, 234.

hardest, they would never reach anywhere near your level. I shall never forget the last evening, when you entertained Victoria, Brocklehurst, and me with your solo performance. I hadn't laughed so much for ages!'

W. T. Stead greatly regretted his absence from the party. 'What I should most have liked to see was the dance which was improvised after the State Banquet . . . The Grand Duchess and Admiral Fisher danced with their hands behind their heads, with all the brilliant company standing round the dancers, until they were tired. Then "Jacky" went on deck, and by requests, which were commands, he brought down the house by dancing a hornpipe in approved nautical fashion.'[1]

'Personally, I had a lovely time,' Fisher reported to his First Lord from the Royal Yacht on the way home. But there was a more serious purpose behind the visit, and the King's charm was as effective with the Russians as it had earlier been with the French. '*The visit has been a phenomenal success. Private.* The Emperor said, for instance, "The whole atmosphere of feeling has altered" . . . The King has just surpassed himself all round. Every blessed Russian of note he got quietly into his spider web and captured!'

But perhaps it was the trivial moments of intimacy with the King that Fisher most treasured: the incident during his arrival at Balmoral on one of his visits. King Edward sent a brougham to meet him at the station and a wagonette to collect his luggage. 'Instead, however, of riding the brougham, the Admiral drove with his luggage on the back of the wagonette. Half way up the drive, they met His Majesty, who was superintending the transplanting of some young trees.' Fisher climbed down at once.

' "This is a nice way to come visiting me," said His Majesty with a smile.

' "I had no idea I should meet your Majesty," said the other, "and, Sir, I am so fond of the air." '[2]

Fisher himself recalled how 'On another occasion I went down to Sandringham with a great party, I think it was for one of Blessed Queen Alexandra's birthdays . . As I was zero in this grand party, I slunk off to my room to write an important letter; then I took my coat off, got out my keys, unlocked my portmanteau and began unpacking. I had a boot in each hand; I heard somebody fumbling with the door handle and thinking it was the Footman whom Hawkins had allocated to me, I said "Come in, don't go humbugging with that door handle!" and in walked King Edward, with a cigar about a yard long in his

---

[1] *Review of Reviews*, February 1910.
[2] G. W. Stamper, *What I Know* (London, 1913), 25.

mouth. He said (I with a boot in each hand!) "What on earth are you doing?" "Unpacking, Sir." "Where's your servant?" "Haven't got one, Sir." "Where is he?" "Never had one, Sir, couldn't afford it." "Put those boots down; sit in that arm chair." And he went and sat in the other one the other side of the fire. I thought to myself, "This is a rum state of affairs! Here's the King of England sitting in my bedroom on one side of the fire and I'm in my shirt sleeves sitting in an armchair on the other side!"

' "Well," His Majesty said, "why didn't you come and say 'How do you do' when you arrived?" I said, "I had a letter to write, and with so many great people you were receiving I thought I had better come to my room." Then he went on with a long conversation, until it was only about a quarter of an hour from dinner time, and I hadn't unpacked! So I said to the King, "Sir, you'll be angry if I'm late for dinner, and no doubt your Majesty has two or three gentlemen to dress you, but I have none." And he gave me a sweet smile and went off.'[1]

Fisher's family life continued on a happy level during these years. He remained devoted to his wife although there were long periods, when he was abroad, or staying in the country, or on official business, when he was away from the family house in Queen Anne's Gate. By 1908 their two younger daughters were both married and, not surprisingly, to naval officers, Pamela to Commander Henry Blackett in 1906, and Dorothy to Lieutenant Eric Fullerton in 1908. In 1908, too, Josiah Vavasseur died, and Kilverstone Hall now belonged to Cecil. Cecil had already retired from the Indian Civil Service in order to help manage the Norfolk estate.

The Vavasseurs remained close and valuable friends to Fisher to the end. A year before Cecil was made Josiah's heir in 1903, Fisher was writing to his son, 'Mother has heard from Mrs Vavasseur telling us to use their house as if it was our own and for just as long as ever we like! They really are the very kindest friends we have ever had, *and they are both absolutely devoted to you*! which I know you will appreciate.' The inheriting of Kilverstone Hall by his son provided Fisher with the next best thing to a country seat of his own at which he could return some of the hospitality he had enjoyed in the past and to which he could look forward to retiring. He loved the old house with its great walled kitchen garden, its dovecot, its lawn and meadows falling down gently to the river. Here he had erected the figurehead from the first seagoing ship in which he had served, the *Calcutta*, at the end of a long yew-bordered grass path. When in residence at Kilverstone, Fisher could

[1] *Records*, 26–7.

often be found, especially early in the morning, pacing up and down this path which inevitably became known as 'the Admiral's walk'. After Fisher had made the decision in October 1909 to retire, King Edward motored over to Kilverstone Hall on a Sunday afternoon from Quidenham where he was staying with Lord Albemarle, and Fisher introduced him to his son—'it was sweet of him!' Fisher commented to Esher. To act as part-host to his King at Kilverstone gave Fisher infinite pleasure.

King Edward's visit to Kilverstone and Fisher's journeyings to Sandringham during the black month of October 1909 symbolically marked the King's 'unfaltering support right through unswervingly' to Fisher during his tumultuous term as First Sea Lord. This mutual loyalty and affection was honourably marked at the end of the month.

FROM H. H. ASQUITH

10, Downing Street
Whitehall, S.W.
October 26th, 1909

Confidential
My dear Sir John,
I have the pleasure of formally proposing to you that, on the occasion of His Majesty's approaching birthday—November 9th—you should be raised to the peerage.

I am much gratified that it should fall to me to be the medium of communicating to you His Majesty's gracious intentions.

I desire, at the same time, to express to you the sincere and grateful acknowledgments of His Majesty's Government for the great work—unique in our time—which you have accomplished in developing and strengthening the Navy, and assuring the maritime supremacy of Great Britain.

I beg, with respect and esteem, to remain,
Yours very faithfully,
H.H. Asquith

It was entirely consistent with Fisher's character, background and political leanings that, while he condemned inherited titles as anomalous and out of date—citing the good examples of Canada and the United States—he considered that he should have been given the superior honour of a viscountcy.

The sources of the conflicts in which Fisher became so deeply embroiled in 1909 stemmed from so many springs, and their courses were so confused, that it is difficult to distinguish the currents which combined to sweep him away on a turbulent torrent by the end of the year.

Although 1909 was a year of social revolution, in which class hatreds were aroused as never before, and many men were publicly pilloried, no individual was more vulnerable than the First Sea Lord. Fisher was the person most responsible for securing the defences against the threat to the nation and empire, to the balance of power and the balance of wealth in Europe, created by German aggrandizement and naval rearmament. In addition to his many enemies within the service, people like Norman Angell and the out-and-out pacifist school regarded him as a warmonger lusting for blood. Then there were the people who took an optimistic view of the intentions of the Germans. And there was the powerful wing of the Liveral Party which assuredly believed in higher taxation—but for the deserving cause of the welfare and social services: pensions before Dreadnoughts. Half the nation was calling him a traitor for depriving the poor to satisfy his lust for battleships and power, and the other half abusing him for neglecting the Navy. He won all his contests, but only narrowly on points; and like an ageing and sorely damaged heavyweight who knocks out his opponent in the last round, he was too weak to get back to his own corner.

In 1908–9 the tide of Liberal idealism was rising as fast as German naval armaments. 1909 was the year of the 'People's Budget'', of renewed enthusiasm for social reform, of new attacks against inherited privilege, riches and titles. It was the year when Winston Churchill was more fearful of class warfare than the war with Germany. 'If we [carry] on in the old happy go lucky way,' he warned in one of his speeches, 'the richer classes ever growing in wealth and in number, the very poor remaining plunged or plunging ever deeper into helplessness, hopeless misery, then I think there is nothing before us but savage strife between class and class . . .'[1] And in this same year, David Lloyd George, whose budget marked a new social epoch for the country, claimed that 'a fully equipped duke costs as much to keep as two Dreadnoughts, and dukes are just as great a terror and they last longer'.[2]

These were the two Cabinet members who were to conflict most fiercely with McKenna and Fisher and the Board over the 1909–10 estimates—an event that developed into the most intense 'navy scare' of Fisher's lifetime. By the late autumn of 1908 rumours, information and events had awakened the Board to new dangers from Germany. All signs now indicated that her Navy was to be increased in strength and numbers beyond her original announced intention that 'if the

---

[1] Randolph S. Churchill, *Winston S. Churchill*, vol. ii (London, 1967), 325. (Hereafter cited as *Churchill*.)   [2] *ibid*.

strongest naval power engaged it, it would endanger its own supremacy.'
Intensification of rivalry and fear in both countries, and the opportunity
to level the score offered by the introduction of the *Dreadnought*, had
evidently decided the German government to devote vast new resources
to the creation of a fleet that would not only equal but actually exceed
the strength of the Royal Navy. By November 1908, the Board calculated that Germany could have not less than thirteen Dreadnoughts
(battleships and battle cruisers) in active commission by 1912. Britain
had authorized only two in 1908; if *three times* this number were ordered
in 1909, the Royal Navy could expect to have eighteen Dreadnoughts
by 1912. Eighteen to thirteen was far below the two-keels-to-one
standard which was generally thought to represent the minimum measure
of superiority for the safety of the nation.

This was bad enough. But reports from Germany indicated that
elaborate and carefully laid plans were being made to accelerate their
programme even further, that Krupp's were involved in a vast scheme
to increase their capacity for manufacturing guns, gun mountings and
armour plate, that German shipyards could already match British yards
—previously the fastest and most experienced in the world—in speed
of construction. A careful examination at the end of 1908 of all this new
information pointed to the alarming fact that Germany might be able
to put to sea *three more* Dreadnoughts than Britain by 1912. Alarm spread
through the land and vigorous attacks were made against 'small navy'
politicians, against the Board and against Fisher for failing to anticipate
the danger.

Fisher and his Sea Lords had been impressing on McKenna throughout 1908 the absolute necessity for laying down not fewer than six
Dreadnoughts in the following year. While navalists considered this
number inadequate the powerful Radical wing of the Liberal Party, led
in the Cabinet by Churchill and Lloyd George, considered such a large
increase as incompatible with all the high ideals of their election
pledges. In fact, so sensitive was the nation's economy to the armaments
business, that unemployment and acute suffering among the working
classes in the shipbuilding, ordnance and heavy steel industries had
been created by the reduction in building in 1908. Lloyd George also
believed that McKenna was bowing to popular and ill-informed demands
because he felt 'his personal position and prestige is at stake', and that
'the Admirals are procuring false information to frighten us'.[1]

In fact, at this time (January 1909) Fisher was already extending his
demands even further than Lloyd George and Churchill feared. In a
memorandum to McKenna the Sea Lords now confirmed that Germany

[1] *Churchill*, ii, 517.

would have seventeen Dreadnoughts by 1912 'for certain', and that Britain's eighteen 'is not considered in any way adequate to maintain the command of the sea in a war with Germany without running undue risk'. The memorandum continued: 'We therefore consider it of the utmost importance that power should be taken to lay down two more armoured ships [Dreadnoughts] in 1909–10—making eight in all . . .'

Lloyd George soon got wind of Fisher's determination to quadruple the previous year's Dreadnought programme. On 3 January 1909, he wrote to Churchill from Cannes: 'The Admiralty mean to get their 6 Dreadnoughts. Murray sent me a message through Clark that the Admiralty have had very serious news from their Naval attaché in Germany *since our last Cabinet Committee* & that McK is now convinced we may have to lay down 8 Dreadnoughts next year!!!

'I feared all along this would happen. Fisher is a very clever person & when he found his programme was in danger he wired to Davidson[1] for something more panicky—& of course he got it . . .'[2]

On the same day, Fisher wrote to the King: 'The outlook is very ominous. Herculean efforts of which we know secretly and *certainly*, are being made by Germany to push on their Dreadnoughts—so much so that McKenna, who was when he came here an extreme "Little Navy" man, is now an ultra "Big Navy" man, and Your Majesty would be astonished by his memorandum to Grey and to the Prime Minister as to building more Dreadnoughts next year than intended, and we shall certainly get them!'

In the first months of 1909 the nation, the government and the cabinet split into three warring factions fighting for four, six or eight Dreadnoughts—a complex statistical conflict which required a slide-rule or a crystal ball to resolve. In the Cabinet Churchill introduced a new quantitive factor by claiming points for Britain's superiority in pre-Dreadnought battleships, which Fisher attacked as a 'red herring trick', and produced a characteristic colourful simile: 'It's the armadillo and the ants—the armadillo puts out its tongue and licks up the ants— the bigger the ant, the more placid the digestive smile! And so the Dreadnought would eat up the [pre-Dreadnought] . . .'

The struggle continued until the middle of the year. At first it was between the 'six-ers' and the 'four-ers'. But soon the extreme militants got wind of the Admiralty's behind-the-scenes demand for eight Dreadnoughts. The news acted like a charge of cordite hurled on the fire of controversy. 'Pacifist' joined 'little Englander' and 'panicmonger' as dirty words, and a Conservative Member of Parliament coined the cry 'We want eight, and we won't wait', which echoed throughout

---

[1] Assistant Private Secretary to King Edward VII.   [2] *Churchill*, ii, 516.

the land—in pubs, political meetings and music halls. Again, Fisher and the rest of the Board threatened resignation.

The danger to the government became so critical that Asquith was forced to search for a compromise, at which he was a past master. He proposed that four Dreadnoughts should be authorized now and four more before April 1910 if information from Germany seemed to make them necessary. Both sides in the Cabinet reluctantly agreed, but McKenna at Fisher's insistence had a footnote inserted in the estimates which allowed for much of the material for the four 'contingent' ships to be included in order that they could be quickly completed. Churchill and Lloyd Gorge spotted the stratagem too late. When they said they would agree to six after all, McKenna and Fisher flatly refused.

No one was happy for long about the compromise. Esher, as influential as ever, was among those who were determined that the contingent ships should be begun without delay. '. . . unless the B. of Admiralty get their 8 ships ordered *at once*,' he wrote to his son, 'they ought to be hanged. I am going to try and put the fear of God into Jackie this morning.'[1] This was neither a necessary nor a practical intention. Fisher was fighting as never before—as Esher himself had to admit. 'Certainly no one could have made a more gallant fight and it reflects the greatest credit upon him,' he wrote at the same time. '. . . I was doubtful as to the reality of the fight he had made.'[2] Yet three weeks later Esher was telling Knollys that 'Jackie will, I fear, prove to be the earthen vessel, between the two iron pots of conflicting parties . . .' and suggesting that he would 'bitterly regret' not tendering his 'qualified resignation'.[3]

The battle continued until July, with accusations of wild extravagance and *hysteria Germanica* blasting from the muzzles of one camp, and of Liberal cowardice and political opportunism from the militants. 'Insist on "the Eight, the whole Eight, and nothing but the Eight", with more to follow, and break any man or faction that now stands in the way,' *The Observer* advised.

Fisher miraculously retained his sense of humour, though its reserves were running low and he was sparing in its use, and an understandable edge of bitterness could be noted.

TO WINSTON S. CHURCHILL

March 4th, 1909

Private and Secret
My dear Winston,

Thanks for your letter just come, and more especially for its concluding

---

[1] *Esher*, ii, 377.　　　[2] *ibid.*, 376.　　　[3] *ibid.*, 380.

French words of your unaltered feelings towards me. It's kind of you to send me these Cabinet revelations. It's too sad and most deplorable. Let us write the word 'Finis'! The Apostle is right! The tongue is the very devil! (N.B. Yours is slung amidships and wags at both ends!)

Yours till the Angels smile on us! (Four more Dreadnoughts!!!)

J.F.

I told Marsh I had burnt your previous letter. No eye but mine had seen it. I have also burnt this one just come from you for the same reason! *'Amantium irae amoris integratio est.'* Have you got the same cook as at Bolton Street?

I think it would be quite lovely to call the four extra Dreadnoughts:—

> No. 1 'Winston'
> No. 2 'Churchill'
> No. 3 'Lloyd'
> No. 4 'George'

How they would fight! Uncircumventable! Read this out to the Cabinet!

The conflict was resolved in an entirely unexpected way. In April confirmation of earlier intelligence began to filter through that both Italy and Austria were about to lay down Dreadnoughts, to the number of four apiece. This emphasized again the high regard in which this new instrument of war was held by the great powers: France, Russia, the USA, Japan, Turkey and the South American republics were already planning and building them. Not only would the balance of naval power in the Mediterranean be entirely destroyed by four Italian battleships. Austria-Hungary was a committed partner to the German empire, and there was nothing to prevent these formidable new ships from reinforcing the German High Seas Fleet in time of war. On 26 July 1909 McKenna announced in the House of Commons that 'after very anxious and careful examination of the condition of shipbuilding in foreign countries' the Government had 'come to the conclusion that it is desirable to take all the necessary steps to ensure that the second four ships . . . should be completed by March 1912' (Opposition cheers).[1]

Had this been a scare, a cheap political sabre-rattling episode, fanned by power-hungry politicians and greedy armament barons? There was no doubt that the degree of German acceleration had been greatly exaggerated, however unwittingly. This soon became evident, but no political advantage was to be gained by pointing this out—besides, Churchill was by that time First Lord himself, and the greatest navalist of them all. But the statistical comparison of German and British Dreadnoughts in home waters on 4 August 1914 was:

[1] *The Times*, 27 July 1909.

Germany	Britain
Battleships 14	Battleships 20
Battle cruisers 3	Battle cruisers 5
——	——
17	25

Lacking the four 'contingent' Dreadnoughts of 1909, the British margin would have been narrow indeed. As it was, and in spite of the expropriation of foreign ships building in Britain at the outbreak of war, when four battle cruisers were hunting for German cruisers in the Atlantic and Pacific at the end of 1914, and a British battleship had already been sunk, the two main fleets were almost on level terms.

Although Fisher had been struggling for all he was worth for the increase in battleship construction, complementing McKenna's magnificent efforts in the Cabinet and the House of Commons, he took much of the public blame for bringing about the crisis. He was widely accused of concurring in the reduced programme of the previous year, and of failing in his duties. A leader writer in the *Daily Express* (20 March 1909) exemplified the views of the half-frightened, the half-informed, and the political opportunists:

'The sole responsibility for the fact that in a few months Great Britain will be in a more vulnerable position than she has been since the battle of Trafalgar belongs to the First Sea Lord . . . Above all, he is responsible for the starving of the Navy during the last three years . . . his notorious "sleep safely in your beds" speech was a direct justification of Radical policy. We arraign Sir John Fisher at the bar of public opinion, and with the imminent possibility of national disaster before the country we say again to him, "Thou art the man!" '

Whether or not Fisher was 'the man' was to be decided not by writers in the *Daily Express* or the *National Review* or any others who were trading on the current wave of fear they had themselves helped to enflame, but by the investigations of the sub-committee of the Committee of Imperial Defence Beresford had persuaded the government to set up. Since he had hauled down his flag and nodded to the cheering crowds who had welcomed him ashore and to London, Beresford had been busy. He had already tried some rather primitive blackmail. Shortly before he gave up his command, Beresford had searched out Balfour, in the expectation of the government's imminent downfall and of Balfour again becoming Prime Minister. For the price of Balfour's promise that he would be made First Sea Lord, Beresford said he would refrain from publicly attacking Fisher and the state of the Navy. Failing the promise, Beresford said he would 'stump the country and agitate'. Balfour replied that he had not given consideration to any future cabinet or Board of Admiralty.[1]

It was as well for Beresford that news of his behind-the-scenes tactics did not leak out. By this time neither party was being very scrupulous about methods of attacking the other. Fisher had had privately printed for circulation among certain officers some of the letters Bacon had written in confidence to Fisher from the Mediterranean in 1906 reporting on Beresford's conduct. The purpose was to impress on them his incompetence. The original request by Fisher to Bacon to write the letters was in doubtful taste; the printing and circulating of them three years later without Bacon's knowledge was inept and foolhardy. The news was bound to get out. It did, in a speech made by one of Beresford's closest and cleverest allies, Sir George Armstrong, on 2 April 1909. This appeared to confirm all Beresford's accusations that Fisher had used serving officers to spy on him. The revelation cost Fisher dear. A number of people who had withheld judgement or had decided that it was their duty to remain above the squalid and damaging battle being played out, now turned on Fisher.

The Cabinet committee, with Asquith presiding, had its first meeting on 27 April and its last on 13 July. It consisted of Haldane, Grey, Lord Morley, a Radical and small-navy man, and the Earl of Crewe, a big-navy supporter. Evidence was offered by McKenna on bahalf of the Board, and by Beresford, who had drawn up charges against the organization and distribution of the Fleet in home waters, against the shortage of supporting small craft and destroyers, and the lack of proper war plans and intelligence. Custance was in attendance on Beresford, like an able junior supporting a counsel of declining powers. Fisher was present at all fifteen meetings but spoke only when questions were directed at him.

Many of Fisher's supporters wanted to counter-attack publicly, but Fisher thought this would do more harm than good and begged them to keep their counsel.

FROM ROLLO APPLEYARD[2]

79 *St Mary's Mansions,*
Paddington
April 4th, 1909

Dear Sir John Fisher,

It is hard to refrain from answering some of these vile attacks. I am refraining solely because you have asked me to refrain, and because you have

---

[1] Marder, i, 189.

[2] According to Fisher's marginal note, 'A very eminent Civil Engineer'. Lennoxlove MSS.

asked me so repeatedly and so emphatically. Is it still your wish that they should be passed over in silence? I am convinced that the war is being carried on not so much by ignorant members of the public as by discontents within the Service.

Yours sincerely,
R. Appleyard

The ever-wise Ponsonby aided Knollys in keeping Fisher in touch with events and trends of thought at Court. 'The King would like to see you on Sunday next between twelve and one or three and four,' he wrote to Fisher (5 May 1909). ' . . . Personally I am glad to hear that Beresford is having every possible chance. If, as I believe, your case is so strong there is nothing to be gained by not allowing him to get off his chest all he has to say on the subject. It seems to me to strengthen your position very much if Beresford is allowed as much rope as he wants. The King however does not take the same view!'[1]

As these remarkable proceedings continued, with their accusations and counter-accusations that were so remote from the formal charges, the need for Fisher's resignation was widely and increasingly discussed. Esher had already stated his views to Fisher on the subject. On the evening of 14 April he 'came up to Town, and had a long talk with Jackie. We agreed that in view of the attacks upon him resignation was impossible. Nothing but a "file of marines should get him out of the Admiralty. I wrote and told the Prince, and I sent him references to the attacks on St Vincent in 1804. A good analogy of what is going on here.'[2]

Archibald Hurd, another stalwart ally, offered the same advice in a letter of sympathy, to which Fisher replied:

TO ARCHIBALD HURD[3]

Admiralty,
Whitehall
5th May, 1909

Secret and Private
My Beloved Hurd,
    Thanks for your valued letter. *I am not going until I am kicked out!*
'And non fugimus nos fugamur.'
    (We are not deserted! We are outcasts! is what those Old Boys said those hundreds of years ago!) I am eating dirt and undergoing humiliation but I am going to stick to it, and stick to it in silence.
    'Only Luke is with me', is what S. Paul said when all his friends had scuttled! I am getting near that!

[1] Lennoxlove MSS.   [2] *Esher*, ii, 382-3.   [3] Lennoxlove MSS.

However, I think of that fine epitaph of one of Nelson's captains. *'Death found him fighting.'*

Yours,
J.F.

The defection of the Prince of Wales, now openly antagonistic, wounded Fisher more deeply than anything else, and accounted for his anti-monarchist attitude after the death of Edward VII.

TO VISCOUNT ESHER

Admiralty, Whitehall
July 3rd, 1909

Private and Secret
My dear E.,

Do you think the Prince of Wales at all realizes what would happen if the Public (*and especially the Radical Party*) knew he was actively taking Beresford's side and saying I must go (and he is now doing and openly said at Royal Yacht dinner last Saturday), and that his bosom friend Captain Campbell had been doing 'Judas'! perpetually at my house, and selling me all the time to Beresford!

The latest development is that Sir G. Armstrong has a pile of my private letters to various people—not printed or typewritten but *the original letters,* so he says, which he is going to produce unless I agree to go in October! Some of the letters stolen and some given (so I am told!). However 'hot' they may be, I don't regret a word I ever wrote, and I believe my countrymen will forgive me. *Anyhow I won't be blackmailed!* There was murder in the King's eye when I told him (*but I didn't tell him all!*). Dear old Knollys was splendid. *I just love him! I am going to fight to the finish! Heaven bless you for your help.*

Yours,
J.F.

The committee's report was published on 12 August 1909. Its General Conclusion, diplomatically worded to give the least possible offence to either of the warring factions, supported the Admiralty's 'arrangements for war, whether considered from the standpoint of the organization and distribution of the fleets, the number of ships, or the preparation of War Plans'. But 'the absence of cordial relations' between Beresford and the Board 'seriously hampered' these arrangements. Beresford was indicted for failing 'to appreciate and carry out the spirit of the instructions of the Board, and to recognize their paramount authority'; while the Board was criticized for failing to take Beresford sufficiently into their confidence. Beresford's complaint about lack of war plans was denied, but the committee reported that they look forward 'with much confidence to the further development of a Naval War Staff'.

The findings (see Appendix 3) represented a qualified vindication of Fisher and his régime, and failed to condemn as roundly as Fisher had expected Beresford's 'gross insubordination'. Its damaging effect on Fisher depended largely on his own public response to it. It was possible to hail it as a victory for either party. By this time Fisher's sensitiveness to criticism had developed into a persecution complex, and he was cast down and angry about the report and the 'cowardliness' of those who had drawn it up. If all his supporters had joined together in a triumphant chorus, far from damaging him the report could have cleared away all public doubts and restored the reputation he had once enjoyed.

Instead, Fisher's dismay and disappointment were fertilized in their growth by letters of commiseration rather than congratulation.

FROM VISCOUNT KNOLLYS

> *Craig Gowan*
> *Balmoral, N.B.*
> *September 19th, 1909*

Private
My dear Fisher,
 . . . I felt so disgusted with the Report of the Beresford Committee that I really could not make up my mind to write to you about it, but I can assure you I felt deeply for you, as you have been most unjustly treated. I was in hopes that the draft report, as it was originally prepared, would have been substantially adopted, but Asquith 'watered it down' to such an extent that it amounts to a verdict in Beresford's favour, and it has given him the opportunity, which he has not been slow to avail himself of, to declare publicly that the Report was favourable to him.

If it is in his favour, it must be unfavourable to the Admiralty, and poor McKenna is in such a ticklish position that if he had remonstrated, it is very probable that Asquith, with the applause of the two moving spirits in the Cabinet, L. George and W. Churchill, would have got rid of him. The fact is the Committee, as I have always said, were afraid of Beresford, and this has been proved by their treatment of him when he was under examination, and by the Report itself.

The King has asked McKenna to come to Balmoral as Minister in Attendance, which I am very glad of, as it is a sort of compliment to him and the Admiralty and will show everybody that H.M. approves of what he has done . . .

> Yours ever,
> *Knollys*

Beresford, on the other hand, was better supported and better advised. With admirably organized staff work, he issued to the press four days after the publication of the findings a circular letter which read like a C.-in-C.'s victory report, expressing 'great satisfaction'. His army of supporting journalists combined in a shamelessly vindictive personal attack on Fisher and all he had accomplished. 'Should it come to hanging,' wrote one in the *National Review*, 'he will be entitled to the nearest lamp-post.' A year which had begun in a frenzy of Teutophobia, fear and panic was ending in an outpouring of vitriol directed against the man who had done most to alert the nation to the danger across the North Sea and prepared the Navy for the war that lay ahead. It was an ironical turn of political fate, which Fisher would have relished, that Churchill, one of his warmest opponents, was to suffer similar denigration from anti-militarists for similar reasons a quarter of a century later with the rise of the Nazi threat.

To sustain his campaign of reform in the face of such public defamation and the 'base innuendos against the Admiralty' in the report signed by '*5 cowards*' was beyond Fisher's powers. To submit his resignation now would be to accept the implied rebukes in the report and to bow before the hostile personal attacks in the press. Answering in a letter to Esher the rhetorical question 'What am I going to do?' he replied, 'Answer—*nothing!* It is the ONLY course to follow! I have thought it all out most carefully and decided to keep absolutely dumb.'

Yet Fisher knew that he could not stay for long. His authority had slipped too far to be retrieved. Asquith and McKenna knew too that it was politically necessary to name a date and find a successor. Late in October the three men conferred together—the wily Prime Minister who had completed one more private and delicate tightrope walk, the First Lord who had fought so stubbornly and loyally for the case of Fisher and the Navy, and the Admiral who had been found not guilty yet was unemployable because of the tarnish to his reputation. This was the occasion when it was decided that Asquith should recommend to the King that Fisher be raised to the Peerage on the King's birthday, and retire on his own 69th birthday in January.

With the decision made at last, Fisher felt a great sense of relief. 'I am all right!' he told a friend on 29 October. 'I told the King I had led a dog's life, but yet every dog has had his day.' On the same day he received 'the very best letter I ever received in my life'.

FROM KING EDWARD

Newmarket
October 29th, 1909

My dear Fisher,

Many thanks for sending me the Prime Minister's letter to you of 26th inst. to read, which I return. It is a charming letter in every respect and one which

I know you would wish to keep. I endorse every word in it and nobody deserves the thanks of your Sovereign and your Country more warmly than you do. Time will show what admirable Reforms you have created in the Royal Navy, and you can afford to treat with the contempt that it deserves 'those back biters' who have endeavoured to calumniate you! When you leave the high and important post which you now occupy in the Admiralty, I hope you will still render the best services that lie in your power for the good of the noble profession to which you belong, and I hope continue a member of the 'Defence Committee'! You possess too much vitality to 'lie fallow'!

Ever, Yours very sincerely and gratefully,
Edward R & I.

After the news became public on 2 December, the honour and tributes came pouring in, as if a dam of caution and discretion had suddenly burst. Many people who had remained silent during the darkest and most dangerous days felt able to write again, to congratulate him on his Peerage and to praise him for all his accomplishments. Those who had pleaded to make public their support could now come out into the open, too. King Edward sent him a silver model submarine as a Christmas present, and Queen Alexandra, to whom he was equally devoted, a Dutch ship in full sail on an old silver ladle.

On the termination of his office, the judgements and summaries inevitably appeared in the press. Those who had most bitterly attacked him remained silent—what more was there to say? *The Times* was forced to acknowledge the occasion. Predictably, the toast was a muted one, for their military correspondent was a firm Beresfordite, and the paper had recently published a series of fiercely anti-Fisher articles co-authored by Custance. 'During these five strenuous years,' ran their judgement (25 January 1910) 'which have seen the consummation and crown of a long career equally strenuous, Lord Fisher has for good or for evil—and in our judgement largely for good—left an indelible mark, a mark deeper than that made by any of his immediate predecessors, on the administration, organization, disposition and equipment of the Royal Navy . . . it is probable that some things may have been done amiss, that some reforms which were . . . necessary in themselves may have been introduced somewhat brusquely, and that the manner of effecting them may not always have been unimpeachable from the point of view of official conventions and service traditions. It is certain, at any rate, that they have aroused much bitter antagonism and much painful controversy . . .' Fisher's methods, concluded *The Times*, had not always been commendable.

The fullest, most fulsome, yet most considered assessment of Fisher and his works came from his old friend W. T. Stead. Fisher's enemies dismissed this as a sycophantic outpouring. Yet it has stood the test of time. In 1910 Stead was editing the *Review of Reviews*. He was a firebrand journalist of the old school. Yet his soul was incorruptible. Morley told Fisher 'that he had never known the equal of W. T. Stead in his astounding gift of catching the popular feeling'. Esher 'loved and admired' him. 'He was one of the few very honest, very single-minded and really good men.' Fisher described him as 'the greatest of all journalists . . . He was absolute integrity and he feared no man.' He told Fisher that 'he would die in his boots', and this prediction, too, came to pass—for he went down in the greatest newspaper story of his time, the sinking of the *Titanic*.[1]

After listing a multitude of reforms Fisher instituted—from the reorganization of dockyards to the development of submarines, from the establishment of a navigation school to minesweepers, introduction of a Fleet reserve and organization of arrangements for mobilization besides the more widely known introduction of the Dreadnought and the redistribution of the Fleets, Stead offered his readers a quick pen portrait: 'For Fisher was a great man—one of our greatest men.

' "I don't know how you feel about it," said a friend the day after Fisher's retirement, "but I feel pretty bad. It is almost as if Nelson had stepped down from his monument in Trafalgar Square." This is not an exaggeration. We all feel more or less like that, from the King upon his throne down to the scurviest of the curs who snapped at the great man's heels . . . His greatness was attested alike by the devotion that he commanded from all the greatest, and the fierce rancour of animosity which he aroused in the worst, of his contemporaries.'

Esher reminded Stead of 'one point about Jackie you omit to mention. His reverence for sacred things. Perhaps you never saw him in church.

'People might think from his frequent use of Biblical phrases that he was not particularly endowed with reverence.

'How wrong they would be! Like all strong characters there is no better friend than Jackie, and no better enemy too.'[2]

---

[1] On his death in the *Titanic* disaster Fisher wrote to Esher: 'This loss of dear old Stead numbs me! Cromwell and Martin Luther rolled into one. And such a big heart. Such great emotions. . . . The telegrams here say he was to the forefront with the women and children, putting them in the boats! *I can see him!* . . . He told me he would die in his boots. So he has. *And a fine death.* As a boy he had threepence a week pocket money. One penny bought Shakespeare in weekly parts, the other two pennies to his God for Missions. And the result was he became editor of a big newspaper at 22! And he was a Missionary himself all his life. Fearless even when alone, believing in his God—the God of truth—and his enemies always rued it when they fought him. He was an exploder of "gasbags" and the terror of liars.' (*Memories*, 264.)

[2] *Esher*, iii, 46.

Churchill, already half-forgiven by Fisher (who understood very thoroughly the needs and the appetites of the political animal) wrote a cheerful letter from the Home Office: 'I am only sorry that the drift of events did not enable us to work together. Your elevation to the Peerage was a real source of pleasure to me; and was a partial recognition of the great services you have rendered to British Naval supremacy.

'I have regretted since,' he went on significantly, 'that I did not press for the Admiralty in 1908 . . . I believe it would have been better for us all.'[1]

Some years later Churchill was to write of the man with whom he had such a tempestuous relationship: 'There is no doubt whatever that Fisher was right in nine-tenths of what he fought for. His great reforms sustained the power of the Royal Navy at the most critical period in its history. He gave the Navy the kind of shock which the British Army received at the time of the South African War. After a long period of serene and unchallenged complacency, the mutter of distant thunder could be heard. It was Fisher who hoisted the storm-signal and beat all hands to quarters. He forced every department of the Naval Service to review its position and question its own existence. He shook them and beat them and cajoled them out of slumber into intense activity. But the Navy was not a pleasant place while this was going on.'[2]

'His English temperament includes the strange contradictions of the English character,' wrote Arnold White in his tribute. 'He can be as hard as Harveyised Steel and as gentle as a woman; but since he is generally fighting he is generally Steel. Contrary to the current conception of his character, Fisher is, however, also a sentimentalist. When H.M.S. *Victory* was rammed in the fairway of Portsmouth Harbour and her salvage and repair were problematical, Fisher travailed for her safety as a man travails and toils to save one he loves much . . . When Fisher buckled to his task of cramming into five years the reforms of forty he was wont to look at the figure of Nelson in Trafalgar Square from the window of the First Sea Lord's Room at the Admiralty . . . When the menace of the North Sea shifted the centre of gravity from the Mediterranean it was met; and the proof that it was met is the fact that there has never yet, since October 21st, 1904, been a division in either House of Parliament on Fisher's administration. Three Premiers have supported him in succession. Yet the Party system has never lassoed him. Nobody knows whether he is Unionist or Liberal. I

[1] Lennoxlove MSS.
[2] Winston S. Churchill, *The World Crisis* (London, 1923–9, 4 vols in 5), i, 74–5. (Hereafter cited as *World Crisis*.)

don't. That is the unpardonable sin to Party men. Our present Naval fitness for the great day of trial was the measure of Fisher's greatness . . . He has the capacity for scorn; knows the value of reserve, and of silence. Some men's influence is talked to death by themselves. He gives the impression of being elemental man in the midst of wax figures. In the stress of his work he has no more idea of attitude than a tempest or a fire. Magnetic to an extent that violently repels or strongly attracts everyone he meets, he has used his power over men and material to the best of his knowledge solely for his King and Country. The proof is in the Navy. It is his monument . . .'[1]

The judgement of Fisher by his contemporaries must always be the most valuable and accurate. But these judgements must be assessed today in their own setting. In the more humble public world today there are many fewer big figures. Seen through the eyes of today, the great public figures are larger-than-life, talk extravagantly and often intemperately, and are more easily aroused to affection and hatred. There was a greater sense of national pride. The group and class divisions were much wider, and those who aspired to move from one to the other were subjected to far greater strains than they would today. Lord Fisher in 1910 must be seen in this richer, more ruthless, more vital environment.

At a time when Britain has for more than two decades been shedding her territory and her responsibilities and has become increasingly dependent on a mutual defence system, it is even more difficult to comprehend the nation's preoccupation with its defences thirty years before air power finally shattered insular illusions. Then half the world in the atlas was painted empire red. The Navy was the great source of national security. Everything about it—its appearance, its strength, its past, its traditions, were calculated to instil pride in its proprietors. At this time, too, a battleship was a more emotive weapon of war than any number of hidden guided missiles and supersonic bombers and polaris submarines. Far from being concealed, or making fleeting appearances, the battleship was always proudly there, to be seen in every port and river estuary, distantly as a grey shape to holidaymakers on the coast, or in startling close-up in harbour, or—most impressive of all— *en masse* at some Spithead Royal Review. The Navy gave the nation its peace of mind, and in return received the confidence and adulation of the people. Every Briton loved a sailor, and the breed was symbolized by the great sea dogs of the time.

Fisher and Beresford were both sea dogs in the popular mind. When they began to scrap, the public was fascinated, and their partisanship

[1] *Daily Chronicle*, 10 November 1909.

encouraged the contestants to greater excesses. The playing of the part of a sea dog was a responsible business and over-acting was a temptation when the public cheered. The rhetoric and gestures of both Fisher and Beresford were superb.

Yet by 1910 Beresford was a hack, and even his most loyal supporters had given up hope of hoisting him into the office of Senior Naval Lord. In January 1910 he returned to Parliament, where he became a joke. Churchill reported (12 April 1912) on his performances to Fisher thus: 'Beresford has made such an ass of himself in the House of Commons . . . He is completely gaga, and his oratory belongs to the class of speaker of whom they said "Before they get up they don't know what they are going to say; when they are speaking they don't know what they are saying; and when they have sat down they don't know what they have said".'[1]

By 1910 Fisher's powers, too, had begun to decline. His mind, undulled by alcohol and heavy living, was as active as ever, but now his judgements were marred by bitterness and rancour. He had lost too many friends and fought too many contests. Like his own country eight years hence, he had won through, but his credit was low and his spirit soured by the wounds and the cost. It was best for the Navy that he should go a year before his time was up. It was urgently necessary to renew a spirit of unity before war came; and it was equally necessary to form and train the new machines of a naval staff to take the place of the one brilliant dynamo which had suddenly been switched off.

Letters of congratulation and commiseration arrived for Fisher in large numbers from complete strangers as well as from the many hundreds of friends and acquaintances in and out of the service. Shrewd judges of the scene believed that Fisher's active days were by no means over. Jacky would be back, they were saying. It was as preposterous to think of the Navy without Fisher as it had been to think of England without Queen Victoria. McKenna actively encouraged Fisher to expect to return to Whitehall. Just before he left he invited Fisher out for a walk one Sunday evening. 'As he left me,' Fisher told Arnold White later, 'he said "You will be First Sea Lord again in a year and bigger than ever . . ."'

A lighter note later sounded out from Buckingham Palace, of all places. 'Fritz' Ponsonby had been invited to continue his private secretarial duties with George V. Ponsonby had always had a soft spot for Fisher and their relationship was close and familiar. 'I think it is a pity,' ran Ponsonby's contribution to the tributes, 'we do not adopt with our big men the methods we find so successful with horses. If after retiring

[1] Lennoxlove MSS.

from the Admiralty you had been sent round the sea ports to breed Admirals with bucks and lasses specially selected on account of their seafaring propensities think what the Navy would gain in twenty years' time!'[1]

<hr/>

[1] *ibid.*

PART THREE

Chapter 1

'A READY AND CONSTANT COUNSELLOR'[1]

Late in January 1910 Fisher made the journey to his son's home at Kilverstone Hall and found there the peace he so sorely needed. 'I've never known till now what joy there is in Nature,' he wrote. 'Even beauteous woman fades in the comparison.' He loved the garden, especially the 10,000 roses, in which he took a special and active interest. 'So Jacky is growing roses, is he?' a friend exclaimed. 'Well, all I've got to say is that those roses will damned well have to grow.'[2]

He seemed to be content to be out of the battles of Whitehall. He has a pension of £2,000 a year, and a joint private income with his wife of around £300. It was enough for their needs, and he was free from financial anxiety. He enjoyed telling his friends of the new, relaxed life he was leading in the country. 'You will remember the Emperor Diocletian doffed the Imperial purple and planted cabbages. My first days are so promising I think I shall find it also a success. Also I am learning golf. Across the river here lives a millionaire with his private links and a professional always attending. The charming thing is there are comfortable seats at each hole where one rests. I hope when the roses are blooming in June you will come and try those seats!'

It is unlikely that Fisher ever took advantage of those seats. He was as physically fit and active as ever. At 69 his enthusiasm for dancing was as keen as ever.

---

[1] 'I shall most sedulously endeavour to carry you with me in my administration at the Admiralty and I have good hope that I shall succeed, and that you will feel free to be a ready and constant counsellor.' Churchill to Fisher, 2 November 1911 (Kilverstone MSS.)

[2] *Bacon*, ii, 119.

TO VISCOUNT ESHER

Kilverstone Hall
February 2nd, 1910

Private
My beloved E.

... I've just got here from Cheshire, where for days running I've had Paradise. 3 lovely girls in the house, a *splendid* ball-room, and music always on hand. 3 young Guardsmen there, but I held my own! ... Dancing till 4 a.m. took it out of me a bit, but it revivified me and I renewed my strength like the eagles! Did you ever meet a Lady Jean Cochrane? Such a dancer! But she was an extra! So good-looking ...

Yours for ever,
F.

Then again, the next year, from Lucerne: 'I've had a lovely time here. Fancy! for 3 whole weeks a dance every blessed night till 3 a.m.! and these lovely Americans DO dance divinely! It was lovely!'

The practice of years of writing in longhand in the early hours could not be halted. From Kilverstone the letters poured forth in a torrent, many of them in extravagant terms to the clever and beautiful women he most admired.

TO MRS REGINALD MCKENNA

Kilverstone Hall
March 17th, 1910

My dear Pamela,

I don't know that I should have quite answered your letter by return of post except to urgently entreat you to take off your spouse *at once*, for a sea trip in the *Enchantress*, or, anyhow, a 'spell off' somewhere! as I hear he looks quite done up, but evidently he's not *hors de combat!* He has fought splendidly! I LOVE HIM!! You have sent me a sweet letter! I LOVE YOU ALSO!! But imagine my delight in quite casually and accidentally finding a fellow-worshipper, who harangues me on two sheets about your brains! (Being a woman, I suppose she doesn't care a d—n about your looks! which I myself much admire!) ...

In haste, Ever yours,
'Jacky'

The frequent references to 'growing cabbages' was a joke which he did not expect anyone to believe. Even the roses took little of his time. For Fisher had not retired into inactivity, nor had he cut himself off from Westminster, Whitehall and Fleet Street: he was only determined to remain physically absent and without direct responsibilities, except to the Defence Committee of which he remained a member. His social life at Kilverstone was a busy one.

'A Ready and Constant Counsellor'

TO JOHN LEYLAND[1]

Kilverstone Hall,
Thetford,
May 9th, 1910.

My dear Leyland,

I have Garvin of "The Observer" and his wife and Sir H-Lucy and his wife coming to stay and it occurred to me suddenly that they would be pleasant company for you to meet so I packed off a telegram and am indeed *delighted* you are coming . . .

Through conversations late into the night, and passionately worded letters to his old friends who still held power and influence, Fisher continued to press for the developments and reforms in which he remained deeply interested—from the lot of the lower deck, to an increase in the submarine service. He fought from afar for 'the greater recognition of our Bluejackets and Marines to attain commissioned rank'. To the editor of the *Daily News* he wrote in his finest evangelical (and indiscreet) vein: *'This is a deadly secret,* so burn and don't talk in your sleep! We have got a submarine that carries two 4-inch guns and goes 21 knots and can cross the Atlantic and wants no convoy and lives by herself for 2 months!'

Fisher so closely savoured his remaining power that no one could believe that his taste for it had altogether gone sour. Within ten weeks of his arrival at Kilverstone, he wrote to Gerald Fiennes, the naval journalist, 'Perhaps in view of these articles you are writing it may not be politic for you to come and stay wtih me. They would say I inspired them! . . . I am in big things just now in the Committee of Defence. *Secret.* Only two days ago I had to send an ultimatum that if any tampering with a certain sacred principle I should "call the cat"! . . . '[2] And to Gardiner of the *Daily News* some months later: ' . . . *Secret* I am more powerful now in the Committee of Defence than when I was First Sea Lord. I had masters then, now I have none and I have a platform.'

The causes were the old ones he had fought over time and again in the past. On this occasion it was a proposal to divert eight million pounds of money for defence to compulsory military service. 'It's not invasion, it's starvation that has to be contemplated. A British Army of 4 millions led by Moltkes instead of Asses no use if we have not command of the sea! . . . Give the Navy every d—d thing they want! . . .'

[1] Late editor *Army and Navy Gazette,* now Naval Correspondent of *The Times.* Kilverstone MSS.
[2] Kilverstone MSS.

There were new causes, too. Besides the submarine, he hurled himself with his old ardour but without sufficient knowledge, into the cause of the diesel engine as a motive power for big ships. Engines using heavy oil rather than refined petroleum (requiring a spark for ignition and a dangerously inflammable fuel) had first been used in submarines. So enthusiastic was Fisher in the promotion of the diesel engine that he might have been its inventor. In his mind it represented one more revolution, like the small tube boiler and the turbine to which he had been such an early convert. 'Motor battleships!' he wrote to Spender. 'No funnels—no boilers—no smoke—no engineers—no stokers—only a d—d chauffeur and prodigious economy! *"Colossal billig"*! as the Germans would say! and imagine the fighting effects of all this!'

Fisher's forecasts in his last years were still sometimes uncannily accurate. But now, as if he feared it might refute the theory already hard-set in his mind, he was taking less and less advice. Diesel power for big warships was only one of a number of ill-advised or little-advised causes which were bound to fail. In fact it was tried with very qualified success only in the German between-the-wars 'pocket' battleships.

In his politics Fisher became a radical authoritarian. 'What this country wants,' he told Spender, 'is a mild despotism tempered by a chastened Bismarck!' His abhorrence of professional politicians remained as powerful as ever as his support for the underprivileged increased. Party politics to Fisher was a giant contest in opportunism; even when party policy favoured the Navy, he considered the politicians' motives as purely opportunistic. 'I said to him [Jellicoe],' he wrote to McKenna, 'it didn't signify what d—d fools we had to govern us—we got on! The Tories gave up Heligoland, the key to the Baltic, and the Liberals gave up Corfu, the key of the German Mediterranean . . . and some other ass gave up Curaçao, the key of the Panama Canal, and Ceuta, more precious than them all . . .' And, on a more personal level, he exclaimed to Esher, 'How funny it is that I did *infinitely more* for the Conservatives than for the *Radicals*, and yet the Radicals have given me all I have got and the Conservatives have only given me abuse and calumny!

'The Radicals gave me £2,000 a year and a Peerage, and I increased the Radical estimates nearly 10 millions! I decreased the Estimates 9 millions and reduced prospective charges by nineteen millions sterling for the Conservatives, and they never lifted even a little finger to help me, *but on the contrary* have heaped dunghill abuse on me!'

Inherited titles and privileges were anathema to Fisher, and he remained a Royalist only so long as King Edward lived. His death came as a fearful blow so soon after his own forced retirement. Esher and Fisher exchanged mutual heartfelt messages of commiseration over the loss of their friend. 'What an *inexpressible* sorrow! How we both know the loss!' Fisher exclaimed. 'What a great National Calamity! And *personally* what can I say? *What a splendid and steadfast friend!* No use saying any more to each other—is it? *I really feel heart broken.*' Two weeks later Fisher still felt that 'I really can't get over the irreparable loss. *I think of nothing else!*'[1] At the end of the year, seven months after the funeral, Fisher was still lamenting the loss.

Official and family arrangements acknowledged the long and close relationship between Fisher and his King. The beautiful widowed Queen Alexandra, whom Fisher loved and admired so deeply, telegraphed him at Kilverstone:

'Being such a friend of my poor King and he was devoted to you will you come and see him once more in his last beautiful sleep. Alexandra.'[2]

Fisher hastened to Buckingham Palace; and later reported to McKenna, 'I had an affectionate half-hour with the Queen—too sacred to talk of. I really felt as I looked at my best friend (as the Queen justly called him) that he was there still! I always knew the Queen in love with him. No one knows what I have lost. I've burnt his letters. Fancy, he was probably coming here yesterday. But he has gone at his zenith like Elijah, Nelson, and Moses: "His eye was not dim, nor his natural force abated." It's the best way to go . . .'

In the mighty funeral procession, which included eight Kings and the German Emperor, Fisher as First and Principal aide-de-camp walked alone. He was 'a striking figure, to whom the attention of all was drawn irresistibly',[3] his chest ablaze with decorations and orders, his head held low in the deep sorrow he was suffering.

Fisher found a measure of consolation in his only son's prospective wedding. Cecil Fisher had fallen in love with Jane Morgan, an American heiress. In October 1910 he brought her to Kilverstone Hall before the wedding. Fisher approved of his only daughter-in-law. 'Cecil desperately in love,' he wrote, 'and she with him, and all is most suitable in all ways in her! Looks, age, character, and means, and I thank Heaven!'

Fisher sailed for New York in the *Baltic* in November for the wedding, and straight away embraced the new Continent like a splendid dancing partner or the blueprint for a Dreadnought. Everything was

---

[1] *Memories*, 198. [2] Kilverstone MSS. [3] *Illustrated London News*.

wonderful and marvellous, and nothing less than an instant *entente* would satisfy him. The accounts of his adventures and reactions written to his friends included evidence of his more accurate prophetic power, especially on the results of the next Presidential election.

TO ARNOLD WHITE[1]

> *Kilverstone Hall*
> *December 20th, 1910*

Private
My dear Arnold White,

The Election being over—a thing of apathy, and no one seeming to care a d—n—you may have time to read a letter.

I enjoyed America immensely, but am overjoyed to be back.
'The heart untravelled fondly turns to home,
And drags at each remove a lengthening chain.'
But I shan't be surprised if I go over there to die! I had a wonderful welcome, and they seem to know me more than in my own land. (But the Scripture mentions that!) The magnitude of Men, Things, and Ideas impressed me tremendously. I think I saw all the great men and had fascinating *tête-à-tête*. Everything is big. St Peter's at Rome will go inside the waiting-room of the new Pennsylvania Railway Station, and they return you your money if the train is late; and one street in Philadelphia is twelve miles long, three times wider than Regent Street, and houses both sides all the way! . . .

They told me their population is now 100 millions; and yet only 25 persons to the square mile, Germany 250, I think, and England 550, about. They are going to be 250 millions.

Seventy multi-millionaires gave me a private lunch, and they asked me to "raise the Middle West" (as they called it), but *festina lente*, and much judgment is wanted. I'm going to begin with Lord Morley and Rosebery. I think it will come about—Germany and Japan are coalescing to exploit China and threaten the United States. No one mentions it any more than Gambetta mentioned 'Revenge,' but it is running like wildfire through the American mind! Hence the plunge about fortifying the Panama Canal dead in the face of our treaty against it. They know England is on their side. And Taft is sowing the seed for an English *entente*, and the next President, Woodrow Wilson, Governor of New Jersey, whom I had a *tête-à-tête* with, is dead on. (Burn this.) I told them it was a d...d fine old hen that hatched the American Eagle, and they madly cheered; and that George Washington was one of the *greatest Englishmen*, because he made England prosperous, by teaching us how to manage our Colonies.

> Yours always,
> F.

After the wedding at Chestnut Hill, Philadelphia, on 22 November

[1] *Bacon*, ii, 145.

1910, Fisher returned to England and Kilverstone. He was nearly seventy years old. He hated the English winter climate. Satisfied that his successor was continuing his policies, he turned an uncharacteristic and non-Nelsonic blind eye to Wilson's bad relations with McKenna and the Defence Committee members and his failure to promote the cause of the submarine. McKenna was apparently doing all right, too—thanks to the ceaseless words of advice with which Fisher plied him. Fisher therefore determined to do what he had promised himself when he was in harness—spend a long time on the Continent, glorying in the sun, the fresh fruits and wines, the friends he would find everywhere, and the dancing they would provide. On 18 February 1911 he and Lady Fisher crossed the Channel, intending to stay in inexpensive small hotels, until March 1912, when Wilson was due to retire and a successor would have to be found. Then perhaps he might even be called back to duty in Whitehall? It was not impossible. Had not McKenna, among others, predicted it?

The distances and the distractions of Continental travel did not deter Fisher from offering information and guidance to those who could still influence events in his absence. From Venice, Bad Nauheim, and Lucerne the letters sped to McKenna and Jellicoe, Spender, Esher and Arnold White, and many others. In return he was kept in touch with events at home. 'I have had a long yarn from Esher full of the inside of things,' he wrote to Mrs McKenna (now 'My beloved Angel') in 4 May 1911. 'He has been staying a fortnight at Windsor Castle! *He really is wonderful.* He says he *"feels as he were staying at a quiet vicarage"!* Don't you think that's lovely? But the gist of the letter is . . . ' And there followed a long and 'inside' account of the latest political machinations.

Five months later the political situation, especially as it related to Fisher, was abruptly altered by the sudden termination of McKenna's appointment as First Lord. Asquith, Haldane and others responsible for the nation's defence against the ever-growing German threat were concerned at the lack of progress towards modernizing the Navy and the creation of a Naval War Staff. The dead hand of Wilson was too tightly gripped on the controls, and McKenna was helpless to remove it. The eagerness of Churchill, then at the Home Office, to get this plum post was almost unseemly, and gave McKenna and others the probably mistaken impression that he had plotted to bring about this coup. McKenna went unwillingly to the Home Office on 25 October 1911; and on the same day Churchill made the first of his two hurricane-like entries into the Admiralty.

Churchill at once acted with dramatic and impetuous speed. Even before he moved offices, he signalled to Fisher, now at Lucerne.

First Sea Lord

FROM WINSTON CHURCHILL[1]

Home Office
25 October 1911

My dear Lord Fisher,

I want to see you vy much. When am I to have that pleasure? You have but to indicate your convenience & I will await you at the Admiralty.

Yours vy sincerely
Winston S. Churchill

At this time Churchill wanted Fisher back as First Sea Lord, and to talk him into acceptance. But Fisher was not so easily persuaded to renew their old friendship. He regarded Churchill's behaviour over the 1910 Estimates as traitorous, and suspected him of all kinds of chicanery over McKenna's displacement. But when the invitation to come to England was repeated, and this time with McKenna's support, Fisher reluctantly agreed, but only on the condition that the visit was kept deadly secret. The waters were muddy enough already, and Fisher did not wish to stir them further by offering his old enemies the chance to accuse him of backstairs influence.

The trip was a weird business. He arrived incognito on 28 October. 'It's so very awkward between McKenna and Winston Churchill,' he wrote to his son. 'Like balancing on tight rope! McKenna meets me at the station and I dine with him and Winston waiting outside with the motor to go to the station!'[2] A meeting had been set up at Reigate Priory. Churchill and most of the Cabinet were present. The old Admiral faced them like the wise old man before his appellants. What was it they wanted of him?

By this time Churchill had changed his mind about inviting Fisher to return as First Sea Lord. No doubt he had also sought the advice of Asquith and other Cabinet members. It was not so much that Fisher was an old man—to those present he was quite evidently in the highest spirits and in better health than ever. But his appointment would create new uproar and new dissension in a service which was just beginning to cool down from the passions of two years before. What the meeting chiefly required was advice on the future constitution of the Board. Arthur Wilson was due to retire shortly—who was to take his place? And who was to be Second Sea Lord? Private talks with Churchill followed, when Fisher also helped him plan his speech on the Estimates.

Fisher slipped away, and then returned, following a further appeal from Churchill, on 17 November. This time the meeting, as secret as the earlier one, took place in the Admiralty yacht *Enchantress* in

---

[1] Lennoxlove MSS.   [2] Kilverstone MSS.

Plymouth harbour. It was evident that some strenuous jockeying for the post of First Sea Lord was going on, with Royal intervention, and that Wilson would be asked to retire before his time was up.

Safely back in Switzerland, Fisher reported on the talks and the advice he had offered to Churchill, to his son and new daughter-in-law.

TO CECIL FISHER[1]

> The *Grand Hotel National,*
> *Lucerne*
> *November 24th, 1911.*

Dearest Cis,

    . . . I had a splendid time at Plymouth and got W.C.'s head perfectly straight I think. He entreats me to come over again. I shall 'wait and see'! . . . [He] thinks I'm a better fighter now than three years ago! Of course McKenna isn't in it with him for genius and audacity! All the same McKenna was a great patriot when Winston wasn't one! Now he is! . . .

> Your loving father,
> *F.*

TO MRS CECIL FISHER

> The *Grand Hotel National*
> *Lucerne*
> *December 2nd, 1911*

My dear sweet Jane!

    . . . *Yes, I have really had an immense triumph over the Board of Admiralty.* The King quite thought he had arranged for Sir John Durnford to be First Sea Lord. *This is very private, of course* . . . Then again, Sir William May, who is a renegade, also thought he was sure. No one suspected any of the new men . . .

> Fondest love to you both.
> Your loving father,
> *F.*

The reliable Fisherite, Bridgeman, was to take Wilson's place, and Battenberg, because it would please the King and because Fisher had a high regard for him anyway, was to become Second Sea Lord. But other, and scarcely less important appointments were also decided at the second meeting at Plymouth.

---

[1] Kilverstone MSS.

First Sea Lord

TO GERARD FIENNES[1]

> *Excelsior Hotel,*
> *Naples.*
> *December 26th, 1911.*

Private
Dear Fiennes,

. . . when Winston asked me to come the third time à la Nicodemus I said I'd see him d——d first so I think he is coming here (*but this is sacredly private*) —(when the mountain wouldn't come to Mahomet—why Mahomet went to the mountain!) The sweet thing in the Admiralty revolution is that not a soul has discovered what it all *absolutely* and *solely* pivoted on! (*And don't you tell anyone!*) Jellicoe to be Admiralissimo on October 21st 1914 when the Battle of Armageddon comes along! He automatically becomes Commander-in-Chief of the Home Fleet in two years' time! . . . Jellicoe about the same age as Nelson at Trafalgar and possesses all Nelson's attributes except Lady Hamilton and there I sympathise with him! . . .

> Yours always,
> F.

Wilson was to be prematurely retired, and this was not gracefully handled—Churchill was not renowned for his tact at this time and was making service enemies at twice the rate Fisher ever achieved. According to Balfour's secretary, J. S. Sandars, 'it was a plain notice to quit, coupled with a olatium that he might have a peerage if he liked . . . Wilson, without any grace whatever, promptly declined the honour.'[2] Now Fisher again had the successor of his choice, who also happened to be sufficiently pliable to match even Churchill's idea of a cipher. In fact, Bridgeman turned out to be a greater disaster than Wilson, truculent in his weakness where Wilson had been granite-like in his obstinacy. But at least there was now a machine happy to do the work of the whole Board in running things. A Naval War Staff was quickly created.

Fisher, the distant but 'ready and constant counsellor', was ever eager with advice for the remarkable young statesman who was to be three times a devoted friend, and three times an implacable enemy.

During the following six months a steady flow of correspondence was exchanged between Fisher in Italy and Switzerland and Churchill in Whitehall. It was prodigious in quantity and unprecedented in its wide-ranging coverage. From time to time, when the urgency seemed to demand, it was augmented by telegrams. The eager, precocious and ambitious young statesman was picking up his new job fast, and he was shrewd enough to recognize that he could learn more in writing from the wisest and most knowledgeable old Admiral of them all than he

---

[1] Kilverstone MSS.   [2] *Churchill*, ii, 542.

could ever hope to learn from anyone else. The teacher conducted his correspondence course on every imaginable subject related to naval affairs. He was moderate in nothing — in his terms of expression, in the nature of his remedies, in his strictures, as a few extracts reveal:

'The most damnable person for you to have any dealing with is a Naval Expert! Sea fighting is pure common sense. The first of all its necessities is SPEED, so as to be able to fight—

> *When* you like
> *Where* you like
> and *How* you like.

'Therefore the super-*Lion*, the super-*Swift* and the super-Submarine are the only three types for fighting (*speed* being THE characteristic of each of these types). AVIATION has wiped out the intermediate types. . .'

'. . . alas! you do not mention the paltry sum about a couple of hundred thousand pounds wanted to open the Navy to all classes. Our officers are restricted now to less than 1/40th of the population. *We want the brains of the other 39/40ths!'*

On the Navy's weak gunnery: 'My counsel is, send [for] Jellicoe about something else and engage him in private talk—he is fearfully sensitive as regards loyalty to the First Sea Lord. So you have to draw him carefully, but I counsel this because I want you to assure yourself by the testimony of the best officer the Navy has ever had since Nelson that I am correct in warning you of the vital danger hovering around . . .'

The correspondence came to an abrupt halt in April 1912. The reason was that Churchill had made a number of appointments which did not find favour with Fisher. With the decline of Fisher's influence brought about by the dismissal of McKenna and Wilson, King George V began to press more seriously and with greater effect for the appointment to senior posts of officers of whom he especially approved. Having failed to get the Admiral of his choice as First Sea Lord, the King was now working hard on Churchill to promote some of his other friends. Among the officers who received gratifying and unexpected appointments were Custance, Lambton (who had recently changed his name to Meux) and Milne, an officer whose startling incompetence was expensively confirmed in the opening months of the war in the chase of the *Goeben*.

Churchill's relations with the King had not so far been happy. To have a Radical as the leader of his beloved Navy was painful enough for King George. A bumptious smart aleck who listened to the advice of Fisher and turned down his Sovereign's candidates was scarcely to be tolerated. Churchill knew how dangerous this could be for him, and this was why he had yielded to Court pressure.

Fisher was furious. ' . . . I fear this must be my last communication with you in any matter at all. I am sorry for it, but I consider you have betrayed the Navy in these three appointments, and what the pressure could have been to induce you to betray your trust is beyond my comprehension . . . You have practically annihilated him [Jellicoe] by your appointments of Meux and Milne. *I can't believe that you foresee all the consequences!*'

To his 'beloved E', Fisher let loose a barrage of abuse against Churchill. 'Winston, alas! (as I have had to tell him) feared for his wife the social ostracism of the Court and succumbed to the appointments of the two Court favourites recently made—*a wicked wrong in both cases!* Winston has sacrificed the Country to the Court . . .'

But Fisher demonstrated no feelings of personal animosity towards the King. In turning down another invitation to return secretly to England to hold conversations with people 'from most influential quarters', Fisher justified himself to Esher thus: 'BUT I DON'T WANT A PERSONAL VICTORY! Neither do I wish to lower the King's prestige. *I should have to.* He has said things in his unguarded and loquacious way that he would have to take back. His sycophants are playing hell with him. A weathercock would be his crest if his character had to be represented . . .'

Churchill energetically set about justifying his actions to Fisher, representing that the appointments did not give the officers the power Fisher had supposed. He replied to Fisher's attack 'very nicely'. 'No matter what I like to say to him,' Fisher wrote to Cecil, 'he is going to stick to me and support all my schemes and always maintain that I am a genius and the greatest naval administrator, etc., etc., etc.'

Fisher's flames of fury died and by mid-May were almost extinguished. The reason was that Mahomet had indeed come to the mountain. The Admiralty yacht *Enchantress* was cruising in the Mediterranean, ostensibly 'to investigate strategical problems, to visit the Fleet, and to inspect Naval Establishements'. On board were Asquith and members of his Cabinet, Battenberg, Bridgeman 'and senior military officers', and of course Churchill and his wife and his Naval Secretary. A message was sent to Fisher asking if he would travel to Naples, and there embark for 'a few days . . . and talk of things that can't be written about!' Fisher agreed.

After the *Enchantress* sailed from Elba, in order to give the impression that the meeting was a chance one the story was put about that the yacht had been driven into Naples by bad weather. 'Every Italian newspaper had it!' Fisher wrote amusedly to a friend. 'It's very curious how every one is always so afraid of its being known that I have anything to do with them! . . .'

TO GERARD FIENNES

Lucerne
May 28th, 1912

Burn.
Secret and Private
My beloved Fiennes,

I was nearly kidnapped and carried off in the Admiralty Yacht! They were very sweet about it! My old cabin as First Sea Lord all arranged for me! I had a good time and came out on top! The Prime Minister is 'dead on' for my coming back, and he has put things so forcibly to me that, with great reluctance to re-enter the battle field, I probably shall do so! *But not a word of this*, except perhaps in *the very deepest confidence* to dear Garvin. I had great talks with the Prime Minister upon every sort of subject ('China to Peru'!). No doubt I am *'all there'* with him! (This sounds rather egotistical, I fear!)Don't breathe a word. I just send you this line to say all went well and I am here at Lucerne. They pressed me for three days to go with them, but I had very good public reasons for not doing so. Winston came ashore with me at 2 a.m. the last night to have last words with me! I thought to myself what a story dear old Stead would have made out of that episode of the early morning hours! I grieve very much for him. He was a great wonder and very attractive!

Yours always,
Fisher

The Naval Secretary, Rear-Admiral David Beatty, reported the encouuter to his wife. 'That old rascal Fisher arrived on board directly we got here looking very well and young, never stopped talking, and has been cossetted with Winston ever since, wasn't that something to come to Naples for? Do not mention to *anyone* that Fisher is in close confidence with Winston. It would be injurious to the Service, if it ever got out, and the Navy would hate it . . .'[1]

Churchill came nearer to wearing out Fisher than any politician before him. 'I had four nights without sleep,' Fisher recounted after the *Enchantress* had sailed. 'When I wasn't talking I was writing. My brain was buzzing like a hive of bees. Winston wants to ride two horses at the same time . . .'[2]

[1] Rear-Admiral W. S. Chalmers, *The Life and Letters of David, Earl Beatty* (London, 1951), 114. (Hereafter cited as *Beatty*.)
[2] To Gerard Fiennes. Kilverstone MSS.

The most important subject that had been discussed was Fisher's own future. Churchill had called him back to duty, not as First Sea Lord, but to head a commission on oil, the available resources 'and their relation to this country and the Royal Navy'. Churchill followed up his talks with a moving written appeal (11 June 1912). 'I recognize it is little enough I can offer you. But your gifts, your force, and hopes, belong to the Navy, with or without return; and as your most sincere admirer, and at the head of the Naval Service, I claim them now, knowing well you will not grudge them. You need a plough to draw. Your propellers are racing in air.'[1]

Fisher had become the self-styled 'oil maniac'. He was convinced that coal-fired battleships were as out-of-date as reciprocating engines. Whether diesel or turbine powered, the Navy would need oil in vast quantities for the war with Germany which, according to his earlier prediction, was now hardly more than two years away. This was a task which must bring him back into the mêlée of Whitehall politics. Fisher considered the offer with grave anxieties. There would be little enough power, yet vast responsibilities. There would be accusations and ill-feeling and resentment that he was back in harness—doubtless with his eyes raised again to the pinnacles of ultimate naval power. Beresford would probably stagger back onto the war-path.

His wife had returned to England. Still searching his conscience, Fisher wrote to her.

TO LADY FISHER

Lucerne,
June 17th, 1912

PRIVATE
Dearest Kitty,
     . . . I think you must be in collusion with the English Chaplain here! for in his extempore, very eloquent sermon yesterday morning, he fixed his eyes steadfast on me and made use of the following language: 'No man still in the possession of all his powers and vitality has any right to say, *"Now I'm going to rest, for I've had a hard life"*, for he owes a duty to his Country and to his fellow-men.' Of course, it was an arrow shot at a venture like the one that killed Ahab! as I met him afterwards, when I was calling on Mrs Dickson, and he was very meek and nervous to a degree!

I expect the end of this week will see the matter settled. I wrote 8 sheets, 1 think, yesterday to Hopwood and 9 sheets to-day to Winston Churchill, in reply to a long letter from him, *but all this is very private and secret.* I really am reluctant about it all, but they are so pressing me and shoving me into it, and I really have to admit that they are right when when they all unanimously

[1] *World Crisis*, i, 133.

say to me that no one else can do it—and also the Prime Minister presses me—
but I never should be in the position you mention respecting Sir J. Fullerton
of 'nothing to do', for I enjoy every minute of the day every day I live, and am
absolutely content and happy! . . .

Best love to all.
Y.l.h.
J.F.

. . . this place is just absolutely perfection now. Such splendid strawberries
and peaches, all free!!!

Two days later Fisher returned to England, and at once plunged into
the work of the Royal Commission on Fuel Oil as well as attending
meetings of the Defence Committee. His capacity for work had in no
way diminished though he complained of the strain and yearned for the
peace and the sun he had left behind. The results of his work were to
have a profound influence not only on the future of the Navy but on
economic and foreign policy for decades ahead. As a result of the findings of the Oil Commission vast storage facilities and refineries were
set up, tanker construction put in hand, and oilfields acquired by the
Government in the Middle East by the Anglo-Persian Oil Company,
in which the Government purchased a controlling interest. All this
presaged the switch from coal to oil as a fuel for the defence of the
country and the Empire. With the signature on 10 February 1914 of the
final report on the Commission's work the momentous step was taken
towards reliance on resources outside the island for Britain's lifeblood.
Before long continuous transfusions would be required, and from
sources of supply that were often in hazard and themselves became the
subject of new foreign and defence policies. The industrial revolution
which had been founded on Britain's coal had by this time advanced so far that it had overtaken its own primitive solid fuel. The
acquisition of the Anglo-Persian Oil Company for which Fisher had
worked so hard at least ensured that the Navy's newest ships did
not starve for lack of fuel in the First World War.

Fisher's vision in his early 70's could still be as remarkable as ever.
Not only did he recognize how oil must revolutionize naval warfare.
During the last months before war broke out he was advocating with
all his old enthusiasm and expertise new inventions and new advances
in *matériel*. There was much 'fierce fighting' and repeated doses of his
now famous 'three R's'. Aviation was one new coming thing that
would revolutionize war at sea. The Royal Navy must have its own air
arm. Merchant ships must be armed, for 'WAR IS HELL!!!' and
there would be no restraints or respect for peacetime promises when
it came. There must be more and bigger submarines. Why not build

great tubes—a dozen— under the English Channel to bring in oil in wartime?[1] There must be 25-knot diesel-engined battleships—semi-submersibles with telescopic masts—capable of circumnavigating the world without refuelling: progenitors of the nuclear-powered giant warships of today.

These and dozens more ideas flowed from his mind, were at once transcribed into his eruptive prose and despatched privately and confidentially, and with orders to 'BURN THIS!', to all his friends in Fleet Street, in politics and positions of influence, and to the members of the Board of Admiralty. The intensity of his salvoes was in relation to the importance of the recipient. Churchill remained the primary target. All was forgiven, and the urgent staccato correspondence was resumed.

With Fisher's enthusiastic encouragement Churchill had already put in hand a new class of battleship, the most formidable in the world and armed with 15-inch guns and having a speed of 24 knots. The 'Queen Elizabeths' were the fruit of Fisher's inspiration and teaching. Other *matériel* and personnel reforms advocated by Fisher—the creation of an air service and improvements in pay and conditions for the lower deck for example—were implemented with the pace, gusto and efficiency which Fisher himself long practised at the Admiralty. The office of the First Sea Lord might not have existed: Churchill *was* the Admiralty, and Fisher observed events with the half critical, half approving eye of the master for his precocious disciple. Here, at last and in spite of the past accusations and disputes, was a man after his own heart, with a huge mind full of 'Big things', intelligent and ruthless, dedicated to the continuing greatness and fighting efficiency of the Royal Navy.

In the months of 1914 leading to the 'Battle of Armageddon' he had for so long predicted and prepared for, Fisher brooded on the scene and the events from the house west of London where he and Lady Fisher now lived, Kilverstone being 'too far away for *anno domini* or to get people to come and see one'. His outraged protests had become muted grumblings. By his own exacting standards there was little enough to find fault with. The vast armada he had created was ready for instant action, the right men were in the Admiralty and before the first blow was struck 'beloved Jellicoe' would take over as Admiralissimo, just as he had planned.

But Fisher could never be content, and he believed things would have been different and better still if he had been at Whitehall with Churchill. There would have been more, and bigger, submarines, for example.

[1] Thirty years later this became 'a new invention': the famous 'Pluto' which fed oil to the Normandy beachhead.

A sense of dark expectancy settled over Langham House, Ham Common, where the great of the day called to see him. His predictions were coming to pass, one by one. In mid-July 1914 war by August was inevitable, and Fisher was ready to play his part. He would be called back, of that he had no doubt.

Chapter 2

'THE REAL FOCUS ...'[1]:
WAR, AND RETURN TO POWER

At the beginning of November 1914 the record, reputation and spirit of the Royal Navy were all at a low ebb. The greatest disappointment was a negative one: the German Fleet had not come out and there had after all, been no great modern Trafalgar in the North Sea. Except for a single confused brush in the Heligoland Bight on 28 August, when three German cruisers and a destroyer had been sunk, very little had gone right for the Royal Navy. As Fisher had predicted, underwater weapons had played a more destructive rôle than most people on either side had feared. The submarine was proving to be a deadly man-of-war and had already scored many victims, including three large armoured cruisers on the same day. A precious modern super-Dreadnought had been sunk by a single German mine. German surface raiders were having great successes against British merchantmen. Trade in the Indian Ocean was paralysed by the *Emden* and *Königsberg*, and a powerful German cruiser squadron was still loose in the Pacific: in a few days time it was to be learnt that without loss to themselves they had sunk two armoured cruisers sent in search of them. There was growing public disquiet at the management of naval affairs, and Churchill's prestige—always a precarious thing at this time—was slipping dangerously.

Of all innocent people, Prince Louis of Battenberg became the scapegoat. After two of his predecessors had suffered rapid dismissal by Churchill, Prince Louis had settled down with reasonable comfort in the office of First Sea Lord. The Prince's Royal blood restrained Churchill from bullying him too hard. He worked vigorously and loyally and wrote 'I concur' at the end of memoranda after they had sped to

[1] 'The Baltic Project was the real focus of all my purposes at the Admiralty'.

him from Churchill's office. Fisher described him as 'Winston's facile dupe'. But this was to underrate him grossly. Although partly because of poor health he was not strong enough to withstand Churchill's pressure nor to prevent him from far exceeding the customary limitations of the First Lord's duties, Prince Louis was a fine administrator. His two handicaps were his Chief of the War Staff (cos) and his German ancestry. Sturdee, Beresford's old Chief-of-Staff and now a Vice-Admiral, possessed neither a clear brain nor the ability to delegate. 'His trouble,' Marder has written, 'was that he thought he was the only man who knew anything about war.'[1] Prince Louis's German blood became an increasing embarrassment when naval affairs failed to prosper and anti-German feeling in the country developed. During October venomous personal attacks on Prince Louis reached such a pitch that it was clear that he would have to go. Churchill told him so, and the Prince with magnanimous dignity handed in his resignation.

Asquith, the Prime Minister, agreed to Churchill's choice of Fisher as a replacement. When the announcement was made the news was received with great popular acclamation. Now at last there would be action! But the appointment did not go through as smoothly as all that. Among certain elements in the Navy there was concern about his age and fitness and about how he would work with Churchill. David Beatty, who now commanded the Grand Fleet's battle cruisers, wrote to his wife, 'I cannot see Winston and Jackie Fisher working very long together in harmony. They will quarrel before long.'[2] King George V was exceedingly vexed. 'I did all I could to prevent it and told him [Churchill] he [Fisher] was not trusted by the Navy and they had no confidence in him personally,' the King wrote in his diary (29 October): 'I think it is a great mistake & he is 74. In the end I had to give in with great reluctance . . .'[3] The King had wanted Meux, or Sir Henry Jackson, or Sturdee even—almost anyone but Fisher.

If the two powerful men could succeed in working in harmony it was evident that there was no limit to what they could accomplish. But there was sound reasoning behind the misgivings of the King, who distrusted both men. Lord Beaverbrook briskly summed up the situation:

' . . . A cold wind was blowing on him [Churchill] in October 1914, and he has since recognised the fact. He therefore pressed hard for Fisher's appointment as a support to his own position—which was really another mistake.

'Churchill co-opted Fisher to relieve the pressure against himself,

---

[1] *Marder*, ii, 9.   [2] *Beatty*, 179.
[3] Harold Nicolson, *King George V: His Life and Reign* (London, 1952).

but he had no intention of letting anyone else rule the roost. Here, then, were two strong men of incompatible tempers both bent on an autocracy. It only required a difference of opinion on policy to produce a clash . . .'[1]

There was no doubt that Fisher was in adequate physical condition to handle the prodigious tasks that lay ahead. Churchill had made certain of this. 'He used to come occasionally to the Admiralty,' he wrote later, 'and I watched him narrowly to judge his physical strength and mental alertness. There seemed no doubt about either. On one occasion, when inveighing against some one whom he thought obstructive, he became so convulsed with fury that it seemed that every nerve and blood-vessel in his body would be ruptured. However, they stood the strain magnificently and he left me with the impression of a terrific engine of mental and physical power burning and throbbing in that aged frame.'[2]

Fisher was as equally confident of his physical fitness. 'REALLY and TRULY I am more fit and virile than [when] I left the Admiralty more than four years ago!' he proudly told Pamela McKenna. 'I can't make it out! *But it's a fact!*' Others have added their testimony to his remarkably good condition for his age. Nevertheless, he *was* an old man who had driven himself unmercifully for most of his life. He was no longer capable of the fourteen hours of hard labour a day which had once been his custom. He was seen to flag towards the evening when Churchill was getting his second wind, and he went home worn out, retiring to bed soon after 8 p.m. He had recently suffered a bad bout of pleurisy, and Sir Bertrand Dawson, the King's doctor, had told him to husband his resources.

The characteristic over-simplification and exaggeration which had once been one of his chief strengths, had now become so excessive, and his language so lurid, that he appeared as a quaint caricature of the younger Fisher who had first stormed into that same office ten years earlier. In the months that followed this practice grew out of hand in ratio with the growing complexities of his tasks and the obstacles in the way of achieving them. His intention was to win the war, no less, with the greatest Navy the world had ever seen—which *he* had built. Starting with 'the mess' he found at the Admiralty, Fisher proposed to accomplish this task in dual harness with a wild young stallion who shared his patriotic destination, but not the means of arriving there. The impatience, intolerance, and single-mindedness which had once helped to revolutionize the spirit and *matériel* of the Navy in less than

[1] Rt. Hon. Lord Beaverbrook, *Politicians and the War 1914–16* (London, 1928), 104.
[2] *World Crisis*, i, 401.

a decade had become so over-developed that they were now a hazard. The last tragic act was to be a cruel self-mockery of past magnificent performances.

Just as his manner, his communications and his working methods had by 1914 become over-size, so Fisher's visionary prophetic images were enacted through an astronomical telescope trained on the Second World War rather than the conflict that was being fought out in the fields of Flanders in his own time. In his eyes, submarines, aviation and 32-knot giant warships of minimum profile and armed with 18-inch guns were the war-winners, and nothing else mattered. Only sudden surprise amphibious campaigns, which exploited the mobility sea power provided, could end the immobile slaughter of trench warfare. As if preparing the nation's defences for the battles of 1940–45, he fought for giant motor-driven landing craft each carrying some five hundred men, just as he had earlier advocated a cross-Channel oil pipeline. Twenty years before the factories of Germany and Great Britain, and the other great powers were mass-producing aircraft for the Second World War, Fisher was writing to the Prime Minister advocating the construction of 'a multitude of bombing aircraft made like Ford cars' and was stating emphatically that 'the Air is going to win the War . . .' But not until the 1940s did the 18-inch naval gun fire more than a shell or two in anger, and the 32-knot Dreadnought come into her own in the Pacific war, and the infantry landing craft eject their assault troops on the mainland of Europe. The giant submersibles carrying big guns and capable of encircling the globe without refuelling which Fisher pressed for in the First World War were no more than the precursors of the Polaris nuclear-powered submarines of the 1960s.

The farsightedness Fisher displayed when he came back to power in October 1914 was uncanny in its accuracy, but now it was leaping a generation; his powers of prophecy had lost the immediate usefulness which had foretold the end of sail, the future of the submarine, the demise of the reciprocating engine and the mixed armament battleship and the revolution of the turbine and the all-big-gun battleship. To anticipate oil fuel was a nation-saving proposition; to foretell the end of the battleship and the omnipotence of air power in 1914 was to leap ahead even faster than the rate of technological development.

Everything and everyone was out of step with Fisher in 1914, not because his drill was poor, but because he marched too fast and was round the corner and out of sight to his sailors and his scientists. It was no reflection on anyone that they could not keep up. As the Director of Military Operations at the War Office complained, 'He covered the ground at such a pace that I was speedily toiling breathless and dishevelled far in the rear . . . After an interview with the First Sea Lord you suffered from that giddy, bewildered, exhausted sort of feeling that no doubt has you in thrall when you have been run over by a motor-bus without suffering actual physical injury.'[1]

According to Fisher, on his arrival at the Admiralty everything was wrong in dispositions of ships, misuse of manpower, inadequate torpedoes and mines, weak gunnery. 'Every day,' he complained to Jellicoe, 'I find evidence of utter incapacity and no one shot!' And later to this same Admiral, the C.-in-C. of the Grand Fleet, '. . . this Admiralty is really a terrible place for apathy. I have to lose my temper everyday to push things.' And to Cecil's mother-in-law in Philadelphia, when reporting how he had at last succeeded in retrieving his own daughter and son-in-law from Germany, where the war had trapped them, he wrote:

TO MRS RANDAL MORGAN[2]

Admiralty, Whitehall
December 4th, 1914

Dear Frances,

You can't think how overjoyed we are at getting Beatrix and Co. back! It's a *resurrection!* We had a most decided and emphatic message from the military German authorities that they would be kept till the end of the war! That really was a *death sentence! . . .*

I am working hard.

I am in the position of playing a game of chess very badly begun by fools I hated. I've got rid of the fools, but it's long and arduous to get back to a good position with a consummate good player for an enemy! But I am *trying! . . .*
Heaven bless you both,

Yours affectionately,
Fisher

Things had indeed begun badly, with the worst naval disaster of the war, and the first of Fisher's many threats of resignation. The difficulties were resolved and tragedy turned almost instantly to triumph by a combination of remarkable good luck, wily diplomacy by Churchill and a brilliant stroke of strategy by Fisher—so that it seemed as if all the popular expectations of a triumphant union between these two powerful naval figures were to be fulfilled.

When Fisher arrived at the Admiralty on 30 October 1914, Sturdee was still cos. Fisher would have none of that 'pedantic ass, which Sturdee is, has been, and always will be!' and told Churchill that this

[1] Major-General Sir C. E. Callwell, *Experiences of a Dug-Out, 1914–18* (London, 1920), 121–2.
[2] Kilverstone MSS.

unfortunate officer would have to resign. Sturdee said he would not go, and Fisher told Churchill he would resign if he did not have a new cos. Sturdee would not listen to Churchill's appeals either, for he knew that his dismissal would be a confession by Churchill that Fisher had forced his hand because affairs had been so mismanaged.

Churchill's opportunity to extricate himself from this nasty situation arrived with remarkably neat timing. Off Coronel in Chile on the night of 8 November, Vice-Admiral Maximilian von Spee with a powerful cruiser force met and annihilated the British armoured cruisers under Rear-Admiral Sir Christopher Cradock. There was not a single survivor. This was Fisher's moment, the culmination of all he had worked for over so many years. He decided to rush two of his beloved battle cruisers out to the South Atlantic, and another to the North Atlantic. There were to be no half measures; von Spee must be instantly crushed to avenge the most humiliating disaster in British naval history since the Dutch sailed up the Thames.

Churchill jumped at the chance to save the situation at the Admiralty, and his own skin. Sturdee should command the avenging force. Fisher at once agreed. This was the only way out of the *impasse*. Sturdee was a good enough sea officer, and besides, there was a savage sort of justice which Fisher relished in sending to correct the dangerous situation the one man whose 'criminal ineptitude' had resulted in the death of Cradock and some 1,600 officers and men. But let him not fail!

Sturdee eagerly agreed and was hustled out of home waters with his two great ships, pursued by demands from Fisher for speed. Sturdee arrived secretly at the Falkland Islands the evening before von Spee obligingly, and by a chance in a thousand, appeared over the horizon with his greatly inferior force. In spite of poor tactics and weak gunnery, the British Dreadnoughts and their accompanying cruisers sent four of von Spee's five ships to the bottom.

It was Fisher's finest hour, and Churchill recognized it, even though it was one of their few mutually happy moments.

FROM WINSTON S. CHURCHILL

December 10th, 1914

My dear,

This was your show and your luck . . .

. . Your *flair* was quite true. Let us have some more victories together and confound all our foes abroad—and (don't forget)—at home . . .

Yours ever,
W.

But from this time, relations between Fisher and Churchill steadily deteriorated.

First Sea Lord

TO ADMIRAL SIR JOHN JELLICOE

Admiralty, Whitehall
December 20th, 1914

Secret and Private
Please burn at once.
My beloved Jellicoe,

I find much difficulty in snatching even a few moments in which to write to you. Winston has monopolized all initiative in the Admiralty and fires off such a multitude of purely departmental memos (*his power of work is absolutely amazing!*) that my colleagues are no longer '*superintending Lords*', but only '*the First Lord's Registry*'! I told Winston this yesterday and he did not like it at all, but *it is true!* and the consequence is that the Sea Lords are atrophied and their departments run really by the Private Office, and I find it a Herculean task to get back to the right procedure, and quite possibly I may have to clear out, and I've warned Winston of this. But please do not mention this to a soul. I only want to explain to you that I have so little time to write you . . .

Yours always,
Fisher

It was not only over Churchill's working methods at the Admiralty that Fisher and he were to fall out. It might have been possible, given time, for Beatty's prediction to be realized that Fisher would 'rule the Admiralty and Churchill with a heavy hand'.[1] It was in the overall naval strategy and the conduct of the war that brought both men to mutual destruction within six-and-a-half months.

It is not proposed to describe in detail the events which led to the catastrophe of Gallipoli and the re-formation of the British Government. These have been recorded excellently and accurately in a number of recent books;[2] and while Fisher took an important part in them, his powers were in such a steep decline that his behaviour and activities no longer reflect the true qualities of the man.

Fisher's profoundly held belief that his country should not become involved in a debilitating Continental land war naturally led to his violent opposition to the despatch of the British Expeditionary Force to France in August 1914. 'He was a strong advocate of keeping the Expeditionary Force ready till the psychological moment, and then throwing it ashore at some point where it would place the enemy at a disadvantage.'[3]

By November, his worst fears had been realized. The 'old contemptibles' had been almost wiped out, and Britain appeared to be committed

---

[1] *Beatty*, 160.

[2] See especially Alan Moorehead, *Gallipoli* (London, 1956) and Robert Rhodes James, *Gallipoli* (London, 1965).

[3] *Bacon*, ii, 181–2.

to a long campaign for which new conscript armies would have to be provided. Meanwhile, the enormous power of the Royal Navy remained unused, for the Germans still showed no desire for a showdown.

Fisher brought with him to the Admiralty a scheme he had been nursing since his visit to Russia with the King in 1908 and the formation of the Triple Entente in the following year. He believed that a major part could be taken by the Navy in a war with Germany by carrying an invasion Army into the Baltic and landing it on the Pomeranian coast ninety miles from Berlin. As early as 1909 he was advocating this amphibious operation, which must occupy the attention of a million German soldiers, and bring about total confusion in the capital. Later he elaborated it further, under the inspiration of Julian Corbett, to include the landing of a great Russian Army from the Baltic.

'The Baltic project,' Fisher wrote, 'meant victory by land and sea. It was simply history repeating itself. Frederick the Great, for the only time in his life (on hearing the Russians had landed), was frightened, and sent for poison.

'Geography has not altered since his time. The Pomeranian coast has not shifted, and a million Russian soldiers could have been landed within eighty-two miles of Berlin.'[1]

The idea commended itself to Churchill, who even then loved the big, bold move in war, and weeks before Fisher joined him at the Admiralty he opened discussions with the Russians on the subject.[2] With Fisher's return to power, the Baltic project was pursued by the Admiralty with new ardour. Churchill backed it one hundred per cent, only making the proviso that an island such as Borkum should be seized first in order to provide a base. Fisher threw himself into the task of creating in record time an invasion fleet to transport and protect this vast landing close to the heart of Germany.

Churchill and Lloyd George, the Chancellor of the Exchequer, 'magnificently responded to the idea of constructing a great Armada of 612 vessels, to be rapidly built . . . to carry out the great project'.[3] It was the kind of rush operation at which Fisher excelled, and there was no sign of any diminution in his physical powers when it came to planning and ordering the landing craft, minesweepers and minelayers, the hundreds of auxiliary craft, and the monitors and the ultra-fast, ultra-big-gun, shallow-draught cruisers that would be required. Most of these vessels were in hand by the end of the year.

[1] *Bacon*, ii, 188.
[2] Churchill to Fisher, 16 March 1918. Lennoxlove MSS. This letter was in reply to Fisher's letter 13 March quoting Churchill: 'A descent on the German Coast and the entry and domination of the Baltic would secure a decisive victory for the allies.'
[3] *Memories*, 55

Not content with supervising every detail of the design of every class of vessel, besides running the Admiralty during a highly critical stage of the war, Fisher also 'prepared my own self with my own hands alone, to preserve secrecy, all the arrangements for landing three great armies at different places—two of them being feints that could be turned into a reality. Also I made all the preparations, shortly before these expeditions were to start, to practise them embarking at Southampton and disembarking at Stokes Bay, so that those who were going to work the Russian Armies would be practised in the art . . .'[1]

Late in December Churchill was still backing Fisher for all he was worth.

FROM WINSTON S. CHURCHILL
Admiralty, Whitehall
December 22nd, 1914

Burn
My dear Fisher,
I am wholly with you about the Baltic. But you must close up this side first. You must take an island and block them in, *à la* Wilson; or you must break the Canal or the locks, or you must cripple their Fleet in a general action. No scattering of mines will be any substitute for these alternatives.

The Baltic is the only theatre in which naval action can appreciably shorten the war. Denmark must come in, and the Russians be let loose on Berlin.

There are 4 good Russian Dreadnoughts.
Yours ever,
W.

On 29 December Asquith recorded in his diary that Churchill and Hankey 'are for finding a new theatre for our new armies. Hankey would like them to go to Turkey and in conjunction with the Balkan States to clear the Turk out of Europe. Winston, on the other hand, wants, primarily of course by means of the navy, to close the Elbe and dominate the Baltic. He would . . . invade Scheswig-Holstein, obtain naval command of the Baltic, and thus enable Russia to land her troops . . . There is here a good deal of food for thought.'[2]

Within a few days these young shoots of the Baltic project had been overwhelmed in the considerations of the War Council by the sudden powerful growth of new and dramatic plans to come to the assistance of Russia in the south rather than promote a great offensive jointly with her in the north.[3] Anxiety about the position of Serbia and the

---

[1] *Memories*, 55.

[2] D. C. Somervell, *The Reign of King George the Fifth, an English Chronicle* (London, 1935), 121.

[3] For the best short summary of the Dardanelles campaign, from genesis to post-mortem, see *Marder*, ii, 199–265.

pressure on Russia prompted the War Council to reconsider earlier proposals for an attack on the Dardanelles.

Fisher then made three errors of judgement which he was later to regret and for which he was to pay dearly. On 3 January 1915 he sent to Churchill a plan he had drawn up jointly with Hankey for a combined military and naval attack on Turkey, utilizing old pre-Dreadnought battleships for the bombardment of the forts in the Dardanelles, while a powerful British Expeditionary Force landed just south of the entrance to the straits; 'the Greeks to go for Gallipoli at the same time as we go for Besika, and the Bulgarians for Constantinople, and the Russians, the Servians, and Roumanians for Austria . . .'

The weakness of the plan was at once evident to Churchill; for one thing it presupposed that the neutral countries of Greece and Bulgaria could be persuaded to come into the war on the allied side. But Churchill by no means rejected the plan *in toto*. His eye was caught by the paragraph proposing the bombardment and forcing of the Dardanelles by old battleships. Here was a chance for the Navy, alone and unaided, to strike a fatal blow at Turkey, redeem some of its past failures and recoup his own declining reputation. Ignoring Fisher's premise that the bombardment would be supported on land, he carried the War Council triumphantly along with him on his wave of enthusiasm for this way out of the muddy impasse on the Western Front.

Fisher then committed his next great error. Instead of pointing out with his customary force the fatal flaw in Churchill's borrowed part-plan, for a few days he actually supported his First Lord, doubtless because the real implications of confining the attack to the Navy had not sunk in. He even went so far as to recommend that the Navy's newest super-Dreadnought, the first with 15-inch guns, should take part in the bombardment. Churchill eagerly gobbled up this idea.

The War Council then took the first positive step towards disaster by concluding that 'The Admiralty should prepare for a naval expedition in February to bombard and take the Gallipoli Peninsula, with Constantinople as its objective.' How was the Navy to take Constantinople? With a contingent of Royal Marines? Everyone was too dazzled by Churchill's excited performance to consider how the Navy with a few mainly obsolete battleships was to change the face of the war. 'So, . . . through the fatal power of a young enthusiasm to convince older and slower brains, the tragedy of Gallipoli was born.'[1]

Fisher seems to have woken to the true implications of Churchill's intentions by the middle of January, and certainly by the 19th, when he

[1] C. E. W. Bean, *Official History of Australia in the War of 1914–18, The Story of Anzac* (2 vols, Sydney, 121–4), i, 201.

wrote to Jellicoe, '*I don't agree with one single step taken . . .*' There was only one way out, he told his C.-in-C., 'and that is to resign! But you say *"no"*, which simply means I am a consenting party to what I absolutely disapprove . . .'

By 28 January Fisher was protesting to the Prime Minister against sending 'the *Queen Elizabeth*, with the only 15-inch guns ready at present', against the whole operation as planned, and offering his resignation. '. . . unity is essential in war, so I refrain from any desire of remaining as a stumbling block.' On the same day Asquith got Fisher and Churchill together before a crucial meeting of the War Council. He was the arbitrator, he told them. '. . . The Dardanelles will go on.' It was scarecely arbitration, least of all between the two recently and dangerously antagonistic naval leaders.

Fisher's opposition was immediately evident at the meeting. 'Bloody-minded' was how he later described his feelings. Asquith overruled him. 'The dramatic scene which followed may one day furnish material for the greatest historical picture of the war. Lord Fisher sat and listened to the men who knew nothing about it and heard one after another pass opinion in favour of a venture to which he was opposed. He rose abruptly from the table and made as if to leave the room.

'The tall figure of Lord Kitchener rose and followed him. The two stood by the window for some time in conversation and then both took their seats again. In Lord Fisher's own words: "I reluctantly gave in to Lord Kitchener and resumed my seat".'[1]

The drama is unmistakable, and the scene matches that in any Greek tragedy: the ageing, bewildered and momentarily indecisive old warrior whose past industry and patriotism had created the war machine he now saw being abused by misguided and opportunistic politicians holding him to his post for fear of their own reputations. It is a sad and unlovely picture.

Fisher's third mistake was to base his opposition less on the folly of bombarding forts from the sea, for which there were numerous precedents of failure, than on the folly of attacking in the Dardanelles rather than in the Baltic. 'This line of talk in January 1915 gave the Dardanelles advocates a beautiful chance to spread the word that the old Admiral's formal objections were based on his preference for an attack elsewhere, and not on any inherent unsoundness in the naval plan.'[2]

Although the Baltic project was once or twice perfunctorily raised again as a subject for discussion in the War Council, this imaginative scheme for shortening the war increasingly assumed in the minds of the

[1] *Memories*, 59 n. [2] *Marder*, ii, 219.

defence counsels the spectre of an old man's deluded obsession. The real tragedy of the Dardanelles campaign was that it blinded the War Council, at first with mistaken enthusiasm, then with growing anxieties, and finally with consuming despair, to the opportunities of diversionary activities elsewhere. Among these places was the Baltic. It is unlikely that all the authorities who have since condemned the invasion of Pomerania as impractical have been wrong in their judgement. But as Bacon fairly put it forty years ago, 'It is impossible to say, now, whether the scheme would have survived the detailed and critical examination essential before such an operation could be justifiably undertaken; but it is unjust to dismiss the project offhand as impracticable, and with a shrug of the shoulders to say that it was madness on Lord Fisher's part to propose it. Scientific and thorough preparation would certainly have caused many of the objections which have been hastily advanced to fall into insignificance. The German Battle Fleet would have been placed in a difficult situation, for they would have been forced by public opinion to take some action, and this would have had to have been carried out in the Baltic, in the face of a large fleet of submarines and of extensive and unknown minefields.'[1]

The incomprehensible blunder on Fisher's part was not to propose and energetically to prepare for operations in the Baltic but to hug jealously to his breast his detailed plans, which he claimed to have prepared but which were never divulged. For there was no doubt that the enemy was acutely anxious about the Baltic project. Though they possessed a superb fighting machine in their Navy, the German people and especially the service itself suffered from a totally unjustified sense of inferiority to the British Navy with its magnificent history and traditions. The return to power of Fisher, so widely feared for so long in pre-war Germany, increased their anxieties. Many senior officers regarded the Baltic as their most vulnerable frontier. 'If the British fleet had attacked in the first week of the war,' said Admiral Reinhard Scheer, C.-in-C. of the High Seas Fleet from February 1916, 'we should have been beaten. Under cover of the British navy, the Russian armies, then available in great numbers, could have been landed on the coast of Pomerania and could have easily marched to Berlin.'[2]

However valid or invalid the criticims of the Baltic project may be, Fisher's dogged fight for it and against any other scheme that might jeopardize it does not provide the evidence of his unfitness for war duty. It was the manner in which he fought against the competing campaign in the Dardanelles which reveals his ailing faculties.

[1] *Bacon*, ii, 190.
[2] Cyril Brown of the *New York World* interviewing the Admiral, 30 June 1919.

The sequence of the events in the Dardanelles, and Fisher's part in them, are best told briefly for it is a melancholy tale.

The Dardanelles forts were first ineffectually bombarded on 19 February. Further efforts were made later in the month with no better results. The shooting was poor and operations were handicapped by elaborate and cunningly laid minefields which proved difficult and dangerous to clear. Before the month was out, the view that the Navy could not accomplish the job without military support was widely held on the spot, and in London. In order to secure the Gallipoli peninsula it was necessary not only to reinforce the naval strength but to bring in military support on a large scale. '*I really don't think I can stand it!*' Fisher exclaimed in despair.

By 12 March a substantial force of troops had been assembled at Lemnos under General Sir Ian Hamilton in preparation for a landing that was to include every conceivable example of ineptitude and mismanagement, made all the more tragic by the supreme bravery of the soldiers taking part. The bombardment and the naval attack to force a passage through the straits had come to a standstill. 'Our experience,' reported the Admiral responsible, 'shows that gunfire alone will not render the forts innocuous . . .' When further attempts at bombardment were made, the Navy began to suffer its first serious losses. One battleship after another was sunk or disabled by gunfire or mine. The casualties were fearful; nor were all the ships sunk or damaged obsolete. The battle cruiser *Inflexible* which Jellicoe sorely needed in the North Sea was crippled and put out of action. Six big ships were at the bottom or out of action by 18 March and further demands were made for reinforcements from home, at the expense of the fleets facing Germany. Fisher had predicted that the operations would cost twelve battleships; the score was already half way there.

A new and more aggressive replacement naval Commander was no more sanguine that he could succeed against the German-organized defences.

By the end of March all hopes of forcing the Dardanelles at modest cost by a cheap and simple naval demonstration had been discarded. On 25 April the Army went ashore at last in a desperate and hopeless attempt to seize the heights overlooking the straits. In spite of prodigious gallantry and the seizure of a toe on the peninsula, the Army was soon in difficulties. Within two weeks the first indications of the Dardanelles' fearful and uncontrollable appetite for reinforcements were recognized in London. The man who most feared these demands, and recognized that the beast he hated would never be appeased was Lord Fisher.

Great numbers of the special craft Fisher had built at record speed for his Baltic project were now diverted by Churchill to the Mediterranean. More aircraft, monitors, repair and auxiliary ships, destroyers, cruisers and battleships were demanded as the situation failed to improve. Fisher's reluctance to deprive the Grand Fleet, whose margin of superiority over the High Seas Fleet was dangerously narrow, was met by the accusation that he was callously prepared to leave the Army in the lurch at the time of its greatest need. It was a horrible and harrowing position to be in. *'The Dardanelles entirely exhausts my time,'* he wrote to Jellicoe on 2 April.

The final crisis between Fisher and Churchill developed on 12 May. The position of the Army was static. The Navy had proved itself incapable of knocking out the Turkish guns and forcing the straits on its own. On that day another battleship was torpedoed and sunk, with the loss of 570 lives. In the certain knowledge that German and Austrian submarines were on their way to the Dardanelles, Fisher now insisted on the withdrawal of the newest and most powerful battleship, and reluctantly allowed it to be replaced by two older battleships and two 14-inch-gunned monitors, intended for the Baltic project. That night Kitchener complained of the 'serious and depressing effect on the army' of the withdrawal of this mighty battleship. Fisher announced that he would resign (he threatened to resign nine times between January and May 1915) if she did not come home, and he got his way.

At War Council meetings no light pierced the total gloom. A bloody offensive in France was failing. There was a fearful shortage of shell for the guns on the Western Front, and *The Times* began to expose this scandal on 14 May. On the same day a War Council meeting called for further naval reinforcements to be sent to the Dardanelles. Now Fisher saw that 'the great projects in Northern waters [i.e. the Baltic project] which I had in view' were no longer to be considered. Only the Dardanelles was to count. All that vast fleet for the invasion of Germany was to be dissipated on Churchill's pet, which had now become a monster. Soon, the more aggressive German naval command which had recently been formed would order out the High Seas Fleet, and Jellicoe would no longer have the strength to crush it.

Fisher returned to his office in deepest gloom and told his Naval Assistant, Captain T. E. Crease, that he would not be staying long at the Admiralty. On this same evening, 14 May, Churchill called in at Fisher's office to give him cheer, and evidently to reassure him that no more than the numbers agreed that morning would be required as reinforcements. Fisher went home early to bed. But Churchill's best and most productive work of the day still lay ahead. Sustained by good talk, food and drink, he normally carried on until 1 a.m., some three or fours hours before Fisher started his day. Among the minutes he wrote that night were four to Fisher, which failed to confirm the agreed figures for further reinforcements discussed some ten hours earlier. The extra proposals were for the most modern class of submarine and monitors, and a mass of other *matériel*. (See Appendix 4.)

This was the breaking point. To see these new figures, 'greatly in excess' of what had been agreed the night before, in the cold light of dawn, was more than Fisher could tolerate. Fisher had made many mistakes in the past four months, and he was to commit more damaging errors of judgement over the next two weeks. But this error of tactics by Churchill was more foolish and damaging than all these added together. It was to destroy utterly his political career.

Churchill himself provided a moving and graphic picture of that momentous dawn in the First Sea Lord's office. 'The old Admiral, waking in the early morning, saw himself confronted again[1] with the minutes proposing the reinforcements for the Dardanelles which he knew he could not resist. He saw himself ever more deeply involved in an enterprise which he distrusted and disliked. He saw that enterprise quivering on the verge of failure. He saw a civilian Minister, to whom indeed he was attached by many bonds of friendship, becoming every day a hard and stern taskmaster in all that was needed to sustain the hated operation. He saw the furious discontents of the Conservative Party at the shell shortage and the general conduct of the war . . .'[2]

The next moring Churchill received a note from Fisher. He did not take it very seriously, for it was not the first of its kind.

TO WINSTON CHURCHILL

May 15th, 1915.

First Lord.[3]

After further anxious reflection I have come to the regretted conclusion I am unable to remain any longer as your colleague. It is undesirable in the public interests to go into details . . . I find it increasingly difficult to adjust myself to the increasing daily requirements of the Dardanelles to meet your views—as you truly said yesterday I am in the position of continually veto-ing your proposals.

This is not fair to you besides being extremely distasteful to me.

I am off to Scotland at once so as to avoid all questionings,

Yours truly,
Fisher

---

[1] In fact only the nature of the minutes and with more modest demands had been discussed the previous evening.   [2] *World Crisis*, ii, 358.   [3] *ibid.*, ii, 359.

But when Churchill arrived at the Admiralty 'I found that he had entirely disappeared. He was not in the building; he was not in his house. None of his people knew where he was except that he was going to Scotland at once.'[1]

In fact Fisher was at the Treasury, telling Lloyd George that he was on his way. 'A combative grimness had taken the place of his usually genial greeting; the lower lip of his set mouth was thrust forward, and the droop at the corner was more marked than usual,' Lloyd George described his appearance. 'His curiously Oriental features were more than ever those of a graven image in an Eastern temple, with a sinister frown.'[2]

When Asquith heard the news from Lloyd George he took the same view as Churchill: 'Fisher is always resigning.' But Lloyd George was convinced that Fisher meant to go through with it this time.

Fisher had meanwhile probably gone first to pray at Westminster Abbey, his custom, and then taken a room at the Charing Cross hotel. Here he was eventually tracked down on this eventful Saturday morning by a messenger from the Prime Minister. It ordered him in the King's name to remain at his post.

Fisher went to Number 10 that afternoon and was subjected to Asquith's earnest appeals to remain. Fisher said his mind was made up, though he agreed to postpone his departure to Scotland. Churchill's own alarm was now as great as Lloyd George's and Asquith's.

FROM WINSTON S. CHURCHILL   *Admiralty, Whitehall*
                                             May 15th, 1915
Private and Confidential
My dear Fisher,

The only thing to think of now is what is best for the country and for the brave men who are fighting. Anything which does injury to those interests will be very harshly judged by history, on whose stage we now are.

I do not understand what is the specific cause which has led you to resign. If I did, I might cure it. When we parted last night I thought we were in agreement. The proposals I made to you by minute were, I thought, in general accord with your views, and in any case were for discussion between us. Our personal friendship is and I trust will remain unimpaired.

It is true the moment is anxious and our difficulties grave. But I am sure that with loyalty and courage we shall come through safely and successfully. You could not let it be said that you had thrown me over because things were for the time being going badly at the Dardanelles.

In every way I have tried to work in the closest sympathy with you. The men you wanted in the places you wanted them, the ships you designed, every

---

[1] *World Crisis*, ii, 359.

[2] *War Memoirs of David Lloyd George* (London, 1933–6, 6 vols), i, 225–6.

proposal you have formally made for naval action, I have agreed to. My own responsibilities are great, and also I am the one who gets the blame for anything that goes wrong. But I have scrupulously adhered to our original agreement that we should do nothing important without consulting each other. If you think this is not so, surely you should tell me in what respect.

In order to bring you back to the Admiralty I took my political life in my hands with the King and the Prime Minister, as you know well. You then promised to stand by me and see me through. If you now go at this bad moment and thereby let loose upon me the spite and malice of those who are your enemies even more than they are mine, it will be a melancholy ending to our six months of successful war and administration. The discussions which will arise will strike a cruel blow at the fortunes of the Army now struggling on the Gallipoli Peninsula, and cannot fail to invest with an air of disaster a mighty enterprise, which, with patience, can and will certainly be carried to success.

Many of the anxieties of the winter are past—the harbours are protected, the great flow of new construction is arriving. We are far stronger at home than we have ever been, and the great reinforcement is now at hand.

I hope you will come to see me to-morrow afternoon. I have a proposition to make to you, with the assent of the Prime Minister, which may resolve some of the anxieties and difficulties which you feel about the measures necessary to support the Army at the Dardanelles.

Though I shall stand to my post until relieved, it will be a very great grief to me to part from you; and our rupture will be profoundly injurious to every public interest.

Yours ever,
W.

Fisher replied on Sunday.

TO WINSTON S. CHURCHILL

Admiralty, Whitehall
[May 16th, 1915]

My dear Winston,

The Prime Minister put the case in a nutshell when he stated to me yesterday afternoon the actual fact that I had been dead set against the Dardanelles operation from the beginning! How could it be otherwise when previously as First Sea Lord I had been responsible for the Defence Committee Memorandum stating the forcing of the Dardanelles to be impossible! You *must* remember my extreme reluctance in the Prime Minister's room in January to accept his decision in regard to the Dardanelles, and at the War Council held immediately afterwards I stated, in reply to a question by the Chancellor of the Exchequer, that the Prime Minister knew my views and I left the matter to him to explain.

Ever since (as, I fear, to your great annoyance!) I have been, as you truly said the other day, in the unpleasant position of being antagonistic to your proposals, until the series of fresh naval arrangements for the Dardanelles you sent me yesterday morning convinced me that the time had arrived for me to take a final decision, there being much more in those proposals than had oc-curred to me the previous evening when you suggested some of them.

YOU ARE BENT ON FORCING THE DARDANELLES AND NOTH-ING WILL TURN YOU FROM IT—*NOTHING*. I know you so well! I could give no better proof of my desire to stand by you than my having remained by you in this Dardanelles business up to this last moment against the strongest conviction of my life, as stated in the Dardanelles Defence Committee Memorandum.

You will remain. I SHALL GO. It is better so. Your splendid stand on my behalf with the King and the Prime Minister I can NEVER forget, when you took your political life in your hands and I really have worked very hard for you in return—*my utmost*—but here is a question beyond all personal obliga-tions. I assure you it is only painful having further conversations. I have told the Prime Minister I will not remain. I have absolutely decided to stick to that decision. NOTHING WILL TURN ME FROM IT. You say with much feeling that *'it will be a very great grief to you to part from me.'* I am certain you know in your heart no one has ever been more faithful to you than I have since I joined you last October. *I have worked my very hardest!*

Yours,
Fisher

Churchill, seeing his own political career shuddering at its foundations and the fearful national and international consequences of Fisher's sudden departure, addressed one more appeal to him.

FROM WINSTON S. CHURCHILL

May 16th, 1915

My dear Fisher,

I am touched by the kindness of your letter. Our friendship has been a long one. I remember how in 1908 you tried to bring me to the Admiralty as First Lord. When I eventually came in 1911 I proposed to the Prime Minister that you should return to your old position, and only the difficulties which your enemies were likely to make at that time prevented the accomplishment of my first wish. As it was I followed your guidance in the important decisions which have given us the 15–inch gun and Jellicoe to-day.

Six months ago in the crisis of this great war you came to my aid; since then we have worked together in the very closest intimacy. One difficulty after another has been surmounted; vast schemes of new construction have been carried through; and tremendous reinforcements are now approaching the Fleet. Over the whole range of war-policy and Naval administration there is nothing that I know of on which we are disagreed—except the series of events which have led us into the 'Dardanelles'. Even then we are agreed upon the immediate steps, for I shall not press my wish about reinforcements beyond the point to which you were willing to go—namely the 6 earliest monitors. We are now fully agreed that the Fleet is not to attempt to rush the Narrows but is to support the Army in its gradual advance upon the forts by land. Orders in this sense have been given with which you were in complete accord. . . .

First Sea Lord

The announcement of your resignation at this juncture will be accepted
everywhere as proof that the military operations as well as the naval at the
Dardanelles have failed. . . . The admission of failure at the Dardanelles, for
so your resignation would be exploited all over the world, might prove the
deciding factor in the case of Italy, now trembling on the brink. The knowledge of these facts forces me, not for my own sake (for the fortunes of individuals do not matter now), to appeal to you not to make your resignation
operative until at least Italy has declared herself, for whish the latest date is
the 26th. Meanwhile Sir Arthur Wilson could, if you desire it, do your work.

There ought to be no reproaches between us, and you, my friend, must at
this moment in your long career so act that no one can say you were unmindful
of the public interests and of the lives of the soldiers and sailors.

In any case, whatever you decide, I claim, in the name of friendship and in
the name of duty, a personal interview—if only for the purpose of settling
what explanation is to be offered to Parliament.

TO WINSTON S. CHURCHILL

May 16th, 1915

Dear Winston,

As usual, your letter is most persuasive, but I really have considered everything and I have definitely told the Prime Minister that I leave to-morrow
(Monday).

Please don't wish to see me. I could say nothing, as I have determined not
to. *I know I am doing right.*

Fisher

On the following day he wrote a letter of explanation and justification
to Bonar Law, leader of the Opposition and an old friend. It revealed
at once his personal bitterness, his agony of mind, his anguish for his
country. The strain which he had been suffering for the past weeks
was evidenced in the handwriting, and the wild interpolations and
deletions. Even the date beneath his initial is shown as July instead of
May.

TO ANDREW BONAR LAW

May 17th, 1915

Private & Personal

This letter and its contents must not be divulged now or ever to any living soul.
My dear Friend,

In reply to your letter, after repeated refusals by him I have written to the
P.M. this morning to say that now my *definite decision* is I am absolutely unable
to remain with W. C. (HE'S A REAL DANGER!) *But he is going to be kept*
(so I go! *at once,* TODAY), only they are 'forking' me till Parliament rises
for 3 weeks or more. I regret to say your *A. J. B.* has been backing W. C. ALL
THROUGH and I have ʀefused to have anything to do with him (A. J. B.) in
consequence! *Keep this private.* I must not see you, BUT PARLIAMENT SHOULD
NOT RISE TILL THE FACT OF MY GOING IS EXTRACTED. Lots of people must

Part of Fisher's letter to Bonar Law informing him of his decision to
resign as First Sea Lord.

(*Beaverbrook Library*)

know—for instance, see enclosed from Lord Esher. You might see him at 2 Tilney St., Park Lane, and let his informant be your source of information. *I could not see you—I have seen no one. I have written to no one.*

Yours,
F.

Don't be cajoled *privately* by the P.M. to keep silence. The danger is imminent and VITAL. I don't want to stay, but W. C. MUST go at all costs! AT ONCE. I see Esher's letter is marked 'Private & Secret', so I am unable to enclose it. (*Be careful of W. C. with F. E. Smith and others!*) Be prepared for the *suppressio veri* and *suggestio falsi*. The P.M. will stick at nothing to keep W. C. *I'm a dead dog! I ceased work last Friday night. W. C. is leading them all straight to ruin. Please send a line by bearer that you have received this letter—* AND BURNT IT. . . . I have not answered Esher's letter or anyone else's or said one single word to a living soul except you, so you must be most prudent and not give me away, but I feel bound to tell you as Leader of the Opposition, because *a very great national disaster is very near us in the Dardanelles!* against which I have vainly protested and did resign long ago, but Kitchener persuaded me to stop. *I was a d——d fool to do so!* (HE ought to have resigned also.) I fancy they will cajole (on supposed public grounds) the others of my colleagues to stay, but as Othello said to Iago, '*My reputation! my reputation!*' and W. C. is a bigger danger than the Germans by a long way in what is just now imminent in the Dardanelles. *Concentrate on the Dardanelles!* Yesterday a member of the Cabinet told me that the present Government is on the verge of being smashed by my going! I DOUBT IT, but I WILL GO!

Please burn and don't mention. Very SECRET AND PRIVATE. This evening Winston sent Lambert, the Civil Lord of the Admiralty, to offer me a seat in the Cabinet if I would return as First Sea Lord with him (Winston) as First Lord![1] I rejected the 30 pieces of silver to betray my country.

For two days the pressure on Fisher to remain continued to mount, while he took refuge in his residence at the Admiralty and refused to meet anyone, least of all Churchill, whose 'persuasive powers' he so feared.

The word was getting around. Fleet Street had the news on 18 May. There were cries of outrage, and the Conversative press which once had helped to drive him out of the Admiralty now appealed to him to stay. 'Lord Fisher or Mr Churchill? Expert or amateur?' began one main story. From his friends, from the fleet, from the Court, the appeals and the demands poured in.

FROM VISCOUNT ESHER[2]

2 Tilney Street,
Mayfair.
May 16th, 1915

Secret.
My dear, dear Jackie,

You will never *permanently* paper up these quarrels. The only thing to be

---

[1] Lennoxlove MSS.　　[2] *ibid.*

done is to revive the office of Lord High Admiral and take it yourself. Otherwise we are beaten presently at sea; and unless Lord K. [Kitchener] takes the war into his own hands . . .

Yours ever,
E.

McKenna was equally dismayed; and from the C.-in-C. of the Grand Fleet came the message that he was 'hoping more than I ever wished for anything in my life before that the fact of your being still in London indicated that the disaster may possibly be averted. I would far sooner lose some ships than see you leave the Admiralty . . .' Beatty was staggered by the news Jellicoe had passed on at once to his battle cruiser commander. 'If it is of any value to you to know it,' he told Fisher, 'the Fleet is numbed with the thought of the possibility. Please God it is NOT possible for we absolutely refuse to believe it . . .'[1]

The Palace, too, deplored the threatened loss. 'The King sees that Fisher's resignation at such a moment is bound to have a deplorable, if not a disastrous, effect upon the public, not only at home, but abroad,'[2] wrote Esher. And Queen Alexandra despatched a peremptory message to the Admiralty.

Private[3]
My dear Lord Fisher,
    Stick to your *Post* like *Nelson!* The Nation and we all have full confidence in you and *I* and they will not suffer you to go. You are the Nation's hope and we trust you!

The effects were as profound as everyone had feared. In anticipation of the inevitable Conservative onslaught on his administration, Asquith decided on 17 May to approach leaders of the opposition with a view to forming a coalition government.

When Fisher heard the news he saw sudden hope. The prominent and eulogistic press comment combined with these appeals from all quarters confirmed him in his belief that he really was essential if the war was ever to be won. Leading Conservatives were behind him, and as a result of the 'shell scandal' and his resignation their power was suddenly in the ascendant. Under a coalition government and after all these public accusations, Churchill was bound to be sacked. Moreover, his closest and wisest intimate, Esher, had planted a new and heady idea. Lord High Admiral! Supreme dictator of the Royal Navy!

With precipitate haste, Fisher proceeded to draw up a document setting down his conditions for withdrawing his resignation and returning to his post. The terms were outrageous. He would serve

[1] Lennoxlove MSS.   [2] *Esher*, iii, 235.   [3] Lennoxlove MSS.

neither under Churchill nor Balfour; his old friend Arthur Wilson, who had been working unpaid, but with failing judgement, at the Admiralty, had to leave.

TO H. H. ASQUITH

May 19th, 1915

Preamble

If the following six conditions are agreed to, I can guarantee the successful termination of the War and the total abolition of the submarine menace. I also desire to add that since Lord Ripon wished in 1885 to make me a Lord of the Admiralty, but at my request made me Director of Naval Ordnance and Torpedoes instead, I have served under 9 First Lords and 17 years at the Admiralty, so I ought to know something about it.

1. That Mr Winston Churchill is not in the Cabinet to be always circumventing me, nor will I serve under Mr Balfour.

2. That Sir A. K. Wilson leaves the Admiralty and the Committee of Imperial Defence and the War Council, as my time otherwise will be occupied in resisting the bombardment of Heligoland and other such wild projects. Also his policy is totally opposed to mine, and he has accepted[1] the position of First Sea Lord in succession to me, and thereby adopting a policy diametrically opposed to my views.

3. That there shall be an entire new Board of Admiralty, as regards the Sea Lords and the Financial Secretary (who is utterly useless). *New measures* demand *new men*.

4. That I shall have complete professional charge of the war at sea, together with the absolute sole disposition of the Fleet and the appointment of all officers of all ranks whatsoever, and absolutely untrammelled sole command of all the sea forces whatsoever.

5. That the First Lord of the Admiralty should be absolutely restricted to policy and parliamentary procedure and should occupy the same position towards me as Mr Tennant, M.P. does to Lord Kitchener (and very well he does it).

6. That I should have the sole absolute authority for all new construction and all dockyard work of whatever sort whatsoever, and complete control of the whole of the Civil establishments of the Navy.

F.

The 60 per cent of my time and energy which I have exhausted on 9 First Lords in the past I wish in the future to devote to the successful prosecution of the War. That is my sole reason for the six conditions. These six conditions must be published verbatim so that the Fleet may know my position.

Next he named the weak men who could only be his ciphers and also drew up a list of orders to be prepared ready for 'Der Tag'—or the day the coalition government took over and he became 'Lord High Admiral'.

[1] In fact he had just refused the post.

The 'NEW MEASURES DEMAND NEW MEN!' memorandum was sent at once to Asquith, who was outraged at this 'extraordinary document'. Others echoed his comments, even such an old friend as Lord Selborne. The Prime Minister commented to the King that the document 'indicated signs of mental aberration'.

'Der Tag' when it arrived took on an entirely new meaning for Fisher, who was now utterly wrought up and scarcely in command of himself. Everyone in power in Whitehall agreed that he could not serve in any responsible capacity. Even the Navy had turned against him. There was another reason for this.

Of all times to choose, the German Admiralty, ignorant of the dramas being played out in the enemy capital, ordered the High Seas Fleet to sea. On the afternoon of 17 May decoded German signals indicated that a battle might be imminent. Jellicoe and Beatty were at once informed, and the exciting news was passed to Fisher. He insisted on remaining in his rooms and replied that he would not be needed. The well-oiled machinery was set in motion, but there was only the Second Sea Lord to take over the controls, and he was quite unfitted for the task of supreme command if this was to be the long awaited 'Battle of Armageddon'.

It could and has been argued that Fisher was physically available if a battle appeared inevitable; that his prophetic powers which told him that this was not a serious excursion were as infallible as ever; and that he was justified in not risking a personal encounter with Mr Churchill. But at this time especially, everyone who heard of his refusal to come to the War Room judged it as a dereliction of duty—and these included the Sea Lords.

This extraordinary behaviour caused Fisher to forfeit the support and respect of all those who had deplored his resignation and appealed to him to remain at his post. The Prime Minister thought he ought to be shot. The King was outraged. Six months earlier he had predicted disaster if the Prime Minister and Churchill insisted on the old Admiral's reappointment, but he had never visualized such an end to two unique and splendid careers—the sacking of the young politician, the inglorious abdication of the old Admiral.

Fisher finally left London for Scotland on 22 May, pursued by the formal acceptance of his resignation, which caught him up by telegraph at Crewe Junction 160 miles north. Much had happened since his delayed departure just a week earlier. The events were to have the most profound effects on the war and on the lives of those who conducted it. It was the most sombre day of a life of which he had given more than sixty years to the Royal Navy.

Chapter 3

THE WILDERNESS

Fisher's destination in Scotland on 22 May 1915 was Dungavel, near Strathaven in Lanarkshire, 'absolutely out of reach of interviews and snapshotters!' He had a standing invitation from the Duke and Duchess of Hamilton, and had stayed there in the past. At this critical period, Dungaval offered comfort, privacy and the certainty of a warm welcome.

Fisher's friendship with the Duchess of Hamilton had begun two years after her marriage (as Nina Poore) to his old friend and shipmate, Midshipman Alfred Douglas Douglas-Hamilton, from his old days in the *Northampton* on the North America station. Fisher had been appalled when this young officer, who was renowned for his bravery, liveliness and athletic prowess, had been struck down by an incurable tropical disease which had made him a semi-invalid for the rest of his life. Douglas-Hamilton had inherited through a distant kinsman the title of the premier Peer of Scotland and the vast estates in 1895.

The Duchess, who bore the Duke four sons and three daughters, possessed all the womanly qualities Fisher most admired. Her energy and vitality were immense. She was well-informed and a stimulating conversationalist. She embraced good causes and worked tirelessly for them, especially for charities connected with the defence of animals: she was a leading anti-vivisectionist and battled for years for the reform of animal slaughter. Her inherited social conscience was as deep and passionate as her religious convictions. From their first meeting, the Duchess was attracted to Fisher's strength of purpose, decisiveness, his rank in the affairs of men, his achievements, and his religious fervour. She responded eagerly to his evident admiration of her.

TO THE DUCHESS OF HAMILTON[1]

The Admiralty,
S.W.1.
March 16th, 1908

Dear Duchess,
    Here is [a portrait of] Nelson! Keep it private! Please send *large* photo of yourself.

Yours till the angels smile on us.
J.F.

By the time Fisher returned to the Admiralty as First Sea Lord, their friendship had become closer, but in their correspondence there is nothing to suggest that it was any different in nature from Fisher's relations with the wives of other of his friends and associates. The use of effusive endearments and rich expressions of affection was much more common then than it is today, and Fisher's mode of address to Pamela McKenna—and Jellicoe, Spender and Churchill for that matter—as 'My beloved . . .' was not unusual. To Mrs Spender he could write without giving embarrassment, 'You are like that very lovely woman who knew me and I didn't know her who said, "The moon looks on many rivers, the rivers only look on one moon"! . . .' The exchange of photographs between friends was also a pleasant and usually innocent social custom at this time. Even in the full throes of cleaning up the Admiralty 'mess' in 1914 and 1915, Fisher's need of the company and the exchange of intimate confidences with women was as great as ever, and he still found time to write affectionately to other of his women friends besides the Duchess of Hamilton.

TO THE DUCHESS OF HAMILTON[2]

The Admiralty,
S.W.1.
December 15th, 1914

My dear Duchess,
    So sweet of you to write. *Do* come and lunch with us even if you are only one day in London at 1.45 (the First Sea Lord's House at Admiralty. Any fool will tell you where it is!) Always room, a big table, so come any day *without notice.* You promised long since a good photo of yourself. I have only a miserable one of you. And I'll give you the best I have.

In Haste,
Yours till Hell freezes,
Fisher.

---

[1] Lennoxlove MSS.   [2] *ibid.*

Drawn by Bert Thomas.

Abandoned

(*London Opinion*)

The correspondence between the First Sea Lord and the Duchess increased during the first months of 1915. He recounted his anxieties over the management of the war and the Dardanelles and his troubles with Churchill, and treasured her sympathy. Fisher, who hated the telephone, even welcomed calls from her, and they met as often as they could when she was in London. They prayed together in Westminster Abbey. This time marked the beginning of their 'perfect communion of souls'[1] and mutual interdependence for their spiritual well being.

It is certain that Fisher had lost none of the tender affection he felt for his wife. Lady Fisher had supported her husband nobly and loyally ever since their marriage, when she had vowed, 'I will never rest till I see Jack First Naval Lord of the Admiralty. Never will I stand in his way, even if it means separation for years.' Lady Fisher patiently fulfilled all her duties. She was not by nature gregarious, but she had always acted the part of hostess and wife of a great and ambitious sailor to the best of her ability. There is no evidence at any time that she ever grumbled at her tedious responsibilities. At heart, 'Kitty' Fisher was first a family woman. She was at ease and at her best at home and with her children about her. Cecil and the three 'Fishcakes', as the Navy affectionately dubbed their daughters, were the centre of her thoughts, plans and affection while they were growing up.

When Fisher's mind was full of the noise and fury of battle, of great events and great personalities, and he unburdened himself of his troubles at the end of the day, his wife would listen patiently and sympathetically. But she could never respond with the wit and understanding—nor really the close attention—that Pamela McKenna or the Duchess of Hamilton could offer, however hard she might try. In short, during his time of great power and his frustrating years in 'the wilderness', Lady Fisher alone did not satisfy his need for the flattery and the sharp feminine response and calmative sympathy for which he longed. Lady Fisher never really understood how subconsciously insecure was her husband.

The Duchess of Hamilton soothed Fisher's ruffled pride and supported his vulnerable self-confidence. Her enthusiasm was fresh, her admiration boundless. She was a person of tremendous vigour and possessed qualities of sympathy and character which matched perfectly Fisher's own formidable but now exhausted vitality. The Duchess was responsive and deeply compassionate, noted for her fighting qualities for causes, from spiritualism to the protection of animals. She had a marked contempt for accepted custom, and a love for the eccentric, and the fighter. So when Fisher's position at the Admiralty became intolerable and he

[1] Duchess of Hamilton to Arnold White, 17 July 1920. Lennoxlove MSS.

was forced to abdicate, and then was rejected on his own terms, Dun-gavel rather than Kilverstone was the natural refuge. Here there was peace and isolation and a restorative hand for his aching brow. Within a few days he was writing from Scotland, 'I shall probably stay on here, as the Duke and Duchess are both very dear friends, and it is like home being here with them.'

To Lady Fisher he wrote (25 May 1915) in red ink above one of his first letters to her: '*Nothing will ever induce me to go to London again till the war is over!*'[1] But he was sorry he had left her to clear up the domestic situation following his departure. 'I feel quite ashamed of being here in such great luxury while all of you are topsy turvy packing up, and all going through so much bother and worry while I am here in extreme luxury, *with a suite of apartments fit for a King!*' he wrote the following day. The Duchess wrote to invite her to come and stay too, and Fisher added his own hopes that she might accept—'but I admit it's a long way to come and absolute isolation . . .'[2]

Instead, Lady Fisher returned to Kilverstone where she remained almost until her death. She was deeply hurt by her husband's defection to the Hamiltons, although they exchanged affectionate letters and she saw him from time to time. The three daughters were greatly shocked by the rift in the family and never forgave the Duchess, nor their father, for bringing anxiety and sadness to their mother's last years. There is some evidence that Lady Fisher made several appeals to her husband to leave the Hamiltons and reunite the family; on one occasion at Kilverstone, when the Duchess and Fisher were both guests there. The atmosphere was tense and unhappy.[3]

There was another reason for the Fisher family's distress at his close relationship with the Hamiltons from 1915. With every justification, they believed that the Duchess, by her admiration and flattery and canvassing of support among her friends, encouraged Fisher in the false belief that he might yet again return to power. They wanted him to rest in peace, restore his tired mind and body, and enjoy his retire-ment. But the Duchess of Hamilton was a stimulating influence and wanted to see him great again. She believed passionately that Fisher could still win the war, and knew that he was right when he told her, 'I'm deliberately isolated by the Authorities. It's quite absurd that in these great convulsions at the Admiralty that no place can be found for me! No, the word has been passed round evidently *"Keep him isolated"* . . .'[4]

---

[1] Kilverstone MSS.   [2] *ibid.*

[3] Countess Jellicoe, who was present, recounted this episode to Professor Marder.

[4] Fisher to the Duchess of Hamilton. Undated but probably December 1916. Lennoxlove MSS.

The return of Fisher to the Admiralty was the Duchess's great war cause. 'Why do you not speak out in the House of Lords and elsewhere?' she demanded of Lord Rosebery, one of several powerful figures to whom she appealed 'and rouse public feeling in the country to the dangerous abyss into which we are slowly and surely being drawn by the lethargy of these lawyer politicians who, alas for us, sit so firmly in the saddle? . . . The Almighty has sent us one of those rare geniuses which only appear in time of need and we have allowed him to be shelved, just because he has a dominant personality which makes the politicians "to shiver and to shake" for fear of their own influence!!!...'[1]

Still in the capacity of Fisher's exponent and mouthpiece, the Duchess similarly attacked the press. From many editors and journalists she received no encouragement. Others were more helpful, or at least showed that they shared the Duchess's belief in Fisher. Among these was the editor of the *Manchester Guardian*.

C. P. SCOTT TO THE DUCHESS OF HAMILTON[2]

The Firs,
Hannofield,
Manchester
June 6th, 1916

Dear Duchess of Hamilton,

. . . What matters is that the spirit and power of Nelson live on this earth again, as may be seen of all men, but that by some league of the powers of darkness they are not being used for the Nation's good. If on June 1st[3] of this present year there was not another Trafalgar it is due to that cause and no other.

Yours sincerely,
C. P. Scott

Fisher's return to the Admiralty was the daily prayer of many people during the darkest days of the war. The stature of the legend and the record of his past accomplishments were both too formidable to be forgotten. Here was a great man who could provide a panacea for all the woes and ineptitudes in the conduct of the war. It was easy enough to forget those threatened resignations and the manner of his departure in May 1915, and that terrible discord he and Beresford had created before the war. The Grand Fleet, their unseen shield from the Germans, was his bequest to the nation. It had been under Fisher's brief régime that the Royal Navy had scored the great victories, like the Battles of

[1] Undated. Lennoxlove MSS.　　　[2] *ibid.*
[3] The morning after the Battle of Jutland.

the Falklands and Dogger Bank.[1] And how right he had been about the Dardanelles, or so it seemed now!

So Fisher's hopes were not kept alive by the Duchess of Hamilton alone. As Archibald Hurd told Fisher (31 August 1915), McKenna believed, 'You are still the idol of the nation and you will be recalled by acclamation to the hearts of the people.' Fisher thrived on such encouragement, and redoubled his output of letters of recrimination and advice on how to win the war to the Prime Minister, to Jellicoe, Churchill's successor, Balfour, and others still in command.

TO H. H. ASQUITH

36, Berkeley Square,
W.1.
October 28th, 1915

My dear Prime Minister,
    At this juncture and amidst such great anxieties, I am trusting to be made some use of, as probably few (or I might say no one) can know as much of Navy work, and I am doing nothing at all.

Yours truly,
Fisher

He would be needed again: there was almost daily evidence of it. 'Bonar Law very anxious to see me,' he wrote to his old friend George Lambert, the late Civil Lord of the Admiralty, 'also the Editor of *The Times* asked to see me urgently yesterday, and he remained two hours. He says the whole country is seething to have me back! But so long as "Wait and See" and the *"Philosophic Doubter"*[2] are where they are, *I am out of it!*' Even Churchill of all people judged later in the war that only Fisher could 'vitalize and animate' the Board, which should recall him to his old post as First Sea Lord.[3]

Fisher's first wartime period as a guest of the Hamiltons was after all a surprisingly brief one. To his delight, he received early in July 1915 'exceeding cordial letters' from Asquith and Balfour inviting him to act as chairman to a newly established Board of Invention and Research. The Scottish climate, the smell of the moors, trout fishing with the Duke, had restored his strength, and he stormed back to London on 5 July, full of expectation that the task offered real opportunities. 'Apparently I shall be able to direct big policies,' he told Cecil. With one early stroke of the pen he renamed his headquarters Victory House,

---

[1] Fisher's 'greyhounds' had scored again on 24 January 1915, sinking German's biggest and fastest armoured cruiser.

[2] Asquith and Balfour respectively.

[3] Speech in the House of Commons, 7 March 1916.

and got down to work with a committee of three scientists, J. J. Thomson, the President of the Royal Society, his old friend, Charles Parsons of turbine fame, and a renowned chemist, George Beilby.

The job was a pale, sad shadow of past challenges, and disillusionment set in rapidly. The committee's findings were only advisory. As an executive administrator for so many years, with ever increasing powers to see that his decisions were instantly acted upon, the offering of mere advice was a tame business. When he realized that even the advice was largely ignored, be became very angry. At the same time there occurred a renewed outcry for his return, which was even more unsettling. In November 1915, following an attack by Churchill on his part in the Dardanelles business, Fisher had made a brief and dignified statement in the House of Lords—his first speech in that Chamber. 'I have been sixty-one years in the service of my country,' he said, 'and I leave my record in the hands of my countrymen . . . It is unfitting to make personal explanations affecting national interests when my country is in the midst of a great war.' This not only put Churchill in his place; it was more widely and jubilantly reported in the press than if he had violently counterattacked.

There were renewed demands for his return, to which Fisher listened expectantly. But Asquith, and later David Lloyd George would have nothing to do with him. In the higher echelons of power, Fisher's judgement was doubted. He was becoming an old eccentric and something of a bore with his frequent appeals for a new post and long letters, full of capitals, and underlinings and exclamation marks, instructing a busy prime minister on how to conduct the war.

For the rest of the war he remained a sharp and vocal critic of the running of affairs, not just at the Admiralty but throughout the ministries and services. Event after event reinforced his pessimism. The Battle of Jutland, at which Jellicoe showed up timorously and suffered greater damage from an inferior German force, was a bitter blow. The submarine was proving to be the dominant weapon at sea, just as he had predicted. Jellicoe was brought down from his Grand Fleet at Scapa Flow to take command of the battle against the U-boats as First Sea Lord. Fisher was stunned. Not only was Jellicoe in his judgement a seaman rather than an administrator, but this appointment appeared to destroy all remaining chances of his own return. In desperation, Fisher wrote (31 January 1917) to the new First Sea Lord offering his services as Third Sea Lord and Controller, a post he had not held since 1897. The reply from his old friend and subordinate, to whom Fisher had given the honour and responsibility of commanding the Grand Fleet in war, was deeply wounding.

February 13th, 1917

My dear Lord Fisher,

I have thought a great deal over the suggestion which you made to me during your visit, but I have been forced to the conclusion that it would not be practicable for such a scheme to be adopted.

There are only two posts which, in my opinion, you could hold here—those of First Lord or First Sea Lord. In any other position, I cannot help feeling that difficulties are bound to arise.

Yours very sincerely,
J. R. Jellicoe

Fisher left behind him a note so deeply melancholy that it marks the low point in his spirit during his last years. 'A *soliloquy!*' he wrote. 'When you have done your very utmost for your Country, then sit down under the Juniper Tree with Elijah and ask of God that you may die! and exclaim with the deepest humility and unutterable self-degradation and self-effacement: "I am an unprofitable servant"!'

Again Fisher found solace at Dungavel. During his earlier retreat there in May 1915, the Duke had revealed to him his anxiety about the condition of the Hamilton estates. The family's affairs were complicated by the provisions of the previous Duke's will and by general mismanagement. The Duke's health was too precarious to participate actively in the estates' business, and Fisher eagerly and thankfully took on the enormous task of getting things running efficiently again. His vast experience as an administrative reformer was invaluable and the 'augean task', which included getting a special Act through Parliament and the setting up of a trust of settlement for the family's children, helped to take his mind off the tragedies of the war and the apathy and mismanagement governing naval affairs.

In his letters to the Duchess at this time, he related that without this work and the support and understanding of the Duchess, he could not have lived through the war. *'No one else understands me as you do!'* There was a quality in their relationship, in their shared compassion for the poor and the underprivileged, in the evangelistic nature of their love of God, in their belief in the ultimate goodness of mankind in the midst of the mass slaughter in France, which sustained them both. All who knew them at this time confirm that their relationship was above all deeply spiritual. 'No woman will ever appear against me at the Day of Judgement,'[1] he wrote. But Fisher was well aware that his old enemies would never give up their witch hunt while he remained alive, and he was fearful for the Duchess's reputation as they stayed together at

---

[1] *Memories*, 113.

Hamilton Palace in Lanarkshire, or one or another of the mansions which the Hamiltons leased successively in Sussex, Hertfordshire and Wiltshire. 'I *must* not let the breath of scandal injure you!' he once told her. But he was not wholly successful in this.

When they were apart, they wrote frequently, sometimes as many as three letters a day, and the tone of their letters was always touched by religious preoccupations.

TO THE DUCHESS OF HAMILTON[1]

. . . We've got to live from day to day! It's the oldest lesson in the world and yet we never learn it! We don't make enough of the Lord's Prayer! 'Give us THIS DAY our daily bread'—not for tomorrow even, *let alone the future,* only our bread for *this to-day.* Yet the Almighty has planted in us as a most right-eous plant (*that grows like horse-radish and spreads like Jerusalem artichokes*), the ever effervescing delight of 'ANTICIPATION'!!!! Like the rich man (*whose soul was required of him that very night!*) we are always in anticipation building barns to hold more riches! The golden sands of Samoa! The grandeur of the Siena sunset, the magnificence of Dawn and Twilight in the Michelangelo Chapel! The Heavenly Partnership! Good Health!
And yet what is the right attitude? The only attitude? 'Thy will be done!'

> 'Seek we no more
> content with these.
> Let present Rapture, Comfort, Ease
> as Heaven shall bid them come and go.
> The secret this of rest below!'

Some Holy Saint (I think Bishop Jeremy Taylor) said, learn a lot of hymns, good hymns, and they'll solace you when dying! 'And let the music of Thy name refresh my soul in death.' . . .

Much of their time together was spent on business with the estate and on the Duchess's numerous charities and causes. Fisher supported her in all this work, and helped her in the arrangements, for example, for 'reprinting the Great Bible in modern print (and spelling that won't spoil her children . . .)' He acquired from her an interest in spiritualism.

The schism in his family which this relationship created deeply troubled him, and he continued to write tender letters to his wife, though he saw her rarely. When he learned in July 1918 that she had been taken seriously ill, he rushed to her side in London. Over the following days while he helped to nurse her, he wrote many times to the Duchess recounting to her every stage of the fatal illness. 'One is

[1] Lennoxlove MSS.

living in a most agonizing condition as any second Death may come!'
he wrote (8 July 1918). 'This is the first day since I came that I have
been excluded from the sickroom and everyone else. She has been told
the reason and fully acquiesces! Simple perfect silence is her hope of
life! . . . The two doctors have just been. The morphia they risk giving
to her has given beatific sleep! The Doctors think *"just a chance"* but
"precarious beyond words" and always may die *"in just one second of
time"* . . .'[1]

Lady Fisher died on 18 July. 'A most perfect, peaceful, blissful end
at 2.30 a.m. I will tell you more when bye and bye we meet. A Kindly
Providence gave a beautiful closed life. May your saintly end be the
same!'[2]

In the midst of the task of answering all the letters of commiseration
that came pouring in from his old friends, Fisher wrote of his wife:

'And such was Katharine Delves Broughton, for fifty-two years the
wife of Admiral of the Fleet Lord Fisher of Kilverstone, having married
him as a young lieutenant without friends or money or prospects, and
denied herself all her life long for the sake of her husband and her
children—to them she was ever faithful and steadfast, and to such as
condemned them she was a Dragon!'

Then he wrote to the Duchess, 'I am going to St James' for communion tomorrow. I hope to get help and forgiveness just once more.
"Seventy times seven" I get forgiven . . .'[3]

Fisher's dependence on the Duchess of Hamilton for his spiritual
and physical survival set in more deeply than ever after his wife's death.
'You have saved my life and you know it!' he wrote to her. *'And can
I ever forget it???'*[4]

More than ever he believed himself an outcast. There was almost no
one left who even listened to him.

One last humiliating act remained to be played out. Fisher was
neither invited to the triumphant and moving ceremony of the surrender
of the German Fleet at sea, nor was his name included in the King's
victory speech to Parliament on 19 November 1918—'Yes! King George
arranged my omission!' he noted sadly, to C. P. Scott.

And yet the sprightliness of Fisher's spirits was never quite stilled,
and his obsessional interest in the state of the Navy was noted by his old
correspondents, and by the editor of *The Times*, who published a number
of his letters, each characterized by the familiar underlinings, capitals
and exclamation marks. In 1919 he dictated his memoirs, without plan
or order. As spontaneous effusions, covering every subject which had

[1] Lennoxlove MSS.   [2] *ibid.*   [3] *ibid.*   [4] *ibid.*

ever interested him, broken by fragments of reminiscences and letters, potted summaries of some of the great men and women he had known, lists of his favourite sayings and anecdotes by the score, they are unique among memoirs, and tell us more of the man than many an orderly autobiography. His memory was prodigious, his choice of words often delectable, and his compassion and sincerity shines through every paragraph. During the preparation of the first draft Beresford died, and he struck out some forthright comments on his old enemy. They were the only uncharitable remarks in all the 200,000 words.

The memoirs were cut arbitrarily in half and Fisher arranged for them to be published, as *Memories* and *Records*, on Trafalgar Day (21 October) and the anniversary of the Falklands battle (8 December) 1919. On the proceeds of the sales, he took the Duchess of Hamilton and her convalescent eldest son to Monte Carlo in Febuary 1920. He was soon telling his friends of his love of the place and the winter sun. *'It's Paradise!!!* And fancy my not finding it till in my 80th year!!! If the Duchess dies (as is quite likely—she troubles about so many things!) *—I shall live here altogether!'*

Sir Frederick Treves, the King's surgeon, who was also in Monte Carlo, strongly advised Fisher to remain and have 'the sun's heat . . . cause my calamities to exude in perspiration, instead of the blight of the English east wind congesting all my interior economy!' He was feeling well and more cheerful. But soon the weather and Fisher's health both changed for the worse. He had a sore throat on 5 March, followed by rheumatic pains. Treves ordered him back to England: it was cancer, an immediate operation offered the only slight hope.

Between 17 March and early July Fisher underwent four painful operations in London. His stoicism and patience impressed all who were with him during those last weeks. The Duchess of Hamilton scarcely ever left his bedside. 'But for your devotion he would have gone long ago,' wrote Garvin after it was all over. 'I give my knee to you for that.'[1]

The surgeons and the doctors attending him were astonished at the powers of recovery of his old body. On 6 June he seemed well enough to be moved, and the Duchess took him down to his favourite retreat in the south, the Hamilton estate at Ferne, near Salisbury. He responded marvellously and for a week the Duchess held out some hope of recovery. He lay outdoors in the sun and watched a little Shetland pony and her foal, which the Duchess had brought near him, playing together. Then his condition gradually worsened, and his surgeon ordered him back to London for one last desperate operation. This took place on 9 July at the Duchess's London home in St James's Square.

[1] Lennoxlove MSS.

Fisher never regained full consciousness. In the early hours of the next morning the Duchess fulfilled the promise she had earlier made to him to offer a last prayer when he was dying. She leaned over and whispered in his ear: 'O Lord, in Thee have I trusted, let me never be confounded.' This appeared to comfort him. At 7.15 a.m. on 10 July the old Admiral died.

His instructions were typically simple and to the point.

'PRIVATE. To be opened when necessary,' was on the outside of the envelope. On a single sheet inside he gave the name and address of his undertakers, then:

> 'The nearest cemetery
> No flowers
> No one invited except relatives
> No mourning

> 'Words under tablet at Kilverstone Church
> as arranged in memorandum in my writing case'

The great funeral procession and service in Westminster Abbey took place three days later. It was a beautiful day, and a crowd with bared heads lined the route. They saw the coffin on a gun carriage, draped with a Union Jack and drawn by bluejackets, move slowly along the wide streets he knew so well: Pall Mall, the Mall, and then down Whitehall—between the monolithic clubs where the worst of the calumnies against him were committed; close to Buckingham Palace where he had often made his adored King Edward laugh; under Admiralty Arch and past the Admiralty, where he had worked for many years from long before the sun rose over Trafalgar Square until after it had set over Carlton House Terrace; beneath the over-lifesize figure of Horatio Nelson high on his column; and then past the still-shrouded Cenotaph in honour of the Great War's dead; and so to the West Door of the Abbey where he had prayed countless times for strength and wisdom.

The Times wrote next day of 'The People's Homage': 'Yesterday morning the mortal remains of Admiral of the Fleet Lord Fisher of Kilverstone, GCB, OM, GCVO, were borne in solemn state to Westminster Abbey, where, in the presence of a vast congregation representing all that is most eminent in our national life, an august ceremonial celebrated the passing of a great spirit from the earthly scene of its stupendous labours.

'And yesterday morning the British public showed that it loved and

mourned one "Jacky Fisher." There is no surer test of public feeling
than the size and the behaviour of the crowd in the streets. Till within
the last weeks of his long and bellicose life, Lord Fisher was a stormy
petrel, bringing the tempests he rejoiced in. Behind him he had, at first,
no one; behind him, he had, in these later years, the whole solid
affection and admiration of the people. And yesterday morning the
people, in its silent, stolid, reverent British way, wrote its affection
and admiration for "Jacky Fisher" upon the social history of our time.'

Then, of the scene in the Abbey: 'With infinite slowness to [the]
music the procession moved up the length of the Nave to the choir,
the choristers, white surplices over scarlet, in front, then the canons
and other dignitaries of the Abbey and the Dean. Behind the Dean was
the crimson cushion on which the dead man's Orders and Decorations
were displayed, a glittering mass of stars and ribbon, and then the
coffin . . . crowned with the Admiral's hat and sword, borne by eight
bluejackets . . .'

'One felt it all *really* worthy of him,' wrote the Duchess of Hamilton
to Arnold White that evening. 'It was beautiful the way not a head
remained covered as his dear body passed, even all the way to Golders
Green . . .'[1]

On the following morning she received many letters of condolence
from Fisher's most faithful friends. 'I walked behind your two boys,'
wrote Garvin, 'and saw you in the Abbey . . . What did content me was
the crowd on either hand as we walked with the drum beating. I have
seen larger crowds in London but never a better—never one more
reverent, regretful, more earnest and true. The faces all the way were
the pick of the creed—no mere mob, no sensation-seekers. All came
because a king of men had passed out of Israel and they knew what they
owed him . . .'[2]

After the cremation, the ashes were taken to the tiny church at
Kilverstone and there buried alongside Lady Fisher's grave.

> 'Seest thou a man diligent in his business?
> he shall stand before Kings,
> He shall not stand before mean men'

was the text he had chosen for his stone; and on the footstone the
booming motto he had selected after much consideration ten years
earlier:

> 'Fear God and Dread Nought'

---

[1] Lennoxlove MSS.   [2] *ibid.*

Appendix 1

Verbatim report of a meeting at the Admiralty, 5 July 1907, between Lord Tweedmouth, First Lord of the Admiralty, Admiral of the Fleet Sir John Fisher, GCB, OM, First Sea Lord, and Admiral Lord Charles Beresford, GCVO, KCB, Commander-in-Chief Channel Fleet. This document, marked 'Most Secret', is to be found in the Robinson Papers, Vol. 1, Admiralty MSS. The report is too extensive to quote in full. The following extracts are from the exchanges following questions (3) and (4) respectively: 'Why do you not try to cultivate good and cordial relations with the Admiralty?', and 'Will you explain to us your reasons for saying that "the Home Fleet is a fraud and a danger to the Empire"?'

(Fisher has just asked if Beresford would be satisfied with the reinforcements as proposed):

Beresford: On those lines. I will let you know that. If I have a Fleet which is a striking force.
Fisher: It is no use haggling over terms and descriptions like this ... as Sir Charles Hardinge said to me this morning, speaking of the Hague Conference, it is perfectly ridiculous to think that anything can happen in the shape of a sudden treacherous attack on our Fleet without some preliminary 'strained relations'.
Beresford: That is a matter of opinion. It is most unlikely that this house, in which we now are, is going to be burnt down, but it is possible.
Fisher: I do not suppose you are not working for the good of the State ——
Beresford: Only we differ. You are doing your level best, and I have got to go out to do war duty. I tell you what I think—the only thing I can do. I never go back on my opinions.
Tweedmouth: If you said what were your reasons; but to say, without giving your reasons, that our policy is a fraud and a danger to the Empire, that is pretty hot ——
Beresford: You have not got that officially; you cannot say that ...
Fisher: Having yielded to all Lord Charles Beresford's demands so as to bring your squadron up to what you say were Admiral Wilson's component parts. We do not agree, but we say 'This is our Chief Executive officer afloat; we do not agree, but we will give him the armoured cruisers, the destroyer flotillas and the attendant vessels, as he presses so for them.
Beresford: I cannot see that thing straight off. I will write to you.

Fisher: You must have thought about it. You have been writing about it for months.

Beresford: I am not sure that I have not asked for more cruisers than that on my plan.

.   .   .   .

Beresford: . . . Then this thing—Question No. 3—You will allow me to smile for at least ten minutes over Question No. 3 . . . Although my views are very drastic, there is not any question of want of cordial relations with the Admiralty. Not privately or publicly have I ever said anything against the Admiralty . . .

Tweedmouth: If you say, in a letter to me, as First Lord, that our Home Fleet 'is a fraud and a danger to the Empire', that is not very pleasant to the Admiralty, and you have repeated that again and again . . . I must tell you that to tell the First Lord of the Admiralty that what is a very important part of his Board's policy is absolutely useless and is a fraud and a danger to the Empire, I do not think that is very friendly to the Admiralty.

Beresford: It is a private letter. We have all written much stronger things than that on important questions of that sort . . . It was only a 'term'. If we went to war suddenly you would find it is true. If I had said officially that the Admiralty had created that, or if I had pitched into the Admiralty about it, it would be different . . . That I had any notion of insubordination I absolutely deny. That letter of mine to the First Lord has no right to go before the Board, a private letter like that . . .

Tweedmouth: It is not marked private. Other letters have been marked private.

Beresford: . . . I ought to have put 'private' and 'confidential' on it.

Tweedmouth: I cannot look on that as simply a private communication to me. I think that is a very important letter.

Fisher: I am quite sure you understand we are all equally interested, as you are, in having friendly and cordial relations, but it is absolutely impossible if the Chief Executive Officer of the Admiralty afloat is going to be 'crabbing' the Admiralty in everything the Admiralty is doing, and writing such letters to the First Lord . . .

Tweedmouth: I think so serious a charge against the Home Fleet ought to be substantiated; you ought to say how it is a fraud, and how it is a danger to the State.

Beresford: It is a 'term'. I can write it all out to you in detail. The public think it is ready for instant action. What is your own term? Without an hour's delay: well, it is not . . .

Appendix 2

BATTLESHIP DESIGN

The Committee, in their consideration of the various designs [for the *Dreadnought*], have kept very carefully in view the extreme importance of the ship being in a constant state of readiness for instant action, and have endeavoured to assimilate all peace requirements to those of war, in such matters for instance as signalling, navigation, boat stowage, &c.

After having carefully examined and discussed various types of battleships, and having had six alternative designs prepared, the Committee unanimously decided to recommend outline design H for adoption. The principal features of this design are approximately as follows:

Length, 490 ft.
Breadth, 83 ft.
Draught, $26\frac{1}{2}$ ft.
Displacement, 17,850 tons.
Horse-power, equivalent to 23,000 I.H.P.
Speed, 21 knots.

Armament.—Ten 12-in. guns in five separate turrets mounted on separate redoubts. Twenty 12-pr. Q.F. anti-torpedo boat guns and five submerged torpedo tubes.

Number and Position of Heavy Guns.—In considering the adoption of a uniform armament of 12-in. guns, it became at once apparent that a limitation to the number of pairs of guns that could be usefully carried was imposed by considerations of the blast effect of one gun on the crews of those adjacent to it.

It is obviously uneconomical to place the guns in such relative positions that the blast of any single gun on any permissible training should very seriously hamper the use of one or more of the remaining guns.

Further, it is exceedingly undesirable to place guns so that there is a danger of the projectile from one hitting the muzzle of an adjacent gun.

The effect of the blast from the 12-in. guns can be best appreciated by recalling the fact that it is produced by a confined volume of 35 cubic feet of gas at a pressure of about 7 tons per square inch suddenly expanding from the muzzle into the open air.

The Committee consider that it would be unwise to rely on any exposed positions, such as unscreened sighting hoods, conning towers,

&c., being tenable inside a sphere of 70 feet radius, whose centre lies on the continuation of the axis of the gun and 55 feet from the muzzle.

The substitution of 12-in. guns for 9.2-in. guns on the broadside, with the attendant increase of charge and blast, has added considerably to the difficulties of placing them so as to obtain large arcs of training on which the guns can be practically fought.

While it is recognised that broadside fire is held to be the most important in a battleship, all-round fire is also considered of great importance, since it lies in the power of an enemy to force an opponent, who is anxious to engage, to fight an end-on action. Superior speed undoubtedly gives the power of choosing the range, but a fleet with inferior speed possesses large powers of deciding the bearing on which the action shall be fought.

In the arrangement of armament recommended, six of the guns are mounted in pairs on the centre line of the ship; the remaining four guns are mounted in pairs on the broadside. Thus eight 12-inch guns (80%) of the main armament) can be fired on either broadside, and four, or possibly six, 12-in. guns can be fired simultaneously ahead or astern. As stated above, each pair of guns is carried in a separate turret mounted on a separate redoubt, thus minimising as much as possible the risk of damage which may be done by a single shell explosion.

Anti-Torpedo Craft Armament.—In view of the potentialities of modern torpedo craft, and considering specially the chances of torpedo attack towards the end of an action, it is considered necessary to separate the anti-torpedo boat guns as widely as possible from one another, so that the whole of them shall not be disabled by one or two heavy shells. This consideration, together with the fact that a new and very powerful 12-pr. gun is in existence leads the Committee to recommend a numerous and widely distributed armament of 12-pr. Q.F. guns for use against torpedo craft.

Conning Tower.—Much importance is attached to having a conning tower with a good view and free from blast. Under some circumstances the forward conning tower might be affected by the blast of the broadside guns, when firing right ahead, and strong screens have therefore been arranged for, so as to minimise this anticipated effect as much as possible. It is further recommended, however, that a second conning tower be also fitted amidships, not only for use under the circumstances mentioned above, but also as an alternative position from which the ship may be fought in the event of the forward conning tower, or the means of communication leading from it, being seriously damaged. This central conning tower is also proposed as the station for the torpedo officer in action, thus relieving congestion in the fore conning tower. It is further arranged that signalling during an action shall be carried out from this second conning tower, the signalmen being thus for the first time provided with a strongly protected position.

Control of Fire.—A position for the control of fire, range, and order instruments has been arranged. It is supported by a strong steel structure which cannot be easily brought down by gunfire, and which, at the same time, is not too large a target. An alternative position will also be provided.

Freeboard forward.—In order to give the ship good sea-going qualities and to increase the command of the forward guns, a forecastle is fitted, giving the ship a freeboard forward of 28 feet.

Armour Protection.—The main belt has a maximum thickness of 11 ins., tapering to 6 ins. at the forward and 4 ins. at the after extremities of the vessel; the redoubts vary from 11 ins. to 8 ins.; the turrets and fore conning tower are 11 ins. and the after conning tower is 8 ins. thick; the protective deck varies from $1\frac{3}{4}$ ins. to $2\frac{3}{4}$ ins. in thickness.

Safety against under-water injury.—With a view to safeguarding the ship against destruction by under-water explosion, the inner bottom has been kept as far distant as practicable from the outer skin, and the magazines and shell rooms have been removed as far from the side of the ship as possible, and have been kept at a considerable height above the bottom. Allowance has also been made for protecting the sides of the magazines and shell rooms by plating from 1 ins. to $2\frac{1}{2}$ ins. thick, in order to reduce the probability of their being exploded by a torpedo or floating mine.* All the main transverse bulkheads below the main deck (which will be about 9 ft. above the water line) are unpierced by openings for water-tight doors, and to enable the necessary supervision to be maintained, lifts and other special arrangements have been provided to give access to the various compartments. The main bulkheads will only be pierced for the purpose of leading pipes or wires conveying power.

Torpedo Nets.—Torpedo nets are provided for, and care has been taken, in the arrangements for their stowage, to protect them as far as possible from the blast of the heavy guns. They will be carried as high as possible to avoid catching the water when steaming in a seaway.

Type of Propelling Machinery.—The question of the best type of propelling machinery to be fitted has also been carefully considered. While recognising that the steam turbine system of propulsion has at present some disadvantages, yet, owing to the great saving in weight and reduction in number of working parts, smooth working, capability

---

* Experiments are being made to test the benefit of this plating.

of being started at short notice, saving in coal consumption and in engine-room complement, and to the increased protection which it is possible to obtain by the introduction of this system, the Committee have decided to recommend that it be adopted in this design.

Stopping and Manoeuvring Power.—The point that chiefly occupied the Committee in connection with the introduction of turbine machinery was the question of providing sufficient stopping and turning power for purposes of quick and easy manoeuvring. There was no difficulty in arriving at a decision to adopt turbine propulsion from the point of view of seagoing speed only, but it was not till after lengthy investigation that the Committee were in a position to decide on the possibility of obtaining sufficient effective backing power without losing the great saving in weight which is one of the chief characteristics of the turbine engine.

The Committee have carefully considered the results of comparative trials between the *Eden* and *Waveney*, the performances of turbine steamers employed in the passenger service of various railway companies, the results of experiments carried out by Mr Froude, the Superintendent of the Admiralty Experimental Works, and the evidence of the Hon. Charles Parsons.

All requirements promise to be met by the adoption of suitable turbine machinery, and it is considered that the manoeuvring capabilities of the ship, when in company with a fleet or when working in narrow waters, will not be impaired thereby.

The necessary stopping power will be obtained by astern turbines on each shaft. These astern turbines will be arranged in high and low pressure pairs in series, and in this way the steam will be more economically used when going astern.

The turbines on the same side of the ship will be, as a rule, worked as one engine; a separate set of telegraphs for each will therefore not be required.

Time for Manufacture of Turbines.—From inquiries made by the Committee on this subject, it appears that there should be no difficulty in getting turbine machinery of the required power manufactured in sufficient time to avoid delay in the completion of the ship, as there are at present several firms familiar with this machinery, and which have work of this kind in hand.

Coal Capacity and Radius of Action.—A total coal-bunker capacity of 2,400 tons, has been provided, and with this amount of coal the ship will be able to steam about 5,800 sea miles at economical speed, and about 3,500 sea miles at 18 knots, after allowance has been made for bad weather and for a small amount of coal being left in the bunkers.

Oil Fuel.—Stowage for oil-fuel has been arranged for, but oil-fuel has not been taken into account in estimating the radius of action.

Navigating Arrangements.—It is recommended that structures in the neighbourhood of compasses, such as chart house, wind screen, &c., which have heretofore generally been made of wood, should be made of some non-magnetic metal, thus avoiding the danger of their being set ablaze by a shell.

Boat Stowage.—In view of the numerous heavy guns to be carried, difficulty has been experienced in providing convenient boat stowage, but in arranging the position of such boats as would be kept on board in wartime, care has been taken so that, in the event of their being damaged by shell fire, their wreckage would, as far as possible, be clear of the heavy guns and conning towers.

Accommodation.—Considerable attention has been devoted to the arrangements for the accommodation of the officers and men. In view of the increasing length and greater power of modern ships, the usual position of the Admiral's and Captain's quarters right aft is becoming more and more open to objection. Up to the present the principal officers have been berthed at the furthest possible distance from the fore bridge and conning tower, where their most important duties must be performed. It is recommended that in this ship the Admiral's quarters be placed on the main deck forward, near the conning tower, a suitable ladderway being fitted from there to the fore bridge and conning tower; also that the officers' quarters be placed forward, both on the main deck and on the upper deck, under the forecastle. Ample accommodation for the remainder of the crew is available on the main and lower decks aft. The latrines for the ship's company have been placed at the extreme after end of the main deck.

Communications.—It is recommended that the internal means of communication should generally be by telephone, leading to a central exchange, except in cases where direct leads are essential. All voice-tube communication should be excluded except where vertical leads only are required, or from fire control positions to the deck, but no bulkheads should be pierced for the purpose of leading voice tubes.

Appendix 3

Report of the Sub-Committee of the Committee of Imperial Defence appointed to inquire into certain questions of Naval Policy raised by Lord Charles Beresford.

Part I.—The Organization and Distribution of the Fleet in Home Waters.

Since March 1909 the whole of the naval forces in Home waters, with the exception of the Atlantic Fleet, have been united in the Home Fleet under the command of a single flag officer . . .

In the opinion of the Committee the above organization . . . satisfies in substance all of Lord Charles Beresford's requirements, the only important difference being that the Atlantic Fleet is retained for strategical reasons as an independent command . . . They concur with Sir Arthur Wilson in regarding the present organization as free from the objections which might, in their opinion, have been fairly urged against the arrangements which preceded it, upon any other view than that those arrangements were of a transitory and provisional character.

Part II.—Small Craft and Destroyers.

Lord Charles Beresford stated that during the period of his command there was such a deficiency in Home waters in small craft and destroyers as to constitute a grave weakness . . . They are satisfied . . . there is no such deficiency as to constitute a risk to the safety of the country.

One of the consequences of the alleged dangerous shortage of cruisers was that, in Lord Charles Beresford's opinion, the Admiralty were not in a position to make adequate provision for the protection of trade . . . there is not sufficient foundation for Lord Charles Beresford's apprehensions.

Part III.—War Plans.

Lord Charles Beresford's original statement in his letter to the Prime Minister that 'upon assuming command of the Channel Fleet I was unable to obtain any strategical scheme or plan for the disposal in war of the forces under my command,' was modified under cross-examination, and the Committee are satisfied that he had no substantial grounds for complaint in this matter.

In connection with the question of War Plans it should be mentioned that Lord Charles Beresford attributed many of the Admiralty's alleged shortcomings to the absence of a proper strategical department.

The First Lord of the Admiralty furnished the Committee with a résumé of the steps which have recently been taken to develop a War Staff at the Admiralty, and indicated further advances in this direction which are in contemplation.

General Conclusion

In the opinion of the Committee, the investigation has shown that during the time in question no danger to the country resulted from the Admiralty's arrangements for war, whether considered from the standpoint of the organization and distribution of the fleets, the number of ships, or the preparation of War Plans.

They feel bound to add that arrangements quite defensible in themselves, though not ideally perfect, were in practice seriously hampered through the absence of cordial relations between the Board of Admiralty and the Commander-in-Chief of the Channel Fleet. The Board of Admiralty do not appear to have taken Lord Charles Beresford sufficiently into their confidence as to the reasons for dispositions to which he took exception; and Lord Charles Beresford, on the other hand, appears to have failed to appreciate and carry out the spirit of the instructions of the Board, and to recognize their paramount authority.

The Committee have been impressed with the differences of opinion amongst officers of high rank and professional attainments regarding important principles of naval strategy and tactics, and they look forward with much confidence to the further development of a Naval War Staff, from which the Naval members of the Board and Flag Officers and their staffs at sea may be expected to derive common benefit.

Appendix 4

FROM WINSTON S. CHURCHILL   *Admiralty, Whitehall*
                                                    May 14th, 1915

My dear Fisher,

I send this to you before marking it to others, in order that if any point arises we can discuss it.

                                        I hope you will agree
                                        Yours ever,
                                        W.

First Sea Lord.

1. The fifth 15-inch howitzer with 50 rounds of ammunition should go to the Dardanelles with the least possible delay, being sent by special train across France and re-embarked at Marseilles. Let me have a time-table showing by what date it can arrive at the Dardanelles.

The two 9.2–inch guns will go to the Dardanelles, either in the two monitors prepared for them or separately for mounting on shore. This will be decided as soon as we hear from Vice-Admiral de Robeck.

2. The following 9 heavy monitors should go in succession to the Dardanelles as soon as they are ready: *Admiral Farragut, General Grant, Stonewall Jackson, Robert E. Lee, Lord Clive, Prince Rupert, Sir John Moore, General Craufurd,* and *Marshal Ney.*

The first 6 of the 9.2–inch monitors should also go unless the Admiral chooses to have two of their guns for work on shore, in which case the first 4 only will go.

A time-table should be prepared showing the dates on which they can be dispatched and will arrive. They can calibrate on the Turks. All necessary steps for their sea-worthiness on the voyage should be taken.

In the case of the 9.2–inch monitors it may be found better to send the actual guns out to Malta separately.

It is clear that when this large accession of force reaches the Vice-Admiral, he should be able to spare a portion of his battleships for service in Home Waters, but it may be better to see how the monitors work and what use they are to him before raising this point.

3. Four of the 'Edgars' with special bulge protection against the mine and torpedo are now ready. They carry ten 6–inch guns each and supply the medium armament which the monitors lack. They should be specially useful for supporting the Army at night without risk from torpedo attack. They would also be useful at a later stage in passing a shore torpedo tube or escorting other ships that were passing.

We have not found any satisfactory employment for them here.

It is not necessary to provide crews for them: working parties which can take them out will be sufficient. The Admiral can man them from his large Fleet for any special service that may be required. They should start as soon as possible.

Let me have a report on the manning possibilities as defined above and times by which they can arrive.

It will be for consideration when these vessels are on the spot whether a valuable ship like the *Chatham* should not be released for other duties.

4. The Third Sea Lord will make proposals for providing anti-mine protection for a proportion of the battleships employed, on the lines proposed at our discussion.

5. The following increased provision will be made for the Air Service.

(D.A.D. [Director of the Air Division] will supply on verbal instructions.)

6. During this month 5 new Submarines are delivered, viz., S2, E18, V2, V3 and S3. In June the Montreal boats come in. Therefore, in view of the request of the Vice-Admiral, I consider that two more E boats should be sent to the Dardanelles.   *W. S. C.*
                                                            14.5.

Secretary.
First Sea Lord.

Although there is good reason to hope that a speedy termination may be reached, it would now be prudent to assume that the operations against the Dardanelles will not take less than three months, and to make all preparations on that basis.

If success is obtained earlier so much the better; but let us make sure that it is not deferred longer. The operations have now reached a point where they may easily develop into a great siege similar to that of Port Arthur, though not so formidable. Our preparations therefore should consider and cover the following points:

1. The provision of siege artillery which could be used against the semi-permanent works, and the mounting on shore of heavy long range naval guns which can from the existing positions held by our troops bring accurate fire to bear on the permanent defences.

2. The provision of landing stages of a semi-permanent character at Seddul Bahr and Gaba Tepe, with cranes, lines of railway and all other facilities for handling large and heavy traffic.

3. Protection against the enemy's Submarines by means of the establishment of regular lines of Indicator nets watched by drifters, joining up Imbros with the Gallipoli Peninsula, and providing permanent protection along the Western coast. In these tideless waters, and with the great quantity of Indicator nets coming to hand there should be no difficulty in this.

4. The battleships of the bombarding Fleet should go by turns to Malta, and there be fitted with the best steel trellis work protection against mines which can be devised. While the present lull in the operations continues, there can be no need to keep the whole Fleet at the Dardanelles, and every opportunity should be taken to afford the ships the necessary protection.

5. Seventy aeroplanes and seaplanes will be required, and preparations must be made to work up to this. Some of the heaviest seaplanes, capable of carrying and dropping 500–lb. bombs, are to be included. I will settle the details of this last provision personally with the D.A.D.   *W. S. C.*
                                                            14.5.15.

Index

COMPILED BY G. NORMAN KNIGHT M.A.
Vice-President of the Society of Indexers

The entry under the name of **Fisher, Admiral of the Fleet,** has been confined to those subheadings which cannot be readily found under other entries. Apart from that heading his name has throughout the Index been abbreviated to JF. Similarly, Lord Charles Beresford is sometimes abbreviated to LCB.

Other abbreviations used are; *f.*, standing for *facing page* (for illustrations); q. for 'quoted'; *qv* for *quod vide* ('which see').

Subheadings have been arranged mainly in chronological order.

Page reference numbers in **bold type** indicate that more than a few lines are devoted to the item in the text. Reference numbers in *italics* denote illustrations or their captions.

bis after a reference number denotes that the item is mentioned in separate contexts twice on the same page, and *ter* three times. *passim* after a group of reference numbers (e.g. 16–20 *passim*) indicates that the item is not referred to continuously but is scattered throughout those pages.

All naval officers are indexed under the highest rank attained.